Human Resource Director's

CORPORATE COMMUNICATIONS MANUAL With Models and Forms

Human Resource Director's

CORPORATE COMMUNICATIONS MANUAL
With Models and Forms

Linda L. Trainor

PRENTICE HALL
Englewood Cliffs, New Jersey 07632

Prentice-Hall International (UK) Limited, *London*
Prentice-Hall of Australia Pty. Limited, *Sydney*
Prentice-Hall Canada, Inc., *Toronto*
Prentice-Hall Hispanoamericana, S.A., *Mexico*
Prentice-Hall of India Private Limited, *New Delhi*
Prentice-Hall of Japan, Inc., *Tokyo*
Simon & Schuster Asia Pte. Ltd., *Singapore*
Editora Prentice-Hall do Brasil, Ltda., *Rio de Janeiro*

Library of Congress Cataloging-in-Publication Data

Trainor, Linda L.
    Human resource director's corporate communications manual : with
models and forms   / by Linda L. Trainor.
        p.   cm.
    ISBN 0-13-445594-0
    1. Communication in personnel management—Handbooks, manuals, etc.
    I. Title.
    HF5549.5.C6T69   1989   89-22865
    658.4′5—dc20   —   CIP

ISBN 0-13-445594-0

PRENTICE HALL
BUSINESS & PROFESSIONAL DIVISION
A division of Simon & Schuster
Englewood Cliffs, New Jersey 07632

Printed in the United States of America

WHAT THIS MANUAL
WILL DO FOR YOU

The *Human Resource Director's Corporate Communications Manual: With Models and Forms* is designed to help you develop effective solutions to increasing internal communication challenges. You can use the examples, techniques and tips included in this *Manual* to improve your communication efforts in a cost-effective way.

Each chapter focuses on one communications medium and tells you "how to" with examples from actual businesses, forms, worksheets, models, preparation tips and checklists. For each communication medium, the *Manual* addresses cost considerations and cost-cutting measures for all types of organization and industry, large and small, with single or multiple locations. For example, you will find ideas on how to communicate new types of benefits and other programs—and changes in existing benefits and programs—in terms the employee can understand.

Steps To Take You From Planning Through Successful Completion Of Any Communication Project

The simple step-by-step approach makes is easy for you to

- assess your communication needs
- develop solid communication action plans
- establish and control communication budgets
- write and produce a variety of employee publications
- prepare better handbooks with less hassle
- produce audiovisuals that enhance your communication objectives
- take advantage of computer technology to personalize communication and reduce administrative burdens
- use unconventional tools to complement your communication campaign
- improve communication effectiveness with better training
- prepare cost-effective communication programs for multiple locations
- use external communication techniques to support internal communication objectives
- prepare more effective reports and presentations for management
- find ways to get more from your communication investment
- get more mileage from each communication tool
- satisfy legal requirements and still communicate effectively
- maximize internal resources
- select appropriate outside resources
- measure the results of your communication efforts

How This Manual Is Organized

This manual is designed to be a quick reference tool for human resources and personnel professionals who want practical answers . . . not theory. You will find a detailed table of contents which is essentially an outline of the information available in each chapter.

Each chapter addresses a specific element fundamental to successful communication programs, including

- how to assess your communication needs
- how to develop strategies and budgets
- how and when to use different communication media
- how to measure results

To get the most from this book, it will be worth your time to peruse Chapters 1 and 2 which focus on needs assessment, planning and budgeting techniques. Chapters 3 through 13 cover different types of HR communication media or organization issues. Within each chapter you will find a variety of approaches, examples, checklists and tips appropriate to the issue at hand.

While each chapter will build on information from the first two chapters, every chapter can also be referenced as a stand-alone element. For example, you may have already developed a plan and are satisfied with most of your current communication tools. Now you want to determine whether or not an audiovisual program will enhance your communication objectives and, if so, which kind of format (film, videotape, slides) will do the best job. You can go directly to Chapter 7, which gives you practical tips on when and how to use audiovisuals, how to produce them and how to budget for them.

You will want to keep the *Manual* handy for quick reference whenever you are looking for creative solutions for a short-term communication problem or undertaking a long-term communication plan. In the final analysis, you will benefit most by using it as a brainstorming tool to inspire your own creative ideas, resulting in better solutions to your ongoing human resource communication challenges.

Acknowledgments

I am deeply grateful to the colleagues, friends and clients who so energetically and enthusiastically permitted me to include their ideas and sample materials.

- Paula Cowan, Vice President Human Resources, *Ashton-Tate*
- Julius Valdez, Executive Vice President, *Coso, Incorporated*
- Gloria Gordon, Editor, *Communication World*
- Patricia K. Lang, Vice President Personnel, *Federal Reserve Bank of San Francisco*
- William Goelkel, President, *Focus III Productions*
- Ken Love, President, *Imagery Source, Inc.*
- John D. Butler, General Director, *General Motors Corporation*
- Lynn Decker, former Manager of Compensation and Benefits, *McDonnell Douglas Helicopter Company*
- Thomas M. Snediker, Director of Personnel, *Morrison Knudsen Company, Inc.*
- Clarence Frayer, President, *Savings Today, Inc.*
- Thomas E. Thomas, former Manager, Health Care Services, *Southern California Edison Company*
- Eloise McGraw, Co-Director, Performance Management System, *The Commonwealth of Massachusetts*
- Joan Edelmann, Manager, Employee Benefits, *TRW Space & Defense*

· George Faunce, III, Managing Director and Chief Administrative Officer, *William M. Mercer Meidinger Hansen, Incorporated*

A special word of appreciation goes to my editor, Olivia Lane. Without her dedication, encouragement and attention to detail, this book would have languished in the Gallery of Good Ideas.

Finally, a special thanks goes to my Dad and Aunt who patiently endured my prolonged negligence and absence from their daily lives while this book was being written.

Linda L. Trainor

ABOUT THE AUTHOR

LINDA L. TRAINOR is principal of William M. Mercer Meidinger Hansen, Inc., Los Angeles, California, a world-wide consulting organization providing consulting services in the areas of employee benefits, compensation, human resources management, and funding and financing of compensation and benefit programs. Her experience spans over twenty years in the communication arts field, including advertising, marketing, public relations, film and video production as well as organizational, benefit and compensation communication consulting. Her clients have included large and small organizations in both the public sector and virtually every industry group in the private sector.

She routinely speaks and conducts seminars for professional organizations across the country and has been published in a variety of national publications ranging from *American History Illustrated* to *Financial Executive*. She is also the author of *Lawyers' Advertising Handbook* and a contributing author to *Writer's Digest* anthology, *Jobs for Writers*.

Ms. Trainor's innovative, results-oriented approach to solving communication problems has enabled her to build and manage a multi-million dollar communication consulting operation, develop and implement time-saving strategic plans for clients, and introduce high-tech solutions to complex communication and human resource management challenges. The communication programs and tools she has developed have consistently won top awards in national and international competitions since 1976.

CONTENTS

LIST OF FIGURES

CHAPTER 9   INTEGRATING COLLATERAL MATERIALS INTO YOUR COMMUNICATION PROGRAM

CHAPTER 10   EDUCATION AND TRAINING

CHAPTER 11   HOW TO HANDLE COMMUNICATION AT MULTIPLE LOCATIONS

CHAPTER 1

HOW TO ASSESS YOUR ORGANIZATION'S COMMUNICATION NEEDS

Human resource communication is a hot topic within organizations these days, but it is not a new one. Peter Drucker and other management luminaries have advocated strong, clear communication for years. In fact, most prominent management books and articles refer repeatedly to the importance of effective communication.

"We have learned, mostly through doing the wrong things, four fundamentals of communications.

> 1. Communication is perception.
> 2. Communication is expectation.
> 3. Communication makes demands.
> 4. Communication and information are different and indeed largely opposite—yet interdependent."*   *Peter Drucker*

The challenge is to move communication from theory into practice. Since basic communication is something we learned to do at a very young age, we generally do not think of it as requiring any special talent or training. Yet when supervisors or managers are given the responsibility to implement any type of **formal** communication program, they often get cold feet. While it is true that some people's communication instincts set them apart from the norm, Dr. Norman Sigband reminds us, "The greatest illusion in communication is to assume that it always takes place effectively."**

Many useful techniques and systems can be learned and used to improve the quality and effectiveness of any organization's effort to communicate human resource issues. But before you put these techniques to work, the first step in assessing your communication needs is to determine where you are, what your current situation is.

HOW TO EVALUATE YOUR CURRENT COMMUNICATION STRATEGY

This chapter will illustrate how to get the information you need to assess your communication needs. A variety of formal and informal methods are available to evaluate your current situation. The most common formal method is to use some type of survey. A less structured approach is to examine the most critical factors that will impact the effectiveness of your current and future communication strategy. These factors are: Communication Policy, Image, Audience Profile, Communication Topics, Communication Tools and Common Communication Pitfalls.

---

*Management Tasks Responsibilities Practices, Harper & Row, New York: 1974. p. 483.
**Pace, Official publication of Santa Fe Southern Pacific Corporation, November, 1985. p. 15.

How To Use Surveys To Assess Your Current Situation

Surveys come in many sizes and shapes. The two basic survey techniques are written and oral. They are often disguised by names such as audit, climate review, attitude survey, sensing session, focus group, and market analysis. The most informal survey approach is to ask one or more people for their opinion. The scope or magnitude of the survey depends primarily on which approach you select, the results you expect, and the price you are willing to pay. The more comprehensive and sophisticated the survey, the higher the cost.The following steps apply to both written and oral surveys.

Seven Steps For Conducting A Survey

Step 1. Identify a Task Force. Choose one or two people who will be responsible for coordinating the project, producing a report which summarizes the survey results, and recommending action items. Include enough people to ensure you have a good representation of human resource specialties (e.g. recruiting, compensation, benefits). Also include a data processing specialist if possible, but try to keep your task force to five or less so it is manageable.

Practical Point   Surveys are very valuable tools. They are also very dangerous because if they are not carefully constructed and administered they can be instrumental in sending a negative message to your audience(s). The result can destroy your communication efforts for years and create huge employee relation problems. If you or someone in your organization does not have practical experience in developing and administering surveys, seek professional advice.

Step 2. Identify Your Objectives and Participants.   Decide what you want to learn from your survey. In some cases you may want to limit your survey to just one issue such as recent labor negotiations, a compensation or benefit change, or an evaluation of a new employee newsletter. On a larger scale, you may want to evaluate employee understanding of the company's business goals or decide which are the most effective tools you can use to regularly communicate with employees. Carefully list your objectives as they will help you structure your survey documents and avoid including superfluous questions.

You also need to determine whether you want to survey your entire employee population or some type of random sample. The more people you include in the survey, the better. People like to be asked their opinions and total population surveys send the message that you value input from all employees rather than just a select few. If time and/or budget make a total population survey difficult, it is statistically possible to survey a smaller number of employees which will reliably mirror the attitudes and opinions of the entire group.

Finally, you must decide whether to process the results manually or with a computer. The more complex your survey objectives, the higher the probability that you will want to use a computer to compile and help analyze the results.

Step 3. Establish a Timetable and Budget.   Developing a timetable will help you keep the project moving. The timetable should be realistic, taking into account your internal and external resources, other project priorities and budget. Even for the most simple survey you should allow yourself a minimum of two or three months.

Your budget will depend on the scope and level of sophistication you expect. Remember to include estimates of internal staff time, computer programming and processing, questionnaire and report production, and external costs such as consulting fees.

Step 4. Develop Survey Documents.   Whether you are doing a more formal, written survey with 180 questions or an informal mini-survey by phone or personal interview, you need to have written documents.

If your survey is intended to be completed in written form, you must spend a good deal of time ensuring that the questions are clear. If your survey is oral, you need to have your key questions written so you will ask each participant for the same information in the same way. Your documents should also allow room for collecting demographic information which will be useful in analyzing the results. (Sample survey documents are shown later in this chapter.)

Step 5. Test, Announce, and Conduct the Survey. Once you believe your document is satisfactory, you should test it. Select a sample cross-section of employees that represent your bigger participant audience. If they have trouble understanding or completing the survey, you will have to refine it. Be sure that you are prepared to keep the results organized and confidential. Dedicating files and or binders to hold the completed survey documents will help you considerably.

Before you actually conduct the survey, give participants advance notice that they are invited to participate. Explain your goal, why their input is important and what you will do with the results. When you conduct the survey, stress confidentiality and commit to reporting back with the results.

Practical Point   If you do not intend to report the results to your participants, you will send a message to the participants that you distrust their ability to understand the significance of the results and that you may not act on them.

Step 6. Compiling the Data and Analyzing the Results. If your survey is extremely simple, you may be able to manually compile the results. More frequently, you will have the results entered into a computer. The program used to compile and analyze the data can be as simple as a PC-based spreadsheet or as complex as a highly sophisticated statistical analysis package. (The processing decision will have been made in Step 2.)

Analyzing the results will be a little more time consuming. You should look for information that will correspond to the objectives you identified in Step 1. This is also the time to look at the demographic profile of the participants to see whether there are differences in the results among demographically unique groups (e.g. age groups, sex, length of service, job classifications, office or plant locations).

Practical Point   Frequently, you will discover other interesting information or trends, you must take care to avoid being distracted from your goals. Remember, too much information is as bad as no information at all.

Step 7. Recommend Action Items and Feedback. Your analysis will help you identify and prioritize action items. If the results indicate employees are very satisfied with the new employee newsletter, your action item is: Don't fix it, it isn't broken. If the results indicate that employees believe the performance review process is not administered fairly, your action item is: Consider implementing more and better performance review communication to employees and perhaps special training for supervisors.

Once you have determined your action items and their priorities, you should feed back this information, along with the survey results, to employees. If you only surveyed a random sample, you still should communicate to all employees.

Practical Point   Make sure you are candid. You may have to acknowledge there is some discontent with respect to a certain issue and you can't do anything about it just now. You will have much more credibility taking this approach than if you try to bury or ignore the issue.

Figures 1.1 through 1.4 are sample survey documents for different survey approaches.

A mini-survey can help you get a general feel about your employees' attitudes toward your communication efforts. It is designed to be a quick perception test rather than a sophisticated analysis tool.

Figure 1.1: MINI COMMUNICATION SURVEY

	TRUE	FALSE
1. I get adequate information about how well I'm doing my job.		
2. I understand how the retirement plan works.		
3. The employee newsletter is a useful way for me to get information about the company.		
4. My supervisor does a good job explaining organizational policies.		
5. The company does a good job keeping me informed about things I need to know in order to do my job well.		
6. The employee handbook is a useful reference tool.		
7. The company does a good job explaining my benefits.		
8. Our employee benefit statement helps me understand our benefit plans.		
9. The company does a good job informing me about our pay policies.		
10. The quarterly staff meetings are a good way to keep me informed about company performance and business goals.		
11. I prefer receiving memos about benefit changes.		
12. I take all benefit communication materials home to share with my family.		
13. My co-workers are my best source of information about how to use my benefits.		
14. I check the bulletin board regularly.		
Demographic Information		
Age ____ Male ____ Female____		
Department _____ Work Location _____		
Years With The Company (Check One)		
Less than 1 year ____1-3 years ____4-6 years ____More than 6 years ____		
Marital Status (Check One)Married ____Single ____		

COMMENTS

The following survey example is more comprehensive than the first because it is designed to help you measure overall job satisfaction as well as communication effectiveness. It also lets you cut the data more finely by giving the respondents more opinion choices.

An important reason to include job satisfaction questions in surveys is that they can give you some clues about communication issues you might otherwise overlook. For example: If employees overwhelmingly report that they do not believe the company has a good career opportunity program, but you know it is one of the best in your area, you will know you have not been doing an adequate communication job.

This survey example identifies job satisfaction topics with headings to help you distinguish the differences among the questions. However, it is not usually desirable to include the headings in your survey because they can be distracting to the survey participants. You will also notice some questions seem to be asked more than once in slightly different ways. This allows you to check for consistency. If respondents generally answer the question one way the first time and differently the next time, you should take this into consideration when interpreting the results. A pattern of inconsistent answers to similar questions suggests that either the respondents don't understand the question(s) or they are ambivalent.

If you want to conduct a survey similar to this, you should consider getting professional guidance as the data analysis can be complex.

Figure 1.2 JOB SATISFACTION SURVEY

INTRODUCTION

In preparation for our five-year business planning process, we would like you to help us identify our company's strengths and weaknesses so we can make appropriate decisions about future goals and priorities.

In order to ensure confidentiality, we have engaged the services of [name of outside survey firm]. The results of the survey will be tabulated and analyzed by [survey firm name]. Highlights of the survey results will be published in the September issue of the Company Newsletter. In October, special employee meetings will be conducted to share more details about the survey and introduce the new five-year business plan.

Put your completed questionnaire in the attached postage paid envelope and mail it directly to [survey firm name] no later than June 1.

Opposite each question, simply check the box that most accurately reflects your opinion.	STRONGLY DISAGREE	DISAGREE	AGREE	STRONGLY AGREE
Physical Work Conditions				
1. My work area has some unnecessary safety hazards.				
2. The bank provides good parking for its employees.				
Supervision				
3. My supervisor criticizes me more than he or she praises me.				
4. I feel comfortable talking to my supervisor about work-related problems.				
5. Overall my supervisor does a good job.				
Career Development				
6. I have a good chance here at the bank to improve my knowledge and abilities.				
7. Getting ahead here is based more on your skills and abilities than who you know.				
Overall Satisfaction				
8. All things considered I'm pretty satisfied working for the bank.				
9. Our pay is better than pay for other banks in this area.				
10. Compared to other people in my department my pay is unfair.				
11. Compared to other employers in this city the bank pays well.				
12. Compared to others in this bank I am paid fairly.				
Personnel Policies And Systems				
13. Our personnel policies are unfair.				
14. The way my job performance is evaluated is fair.				
15. My job description clearly tells me what I need to do to be successful on my job.				
Communication With Management				
16. Management doesn't tell employees enough about present and planned activities for the bank.				
17. What employees say on this survey will be given serious consideration by management.				
18. My supervisor keeps me informed about what's going on in the bank.				
Work Climate				
19. The bank provides a good environment for employees to get involved in their work.				
SURVEY DOCUMENT - PAGE 2				

20. Most of the people at the bank are friendly.				
Benefits				
21. Our medical coverage is good.				
22. The benefits here are not as good as the benefits of other banks in this area.				
23. Employee claims with (name of medical claims administrator) are handled quickly and fairly.				
24. Dental insurance claims are paid quickly and fairly.				
25. My supervisor administers sick leave policy fairly.				
26. My overall understanding of the benefit packages is not very good.				
27. Our retirement program won't provide me enough money when I retire.				
28. The deductible on the bank's medical coverage is $100 per year.				
29. The bank matches each employee's contribution to Social Security, dollar-for-dollar.				
30. If an employee leaves the bank before completing 10 years of service, he/she will not get any pension benefit.				
Organizational Image				
31. This bank provides good service to its customers.				
32. I am proud to say I work for this bank.				
33. I would recommend this bank as a good place to work.				
General Communication				
34. The employee newsletter is a useful way for me to get information about the company.				
35. The employee handbook is a useful reference tool.				
36. Our employee benefit statement helps me understand our benefit plans.				
37. The quarterly staff meetings are a good way to keep me informed about company performance and business goals.				
38. I prefer receiving memos about benefit changes.				
39. I take all benefit communication materials home to share with my family.				
40. My co-workers are my best source of information about how to use my benefits.				
41. I check the bulletin board regularly.				

SURVEY DOCUMENT - PAGE 3

Rate the value of the following communication tools using the following rating system.
0=Not Valuable at All; 1=Somewhat Valuable; 2=Very Valuable; 3=I Don't Know.

	0=NOT VALUABLE AT ALL	1=SOMEWHAT VALUABLE	2=VERY VALUABLE	3=DON'T KNOW
42. Employee Orientation Audiovisual				
43. Employee Handbook				
44. Benefit Statement				
45. Annual Health Care Enrollment Kit				
46. Company Newsletter				
47. Compensation and Benefit Newsletter				
48. New Employee Welcome Package				
49 Bulletin Board Announcements				
50. Supervisor				
51. Co-Workers				
52. Benefit Plan Booklets				
53. Employee Meetings				
54. Memos				
55 Letters from the President				
56. Bulletins in Brochure Form				
57. Retirement Plan Statement				
58. Savings Plan Enrollment Kit				
59. Other _____				
60. Other _____				
61. Other _____				

Please complete the following information as it will help us understand how employee
groups with different demographic profiles feel about the issues covered in this survey.

Age ____	
Years with the Company (Check One)	
Less than 1 year ____	
1-3 years ____	
4-6 years ____	
Over 6 years ____	
Marital Status (Check One)	
Married ____ Single ____	

SURVEY DOCUMENT - PAGE 4

Other
_____Male _____Female
Department _____   Work Location_____
Salary Under $12,000 per year _____
$12,000 - $17,999 per year _____
$18,000 - $24,999 per year _____
$25,000 - $29,999 per year _____
$30,000 - $44,999 per year _____
Over $45,000 per year _____

If you have other comments or suggestions, please include them at the bottom of this page. Thank you for your help. Return this survey to (survey firm name) before June 1.

COMMENTS

Personal and phone survey techniques can be difficult because the participants frequently want to discuss other topics. It is critical that the interviewer retain control.

This phone interview guide is designed to help the interviewer ask consistent questions and keep to the subject at hand.

Figure 1.3: PHONE INTERVIEW GUIDE

Date_____
Survey Topic _____
Interviewer _____

OPENING REMARKS
Good (morning/afternoon). I'm _____ from _____. We're doing an informal survey to find out what you think about our new employee benefit statement. Can you spare a few minutes? (*Note: If interviewee is busy, offer to call back at a more convenient time. Schedule a specific date and time.*)

Q1. Did you receive our new benefit statement at home? ___Yes ___No

If yes, ask Q2.

If no, confirm employee's length of service.

If employee did not receive the statement because he/she is not yet eligible, explain the reason and thank them for their time.

Q2. Did you look it over? ___Yes ___No

If yes, ask Q3.

If no, ask why. _____

Q3. Did you find the information useful? ___Yes ___No

If yes, ask what he/she liked best and least.

Best_____

Least_____

If no, ask why. _____

Q4. Did you share it with your family? ___Yes ___No

If yes, ask Q5.

If no, ask why. _____

Q5. Would you like to get a statement like this every year? ___Yes ___No

Q6. Do you have any other comments or opinions about the statement you would like to share?

_____

DEMOGRAPHIC QUESTIONS

I have just a few more questions that will help us understand how different employee groups feel about the statement, but you don't have to answer them if you don't want to.

Job Classification _____

Salary Grade ____

Department _____

Work Location _____

Length of Service _____

Age _____ Sex _____ Married _____ Single _____

Number of Dependents _____

OTHER REMARKS

Focus groups are small groups of randomly selected employees. There are usually no more than 10-12 people in each meeting because larger groups are more difficult to manage and you want to encourage each person to participate.

Like phone and personal interviews, focus group surveys can quickly get out of hand if the meeting leader is not well prepared and skilled in managing group dynamics. It is best to have two people sharing the burden of leading the meeting and documenting the results.

The following sample is similar to the phone interview guide but somewhat less structured because you must record attitudes and comments of the entire group very quickly.

Figure 1.4: FOCUS GROUP MEETING LEADER GUIDE

MEETING DATA

Date _____

Meeting Location _____

Meeting Leaders _____

_____

Elapsed Time _____

PARTICIPANT DATA

No. Participants Scheduled _____

No. Participants Attended _____

No. Male _____

No. Female _____

Job Classifications/Length of Service

_____

_____

_____

_____

INTRODUCTION

Good (morning/afternoon), I am _____ from _____. This is _____ from _____. Does everyone understand why we are here today?

Purpose	We would like to get your opinions and ideas about communication issues. For example, we'll be talking about whether or not you get enough information, how you currently get it and how you would prefer to get it.
Rules	In some cases, we may discuss specific topics such as benefits. It is important to understand that we cannot discuss things like benefit plan designs or company policies and procedures unless they relate specifically to a communication topic. Our objective is to get your opinions and feed them back to management.
Stress Confidentiality	Each of you were invited to participate based on a random sample of employees throughout the organization. Since you are like a representative, you are encouraged to share opinions of your co-workers to the extent you know how they feel. Your comments and opinions will be strictly confidential. We will take notes so we can be sure we are reporting your opinions accurately. Your comments will be combined with those from other meetings like these and reported to management in a general report. Are there any questions?
Roundtable Introductions	Since we will be together for a couple of hours, it will make it easier for all of us if we get acquainted a little better. I'd like to ask each of you to give us your first name and a brief description of your job.

BEGIN FOCUS QUESTIONS

(Note to meeting leaders: If participants are reluctant to begin talking, help them get started by giving specific prompts. It may be necessary to pose the first few questions directly to one or more participants until they become comfortable with the process.)

Q. How do you feel about the company's communication efforts in general? (*Probe*)

Q. How do you find out about compensation and benefits issues? (*Probe*)

Q. Who do you consider the company's most significant competitors? (*Probe*)

Q. How do you think the company ranks among those competitors as a place to work? (*Probe*)

Q. Do you get enough information about company business goals? (*Probe*)

Q. How would you prefer to hear about the company's business issues? (*Probe*)

Q. Do you get enough information about personnel policies and procedures? (*Probe*)

Q. What is the best source of information about personnel policies? (*Probe*)

Q. Do you get enough information about benefits? (*Probe*)

Q. What is your best source for benefit information? (*Probe*)

Q. Which of the following communication tools are best for giving you the information you need? (*Probe*)

___ Employee Orientation Audio-Visual

___ Employee Handbook

___ Benefit Statement

___ Annual Health Care Enrollment Kit

___ Company Newsletter

___ Compensation and Benefit Newsletter

___ New Employee Welcome Package

___ Bulletin Board Announcements

___ Supervisor

___ Co-Workers

___ Benefit Plan Booklets

___ Employee Meetings

___ Memos

___ Letters from the President

(cont.)

___ Bulletins in Brochure Form

___ Retirement Plan Statement

___ Savings Plan Enrollment Kit

___ Other _____

___ Other _____

___ Other _____

Q. Is the employee handbook useful? (*Probe*)

Q. Do you get the opportunity to tell management how you feel about things? (*Probe*)

Q. What is the one thing the company can do to improve communications?

END OF FOCUS QUESTIONS

Wrap-Up   Thank you for taking the time to share your opinions with us. We expect to
                                   give our report to management by _____. A summary
                                   of the report will be published in the _____ issue of the company
                                   newsletter. Have a good day.

MEETING LEADER NOTES

Immediately after each focus group meeting, take a few minutes to debrief and compare notes. Use this space to summarize the highlights and the most significant issues that emerged from the meeting.

DEBRIEFING NOTES

HOW TO EVALUATE YOUR COMMUNICATION NEEDS WITHOUT SURVEYS

In addition to surveys, there are other ways to assess your communication needs. You will find it useful to examine your organization's current cultural and communication practices using information that is already available to you.

```
CHECKLIST: Six Cultural and Communication Factors to Consider
```

There are six basic factors to consider. Evaluating these factors will help you identify the strengths and weaknesses of your current communication activities.

Communication Policy.   If you do not have a communication policy, you should develop one. A communication policy is similar to magazine and newspaper editorial policies. It will help ensure that, no matter what the topic is or which medium you use, you are sending consistent messages every time you communicate. (See pages 16 and 17 for example policy statements.)

Image.   When you try to define your current situation, there are two questions to ask: What is the real situation? And what is the perceived situation? How the organization is perceived is important because it has a powerful influence on your real situation. Knowing how the organization is perceived internally and externally will enable you to develop more persuasive communication techniques. (See the example on page 18.)

Audience Profiles.   No matter how small your organization, you will have more than one audience with which to communicate. Understanding your audiences is fundamental to effective communication. Developing a profile of each audience will simplify your communication challenges because you will have a clear idea of what approach works best with each audience. (See Audience Profile checklist and example on pages 19 and 20.)

Communication Topics and Categories.   The two primary communication issues are organizational and human resources. When you begin to create your communication plan it will be helpful to develop a checklist of the subjects under each topic you might need to address. There are essentially seven categories or methods which dictate how you may want to approach a given topic. Matching the topics to the methods will help you avoid crises. (See examples on page 22 through 28.)

Communication Tools.   Communication tools are the tangible media (e.g. memos, brochures, audio-visuals) you choose to implement your communication strategy. Selecting the right tool for the task at hand is an important part of your communication plan. (See examples on pages 28 and 29.)

Common Pitfalls   There are nine mistakes commonly found in communication tools. Examining your communication tools, identifying the mistakes and correcting them will immediately improve the effectiveness of your communication efforts. (See pages 33 and 34.)

Knowing where your organization is currently positioned with respect to each of these factors will give you enough information to determine your communication needs. You will use this information to build your communication plan which is covered in Chapter 2.

HOW TO WRITE A COMMUNICATION POLICY

The purpose of a communication policy statement is *not* to write an inflexible rule, but rather the opposite. Your statement should provide a dynamic model that will help promote all communication efforts in a clear, concise, and consistent manner. The policy should be harmonious with the way the organization actually does things, both publicly and privately. The best statements will encompass all facets of employee communication activities. Following is a concrete illustration of Drucker's reference to the difference between and interdependency of communication and information.

Human Resource Communication Policy Statement. Figures 1.5 and 1.6 are examples of a broad-based human resource communication policy. Figure 1.6 is a better policy than Figure 1.5. However, note that this type of statement assumes that every department and unit in the organization will use the same standards when communicating with employees.

If an organization uses the second statement, there is a good probability that they will more than satisfy legal requirements. If they use the first statement, they will probably suffer ongoing employee relations and human resource management problems.

Total Compensation Communication Policy Statement. The examples in Figures 1.7 and 1.8 are total compensation communication policy statements. The difference between these and the previous examples is that only direct compensation and benefit department communications would be subject to these guidelines.

As with the previous examples, these statements show the difference between a commitment to communicate and a mere willingness to pass on information.

Publishing policy guidelines gives you an opportunity to quickly review every communication tool to see whether or not your message is consistent and complete. If the tool has ignored any policy points, it should be modified before it is given to employees.

One way to establish an editorial policy is to develop a checklist that includes:

- what you're required to communicate
- what you should communicate
- what you're willing to communicate
- what you're not willing to communicate
- special situations

It would be very difficult to create a comprehensive list to handle every potential situation but the chart in Figure 1.9 should help.

Figure 1.5: POOR HUMAN RESOURCE COMMUNICATION POLICY

We will communicate employees' rights and responsibilities as specified by law.

Figure 1.6: GOOD HUMAN RESOURCE COMMUNICATION POLICY

Our communication objective is to help people understand
1) how the organization operates
2) why it exists
3) their role as employees
4) their privileges, opportunities and responsibilities
5) legal requirements

Figure 1.7: POOR COMPENSATION AND BENEFIT COMMUNICATION POLICY

We will communicate direct compensation issues on a need-to-know basis.

We will communicate benefit issues as specified by law.

Figure 1.8: GOOD COMPENSATION AND BENEFIT COMMUNICATION POLICY

Our communication objective is to help people understand
1) how and when they are paid
2) how performance is measured
3) how performance, pay and benefits are related
4) benefit privileges, opportunities and responsibilities
5) legal requirements

Figure 1.9: A HELPFUL GUIDE FOR ESTABLISHING EDITORIAL POLICY

DESCRIPTION	REQUIRED	SHOULD	WILL	WON'T	SPECIAL
Business Goals		X			
EEO Policies	X	X			
Worker's Compensation	X	X			
Work Rules		X			
Direct Compensation Policy		X			
Benefits	X	X			
Career Opportunities		X			
Quality Control Standards		X			
Productivity Standards		X			
Training Opportunities		X			
Proprietary Information		X			
Other					

NOTE: State and local laws may impact whether or not there should be other "x"s in the required column. "X" has been marked in the *Should* column for virtually every situation because experience shows that the more employees understand, the easier it is to fit their needs and perceptions to an organization's objectives.

WHAT IMAGE HAS TO DO WITH COMMUNICATION

All organizations have a distinctive culture that projects a specific image to a variety of audiences. There is a public image, that is to say, how the organization is perceived by the outside world. The corporate image is a reflection of how the organization's management perceives itself and the organization. The employee image is more complex since employees tend to rank the organization according to how it responds to their personal needs, how the public image affects their pride as employees and whether or not management's perception is in sync with the employees' perception.

EXAMPLE: What Image Means at One Hospital

A vivid example of the influence image and perception have in evaluating where you are is the case of a prominent children's hospital.

Public Image   The hospital has an outstanding local and national public image.

Corporate Image   The hospital management is justifiably proud of its prestige and points to its dedicated employees as the primary reason for success. Management constantly re-evaluates and adjusts compensation, benefits and other human resource programs to be sure that employees are properly rewarded for their contributions.

Employee Image   Employees are extremely proud that they work for this hospital. However, they do not believe that management appreciates their dedication, loyalty, and extra effort to maintain the quality image. They believe they are underpaid and have fewer benefits and privileges than less prominent hospitals in the community.

The only consistent perception relates to the hospital's public image. But even that is endangered. When breaking news stories focus on unfavorable events at the hospital, the hospital management is absolutely astounded to find employee discontent growing to such proportions that a unionization campaign is threatened.

Management misjudged employee perceptions. The real situation is not based on fact but management's *perception* of employee attitudes. Employee assessment of the situation is equally inaccurate.

The core of the problem is poor communication technique. Management's communication was so obtuse that even outside compensation and benefit specialists had a difficult time understanding what management was trying to say.

This is an extreme example of too little time spent thoughtfully evaluating the situation. It demonstrates why organizations frequently find themselves struggling with volatile human resource management problems. Too often, top managers assume they know more than they do about their employees' attitudes. This hospital's inaccurate assessment of employee attitudes adversely affected communication effectiveness.

How To Understand Audience Attitudes And Biases

Understanding the probable attitudes and biases of your audience is critical to successful communication efforts. If you conduct a survey and collect demographic information, you will be able to see unique groups of employees distinguished by such characteristics as age, length of service, plant or office location, marital status and pay grades or job descriptions. If you do not conduct a survey, you should still access this data from your payroll or other management information systems.

How Audience Profiles Influence Communication Needs

Knowing certain information about your various audiences will make your communication effort easier. If you know that the majority of your employees are under age twenty-three, common sense tells you that they are probably interested in different issues than employees whose average age is fifty-seven. Twenty-three-year-olds will respond to certain words, graphics, pictures, values, or performance expectations differently than fifty-seven-year-olds.

All of us instinctively tend to communicate in a style consistent with our own experience and value systems. This isn't wrong, but it is less likely to succeed if you have several drastically different audiences.

The more you know about your audiences, the more comfortable you will feel with handling communication challenges. If you feel comfortable, you will approach every task more creatively and positively and you will see favorable results for your efforts.

How To Develop Audience Profiles

An easy way to get to know your audiences better is to maintain an audience profile checklist. Most of the checklist data is already available to you. You probably use this data for making other important decisions and so you are merely developing another application for using the data. Updating the checklist will be necessary, the frequency of which will depend on business and operating influences. If your organization has a high turnover factor, more frequent updates will be necessary. If the organization's business is more stable and predictable, updating will be correspondingly less frequent. The checklist in Figure 1.10 includes the minimum audience information that you should review before you decide who, what, when, where, and why to communicate.

You can refine and isolate the profile to help identify the statistical profile of your employee group(s). There are only three sociological references in this list: educational background, native language and participation in voluntary plans. These three factors can help you predict how your audience(s) will act or react to any given issue. If performance standards of your organization are more oriented to individual values, you should add more cultural value measures or sociological items to your checklist.

Figure 1.10: AUDIENCE PROFILE CHECKLIST	
Number of Employees	
Sex	
Age	
Marital Status	
Number of Dependents	
Educational Background	
Native Language	
Salary	
Salary Classification	
Years of Service with the Company	
Turnover Rate	
Participation in Voluntary Plans	

What The Profile Will Tell You

Even the most broad generalizations will give you some insight into your audience which can be very useful. The more specific and precise your profile is, the easier it is to target your messages to the audience. The following example shows how you can use a general profile to more effectively deal with a specific communication task.

EXAMPLE: HOW TO USE THE AUDIENCE PROFILE CHECKLIST

Number of Employees	853
Sex	58% male/42% female
Age	27
Marital Status	37% married/67% single
Number of Dependents	1
Educational Background	some college
Native Language	78% English/22% Oriental
Salary	$32,000/year
Salary Classification	45% Professional/32% Production/18% Administrative/5% Management
Years of Service with the Company	4
Turnover Rate	18%
Participation in Voluntary Plans	54%

If this were a profile of your organization's employees, the following are some of the broad inferences you could make from the data.

Communication Tools. The size of your total population is big enough to make one-on-one communication techniques difficult. You would have to use other tools such as memos, brochures or audio-visuals. If you want to use supervisors to help communicate, you will have to be sure they are conversant with the issues, content, and administrative details of the subject to be communicated. If you do not use supervisors, you may be overlooking a powerful tool.

Communication Tone and Style. The age, sex, marital, and dependent status of the employee group probably will relate to a crisp, efficient, high technology style and tone, and one that emphasizes quality of life, personal choice, and flexibility. The educational level suggests an ability to understand reasonably sophisticated issues.

Cultural Issues. There are sufficiently large and varied professional and multi-cultural populations to justify more than passing attention to potential cultural biases. Such biases are not limited to language barriers. Colloquial expressions and lifestyle priorities are evidence of cultural biases. Some are learned; some are reflections of conscious adaptation to the existing environment.

One way to communicate effectively with a group of employees who have unique cultural characteristics is to identify a peer leader who can help bridge the gap. A peer leader is usually bilingual or multi-lingual and has learned to identify with more than one culture. This individual is usually easily identified.

How To Find Common Denominators When You Have More Than One Audience
By now, you have probably confirmed that you do have more than one audience with which to communicate. But lack of time and money will make it nearly impossible for you to deal with each audience optimally. What do you do now? Look for the common denominators. Answer the basic questions all employees will have. What are they?

- what is it
- what will it do for me
- how do the rules work
- what happens if I don't follow the rules
- how much it will cost in money, independence or loss of benefits

If you can afford the time and/or money to enhance the basics with information or tools directed to a specific audience, all the better. But don't forget the basics.

USING TOPICS AND CATEGORY LISTS TO FOCUS YOUR COMMUNICATION PROJECTS

Anticipating your communication needs will make your communication tasks easier. One way to anticipate your needs is to create topics and category lists.

Topics To Communicate
Preparing a list of probable topics is a valuable exercise because you can quickly prioritize which issues require immediate attention, which ones should be targeted for ongoing efforts and which ones can be dealt with over the long term. There are two broad types of communication topics: organizational and human resource issues. You can use the Figure 1.11 worksheet to identify your priorities.

Understanding How Much Your Audience Knows About A Topic
Employers frequently make inaccurate assumptions about what employees know about a specific topic or issue. The most common assumptions fall at one extreme or the other—employees know as much as management or they know nothing. Management may spend weeks or months learning and studying a given topic before information is passed on to the general employee population. By that time, everything is old news to management. At the opposite extreme, it is very easy for management to convince themselves that employees live in some kind of sheltered vacuum. If you start from either premise, there is a high probability you will offend your audience and lose credibility. Surveys are one way to find out how much your audience knows. An easier way is to observe how well employees follow procedures and how often you get the same question. If procedures are consistently ignored or you get the same question again and again, you can see that employees need to know more.

Seven Communication Categories
Once you feel comfortable with your communication policy statement, your organizational image and your audiences, you can revisit the issues you need and/or want to communicate. As you review them, you will find that they can be grouped into several categories with unique characteristics that will influence how you communicate. The most common types fall into the following categories:

Figure 1.11: PRIORITY COMMUNICATION TOPICS WORKSHEET

Place an A in the Immediate column opposite each topic you think needs immediate attention.
Place a B in the Ongoing column opposite each topic that will require ongoing communication.
Place a C in the Long-Term column opposite the topics you will deal with later.

If you have marked both A and B opposite any topics, put them at the VERY TOP of your list of things to do and plan your communication efforts to include the ongoing communication requirements. This approach will enable you to accomplish two tasks at once.

ORGANIZATIONAL ISSUES	IMMEDIATE	ONGOING	LONG-TERM
History About the Business(es)			
Reporting and Operating Structures			
Short- and Long-Term Company Objectives			
Community Image			
Human Resource Philosophy			
Quality and Performance Standards			
Competition			
Facilities Guide (Map)			
Technical and Business-Related Resources			
HUMAN RESOURCE ISSUES			
Direct Compensation (Wage & Salary)			
Benefits (Mandatory & Company-Sponsored)			
Career Opportunities			
Education/Training Opportunities			
Work and Safety Rules			
Performance Evaluation Standards			
Affirmative Action/EEO Policy			
Rehabilitation Policy			
Labor Relations			
Employment Practices			
Employee Assistance Program			
Manpower/Succession/Management Planning			
Job Posting Policy			
Special Recognition Programs			
Internal Resources			
Community Service Resources			

- legally required
- good news
- bad news
- what if or just in case
- promotional
- educational
- informational

Your approach to topics in each of these categories will vary. For example, the way you address a legally required topic will be different than how you address an educational topic because your objectives in influencing employee behavior will be different. Occasionally employers confuse the *what* issue with the *why* and the *how* issues. The following examples illustrate how you can integrate what, why and how into a productive communication effort.

Legally Required Communication. If an employer focuses on the primary business objective of communicating clearly and honestly with employees, the end result will almost always exceed the minimum government standards. However, if an employer emphasizes meeting government regulations over communication objectives, the result is usually dangerous at best.

One of the most frustrating and enigmatic laws employers have had to deal with since 1974 is the Employee Retirement Income Security Act (ERISA). It requires that most employers provide employees with Summary Plan Descriptions (SPDs) for all defined benefit and defined contribution plans. Many organizations have experienced an increase in employees whose native language is not English. In some cases, these employees speak little, if any English. ERISA regulations stipulate that a notice explaining the intent of the SPD and where to get help understanding it must be provided in the native language (other than English). This applies to plans with less than 100 employees if 25 percent of the entire employee population speak the same non-English language. For plans with 100 participants or more, such a notice is required if those speaking the same non-English language is 500 or 10% of all participants, whichever is less. This is another example of how common sense should dictate a reasonable approach, with or without regulatory enforcement. If an employee can't understand what your are trying to say, how can you expect that person to respond appropriately?

In addition to ERISA, most organizations are subject to certain disclosure requirements under other federal laws such as the Comprehensive Omnibus Benefit Reconciliation Act (COBRA) and virtually every tax act passed in recent history. Disclosure is also mandated through regulatory bodies such as the Department of Labor (DOL), and even the Securities and Exchange Commission (SEC), if you provide company stock as an employee benefit. Finally, state and local laws may contain disclosure provisions with which you must comply. Legally mandated communication requirements for non-profit and public sector organizations are frequently less stringent and may even be waived.

Virtually every law or regulation provides recourse for employees if their employer fails to comply with the communication or disclosure guidelines. For example, if an employee cannot understand an SPD and decides to implement legal recourse, legal precedent is in favor of the employee even though government regulations are obscure themselves. However, complying with legal requirements would usually qualify as information as opposed to communication.

The following examples show how to approach the what, why and how of legally required communication.

EXAMPLE: Taking a Traditional Approach to Legally Required Communication

What to Communicate   Explain the provisions of each defined benefit or defined contribution plan.
Why Communicate   The Employee Retirement Income Security Act (ERISA) requires it.

How to Communicate   Follow the government regulations and guidelines. Publish a document that will comply with all regulations.

EXAMPLE: Consider an Alternative Approach to Legally Required Communication

---

What to Communicate   Explain how each defined benefit or defined contribution plan works.

Why Communicate   Employees should be able to understand their rights and obligations under the provisions of each plan and know how to use the plan efficiently.

How to Communicate   Create a useful reference tool which will be simple to understand, complete and useful to employees.

COMMUNICATOR'S TIP: Understanding SPD Requirements

Summary Plan Descriptions (SPDs) are probably the most challenging type of legally required communication you will have to deal with.

Section 102 of ERISA sets forth the philosophical and specific intent of ERISA with respect to summary plan descriptions. Essentially, it says employers will:

> *"..communicate the rights and obligations of plan participants and beneficiaries in a manner calculated to be understood by the average plan participant... will not fail to inform, mislead or misinform any plan participant about their rights and obligations under the plan...."*

FOR MORE EFFECTIVE COMMUNICATION, READ THE ABOVE AS FOLLOWS

Tell employees:

- what it is
- what it will do for them
- how the rules work
- what happens if they don't follow the rules
- how much it will cost in either money or loss of benefits

The message and intent of each approach is the same. The results can be dramatically different. Sample SPD table of contents and language can be found in Chapter Six.

Good News Communications.   Most organizations are willing, if not eager, to communicate good news. There is nothing wrong with communicating good news as long as the approach is consistent with the way neutral and bad news is communicated. In other words, remember your human resource editorial policy. Also, double check your evaluation of the current situation. Sometimes, management's idea of good news is not shared by employees.

EXAMPLE: Explaining a Retirement Plan

An employer has a retirement plan which requires employee contributions. Employees have complained for years that no employee contributions should be required. As a result of competitive studies, bargaining unit negotiations and restructuring the total compensation package, the retirement plan remained contributory but the amount of employee contributions was reduced.

Management's View:	This is good news. The employees won't have to pay so much to participate in the retirement plan.
Employee's View:	The company was reducing their retirement benefits.
The Problem:	Management had forgotten that employees didn't really understand how their contributions related to the benefit they would actually receive at retirement.
The Solution:	It was necessary to explain the contribution/benefit relationship and demonstrate that, due to other changes in the benefit formula, retirement benefits would not be reduced. A reference tool approach was not sufficient. It required a combination of educational and promotional approaches.

Bad News Communication. No one likes to be the bearer of bad news. The tendency is to delay and deny the inevitable. This is an unwise decision. Bad news travels faster than good news and management's credibility will be jeopardized the longer bad news is covered up. Consider the effect of Watergate on this country's people and their perception of their government representatives. Like good news, bad news is in the eyes of the beholder. Occasionally management's view is a result of their self-inflicted paranoia rather than the employee's real view of the situation. Once again, having a realistic understanding of the current situation is critical.

EXAMPLE: Announcing Work Force Reduction

Work force reduction is one of the most traumatic messages organizations are forced to communicate. Over a period of months, local newspapers published feature articles about the financial dilemmas facing the high tech industry. Periodically, print and broadcast media would highlight the declining financial health of a specific company, predicting layoffs or outright closure. The organization had made a series of expense control announcements but repeatedly denied that layoffs or permanent staff reductions would be necessary. To reinforce their position, they even announced that a new profit sharing plan would be introduced later in the year.

Management's View:	They didn't want to lose key management, professional and research staff. They rationalized that they needed to reassure this segment of their employee population until they could find an acceptable way to deal with the less critical employee groups.
Employee's View:	The key employee group saw the inevitable and decided to find other employment, just in case their jobs fell into the unnecessary category. The less important group was worried as well. They spent most of their time discussing their concerns with coworkers trying to figure out what to do.
The Problem:	The organization lost the key people it was trying to retain and suffered more productivity and quality control problems. Neither of these situations went unnoticed by their customers or the press.
The Solution:	Management discovered too late that their employees made decisions based on the information they had available. The news stories were more credible than management's memos. Now they have to start from scratch and it is not yet clear whether they will succeed. This situation requires a very honest and frequent information approach.

What If Or Just In Case Communication. Frequently an organization finds itself in a situation that will probably mean change and finds it necessary to consider two or more alternatives. The more variables, the more complex the decision making process. Conventional wisdom has suggested that it is dangerous to communicate something that hasn't been resolved. The contrary view holds that honesty is therapeutic and that it is ok to admit that you don't know.

EXAMPLE: An Organization Expands Services

A professional organization had decided to expand the scope of its services. That decision out of the way, all that remained was to decide how to do it. They considered three basic alternatives: (1) train existing staff, (2) hire trained professionals from competitors, (3) buy a competitor. There was a fourth option, to do all three.

Management's View:	Most of its current professional staff would feel threatened and would ask too many hard questions. They will lose faith in our leadership if we don't have all the answers.
Employee's View:	Why can't management see that we should expand our scope of services? It would add to our resources and give us a competitive advantage in the marketplace.
The Problem:	Management did not have faith in their employees understanding of the market and long term organizational goals.
The Solution:	An interactive focus including information and some promotional flavor is often very effective. Solicit opinions from the employees and be willing to feedback unbiased results. Frequently, rank and file employees can offer more effective solutions to management dilemmas because they have a more realistic view of the world in which the organization is operating.

Promotional Communication.   For many years, employers viewed employee communication as something akin to religion. It must be taken very seriously and administered with extreme care so as not to be perceived as theatrical or selling snake oil. This position is usually exactly opposite the approach they take to sales and marketing of their products or services. The low key approach can very often insure that employees will never get an important message. If they don't get the message, it will bias their perceptions.

EXAMPLE: Promoting Educational Funds

A pharmaceutical manufacturing organization had earmarked a great deal of money for education and career advancement training programs.

Management's View:	This will permit us to develop talent and offer new career opportunities to our people as we grow.
Employee's View:	If I want to get ahead, I'll have to go to a competitor because I'm at the top of my salary range here and there are too many people above me.
The Problem:	The only place information about the education and career advancement program was available was in the corporate policies and procedures manual. Employees saw the salary administration program as the only issue driving their career opportunities.

The Solution: Promotion is not a bad word. Promote the program during recruiting, new hire orientation, in the employee handbook, and, through special periodic poster and payroll stuffer campaigns.

Educational Communication.   Educational communication does not mean encouraging employees to attain higher degrees or more specialized training for their job. It is really a method of helping employees understand the complexities of your human resource management challenges. At one time or another, almost all of us fall into the trap of assuming that everyone else is operating from the same base of knowledge that we are. Educational communication techniques are frequently necessary to provide a minimum base of information before the real communication objective can be addressed.

EXAMPLE: Teaching the Whys of Cost Containment

A large manufacturing organization was facing the inevitable challenge of controlling health care costs or reducing benefits. They decided to offer employees managed health plan choices [Health Maintenance Organizations (HMOs) and Preferred Provider Organizations (PPOs)] as well as their conventional health plan. In addition, they added cost containment provisions to their conventional plan.

Management's View: Tell the employees about these new types of plan options and sell them on the idea that they can help insure good quality health care at more efficient costs.

Employee's View: Those newfangled options can't be any good. It's just the company's way of trying to take away benefits.

The Problem: Employees needed to learn that they could become discriminating health care consumers in the same way they were food or automobile consumers, by shopping and comparing.

The Solution: Education had to precede promotion. Develop an ongoing health care communication program, using different media and tools to help take the mystery out of the health care delivery system and encourage employee participation in managing health care providers and dollars.

Informational Communication.   Informational communication is reasonably straightforward. It can and should be used when you are certain there is a common base of knowledge and you need to issue a reminder, update or, clarification. Unfortunately, many organizations approach all communication challenges from this perspective which is why their efforts often don't get the desired results.

EXAMPLE: Updating W-4 Forms for the Coming Tax Year

While preparing federal tax returns, many middle-aged employees in a service organization discovered they would have to borrow money to pay unexpected taxes. Most of the affected employees had lost deductions because their children had gone out on their own. The employees had not thought about the need to alter their W-4 filing status to adjust federal tax deductions to a more realistic level. Changes in tax law simply compounded the problem.

Management's View: Everyone knows they should change their W-4 forms when there is a significant change in their filing status.

Employee's View: Why didn't someone tell me before?

The Problem: Tax laws and regulations are increasingly complex. Employees believe that since employers manage their pay checks (including tax deductions), they understand the tax laws. As a result, they also trust the employer to tell them if they should do something differently.

The Solution: A short memo circulated toward the end of each calendar year alerting employees they should re-evaluate their filing status and/or consult their tax advisor. This action will go a long way to promoting good will. If the employee fails to use the information, he or she is less likely to blame you for resulting problems.

Interactive Communication.   Interactive communication techniques can use all of the other approaches and is probably the most powerful tool of all. Encouraging participation in the communication process establishes ownership. It also changes a primarily directive or downward communication style into an upward/downward partnership.

EXAMPLE: Sharing Limited Equipment Purchase Funds

A medium-sized advertising agency was trying to satisfy each department's request for new or improved computer equipment. Each time a request was granted, outcrys were heard from all the departments that had been denied or were waiting for their turn.

Management's View: We do not have unlimited capital to supply the entire organization with new equipment every time the computer industry announces a new and improved product (which is almost every day). Besides, we aren't using the equipment we have to full capacity.

Employee's View: I could save the company money if I only had the right tools.

The Problem: Management had never asked the departments to share equipment or submit a combined equipment purchase request. Therefore, each department was submitting requests with no consideration of equipment already available within the organization. They became more preoccupied with getting equipment than servicing their clients. The result was declining productivity, increasing expenses, and dissatisfied clients.

The Solution: An enterprising account executive invited all the department heads to a brown bag lunch. He asked each one to bring an inventory of hardware and software currently being used as well as a wish list of what they needed in the coming six to twelve months. The lunch resulted in the department heads developing a plan that called for sharing some existing equipment, reassigning some equipment, and requesting new equipment that was equal to one-quarter of their previous combined requests. They were also able to demonstrate an immediate $20,000 per month return on the investment through lower expenditures and increased productivity.

HOW TO EVALUATE YOUR CURRENT COMMUNICATION TOOLS

One of the easiest ways to evaluate your current communication approach is to identify the communication tools you currently use and grade their effectiveness. The following worksheet lists a variety of communication tools. There are also spaces for you to add other tools commonly used in your organization. Place a checkmark by each tool you currently use. Decide how effective the tool has been by checking the appropriate column: Very Effective; Somewhat Effective; Not Effective.

Figure 1.12: COMMUNICATION TOOLS EVALUATION WORKSHEET

To get a quick picture of how effective your current communication tools are, check the appropriate column.

COMMUNICATION TOOL	VERY EFFECTIVE	SOMEWHAT EFFECTIVE	NOT EFFECTIVE
Newsletters			
Employee Annual Report			
Employee Handbook			
Benefit SPDs			
Bulletin Boards			
Audiovisuals			
Benefit Statements			
Retirement Statements			
Profit Sharing/Thrift Plan Statements			
Job Posting Systems			
Quality Circles			
Legal Notices			
Facilities Guide			
Hot Line			
MBO System			
Message Center			
Personal Computers/Computer Terminals			
Payroll Stuffers			
Bulletins			
Memos			
Letters			
Employee Clubs			
Credit Union			
Cafeteria/Lunchroom			
Fitness Center			
Social Events			
Other			

Once you have completed the checklist you will notice two things. 1) There are a number of tools that you have not used. You may want to consider expanding the variety of tools you use on a regular basis. 2) There are a number of tools you are using that should not be used or should be refined to improve their effectiveness. If you know a tool is not well received, you should concentrate on improving it or eliminating it as soon as possible. You will find tips on how to improve each type in later chapters.

Where To Find Hidden Communication Tools

Most organizations have a variety of communication tools that are overlooked but can work exceptionally well. The following list represents only a few of the most likely hidden tools available in your organization. You will probably think of many more that are unique but nonetheless provide powerful communication opportunities.

- Cafeterias and lunchrooms
- Menu boards, napkins, place mats, table tents, posters
- Special interest groups such as sports teams and clubs
- Tee shirts, newsletters, meetings
- Employee picnics, holiday functions, TGIF parties, health fairs
- Theme games, gifts, gags
- Credit Unions
- Newsletters, bulletin boards, statement stuffers
- Libraries, reference rooms, research facilities
- Newsletters, bulletin boards, reference racks
- Employment, personnel, benefit offices
- Bulletin boards, reference racks, audio-visuals, interactive communication tools such as computers and telephone hotlines

Most of these should be considered as reinforcing tools, not primary. They must be used carefully, with a good deal of sensitive and thoughtful consideration or their potential power can backfire.

In-House Communication Talents And Resources

In addition to hidden communication tools, most organizations also have in-house talent and resources that are overlooked. Frequently, they are there because they are engaged in marketing or supporting your business. This means that they usually don't have much time to work on internal human resource problems. But they can be invaluable as peer reviewers and sources of advice and ideas. Many of these helpers are

Figure 1.13: TALENT AND RESOURCE CHART	
SKILLS	**WHERE TO FIND THEM**
Writers	Corporate Communications, Advertising, Public Relations
Artists	Advertising/Marketing, Corporate Communications
Typesetters	Advertising/Marketing, Corporate Communications, Print Shop
Printers	Advertising, Corporate Communications, Print Shop, Company Newsletter Editor
Audiovisual Producers	Advertising, Training Department, Corporate Communications
Photographers	Advertising, Corporate Communications, Public Relations

connected with the groups mentioned above. Others include public relations, advertising/marketing, computer and administrative services. Get acquainted with these folks. They may be more help than you think. The chart in Figure 1.13 shows technical knowledge or skills you may need and likely sources to be found within an organization.

The types of skills you will most likely require are shown on the left. Usually you can find such skills in most of the in-house departments on the right. If they cannot commit resources to help you, they can usually recommend outside freelancers or vendors they have used. Your own compensation, benefits and human resource consultants are also a good resource. More specific details about technical skills, where to find them and how to manage them can be found in later chapters.

HOW TO ASSESS YOUR CURRENT COMMUNICATION ACTIVITIES

As you begin to evaluate your current communication activities, you may notice that you have more communication tools and procedures in place than you thought. You may even become a little indignant as you start to tick off all the things you're doing and still not seeing the desired results. This is when you start asking yourself three key questions

- why don't employees follow the guidelines?
- why don't employees read?
- why don't employees listen?

They don't for the same reason you don't. The list of excuses may sound familiar. There is too much information, not enough, not relevant, not inviting to read, takes too much time and study, not clear, or its dull and boring. These may seem like very flip replies, but think about them.

We are all on the edge of collapse from information overload. We are constantly barraged with information in every aspect of our lives. The more information we are asked to deal with, the more our survival instincts instruct us to be selective about how much and what kind of information we will accept. Accept is a key word. Each of us has the power to accept or reject any and all efforts to communicate. That is why technique is just as important as content or tools. Some techniques work better than others in certain circumstances.

Who Communicates What

Putting the right *who* with the right *what* can be critical to the potential acceptance of your message. Precedent and the organization's culture will dictate some who/what decisions, but these may or may not be the best decisions. And you may not be able to change poor decisions immediately. A classic example is how and when to use the CEO as the primary communicator.

When to Communicate through the CEO.   Organizations often assume the most senior management person is the best person to get people's attention. In small organizations, it is probably a good idea. Employees know the boss, usually on a first-name basis and they know that is where all the decisions are really made. In medium-sized organizations, where intimacy with the boss is diluted but still predominant, it usually makes sense to use the CEO selectively. In large organizations, it is probably a bad idea unless the topic is clearly an organizational issue of global proportions such as an acquisition, merger, or change of business direction.

When to Communicate through Supervisors.   Over time, studies have repeatedly confirmed that employees prefer getting information from their immediate supervisors. The reasons should be obvious. Employees have an intimate knowledge of their supervisor's philosophies, habits, biases and technical and professional skills. That relationship enables an employee to better assess the information communicated from their supervisor than from a relative stranger, even if they don't like the supervisor. Some of the most obvious situations which call for proactive supervisor participation arise when something changes

- staffing changes (including increases or reduction of work force and reporting relationships)
- policy and/or procedural changes
- compensation and/or benefit changes
- changes in the organization's goals, products or services

When any change occurs, it is normal for employees to approach their supervisor with questions like

- Why?
- What does it mean to me (or us)?
- What do I have to do?
- When?
- What is different?

The last question is key to successfully using supervisors as communicators. If they didn't have a reasonable understanding of the situation before the change, they will be hard pressed to be convincing in their communication role. Therefore, it is important that organizations make a conscious effort to be sure supervisors have the information and knowledge base they will need in order to answer questions under routine circumstances. In all cases, supervisors should know about things before they become common knowledge.

When to Communicate through Employees. Frequently, peer leaders are more effective communicators than any authority figure. Most people feel less threatened by their peers so they are willing to listen more freely. It is also easier to admit ignorance or insecurities in discussions with peers. Finally, there is a stronger bond of intimacy, trust, and common experience among peers. This is especially true of employee groups that have unique cultural similarities such as heritage or language, profession, education or job classifications. Some examples are

- foreign language speaking groups (e.g. Hispanic, Asian)
- political or religious activists
- engineers, health care professionals, scientists
- PhDs, MBAs, FSAs, etc.
- computer departments, word processing departments, mail rooms

Employee peer leaders can effectively reinforce or counteract management's efforts and are the real grapevine managers. The ideal communication process model would have employees, especially peer leaders, as active parts of every communication effort. This is not always a practical option. There are a number of situations, however, that should not be attempted without enlisting help from the rank and file employee population. These are

- acquisitions, mergers, divestitures
- major changes in compensation or benefit plans
- efforts to increase quality or productivity
- cost containment programs

As with all human resource management challenges, this is easier said than done. How to use employees as communicators is covered in later chapters as a part of specific techniques and tools.

Avoiding The 10 Most Common Communication Pitfalls
There are ten mistakes most organizations make that compromise their ability to produce effective communication. You can avoid these mistakes and improve your communication efforts dramatically by keeping the following checklist handy.

Figure 1.14: THE 10 MOST COMMON COMMUNICATION PITFALLS

Poor Writing.

Make sure all written material is crisp and to the point. Use action verbs and use more periods than other punctuation marks. Eliminate prepositional phrases, long words and acronyms.

Mixed Messages.

Don't waffle. Be certain that your message is consistent. The most classic example of sending mixed messages is to set down specific procedural rules or guidelines followed by vague exceptions. If the guidelines are specific, the exceptions should be equally specific.

Unrelated Topics.

Overpowering workloads or just plain laziness cause many people to try to deal with several unrelated topics in one communication tool. While on the surface, this may seem like a timesaving technique, it usually confuses the audience. The typical result is that phone calls and queries increase dramatically and these defeat the timesaving purpose. More often, the communication is disregarded altogether because it's too difficult for the reader to figure out which of the many topics is really significant.

Trying to Cover Up Bad News.

No matter how skillfully you embellish bad news, it is still bad news and your audience will know it instinctively. The more you try to cover it up, the more your credibility will suffer. Employees will accept bad news better if you do not try to cover up.

Clouding the Real Message with a Series of Add-ons.

A variation on the theme of covering up bad news is clouding the issue. If the real issue is that 50 people will have to park a block away because the building management gave those spaces to a larger tenant, don't cloud the issue with a promise to try to get the building to add two more floors to the parking structure. Employees will know it is an unrealistic goal and resent your attempt to mollify them.

Assuming Employees Don't Care.

Employees are more interested than ever about circumstances that can affect the company as well as themselves. The more they know about company goals and performance, the more prepared they are to make personal commitments (or even sacrifices) to benefit the organization.

Assuming Employees Don't Understand the Issue.

Employees are not ignorant. When conducting focus group meetings, I frequently find that employees clearly understand most of the issues confronting the organization. Sometimes they understand issues better than management does because they are on the front line. It never hurts to state the issue, but do it in a way that conveys your regard for employees' intelligence.

Assuming Employees Have the Same Information You Do.

When you work with a set of information for an extended time, it is easy to forget that others have not had the benefit of such concentrated exposure. While employees usually understand general issues, management often forgets or is reluctant to share specifics. Except for very confidential data, it is a good idea to make sure employees have the same information you have.

Forgetting that Honesty Is Therapeutic.

Bending the truth or trying to deceive employees is a waste of energy. Employees may not be happy about what you have to tell them, but they will give you a lot of credit for guts and honesty. Furthermore, they will usually rally to your support, which is the most therapeutic result you could hope for.

Assuming that More
Is Better.

When organizations are insecure about a message they have to communicate, they tend to succumb to all of these pitfalls and get carried away with verbosity. You do not need a five-page memo to explain why the organization must institute a hiring freeze. You can effectively explain the issue in a one-page memo. Finding the right balance between too little and too much information will be your most significant challenge.

CHAPTER 2

HOW TO DEVELOP A HUMAN RESOURCES COMMUNICATION PLAN AND ESTABLISH A BUDGET

There are three basic steps to creating a sound communication plan:

1. Prioritize your needs
2. Identify your tools and resources
3. Prepare and manage your budget

After working through the steps discussed in Chapter 1, you are ready to begin preparing your plan. This chapter will show you how to apply the information you acquired while you were assessing your communication needs. If you skimmed Chapter 1, you might want to go back and look at the forms there. They are designed to provide a foundation upon which to begin prioritizing your needs. They will also help you identify which communication tools have worked best for you in the past and where your best resources are. This information will be very helpful when you begin developing your plan and establishing your budget.

You may have already experienced the good news/bad news realities of improving your communication techniques. The good news is that management supports the idea. The bad news is that you are expected to get the job done for little or no investment. This is especially disconcerting when you know it may cost you twenty, fifty or one-hundred and fifty thousand dollars or more to implement a program. So now you must try to improve communications for less money than you expect it to cost. Don't give up. You have the opportunity to test your management skills and creativity. The first step is to establish a process that is most likely to enable you to succeed. This step is called prioritizing your needs.

PRIORITIZE YOUR COMMUNICATION NEEDS

To develop a communication plan that will stand the test of time, take a look at the big picture then begin scaling back to your short-term needs. You may be asking yourself, what is new about this approach. Nothing really. This process is a classic. Visualize your needs three to five years into the future. List all the communication tools and processes you would have in place if you could play Merlin the Magician. Don't concern yourself at the moment with whether or not management would support these goals. Don't think about whether or not you will be here to implement those goals.

The checklist in Figure 2.1 illustrates one organization's needs with notes about which of them are legally required and which are urgent. As you review this checklist, notice that communicating certain items such as work rules, educational assistance and employee assistance programs can cost very little money and require very little approval from superiors. Other items like performance appraisal training or a flexible compensation enrollment could require a tremendous amount of capital and approval from several levels of management.

Figure 2.1 CHECKLIST OF COMMUNICATION NEEDS AND PRIORITIES

COMMUNICATION NEED	URGENT	REQUIRED	IDEAL
Summary Plan Descriptions	X	X	
Health Care Open Enollment	X	X	
Performance Appraisal Training			X
Work Rules			X
Total Compensation Practices			X
Educational Assistance			X
Recognition Awards			X
New Retirement Plan	X		
Attitude/Climate Survey			X
New Hire Orientation			X
Supervisor Training			X
Employee Assistance Program			X
Voluntary Benefit Enrollments			X
Flex Comp Enrollment			X
Worker's Compensation/EEO Guidelines		X	
Health Care Hot Line			X
Interactive Recruiting Tools			X
Pre-Retirement Counseling			X

Organize Your Priorities For Short- And Long-Term Plans

By putting your communication needs into the framework shown in Figure 2.2, you will see the beginning of your short- and long-term communication plans.

Put the items that will take longer to approve and that require major budgets in the 2-, 3- or 4-year columns.

Figure 2.2 LONG-TERM PLAN				
NEXT 6 MONTHS	YEAR 1	YEAR2	YEAR 3	YEAR 4
REVISE SPDs	Review/Update	Review/Update	Review/Update	Review/Update
ENROLL HEALTH CARE	Annual Enrollment	Annual Enrollment	Annual Enrollment	Annual Enrollment
NEW PAY EQUITY	Announce January 1	Annual Reminder	Annual Reminder	Annual Reminder
	ATTITUDE SURVEY	Review Objectives	Comparison Survey	Review Objectives
	ORIENTATION	Refine/Update	Refine/Update	Refine/Update
		TRAINING PROGRAM	Refine/Update	Refine/Update
		RECRUITING	Refine/Update	Refine/Update
			BENEFIT STATEMENT	Refine/Update
				NEW TOTAL COMPENSATION PLAN

List the essential tasks and items that require virtually no budget and lower-level approval as tasks to accomplish this year or early next year. Be sure to list short-term items as update or refinement projects to do every year. Each year add one or two major new projects to your list.

Organizing your priorities over a period of three to five years allows you to develop a true ongoing system that you can easily administer and update on a regular basis.

What have you done? You have, in fact, created a process that helps you avoid crisis communication problems and allows you to anticipate costs and manage each objective as if you had all the time in the world to dedicate only to that problem. At this point, you are probably thinking it looks simple and even possible except for all of the last minute crises that arise on a daily basis. When you have to deal with mergers or acquisitions, work force reductions, denied medical claims, or early retirement windows, little time remains for worrying about what you are going to do five years from now. That's why it is important to develop subsets of your master plan that will help you minimize your crisis intervention needs. Breaking each project into smaller tasks gives you a useful management tool. A six-month plan like the one in Figure

Figure 2.3 SIX-MONTH PLAN

JULY	AUGUST	SEPTEMBER	OCTOBER	NOVEMBER	DECEMBER
SPDs	SPDs	SPDs	SPDs	SPDs	SPDs
Edit/Add New Provisions	Approve Text and Layouts	Typeset and Camera-Ready Art	Print and Bind	Distribute	Plan Next Year
ENROLL HEALTH	ENROLL HEALTH	ENROLL HEALTH	ENROLL HEALTH	ENROLL HEALTH	ENROLL HEALTH
Finalize Plan Design	Creative Design	Typeset and Art	Supervisor Training	Payroll to Process Results	Confirm Elections to Employees, Plan Providers
Decide on Tools	Write Text	Print	Distribute Material		Plan Next Year
Identify Resoures	Approvals	Schedule Distribution	Employee Meetings		
Confirm Budgets			Enrollment Period		
PAY EQUITY	PAY EQUITY	PAY EQUITY	PAY EQUITY	PAY EQUITY	PAY EQUITY
	Finalize Plan Design	Design and Write Materials	Typeset and Art	Print	Mail Dec. 26 Plan Next Year

2.3 will help you keep your priorities straight and gives you a quick way to measure your progress on each project.

How To Minimize The Daily Crises That Distract You From Communication Goals

"A crisis is a problem you didn't recognize when it was a nit," so wrote Bob Orben.*

Planning and prioritizing communication needs will help you manage them despite the need to occasionally deal with an unrelated crisis. Most crises aren't crises at all. We just perceive them that way because a situation arises that interferes with or adds to our long daily list of things to do. Most crises can be traced

*American Way, "Quip Trip," May 27, 1986

to bad planning. For example, you may have known about a plant closing or layoff for several months. Dealing with the mechanics of the situation more than likely took all of your time and attention. You knew that somewhere in the future you would have to communicate about it but that time seemed a long way off. You had time to plan and avoid trouble, but you didn't do it and now you perceive a crisis. If you took a few minutes to add the plant closing to your planning charts as soon as you knew about it, you could easily avoid a crisis. If you are honest with yourself, you will have to admit that there are very few situations that you couldn't have anticipated.

COMMUNICATOR'S TIP:
Four Ideas for Beating the Crisis Intervention Game

Add communication as a task to every project you undertake.

Delegate a planning responsibility immediately.

Make a task timetable that gives you a graphic illustration of the time available to accomplish the entire assignment. Include communications.

Develop a project model that graphically illustrates each communication task and drop dead dates.

Take just a few moments to think about short- and long-range implications of any action, yours, management's, labor's, or that of the marketplace. Here is a classic example of why this is essential.

EXAMPLE: How One Firm's Plan Backfired

Management at one service organization decided to close early on the Friday before a long holiday weekend. The decision had been made at least two weeks before the holiday. However, management thought it would be wonderful to surprise the employees and announce the early closing at noon that day. Because the organization's business depended heavily on service issues, much employee antagonism resulted from the decision. The reason? Because the people responsible for delivering services to customers found themselves with no support staff. Employees had planned to meet certain commitments to clients but the early closing left them no way to fulfill their promises. The secretarial staff, the mail room, the photocopying services all happily closed as soon as the announcement was circulated. The people who were bringing revenue into the business were furious. The issue became a significant employee relations crisis that could have been avoided.

HOW TO IDENTIFY THE TOOLS AND RESOURCES NECESSARY TO
IMPLEMENT YOUR PLAN

The tools you choose will influence which resources you need in order to implement your communication plan. For example, if your task requires nothing more than a memo or bulletin, your resource needs are limited to photocopying and the mail room. If you plan a multi-media, flexible benefit, open enrollment, campaign, you will need writers, artists, photographers, typesetters, printers, audio-visual producers, and many other resources. But before you can decide which resources you will need, you must decide on which tools you are going to use.

Defining The Scope Of The Project And Identifying Communication Tools

Organizations have a bad habit of deciding what tools they need before they have fully evaluated the scope of the project, its purpose, and the complexity of the message. It's not unusual to find a group of executives saying We want an audiovisual, without even considering why. It just seems like a good idea. They may say, We want a handbook, or, We need a benefit statement. This approach leads to inordinate expense, inefficiency, and poor communications. Sometimes the tool the organization selects is wholly inappropriate for the circumstances. The net effect is that a lot of money is spent with no return on investment. Given sufficient planning and thought about the scope and objectives of the project, however, the appropriate tools will become apparent.

One communication project leader in a large corporation was assigned to research employee communication activities in a number of human resource units, but primarily focusing in the benefit area. When asked whether his informal survey revealed if much communication was going on now and if so, what was being relayed, he answered, "Oh yes, here is a list. We are doing statement stuffers, news bulletins, audio-visuals, handbooks, brochures, slides, and overheads." Pointing to a stack of printed materials, he said that this was maybe one-tenth of what he thought was out there. The problem was that he was talking about the media, not the messages. The first challenge in developing an effective communication plan is to streamline and consolidate messages whenever possible, identify overlapping goals and then analyze the media options.

Three Steps for Defining the Scope of the Project

Step 1. Identify your various audiences and decide whether one communication approach will meet the needs of all audiences. For example, if you decide to include employee meetings in your project plan, but forty percent of your employees are field salespeople, it is unlikely you will be able to effectively organize meetings for them. You might have to hold employee meetings at your major location and prepare special direct mail materials for the sales staff.

Step 2. Determine whether the communication effort is informational in nature or requires employees to take action. If employee response is required, your project will be more complex. In addition to employee tools, you should prepare managers and supervisors for their roles in the project. Typically, this means preparing special supervisor-oriented tools, management briefings, and conducting supervisor training sessions.

Step 3. Evaluate the complexity of the message. If the message is simple, such as announcing a change in the credit union's location and business hours, a simple memo and notices on the bulletin board are probably adequate. At the opposite extreme, trying to achieve a reduction in force by offering a special early retirement window will be a complex undertaking. You will have to be prepared to respond to very specific questions, provide clear explanations and examples of the options available and be certain that all employees understand the business reasons for implementing the reduction.

Once you have a sense of the scope of your project, you will have a better idea of what kinds of tools you will need to implement the communication plan.

Tips for Identifying Appropriate Communication Tools

Review Existing Tools.	Examine your current tools and determine whether or not they are appropriate vehicles for the project task at hand. You can almost always take advantage of employee newsletters, memos, and regularly scheduled staff meetings for any employee communication project.
Identify New Tools You Need.	Decide whether you need to create new tools to meet your objective. If you are changing an existing policy, procedure, compensation, or benefit program, or introducing something new, you will need to consider incorporating new or revised tools in your project plan.

Evaluate the Probable Effectiveness of Each Tool for Each Audience. Some tools will be more effective with one audience than another. For example, newsletters are usually more effective with the general employee population than with supervisors, managers, and field sales personnel. That is because these audiences are more directly responsible for day-to-day business activities which consume a great deal of their time. Therefore, they tend to read newsletter-type publications at leisure. Communication tools targeted specifically to these audiences are likely to receive more immediate attention than tools targeted to the entire employee population.

Ask for Suggestions from Operating Departments and Field Supervisors. Effective managers always know which techniques are most effective with their subordinates. If you ask for their input, you will frequently discover options you had not considered. Plus, you will get more support from them, which is paramount for any effort.

Practical Point The quantity, variety, and frequency of your messages should increase in relation to the scope and complexity of the communication objective.

A Quick Way To Match Communication Tools With Communication Projects

Chapter 1 includes forms and checklists designed to help you choose the most effective tools for your organization. Now that you have specific projects identified, you need to match specific tools to them. For example, if you plan to publish revised summary plan descriptions, you know you will have to use some kind of booklet or handbook format, but you will not need an audiovisual. If you are going to introduce a new paid time off program, you will likely use a variety of tools such as memos, the employee newsletter, booklets, audiovisuals, training guides, and employee meetings. A quick way to choose the tools you will need is to use a project tools worksheet like Figure 2.4. Simply put the project name under the project column head and check the tools you need to communicate effectively.

Why Successful Implementation Begins With Writing Detailed Specifications

Once you define the scope of the project and identify the correct communication tools, it is important to write detailed production specifications for each of the tools and to get competitive bids for production costs. This can be a very chancy area if you aren't careful. Typically typesetters, artists, printers and a-v producers will tell you what you want to hear. They usually won't bother you with details or tell you in advance that what you want is going to cost you three times what you want to pay. These suppliers may not be trying to gouge you. Rather, they are accustomed to clients who do not understand the technical requirements of a job and who often neglect to write detailed specifications in the beginning and don't monitor the project carefully as it goes along.

You should be familiar with three primary types of specifications. One for printed materials, one for conventional audiovisual materials (videotape, film, slides, overheads), and one which will become more and more important, computer-related specifications. Each one has certain very specific and peculiar parameters that, if not carefully managed, can destroy your budget.

The specification lists in Figures 2.5, 2.6 and 2.7 highlight the minimum information you will need to project production costs. More detailed specifications and examples can be found in the specific chapters covering theses topics.

How To Get Accurate, Fixed Costs From Suppliers

Once you have specifications, you are in a position to get reasonably accurate costs. Beware of quotes in ranges. If a supplier tells you that something will cost between fifteen and twenty-five hundred dollars, it means one of two things.

Figure 2.4 SAMPLE PROJECT TOOLS WORKSHEET			
COMMUNICATION TOOL	PROJECT 1	PROJECT 2	PROJECT 3
	SPDs	*Health Care*	*Pay Equity*
Newsletter		*X Sept.*	*X Nov.*
Employee Annual Report			
Employee Handbook			
Benefit SPDs	*XX*		
Bulletin Boards			
Audiovisuals		*XX*	
Benefit Statements			
Retirement Statements			
Profit Sharing/Thrift Statements			
Job Posting System/Quality Circles			
Legal Notices			
Facilities Guide			
Hotline			
MBO System			
Message Center			
Personal Computers/Computer Terminals			
Payroll Stuffers		*XX*	
Bulletins			
Memos/Letters	*XX Transmit*		
Employee Clubs			
Credit Union			
Cafeteria/Lunch Room			
Fitness Center			
Social Events			
Enrollment Kits		XX	
Enrollment Forms		XX	
Administrative Manuals			
Supervisor Guides		XX	XX
Training Meetings		XX	
Employee Meetings		XX	
Other		Computer Program	
Other		Verfication Forms	

Figure 2.5 PRINTED MATERIALS SPECIFICATIONS

PRODUCTION COST ITEMS	THINGS TO CONSIDER
Writing	Will You Use an Internal or External Resource
Design/Art	Will You Use and Internal or External Resource
Typesetting	Amount and Complexity of Text, Charts, Tables
Mechanicals	Prepare Copy and Art for Use by Printer
PRINTING	
Quantity	Number of Pieces to Be Printed
Finished Size	Measurement of Finished Piece (e.g. 8"x10")
Number of Pages	How Many Pages in Finished Product
Stock	What Kind of Paper to Print On
Colors	How Many Colors of Ink, On One or Two Sides
Finishing	Special Instructions such as Folding, Punching Holes, etc.
Delivery	How and Where Will Finished Piece Be Delivered

Figure 2.6 AUDIOVISUAL SPECIFICATIONS

PRODUCTION COST ITEMS	THINGS TO CONSIDER
Length/Number of Slides	Number of Minutes Finished Show Will Be
Scriptwritng	Will You Use an Internal or External Resource
Design/Art	Will You Use and Internal or External Resource
Typesetting	Amount and Complexity of Text, Charts, Tables
Producer	Will You Use an Internal or External Resource
Talent	Number of Actors and/or Narrators
Place	Shoot in Studio, On Location(s), Both
Crew	Photographers, Sound, Make-UP, Grips, etc.
Props	Types (e.g. furniture, pens, paper, bicycles)
Post Production	Editing, Mixing, Dubbing, Special Effects
Contingency	Always Plan for Contingencies

Figure 2.7 COMPUTER PROGRAM SPECIFICATIONS	
PRODUCTION COST ITEMS	**THINGS TO CONSIDER**
Data Sources	Where Will Data Come From (payroll, personnel system, outside vendor)
Hardware	On What Type of Computer(s) Is Data Maintained
Employee Identification	If More Than One Data Source, Are There Common Employee IDs
Compensation	Are There Multiple Compensation Structures and/or Pay Periods
Benefits	Are There Multiple Benefit Structures
Data Content	Is All The Data You Need Available (Age, Sex, Salary, Birth and Hire Dates, Address, Dependents, etc.)
Internal Skills	Do You Have Qualified Internal Programmers and Systems Analysts
Quality	Is Data Reliable

1) Your specifications are unclear, or

2) Your supplier wants more latitude than you should be prepared to give.

As long as you have detailed specifications, you should be able to develop fixed costs for any project. At times, you or a supplier will guess wrong about the time required or the complexity of the project. You can easily budget for that by including a contingency factor in your initial estimating process. If the rules or guidelines change after you are into the project, you must be prepared to pay a penalty. You still have a lot of control however, because the moment it becomes clear that your specifications will change, you develop the new specifications and re-estimate the costs. You will be able to immediately see the impact of the new parameters. This is important because some project changes are a result of someone's whim rather than necessary changes. If you quickly re-estimate the financial impact of the proposed changes, you can veto the changes if the cost/benefit ratio is not reasonable.

Effective Techniques For Matching Resources To Needs

Once you have your projects prioritized and your tools identified, you will need resources to help get the work done. Having your resources available and tuned in to your priorities will help you respond quickly and effectively to both short- and long-term needs, and it will permit you to manage the process with less stress. The idea is to develop an informal network of internal and external helpers.

Tips for Cultivating a Communication Network. Don't underestimate anyone's talent, expertise, or willingness to help. This includes everyone from the janitor to the CEO. For example, everyone in the organization should be viewed as a potential door to your internal grapevine. When all else fails, you can get messages throughout the organization quickly by spending only a few minutes chatting with two, three, or four people.

Conventional resources can also be powerful helpers on very short notice. Following is a list of considerations of the most logical resources to have in your informal network.

Considerations for Potential Network Links	

Corporate Communications Staff. — In addition to being familiar with internal and external production resources such as writers, typesetters and printers, corporate communication resources usually know a lot about how to successfully present information and ideas to top management.

Public Relations Staff. — Like corporate communications, the public relations professionals know how different audiences think and can help you sell your ideas. They are usually very skilled writers but are not as knowledgeable about production resources.

Marketing Staff. — Marketing specialists normally focus on selling the company's products and services. While they usually have little patience for human resource issues, they are excellent advisors with respect to production resources.

Mail Room Staff. — The mail room can make you or break you. In addition to having control of distribution, they frequently can direct you to inexpensive production resources.

Word Processing Staff. — Word processing, like the mail room, has incredible power over your communication destiny. They can also give you a variety of solutions to in-house production challenges such as personalized letters to employees or policies and procedures customized by location.

Office Services/ Photocopying/ Print Shop Staff. — These groups usually know more ways to get something accomplished than most of us would ever imagine. More important, they are always eager to share their creativity and resourcefulness.

Typically corporate communications, public relations, advertising, and marketing departments will have information that can be useful to you in planning and implementing your communication programs. For example, what corporate guidelines determine how the company logo can be used? What are the rules about colors, typefaces, and paper? Can they be broken for internal purposes? Cultivating these resources will give you access to key technical people such as writers, artists, and photographers who can often tell you how to accomplish tasks you thought were impossible.

Frequently the reporting relationships of various groups within an organization are structured in such a way that you might not think of using them. That's why you need to develop a network. Rare is the person who will not be flattered by your asking for advice or help, even though this person may have no direct reporting responsibility to you or your manager. As you get acquainted with one another, you will find ways to return the favor.

How To Develop An External Network

Outside the organization, independent professionals such as writers and artists as well as consulting organizations, design firms, printers, typesetters, and audio-visual producers are frequently called upon to help clients find resources to get a job done. They are often willing to help. A number of professional organizations can put you in touch with the type of talent and resources you need to accomplish a specific goal.

Marshaling your internal and external resources can make you more confident of your ability to deal with almost any situation at any time, particularly when it has to be done tomorrow.

Figure 2.8 lists some national organizations which can help you locate outside resources in your area. Some of these organizations also publish useful newsletters. Figure 2.9, a Resource/Needs Worksheet, can help you identify both internal and external resources and give you a reference list to keep at your fingertips.

Figure 2.8 EIGHT PLACES TO LOOK FOR EXTERNAL RESOURCES

CHAMBER OF COMMERCE OF THE UNITED STATES   (202) 659-6000
1615 H Street, N.W.
Washington, DC 20062

INTERNATIONAL ASSOCIATION OF BUSINESS COMMUNICATORS   (415) 433-3400
One Hallidie Plaza, Suite 600
San Francisco, CA 94102

ADVERTISING SPECIALTY INSTITUTE   (215) 752-4200
1120 Wheeler Way
Langhorne, PA 19047

TYPOGRAPHERS INTERNATIONAL ASSOCIATION   (202) 965-3400
2262 Hall Place, NW, Suite 101
Washington, D.C. 20007

PROFESSIONAL PHOTOGRAPHERS OF AMERICA, INC.   (312) 299-8161
1090 Executive Way
Des Plaines, IL 60018

NATIONAL ASSOCIATION OF INDEPENDENT PUBLISHERS   (813) 946-0283
Box 850
Moore Haven, FL 33471

ASSOCIATION OF VISUAL COMMUNICATORS   (818) 441-2274
900 Palm Avenue, #B
South Pasadena, CA 91030

AMERICAN INSTITUTES FOR RESEARCH   (202) 342-5000
Document Design Center
1055 Thomas Jefferson Street, NW
Washington, D.C. 20007

Figure 2.9 RESOURCE/NEEDS WORKSHEET				
TYPE OF RESOURCE	INTERNAL OR EXTER-NAL	NAME	PHONE	COMMENTS
WRITERS				
Audiovisual				
General				
Technical				
ARTISTS				
TYPESETTERS				
PRINTERS				
Low Budget				
Quality				
PHOTOG-RAPHERS				
PROGRAM-MERS				

Understanding the Art of the Possible.   Keeping your Resource/Needs Worksheet up-to-date lets you get projects done under the most difficult circumstances. Prioritizing your needs, developing critical event timetables, and matching your resources to your timetables will keep you ahead of the tasks rather than trying to play catch-up. You are devising mechanisms to put a system in place that can be administered. Work can also be delegated because all of the primary decision-making tools are at hand. Even if you have your act together, your view of priorities may be in apparent conflict with management's.

Clues To Help You Learn Why Management's Priorities Don't Match Yours

When a discrepancy between your priorities and management's becomes evident, a natural reaction is to assume that the discrepancy lies in priorities. For example, you may wonder if management is worried about the bottom line while you concern yourself with the human issues.

In most cases, the true discrepancy is that senior management has dispensed with the matter altogether. After making the critical decisions and delegating the assignments management went on to other issues. As far as these people are concerned it's a dead topic. There's no good reason why they shouldn't think this way, but doing so can create problems for you if you haven't mobilized your resources to finish the project. How do you do that? Get all of the decisions and priorities out of the way as soon as the issue surfaces, while management is still attentive to the issue. That way, when they are on to other things, you do not have to keep going back for approvals.

KEY FACTORS IN DEVELOPING HUMAN RESOURCES BUDGETS AND MANAGING COSTS

Most organizations do a very poor job of budgeting within the human resource communication area. When asked what is to be budgeted to implement a particular assignment, there are usually two answers. The first answer is some unrealistically low assessment of the value of the task. Worse yet, the question is answered with a question—How much will it cost? It stands to reason that if you are asking how much it costs just before you start to do it, you are not going to like the answer. Furthermore, if a significant budget has not been anticipated in the business operating plan, you will have to scramble to get it approved. What is the answer? Develop realistic annual communication budgets. Don't try to find the money in the catch-all fund!

How To Construct A Realistic Annual Communication Budget

You might use one of several ways to develop an annual budget. There isn't a right or wrong way. The best way is the one that works best in your organizational culture. The three most frequent budgeting methods are: Totaling Costs Per Project, Arbitrary Guestimating, and Traditional Business Budgeting.

Totaling Costs Per Project.   If you know you will undertake three projects next year, you can compute the costs for each project and add them together to construct your annual budget. First, delineate the scope of the project and the tools required for each job. Next, attach budget costs to each project and total them. This will give you a sense of what your communication costs would be for the year.

Arbitrary Guestimating.   If you don't have a communication plan, you can guess that your communication costs will be based on past experience. The method is simple. List all the communication activities you did last year and their costs. Add new projects you expect to do this year. Assign a budget amount for each project. The total will be your communication fund.

PROJECT DESCRIPTION Summary Plan Descriptions	RESOURCES Internal -External	EXPECTED COSTS	PROJECT TOTAL	ANNUAL COSTS
Writing	✓	750		
Design/Art	✓	500 ✗		
Typesetting	✓ OR ✓	2000		
Mechanicals		✗		
PRINTING	✓	5000		
Quantity				
Finished Size				
Number of Pages				
Stock				
Colors				
Finishing				
Delivery				
HEALTH CARE ENROLLMENT				
Pre Announcements	✓	200		
Employee Newsletter	✓	500		
Enrollment Kits	✓	10,000		
Supervisor Guides	✓	2,000		
Field Training	✓	2,000		
Audiovisual	✓	25,000	✗✗	
Employee Meetings	✓	5,000		
Computer Programming	✓	3,000		
Verification Forms	✓	1,000		
Other			48,700	48,700
PAY EQUITY PLAN				
Employee Newsletter	✓	500		
Supervisor Guides	✓	2000		2,500

Figure 2.10 appears above as a table titled **Figure 2.10 SAMPLE ANNUAL BUDGET BY TOTALING COSTS OF THREE PROJECTS**

✗✗ One-Time Cost - Amortize Over 3 years TOTAL 59,450

Figure 2.11 ANNUAL BUDGET BY ARBITRARY GUESTIMATING				
PROJECT DESCRIPTION	**RESOURCES** Internal-External	**LAST YEAR PROJECT COSTS**	**THIS YEAR EXPECTED COSTS**	**TOTAL BUDGET FUND**
Employee Handbook-Newsletter-12 Issues	✓ AND ✓ ✓	$10,000 $60,000	N/A $60,000	0
Health Care Enrollment	✓ AND ✓	$49,000	$35,000	
Orientation Audiovisual	✓	$25,000	N/A	
New Supervisor Training	✓ AND ✓	N/A	$20,000	
Benefit Statement	✓ ✓	N/A	$39,000	
	TOTAL	$144,000	$145,000	$145,000

Figure 2.12 SAMPLE TRADITIONAL BUSINESS BUDGETING TECHNIQUES

Active Employees Beginning of Year 2,000	Total Annual Comp/Benefit Budget $40 million
Current Turnover Rate (%) 10%	% Budget for Communication .005
Expected Gains 300	
Expected Loses 0	
Expected Employees End of Year 2,500	Total ANNUAL Communication Budget $200,000

PROJECT DESCRIP-TION	RESOURCES Internal-External	PROJECT BUDGET	TOTAL EX-PECTED COSTS	BUDGET (%) OF COMP AND BENEFITS
S P D's	✓ AND ✓	$10,000		
NEWSLETTERS (12)	✓	$60,000		
HEALTH CARE ENROLLMENT	✓ AND ✓	$49,000		
PAY EQUITY PLAN INTRO	✓	2,500		
BENEFIT STATEMENT	✓ AND ✓	$30,000		
OTHER — CONTINGENCY	✓ OR ✓	$20,000		
			$171,500	.004
TOTAL BUDGET ESTIMATES			↓	↓

Traditional　　　　　　　Developing a communication budget in much the same way you would any other
Business　　　　　　　　operating budget is undoubtedly the most sound approach. Some organizations start
Budgeting.　　　　　　　looking at an annual budget by assuming they will spend between five hundredths
　　　　　　　　　　　　of one percent to one percent of the total compensation and benefit budget for
　　　　　　　　　　　　communication purposes. That certainly is a good starting point. To use this tech-
　　　　　　　　　　　　nique effectively, however, you will want to use a more structured approach.

Five Steps to Better Communication Budgeting

Step 1. Determine the Probable Number of Employees You Will Have.   Start with how many you expect
to have at the beginning of the year. Factor in your current turnover rate and anticipated gains or losses
due to acquisitions, mergers or layoffs. This will enable you to anticipate the quantities you will need for
each communication tool. For example: If your current population is 2,000, your turnover rate is 10% and
you expect to acquire a firm with 300 employees, you will need at least 2,500-2,600 units of printed
materials.

Practical Point　　　　It is much less expensive to print more than you need the first time than to go
　　　　　　　　　　　　back to the printer two or three times.

Step 2. Prepare Detailed Specifications and Cost Estimates for Each Communication Tool.   If you
spend the time to prepare thorough cost estimates for each tool, you are almost guaranteed to meet your
objectives and stay within your budget. The checklists in Figures 2.5–2.7 summarize the information you
will require for different types of media. You will find more detailed specification and budget worksheets
in Chapters 4-13, which discuss each media type.

Step 3. Complete Your Communication Budget Worksheet.   Transfer the costs from each project cost
estimate worksheet to your budget worksheet and total them to arrive at your expected costs for the year.

Step 4. Test Your Cost Estimates Against the Percent of Your Total Compensation and Benefit Budget.
Calculate a percent (e.g. .005) of your total compensation and benefit budget. If your total direct
compensation and benefit budget is $20 million, .005 of that is $100,000. Considering the amount of
money you are spending for compensation and benefits alone, $100,000 is petty cash. Yet, you can
implement a very good communication program for that much.

Step 5. Compare Estimates.   Compare your project cost estimate total to your percent of compensation
and benefit total. If your project cost estimate total is significantly lower than the percentage total, you
may be underestimating your communication needs. If it is significantly higher than the percentage total,
you may need to consider increasing the percentage of the compensation and benefit budget for a year or
two because your project cost estimates are presumably a reflection of your real minimum needs.

Practical Point　　　　If you follow this budgeting process annually, you will find that after two or
　　　　　　　　　　　　three years, you will have a good program in place and you will be able to
　　　　　　　　　　　　control costs without sacrificing your communication objectives.

Looking beyond the current task or even the current year's needs reveals ways to develop tools that have
more than an immediate application. You will recognize that you can amortize the investment over a longer
period of time. The more mileage you can get out of one tool or effort, the more cost effective it is.

How To Get Management To Approve The Budget

There is nothing unique about a communication budget. It should be a component of your overall budget.
Approach it the same way. Do your homework and present to management the rationale in terms that they
understand.

What is it?
What will it do for us (i.e, the organization)?
How much does it cost?

To the extent that you can show a return on the investment, and/or a savings from prior communication investments, it will be reasonably easy to get management to review your proposed budget with an open mind. Showing a cost/savings ratio against prior year investments probably will not be very difficult if you have been developing communication solutions and tools in a crisis mode. For example, make a list of all the activities in which you were involved last year. Identify all the costs connected with implementing each, item by item. Then use your planning and budget worksheets to cost out the same projects. Factor in the long-term applications that will permit you to amortize the costs over more than one month, six months, or twelve months. You should be able to find a twenty to thirty percent savings.

Why Spreading The Cost Of Your Plan Is A Key To Successful Implementation

Once you have established a budget, you may feel that the cost of your plan is prohibitive. Don't give up! There are many accounting techniques to enable you to spread the cost and reduce your projected budget. You may spend the amount of money you budgeted and end up with more than you expected. One of the quickest and easiest ways to look for additional funds is within your own organization.

Where To Look For Money Within Your Own Company

It's disappointing how often departments and units within an organization overlook their overlapping needs. For example, in larger organizations, a human resource unit may include several departments such as employment, recruiting, compensation or benefits. If an organization is not large enough to have several human resource departments, operating departments typically assume some of the human resource duties such as recruiting and hiring. For example, the sales and manufacturing departments will do their own recruiting and hiring and personnel will process the paperwork.

In either case, each department has a separate budget and the staffs may plan global strategic issues together without ever mentioning specific needs such as communication activities. This is unfortunate. By comparing laundry lists of communication needs, overlapping needs would become apparent. Such overlap presents an opportunity to share expenses and develop better tools to serve each department. As an aside, another substantial benefit which can accrue to the organization insuring that a prospective employee sees and hears the same story throughout his or her experience with the firm, from recruitment to retirement.

EXAMPLE: How One Firm's Combined Effort Solved Problems

A public utility company changed several benefit plans and was rewriting their entire employee benefit handbook. Managers were looking for a way to communicate the changes to employees without spending an inordinate sum. Quite by accident their discussions on how to approach the project revealed that an interim communication tool was necessary. The people in the employment area were doing a poor job of explaining the benefit options to newly hired employees. People from the benefit department perceived that they were spending too much time correcting Employment's mistakes. Recruiters on college campuses and at job fairs also came under criticism for how they represented the total compensation package.

Someone suggested that all departments participate in producing a brochure to highlight benefit issues as well as other factors important to employment, recruiting and direct compensation. With some reluctance, the benefit manager agreed to meet with the respective department heads to discuss the possibilities. Once they were together, it didn't take long for each department to see a real need for the tool that the benefit manager wanted. Also, they could easily see that by sharing the development and production costs, they each could get more than they had independently envisioned. A concise, but very professional-looking, brochure resulted. It met the needs of four departments. The cost to each department was reasonable. For the first time, the organization was communicating a consistent, easy-to-understand message about how its compensation, benefit, and human resource management structure worked. Sometimes doing a little research with your colleagues will uncover some exceptional opportunities. Inter-department cooperation can help everyone get more for their investment.

Ideas For Finding Funding Outside Of Your Company

Even if you have developed a sound budget plan and manage your communication costs well, the scope and complexity of a project may impose prohibitive costs. Production expenses, for example, seem to be a perennial problem. At times like these, remember to look for resources outside your organization that might provide funding. The effect can be the same as with sharing costs internally. Everybody benefits. One of the easiest examples relates to developing employee benefit communication tools where insurance companies, HMOs or other outside vendors have a vested interest in an effective communication campaign with your employees.

EXAMPLE: Sharing the Costs of Health Plan Information

Consider how this idea worked with annual health care open enrollments. Before HMOs gained credibility as alternative health care delivery systems, they could force employers to give them an opportunity to enroll employees in their health care plans. HMOs were just entering the business so they took advantage of their mandate under the Knox-Keene Act. Employers were naturally antagonistic in the beginning because something was being foisted on them by the federal government.

As the health care marketplace became more competitive, some HMOs recognized that they had to make significant investments in marketing and advertising to attract employee membership. Each year, the marketing and advertising budgets increased, as did the level of sophistication of their communication tools. Unfortunately, this created a dilemma for employers. During an annual enrollment, employees were deluged with materials from more than one company-sponsored HMO, plus the company's own indemnity or self-insured medical plan. Employees became more confused. Often they made no decision in hopes it would all go away.

When companies decided they had to do something about health care cost containment, they took another look at this situation and accepted a proactive responsibility to help employees make a reasonable decision from among the company-sponsored health care alternatives.

In 1978, one employer was persuaded to eliminate all of the HMO-produced materials from the enrollment process and develop a tool that fairly represented all of the options. This meant an increased communication cost to the company for which there was no budget. So they met with the various health care providers and proposed a joint funding plan. The resulting tool was much more effective and better served the needs of the company, its employees and the health care providers. Since then, many organizations have formed a joint venture or partnership with HMOs and other health care providers. They all work together and share the cost of developing a useful, effective health care enrollment package.

Methods Of Amortizing Initial Investment

Too frequently organizations are very short-sighted when it comes to developing communication programs and tools. They see a very narrow and limited use. More often than not, they could find ways of extending the use of a given tool or program. Just as the benefits and employment departments did in their joint brochure, the objective is to amortize the investment over a period of time.

Most tools don't have to be one-time undertakings. In fact, they're typically communicating subjects on an on-going basis (or they should be.) Therefore, in planning and designing the tools, it makes sense to design them in such a way that they can be used year after year with only slight, modifications, if any.

EXAMPLE: How an Aerospace Firm Recycled a Successful Campaign

---

An education campaign that was developed for an aerospace company introduced a deferred compensation program to its salaried employees in Southern California. An extensive set of communication tools and training devices were developed for introducing the plan, including an audiovisual, enrollment guides, administrative handbooks, posters, payroll stuffers, and masthead bulletins.

About six months after the campaign was completed, the same plan was introduced to salaried employees in Arizona. About a year after that, the bargaining unit in Arizona negotiated for a similar plan. And a year later, the California bargaining unit got a similar plan. During that three year period, the same fundamental tools were used in each of the campaigns. Because of slight plan design differences, differences in the cultures, and audiences' biases, some fine tuning had to be done each time the program was used. However, the efficiencies gained from careful design, which allowed for changes at relatively small expense, has resulted in saving tens of thousands of dollars. The cost of the initial program was $163,000. Modifying the tools for the Arizona salaried employees was only $15,000; for the Arizona bargaining unit, only $8,000 and for the California bargaining unit, only $13,000. If they had approached each project separately, the total cost would probably have been $50-75,000 more.

Beyond the application of direct employee communication activities, the tools have also served as training tools in various locations throughout the organization to help benefit administrators, recruiters, employment, compensation, and personnel managers gain a better understanding of how the plan works. They have also been modified and used in new hire orientation programs.

Whether your budget is $20,000 or $200,000, you can achieve significant cost efficiencies by planning ahead.

No Budget Or Low Budget Situations

No matter how well you plan and budget, at times you must relate unanticipated issues. You need to convey the message quickly, effectively and cheaply. Here are some ideas:

- Existing information hot line . . . . no budget
- Existing employee publication . . . . no budget
- Bulletin board notices . . . . no/low budget
- Special bulletins on masthead . . . . no/low budget
- Regularly scheduled meetings . . . . no/low budget
- Payroll/credit union stuffers . . . . low budget
- Cafeteria menus/table tents . . . . low budget
- Rest room bulletins . . . . no budget
- Supervisors . . . . no budget
- Internal public address system . . . . no budget
- Electronic mail boxes . . . . no/low budget
- Employee clubs/special interest groups . . . no budget

This list is not exhaustive. You'll notice however that two frequently used tools are glaringly absent: memos and letters from the President. The reasons are that memos frequently get lost or overlooked for days at a time.

Letters from the president often lack credibility unless the organization is very small and employees are accustomed to getting most of their information directly from this person. We'll explore these two media further in Chapter 3.

Look around your organization and compile a list of existing communication vehicles that could satisfy your needs. Add them to your list of resources. Remember that using a variety of vehicles simultaneously can make your job easier and reinforce your message in a non-threatening way.

By now, you have most of the tools and information you will need to set your plan in motion. Many plans get derailed at this point for lack of action. The most common excuse is that implementation had to be delayed because an unexpected crisis took priority. You cannot afford to fall into this trap or all your hard work will have been wasted and you will probably have to start over. Remember that you can control the crisis syndrome. Furthermore, you have been developing a system that will help make your challenges routine.

How to Maximize Short-Term Opportunities

Many short-term communication issues are a result of the crisis mentality. Instead of viewing these projects as burdens, see them as opportunities. Each time you communicate, no matter who the audience or what the topic, take a few minutes to think beyond the immediate need.

- Will you ever have to do this again? If so, how often?
- Is this a small component of a bigger communication challenge?
- Are there other departments or units that also communicate on this topic?
- How do they do it?
- How does their communication effort affect yours?
- Is there a way to use this communication opportunity to establish a precedent for future communication needs?
- How much of this communication effort can be standardized, how much must remain variable?

Few short-term issues lack long-term implications. Filling a short-term need can give you a cornerstone upon which to build a long-term solution.

EXAMPLE: How One Company Implemented a Long-Term Solution to a Short-Term Need

Short-Term Need:	Hire the best young information processing talent available in order to meet current marketplace demands and be cost competitive.
Long-Term Challenges:	Retain the newly hired talent and groom them to help build the company's market share and pre-eminence in the industry.
The Problem:	The talent pool was very small so the competition to hire the best people was fierce. This firm was unable to offer salaries as high as their competition. They repeatedly lost potentially valuable employees to their competition.
The Short-Term Solution:	After asking two or three people why they chose to go to a competitor, it became apparent that salary was not the primary motivator. Each person said the competitor seemed to have better skills training and professional career development programs. The firm quickly realized that their recruiting materials and interview process were focusing almost exclusively on salary and benefits. They revised their recruiting materials and conducted interview

training workshops to place more emphasis on their training and career development programs.

The Long-Term Solution: In order to avoid making similar mistakes in the future, the interview process was revised to ensure that the organization knew why a prospective employee chose to join the firm or a competitor. This informal survey technique will enable the company to constantly review and revise their recruiting and interviewing approach.

HOW TO PREDICT YOUR FUTURE COMMUNICATION NEEDS

Predicting future communication needs is much easier than you think. You have already organized the information you need to make reasonable projections with respect to the organization as it exists today. But what about circumstances that are not part of your current culture? Even those things are more predictible than you may think. Organizations don't change so quickly that you can't be prepared. This list shows events that can arise and affect your communication practices.

- Potential acquisition, merger or sale.
- Change in financial health of the organization.
- Change in marketplace conditions.
- Change in senior management.
- Change in compensation/benefit structures.
- Relationship with unions.
- Emerging trends in community opinion.
- Changes in legislation.

You will more than likely be aware of these issues long before you actually have to relate them to the general employee population. That does not mean that you should wait for the event to occur or details to be finalized before you develop a strategy. If you do, you run the risk of doing a poor job because you weren't prepared and are now facing another crisis intervention task.

How To Beat Murphy's Law: Have A Detailed Schedule

I don't know anyone who doesn't have a lot of Murphy's Law war stories. However, the probability of experiencing the inevitable, if anything can go wrong, it will, increases exponentially when you are trying to implement a communication plan. That is because an infinite number of people and circumstances outside your control can inadvertently sabotage your program. The key to increasing the odds of coming out of the process reasonably whole is to be able to anticipate the greatest risk.

The easiest way to anticipate problems is to be certain that every project has a detailed schedule, allows for Murphy's Law along the way, and is immediately revised the minute a deadline is missed. That way you'll rarely be surprised at the outcome of your project. It will also help you make decisions when someone wants to make changes just as you are ready to cast it in stone. If the changes are absolutely necessary, you must make them and do the best you can to get it done on time. In most cases, changes suggested this late in the project are not mandatory, and showing how they will adversely impact the schedule is often enough to eliminate them.

Three Pitfalls Guaranteed To Cost Time And Money

Several stumbling blocks are sure to destroy your project schedule and budget if you let them. Don't!

1. Rough Drafts. Whether your communication tool is printed, audiovisual, or computer-based, you can count on sloppy peer review if you present the material in anything less than its best dress. The more people you need to sign off on something, the more important it is to present it as if this were the first and last chance to make any suggestions or changes. Use an approval stamp that requires the reviewer to sign and date the draft. However, if designs, words, scripts, or programming specifications look like they will have to be revised, you can be sure that they will not take their review very seriously. If you attach a production schedule to the material, highlighting the reviewer's drop dead date for returning it, you have a better chance of getting it checked more carefully and on a timely basis.

2. Show Me When It's Final. A more dangerous situation is when top management will not look at anything until it is final. You must make every effort to avoid this trap. This approach can be very costly. By using the best dress presentation techniques, you can usually overcome this stumbling block.

3. Multiple Choice. Avoid presenting multiple choices. Most of your reviewers will not be sufficiently conversant with the specifics of the assignment to give any more than biased opinions. Furthermore, they will get confused and you will end up with the proverbial horse that looks like a camel, which will not be very effective. If the design, tone, theme, and tool respond to the audience and project objectives, you can usually get concept approvals by presenting only one option.

EXAMPLE: Flexible Modeling, How to Deal with the Unexpected

The best way to deal with the unexpected is not to panic and not to overreact. One day a printer's representative called to advise that the printer was going into bankruptcy and would close its doors in two days. A client had printing jobs ready to go to press with delivery dates ranging three to ten days from the date of the call. Three tasks had to be done immediately.

> 1) Obtain all mechanical art, film, and other materials the printer was holding.
> 2) Find a new printer or printers who could take the jobs and deliver them on time without additional cost.
> 3) Advise clients what had happened, what was being done about it and what might happen if they were unsuccessful on either points one or two.

Since they are very careful to select reputable suppliers, it was not difficult to handle item number one. Since they always get three bids on every project, they had a place to start looking for a new printer without starting from scratch. We already knew what their bid cost was and we only had to reconfirm it. Since there was a plan and the clients are accustomed to frequent and specific communication about the status of any project, they were almost blasé about the phone calls. They didn't have to panic because they had done proper planning in the beginning. Problems of this magnitude don't occur often, but it only takes one time to create a disaster. Most unexpected problems are only minor irritants if you have an action plan and follow it.

MEASURING THE RESULTS OF A COMMUNICATION PLAN: A KEY TO SUCCESS

It's hardly worth the time and effort to develop and implement any plan if you can't measure the results and see how you're doing. The degree to which you can quantify the results of your efforts depends on your specific objectives. Like all human resource-related activities, there is a gray area that is always subject to interpretation, bias and perception. You can reasonably expect most of the world to agree that one plus one equal two. You will have a difficult time getting agreement that you plus me equal two. The dynamics and complexity of human relationships allow someone to judge that you plus me equal one-and-a-half or two or three or ten.

What Can Be Measured
If you spend enough time at it, you can probably build a case for quantifying anything. The question is, is it worth it? Perhaps. Organizations tend to spend more time and money trying to justify a particular posture through committees, surveys, and superfluous analysis than by just getting on with the job. There

are basically two measuring sticks you can use to evaluate your communication situation. These are fuzzy stuff and hard data.

Measuring the   Trying to measure the fuzzy stuff is frought with danger and frustration but can be
Fuzzy Stuff   useful if not taken to the extreme. Perceptions are powerful regulators of any
(Perceptions).   organization. How things are perceived will influence how people behave. Behavior
                      patterns are a good barometer for evaluating perceptions. The trick is identifying
                      which issue or combination of issues contribute to a specific perception.

EXAMPLE: How Perceptions Affect Communication Efforts

A prominent hospital had contracted for an employee attitude (or climate) survey. The main purpose of the survey was to help determine how the hospital could change their employee communication processes to improve morale and perceptions about the hospital as a place to work. When the results were presented, the hospital was confused and concerned. The results seemed to indicate that employees felt very positive about the hospital and its communication process and had an unusually high level of understanding about human resource policies, procedures, compensation, and benefits. While all these things were measured favorably on the survey, day-to-day behavior patterns indicated low morale and dissidence.

The obvious question: How could daily behavior patterns be in such apparent conflict with the survey results? A post mortem focus group meeting was arranged with respresentatives of human resources and various operating departments within the hospital. After some discussion and deliberation, a clue to the mystery began to emerge. Staff physicians, who traditionally are very powerful in the hospital environment, were intentionally eliminated from the survey because their input was expected to be negatively biased. Their traditional role in the hospital was preeminence and was perceived that way by all hospital employees. This perception, connected with the conflicting messages coming from the physicians and the hospital adminstration created daily confusion. This situation is a classic example of the part audience demographics plays in evaluating your communication strategy. The hospital had a textbook model communication plan in place for everyone except the doctors. The real challenge was to get the doctors to play, to get them to reinforce the hospital's human resource goals. That required a communication effort tailored to the doctors.

Figure 2.13 CHECKLIST FOR UNDERSTANDING AUDIENCE PERCEPTIONS

Following are some of the barometers for measuring how effective your efforts are with respect to influencing perceptions.

- Do employees ask emotional or factual questions?
- Can employees accurately explain the organization's culture?
- Is the organization experiencing quality problems?
- Do employees make emotional or practical suggestions?
- Is productivity static or declining?
- Do employees say one thing and behave differently?
- Do work areas reflect personal/professional pride?

In order to answer the barometer questions, you need to have some mechanisms in place to get periodic feedback. The possibilities are limited only by your creativity and imagination. Following are only a few:

- formal suggestion program
- formal Q&A forum (hot lines, employee publications, surveys)

- quality circles/formal quality assurance reward programs
- periodic mini-opinion surveys
- periodic focus group meetings
- MBWA (management by walking around)
- periodic climate (attitude/job satisfaction) surveys
- periodic customer opinion surveys

You may have guessed by now that there is an important link between how you communicate and how you operate. If actual practice doesn't support what you are saying, it doesn't matter how clearly or consistently you communicate.

Hard Data Analysis Measuring communication effectiveness is much easier when you have some quan-
(Results).   tifiable goal to achieve. For example:

- getting one hundred percent participation in a United Fund campaign
- increasing output by ten percent
- moving fifty percent of all eligible employees into managed health care programs
- getting two hundred and fifty targeted employees to willingly accept early retirement

If you meet or exceed your goals, your communication efforts can be considered successful, provided employees perceive the resulting changes are in their best interest.

How To Establish Realistic Benchmarks

To measure results, it makes sense to establish some measurement benchmarks. It is critical that they be realistic and surveys are the most conventional tool used to establish benchmarks. Unfortunately, there may be a tendency to assume that surveys are the ultimate authority. While they can be a useful tool, they should be used carefully and with a healthy skepticism. After all, other than demographic data, they only reflect opinions and perceptions of a given group of people at a given point in time under a given set of personal and professional circumstances.

What Is the Current Situation?   Benchmarks should be set in the context of the current situation, not what you want it to be but how it really is. If you want to move 50% of your employees into a managed health care plan, but currently 75% of your employees live outside the plan's service area, your goal is not very realistic. You should revise your current target to something less than 25%.

What Are the Criteria of Your Objectives? The communication challenges you face will be directly related to the complexity of your criteria. If you want to encourage two hundred and fifty employees to take early retirement but have three hundred and fifty who are eligible, you must realize that you probably can't control which two hundred and fifty may elect the option. So you have to decide whether retiring any two hundred and fifty of the three hundred and fifty is your measuring stick or if you will complicate it by adding other criteria to your objectives statement.

When to Measure Results.   You should measure results after you have completed the project and there are some results to measure. Remember, however, that the most successful communication efforts are ongoing. There really isn't a beginning and an end. This is particularly true of fuzzy stuff. After you have a suitable set of benchmarks against which to measure, perception and attitudes should be re-evaluated periodically. How often depends on things like the measurement tools you use, your culture, turnover, and objectives. Many organizations rely heavily on attitude surveys and conduct them every year or two. Remember to factor in cultural changes that may have occurred since the last survey.

Measuring hard data is obviously easier. Whether or not you met your specific goals, it is worthwhile to spend a little time evaluating *why.* You will want to use the most successful techniques again and discard those that were either marginal or unsuccessful. One of the most productive ways to accomplish this evaluation is to sponsor a feedback meeting with appropriate managers and supervisors from units, departments, locations, divisions, and other groupings. If the meetings are held soon after a campaign is completed, these people can usually give you candid and accurate feedback regarding results.

Finetuning Your Plan

No matter how successful your communication efforts appear to be, there will always be room for refinement. But there is a fine line between tinkering and refining. The following case studies illustrate three guidelines to remember when you're finetuning.

Don't Fix It if It Isn't Broken.   A financial institution had committed a substantial budget to developing more sophisticated employee communication tools. This meant dispensing with the prior tools including an exceptionally well-done employee newsletter. Virtually no research or planning was done before new tools were developed. There was no evaluation of the effectiveness of the new tools after they were introduced to employees. After several months, management began to sense that employee attitudes and perceptions were deteriorating rather than improving. Subsequent research revealed that the former newsletter was the most powerful and effective formal communication tool the organization had before or after the new communication tools were introduced.

> *Guideline: No matter what your personal bias is, if something*
> *works, keep it. Monitor it to be sure it continues to be effective*
> *and take advantage of it as a component of your overall com-*
> *munication activities.*

Throw It Out if It Doesn't Work.   A high tech organization decided that they needed a personalized benefit statement for their employees. They reasoned that knowing specifics about their benefit plans was important to employees and that this tool would give the firm an opportunity to gain a greater appreciation of the company's cost of providing the benefits. Again, no research was done before producing the statement. After two years, there was no obvious change in employee knowledge, attitudes, or apprecia-tion. A study of the situation revealed that many employees just threw it away or filed it and weren't even sure why they got it.

> *Guideline: Don't do something because it worked somewhere else*
> *or everyone else is doing it. If employees do not perceive any real*
> *value in the tool, no matter how sophisticated, they just won't use*
> *it or even relate to it.*

Change It when Circumstances or Objectives Change.   An entrepreneurial health care services or-ganization experienced rapid growth in the three years following the start up. Initially, internal com-munication problems didn't exist. The handful of employees talked with one another regularly and informally. All had healthy respect for the importance and power of good communication and vowed to make sure it was always a top priority. Two hundred people later, they were perplexed by their inability to spread the word. "We all are like family here," they lamented. With one minor caveat. They had two hundred perceptions of the world rather than eight.

> *Guideline: When you've found a communication technique or*
> *methodology that works, don't kid yourself that it will last forever.*
> *It won't.*

CHAPTER 3

HOW TO WRITE EFFECTIVE MEMOS AND LETTERS TO EMPLOYEES

Memos and letters are the staples of organizational communication. Your challenge is to ensure that your memos and letters are effective and help meet your communication objectives. These objectives will dictate which tools are most appropriate, the style and tone of the message, and who should write it. Different situations may call for different solutions.

This chapter shows you how to use memos and letters to address internal communication issues including letters to applicants, memos regarding benefit changes, or organizational changes or promotions. You will find:

- scores of ready-to-use models of letters and memos
- highly effective format alternatives
- guidance for deciding what format to use and when
- communicator's tips such as how to reduce the length of your memo or letter and increase its effectiveness

Since most memos and letters rely soley on words to send a message, you must carefully consider which techniques can help increase their effectiveness. Authors of the most effective memos and letters focus their attention on content, layout, format and brevity.

FACTORS THAT LIMIT THE EFFECTIVENESS OF LETTERS AND MEMOS

Unfortunately, memos and letters frequently are not read, or they are read too late, because they are poorly written, too long, and employees receive too many of them in any given day. A more subtle reason has to do with how the memo looks on the page. Many memos and letters look uninviting. A common mistake is trying to communicate more information than is appropriate for that format. How many memos or letters do you see that use almost every inch of white space on a page, with long fat, paragraphs and multiple pages. Which of the memos shown in Figures 3.1 and 3.2 are you more likely to read first?

While the memo in Figure 3.1 is only a page long, it is less inviting to read and does not give the reader any more information than the version appearing next. One reason letters and memos tend to be longer than necessary is that the writer waffles. Most people don't like to say no and feel very uncomfortable delivering messages that may be perceived as negative. So he or she tries to soften the message by adding irrelevant or flowery prose.

In these illustrations, the second version is 30% shorter than the first. With careful editing, it could be shortened further without sacrificing the meat of the message. Rare is the person who can write a tight, effective letter or memo in the first draft. Carefully reviewing your draft will reveal ways to communicate the same message in 50 percent or less of the space required originally.

Figure 3.1 FORMAT ALTERNATIVE

XYZ SERVICES
1234 Berendo
Oroville, CA 91344

April 13, 19xx

TO:

FROM:

RE: FLEX AND CHILDCARE BENEFITS

Thank you for your recent memo regarding childcare. I also saw the Tribune article on Section 125 last Sunday.

The 125 or Flex Plan idea has been available for a few years now and is something we are already looking into. As you are aware, this sort of program provides a certain dollar value to each employee in a spending account and the employee spends his or her funds on benefit items of value to them personally. The arrangement would allow those with children to use monies for childcare and others could use the money for insurance benefits or health programs as they choose.

As you recognized, the effective administration of such a program is extremely complex and in the assessment of Finance and Human Resources, probably beyond our current system's capacity. We are evaluating its feasibility, cost, and impact on the organization and will have a better feel for its potential later this year.

Childcare is an important subject to several of our employees and for your information, Jill Sampson and I have been involved in a number of meetings with local employers and outside consultants attempting to identify an effective alternative to the need. Unfortunately, at the moment, the local employers (fifteen of which I called personally) are unwilling or uninterested in working with us to set up some sort of childcare center. With the costs, insurance, and legal liability extremely high, this is not really a program that XYZ can undertake on its own.

Although I haven't given you a great deal of hope for an immediate answer on childcare, I do want you to know that it is a priority and we are evaluating every alternative we can find and we'll keep trying.

COMMUNICATORS' TIP:
How to Quickly Shorten Your Letter or Memo

Eliminate unnecessary words, replace big words with simpler ones and allow only one or two prepositional phrases in any sentence.

What Makes Letters And Memos More Effective?

Like every other tool, there is a time and a place for letters and memos. The larger or more dispersed your target audience, the more likely you want to use memos and letters. They are particularly valuable when you want to send information quickly and in an abbreviated format. Ideally, memos and letters merely highlight issues the writer wishes to communicate while other documents and communication tools provide more detail. The easiest way to construct an effective memo or letter is to limit the information by answering the three basic questions your reader will subconsciously ask. What is it? What will it do for me? How much does it cost (in time, money, inconvenience)?

Figure 3.2 FORMAT ALTERNATIVE

XYZ SERVICES
1234 Berendo
Oroville, CA 91344

April 13, 19xx

TO:

FROM:

RE: FLEX AND CHILDCARE BENEFITS

Thank you for your recent memo regarding the Tribune article about flex plans and childcare benefits.

We have been studying the possibility of offering a flex plan to our employees. We like the idea because it would give all our employees more opportunity to select the benefits most important to them.

However, there are some obstacles we will have to overcome before it would be practical to develop a flex plan for XYZ. The most significant issues are:

- the need to expand our systems capabilities so we can manage such a plan effectively
- assessing which benefits are most needed and wanted by the majority of our employees
- evaluating the overall feasibility, cost and impact on the organization
- limiting the potential legal liability connected with offering childcare

We have tried to interest other local employers in working with us to set up some sort of childcare center. Unfortunately, to date, there is no interest from them.

While I do not have an immediate solution to the childcare issue, I can assure you we will continue to look for alternatives that will be in the best interest of our employees and the company.

For example, in Figures 3.1 and 3.2, the answers to the questions are:

What is it? The topic is childcare and flex benefits.

What will it do for me? It would fill a perceived personal need.

How much does it cost? It will cost the employee time and inconvenience because the company has explained they are not prepared to implement such plans in the forseeable future.

Notice that it was possible to answer the three questions in only thirty-nine words. If you use this technique to answer the questions before you begin writing your letter or memo, it is likely the result will be a more concise, effective communication.

The employee will probably be disappointed that these plans are not immediately forthcoming. However, knowing that enables him or her to accept the reality and move on to other things.

Will A Memo Or Letter Do The Job?

How many times have you asked someone if they got your memo? You may get a response like, Oh, yes but I haven't read it yet, or Gee, I may have, I'm not sure, it's probably among that stack of reading material on my desk. These responses illustrate the risk of relying on letters and memos. You have probably asked yourself more than once why you bother sending out the memos if no one will read them. There are appropriate and inappropriate times to use a memo or letter. Sometimes a post-it note, a phone call, a poster on the bulletin board, a brochure, a booklet or an audio-visual will do the job better. I know one executive who irritates his colleagues, superiors, and staff because he generates an extraordinary volume of non-essential memos. He wastes his time, his secretary's time, and a great deal of stationery just to send a formal memo saying the attached is for your information. Before you dash off a memo or letter, stop for a moment and consider whether it is the right tool for the job.

What To Do If Your Letter Or Memo Doesn't Work

Even if you have correctly assessed the situation and have decided that a memo or letter is the best communication vehicle, there may be times when you are dismayed to find it didn't work. The most common situations are when employees take offense or when nothing happens.

When Employees Take Offense. Employees are usually offended by a letter or memo if they believe they should have been told more, been told earlier or that they should have had some input into the issue at hand. The classic example has to do with the somewhat natural conflict between product development and customer service functions. Product development employees focus on quality, competition, and real production problems. Customer service employees focus on sales, customer satisfaction, and personal credibility issues. This is true whether the organization's business is manufacturing- or service-oriented. Product development gets upset if customer service promises something without asking if it can be done. Customer service gets upset if product development doesn't tell them before the product is made public or fails to deliver when they agreed to.

EXAMPLE: Why It's Important to Tell Employees First

The new product development unit of a local savings and loan company was quite proud of a program they devised. It would give them a competitive edge in the market for at least three months while their competitors scrambled to design a similar product.

They worked diligently with the data systems department to ensure that they could handle the expected volume of business the new product would generate. Meanwhile, the advertising department worked furiously to develop brochures, enrollment forms, and a massive media campaign.

The day the product was announced to the public was near disaster. Prospective customers flocked into the branches only to find that the tellers, the customer service representatives, and even some branch managers could not answer the most basic questions about the new product.

Not only did the company forget to include adequate training in their new product plan, they did not even advise employees when the new product would be made public.

The employees were naturally embarrassed in front of customers. Both employees and customers were furious and the savings and loan lost business and employees as a result.

In the broader human resource context, all employees take offense when they read about company business in the newspaper or hear about it from the competition before the organization gets around to advising them. It is embarrassing to feel like you are the last to know.

COMMUNICATOR'S TIP: Beat the Press and the Competition

Advise employees of pending events or circumstances on the horizon. Even if you can't give them details, they will be less critical and more patient than if they hear it from the outside.

Figure 3.3 ADVISING EMPLOYEES OF A SPECIAL EVENT

August 15, 19xx

TO: Account Executives

FROM: Stanley Miller

RE: Business Trends Seminar

We will be sponsoring a business trends breakfast seminar on October 7 for the senior executives of our 20 largest customer firms. The purpose is to provide a discussion forum to encourage sharing ideas about how we can all more effectively deal with the current tax legislation requirements.

Attached is a preliminary agenda of topics we expect to cover. You will receive more details as soon as plans are finalized and the invitations are ready.

In the meantime, if you have any suggestions for improving the topics agenda, please submit them to Harriet Grant by September 1.

In addition to giving Account Executives advance notice about an event that could impact their customer relationships, the memo shown in Figure 3.3 invites their participation.

Figure 3.4 ADVISING EMPLOYEES OF HOSTILE TAKEOVER BID

March 3, 19xx

Dear

We expect the City Journal to publish an article in Sunday's Business Views section about the intention of XYZ company to buy this company. The announcement is not a cause for alarm.

Based on preliminary discussions, I do not believe their expected offer is in the best interest of our employees, stockholders, or customers. However, under the right circumstances, a merger of our two organizations could be very beneficial to all concerned.

It is not possible to discuss all the details at this time. Over the next few weeks, I will keep you advised of developments surrounding this issue. In the meantime, please direct any specific questions you may have to John Hauser, Human Resource Vice President. Send your questions to John in writing, using our standard Q&A communication form.

Starting next week, we will dedicate a column in ABC NEWS Briefs to answer your questions as quickly as possible.

Sincerely,

President

Taking the initiative to communicate with employees as soon as possible when a significant issue arises sends a reassuring message. This letter (Figure 3.4) sends two important messages: 1) Senior management is proactive about communicating with employees, and 2) There is a plan to keep employees informed about future developments. The power of this approach is that employee attitudes and perceptions are less likely to be influenced by the inevitable publicity, uncertainty and speculation that surrounds mergers and acquisitions. They will instinctively rely on the company-provided information.

Figure 3.5 ADVISING EMPLOYEES OF CAREER OPPORTUNITIES

June 1, 19xx

TO: All Employees

FROM: Vice President, Human Resources

RE: JUNE JOB POSTINGS

Three departments have new job openings this month. They are:
- Marketing
- Information Service
- Quality Control

Position descriptions and qualification requirements are posted in the CAREER section of all bulletin boards along with other positions which have not yet been filled. If you are interested in applying for any opening, complete a Career Opportunity Form and send it to Jane Sims in Personnel. She will arrange an interview for you with the appropriate manager.

Issuing this form memo (Figure 3.5) monthly helps reinforce the idea that the company is committed to career development. It also sends a more subtle message that the employee must take some personal initiative (i.e. checking the bulletin board and submitting an application form).

Figure 3.6 ADVISING EMPLOYEES OF COMPETITIVE SITUATION

February 1, 19xx

TO: All Employees

FROM: Sales Manager

RE: New Business Opportunity

It has come to my attention that Mitchell and Marks recently advised their clients that they will have to pay for user application updates and telephone troubleshooting support.

Their decision gives us an exceptional opportunity because it means that their customers will have to pay ten percent more for the same services. It will also make it more inconvenient for their customers because M&M will not provide these services until they have confirmed the client has paid for them under a separate contract.

Since our comparable software package includes quarterly application and telephone troubleshooting support, we have the opportunity to increase our market share substantially.

We will begin an aggressive direct mail campaign featuring our advantage over the M&M product and expect to experience a substantial increase in client and prospect interest in our product.

We need your help. Next week, you will receive our new promotional brochure. Please get acquainted with the advantages we offer over M&M so you can be a part of promoting our product. If we all promote our advantages, we can reach our 19xx sales goal six months ahead of schedule. If you would like to see how our product compares to theirs, the Sales Staff will be conducting demonstrations in the lunchroom from 12:00 to 1:00 p.m. every day next week.

The memo shown in Figure 3.6 is sent to all employees with the specific objective of creating pride and interest in building company sales and image. The premise is that it isn't only the sales staff that is responsible for building the business. The more the switchboard operator knows about what the company does and why it is better than the competition, the bigger your competitive advantage.

When Nothing Happens.   The most common reason nothing happens when you write a letter or memo is that it didn't contain a call for action or the call to action was too obscure. BP America's Robert B. Horton was quoted in the Wall Street Journal as follows:

> *"When I ask a subordinate to do something, I tend to say, 'When you've got a minute, would you mind doing such-and-such.' I found that, at first, they were taking me literally."*

If you want a specific action to result, be specific about what it is and when you want it.

EXAMPLE: Weak Call to Action

Please decide whether or not you think this recommendation is valid.

EXAMPLE: Better

Please advise me by Friday whether or not you will support this recommendation.

EXAMPLE: Weak Call to Action

You should decide which health plan is best for you and your family.

EXAMPLE: Better

Decide which health plan is best for you and your family and return your completed enrollment form to Employee Benefits before April 1.

CHECKLIST: Deciding when to Write a Letter or Memo

Write a memo if:

- it is appropriate to communicate the topic informally (e.g. change in parking space allocation, confirming time and place of a scheduled meeting)
- you can limit the length to one page or less
- the audience does not require a lot of support information to understand the message
- you expect actions or results from the reader(s)
- a phone call or personal discussion would not get the same results as a memo
- the audience really needs the information

Write a letter if:

- the topic should be communicated more formally (e.g. offer letter to prospective new hire, congratulations on promotion, termination notice)
- you can limit the length to one page or less
- the audience does not require a lot of support information to understand the message

- a phone call or personal discussion would not be appropriate
- the audience really needs the information in the letter format

Select a different medium if:

- the information requires more detail than can be covered in a one-page letter or memo
- examples, charts, illustrations, sound or motion will help communicate the message
- the information should be kept by the recipient(s) for future reference

---

Figure 3.7 INFORMAL SKILLS TRAINING

January 1, 19xx

TO: All Employees

FROM: PC User Group

RE: 19xx PC User Group Brown Bag Lunch Schedule

Our 19xx PC User Group schedule is attached. We are happy to welcome eight new participants to our monthly brown bag lunches. The list of our new and regular participants is attached.

The January meeting will be lead by Les Johnson who indicates that his Lotus 1-2-3 team will demonstrate six new timesaving templates. Bring your formatted disks so you can copy them and take them back to your work station.

If you haven't attended one of our brown bag lunches and are interested in learning about how our user group network can help you get started or improve your skills on the PC, contact any of the regular participants.

Plan to join us at our next meeting on January 12. Also please bring your latest problem or solution to share in our Q&A forum at the end of the formal agenda.

Encouraging informal employee-sponsored and managed communication activities such as this brown bag lunch (Figure 3.7) is a powerful communication technique.

Figure 3.8 INVITING EMPLOYEES TO MEET A DISTINGUISHED VISITOR

May 16, 19xx

TO: All Employees

FROM: VP, Human Resources

RE: Meet Mr. Murphy

Mr. Samuel Murphy, a distinguished scientist from our Atlanta plant will be visiting our office June 3 and 4. As you may know, Sam has received tremendous support for his innovative aircraft engineering ideas.

Figure 3.8 Continued

Sam will be conducting a technical seminar for our clients on June 4 but has expressed a desire to meet the Santa Clara staff and learn more about our activities.

Therefore, the South Room of the cafeteria will be dedicated to Meet Mr. Murphy on June 3. The entire day will be dedicated to ongoing informal rap sessions with Sam. If you would like to join the sessions, please make arrangements with your supervisor.

Coffee and soft drinks will be available throughout the day in the South Room. However, all food items must be confined to the Main and North Rooms of the cafeteria. If you are unable to Meet Mr. Murphy during the day, you are invited to join him at an informal reception in the commons area between 5:00 and 7:00 p.m.

Advising employees when and why an internal or external dignitary is visiting reduces speculation even if you can't arrange meeting opportunities for all employees as this firm did. (See Figure 3.8.)

Figure 3.9 COMMUNICATING A TRAGEDY

November 6, 19xx

TO: All Employees

FROM: President

RE: Justin Smith-Jones

I am sorry to advise you that our Chief Financial Officer, Justin Smith-Jones was killed in a freak auto accident over the weekend. It is a tragic loss.

Private services will be held on Wednesday at the Church of the Holy Cross. His family requests that we make donations to his favorite charity, [name charity], rather than send flowers or other remembrances.

The company will make a $5,000 contribution to [name charity] on behalf of all ABC employees.

Tragedies are always difficult to communicate. It is best to be clear and brief, as illustrated in Figure 3.9.

Figure 3.10 STOCK PURCHASE OFFERING TRANSMITTAL

December 1, 19xx

TO: All Eligible Employees

FROM: Benefit Manager

RE: Stock Purchase Offering

Enclosed is your Stock Purchase Enrollment Kit for the new plan year beginning January 1.

The kit contains:

- a highlight brochure summarizing the features of the plan, including questions most frequently asked

Figure 3.10 Continued

- a personalized participation form showing your status in the current plan and your options for the new plan offering
- a personalized enrollment form

Employee Meetings. Information meetings will be held from 8:00 to 9:00 a.m. during the week of December 5. The purpose of the meetings is to answer any questions not covered in your enrollment kit. Attendance is voluntary.

Enrollment Deadline. If you wish to participate in the new offering, complete the personalized enrollment form (include any changes such as address or family status), sign it and return it to Veronica Small not later than December 20. If your completed enrollment form is not received by that date, you will not be eligible to participate in the plan until the next offering at the end of next year.

Tips For Improving Your Memo- And Letter-Writing Skills

The following tips will help keep your letters and memos concise and increase the probability that they will be read.

DO:

limit your message to 250 words, double spaced
keep prepositional phrases to a minimum
use common words
avoid multi-syllable words
use periods generously
use active rather than passive verbs
eliminate unnecessary information
avoid acronyms or facsimilies

DON'T:

use all the space available just because it's there
refer to unfamiliar people, places or things (e.g. The NPG members suggest...)
allow a sentence to be longer than 2 lines.
allow a paragraph to be a half page long.

Employee Situations: When Letters Are More Appropriate Than Memos

The most important situations calling for letters relate to more formal, individual or personal issues. These are typically situations that suggest the information has been somewhat personalized for the specific reader and should be considered more private. It is important to be sure that the right person is writing the letter. Usually, letters come from senior management, but level within the organization is not the primary criterion. Figures 3.11 through 3.16 illustrate letters.

CHECKLIST: Common Situations which Require Letters

- offer letter to prospective employee
- welcome letter to new employee

- major organizational change (e.g. acquisition, merger)
- termination letter
- retirement congratulatory letter
- major change in business objectives
- change in senior management
- major change in condition of organization (e.g. big loss, quality control problem publicized in the news media)
- special recognition to employee
- professional courtesy
- invitation to a formal organization function
- acknowledging a resignation
- refusing employment, raises, bonus
- congratulations for achievement, promotion, anniversary

Figure 3.11 OFFER LETTER

April 24, 19xx

Dear

I am pleased to offer you the position of Director of Product Marketing with [firm name].

The specific elements of this offer are as follows:

> You will report directly to [name], Vice President, Marketing and your duties will be those discussed during your interview.
> Your start date will be March 16.
> Your base salary will be $_____ annually. You will also participate in the fringe benefit package provided to employees at your level.

I will recommend that the Board of Directors grant you options under the Company's Stock Option Plan. Your total number of exercisable shares will be 7,000. The exercise price will be the fair market value on the grant date (which would be the next meeting of the Board of Directors following your hire date). All shares are subject to the 4-year vesting schedule with 25% of the shares vesting on each anniversary of the grant date.

As a participant in our Executive Bonus Plan, you will be eligible for bonus payments between 20% and 45% of your base salary. The bonus formula is based on your attaining personal performance objectives as established by [name of supervisor] and yourself and the Company's attainment of sales/profitibility targets. Your personal performance accounts for 67% of the formula. Company performance accounts for 33%.

This offer is contingent upon your successful completion of a physical examination with our Company physician and our reference checks. If you agree, please indicate your acceptance by signing below and returning a copy to me.

We are enthusiastic about you joining [firm name] and look forward to our future working relationship.

Sincerely,

Paula Cowan, Vice President, Human Resources

Accepted and Agreed:

By: _____ Date: _____

Figure 3.12 WELCOME

April 24, 19xx

Dear

Welcome to [name of firm]. I am pleased that you have chosen to accept our employment offer and know that this is the beginning of a mutually beneficial association.

Enclosed is our welcome kit which includes material designed to help you get acquainted with your new work location, our community, and your co-workers.

As part of our career development program, we encourage our employees to take advantage of continuing education courses available in this vicinity. The courses and their corresponding registration dates are included in your welcome kit. If you decide to attend one of these courses, please advise your office manager and he will make the necessary arrangements.

If there is any other way I can help, please give me a call. Looking forward to seeing you on May 1.

Sincerely,

John Doe, Vice President, Specialty Operations

Figure 3.13 THANKS AND A BONUS

April 24, 19xx

Dear

Your extra effort and contribution to the [description of project] was truly outstanding. It is clear that we were awarded this project due to your fine work.

Please accept the enclosed check as our way of saying thank you for a job well done.

Sincerely,

John Doe, President

Figure 3.14 LAYOFF

April 24, 19xx

Dear

You are aware that our recent reorganization has been a difficult period for all of us. We had hoped that our efforts would enable us to keep all of our employees with the company. Unfortunately, this is not the case.

It is with regret, therefore, that we must inform you that we will be unable to utilize your services after [date]. We have been pleased with the qualities you have exhibited during your employment with us, and will be sorry to lose you.

Figure 3.14 Continued

Please accept our best wishes for your future.

Sincerely,

John Doe, Director of Personnel

Figure 3.15 THANK YOU TO YOU AND YOUR STAFF

April 24, 19xx

Dear

This letter is to thank you for the hospitality and courtesy that was extended to our Australian visitors during their recent tour of your facilities.

Your staff went out of their way to ensure that our visitors understood your operational systems and procedures. Their enthusiasm speaks well for your management skills and it's rewarding to see that they are apparently very proud of their association with our firm.

Please accept my thanks and express my gratitude to your personnel.

Sincerely,

John Doe, President

Figure 3.16 SPECIAL RECOGNITION

April 24, 19xx

Dear

You have proven the skeptics wrong and accomplished what most said was impossible.

There is no doubt that your recent achievements will be spoken of for some time to come and that the admiration for your accomplishments is felt by all of us within the industry, as well as the general public.

Please accept my heartiest congratulations for your success.

Sincerely,

John Doe, President

Employee Situations: When Memos Are More Appropriate Than Letters

Don't forget that memorandum means "a note to help the memory." A note is not a book-length position paper.

Think of memos as the organization's equivalent of advertising's billboards. The most effective billboards are concise and typically lead you to other sources for more detail. A rule of thumb for the advertising industry is that a billboard should not contain more than 10 words, less if possible. The sign must be able to be viewed and understood within seconds. It relies on both emotional and logical responses. The appeal to the target audience's emotional response is based on their biases. The appeal for a logical response requires motivating an individual to get more details. The most effective billboards are a combination of pictures and words. Typically you will not include pictures in a memo. However, if the memo is attractively formatted so the prospective reader can absorb the information quickly, the net effect will be very similar to having used pictures. The examples shown in Figures 3.17 through 3.19 communicate the same message, but notice, by deleting unnecessary words and changing the format, the clarity and effectiveness of the message increases. Figures 3.20 through 3.24 illustrate a variety of memos.

CHECKLIST: Occasions when Memos Are More Appropriate than Letters

- alerting impending organizational change
- announcing impending change to compensation and/or benefits policies
- announcing changes in hours, availability of services or resources, or any change affecting established day-to-day routines, habits, or patterns of operation
- confirming verbal agreements and/or commitments
- requesting or responding to requests for recommendations
- announcing employee meetings or social events
- publicly commending an individual or group for extraordinary efforts or successes

---

Figure 3.17 DRIVING EXPENSE POLICY—FORMAT 1

April 24, 19xx

TO: All Employees

FROM: Director of Personnel

RE: DRIVING EXPENSE REIMBURSEMENT

It is essential that any of our personnel who drive company and personal vehicles in connection with company business maintain a thorough record of any expenses incurred. It is our desire to be certain that you are reimbursed for any expenditures that you make in this regard and your good record keeping will make this possible.

Receipts must be submitted for gasoline purchases, parking expenses, and repairs. In addition, we will require your daily record of the number of miles driven, the odometer reading, before and after, and the amount of time spent driving. This information should be contained in your weekly report to [name].

Thank you very much for your cooperation in this matter.

Figure 3.18 DRIVING EXPENSE POLICY—FORMAT 2

April 24, 19xx

TO: All Employees

FROM: Director of Personnel

RE: DRIVING EXPENSE REIMBURSEMENT

It is our desire to be certain that you are reimbursed for any expenditures that you make in this regard, and your good record keeping will make this possible.

Driving Reimbursement Policy. It is essential that any of our personnel who drive company and personal vehicles in connection with company business maintain a thorough record of any expenses incurred.

Records Required. Receipts must be submitted for gasoline purchases, parking expenses, and repairs. In addition, we will require your daily record of the number of miles driven, the odometer reading, before and after, and the amount of time spent driving.

When and How to Submit Expenses for Reimbursement. The records listed above, along with an Expense Reimbursement Request form must be submitted weekly to [name].

Thank you very much for your cooperation in this matter.

Figure 3.19 DRIVING EXPENSE POLICY—FORMAT 3

April 24, 19xx

TO: All Employees

FROM: Director of Personnel

RE: DRIVING EXPENSE REIMBURSEMENT

If you drive a company or personal vehicle in connection with company business, you must submit detailed records of all expenses so you can be properly reimbursed.

Quick Check Procedure

1. Submit a Driving Expense Reimbursement Form on the last day of each week.

2. Attach all receipts for:
- gasoline purchases
- parking expenses
- repairs

3. Attach your daily mileage record including:
- number of miles driven
- odometer reading at start of trip
- odometer reading at end of trip
- amount of time driven

Submit this with your weekly report to [name].

Thank you very much for your cooperation.

Figure 3.20 STAFF CONGRATULATIONS

April 24, 19xx

TO: Sales Department Members

FROM: John Doe, Director of Marketing

SUBJECT: Monthly Results

The numbers are in and I am proud to inform you that our total sales for the period of April 15th through May 15th amount to $358,466.00, which represents a 10% increase over our sales for the preceding period.

You have achieved the goal we established in the first week of April, and you are all to be highly commended for your achievement. Congratulations!

Figure 3.21 EMPLOYEE MORALE

April 24, 19xx

TO: President

FROM: Vice President, Human Resources

SUBJECT: EMPLOYEE MORALE

There is such a high degree of anxiety about the proposed merger with [name of firm] that I can see increasing negative effects in my department daily. I do not feel that the newsletter put out last week helped reduce the fears of the other employees.

I believe that it might be beneficial to meet the issue head-on by holding meetings to answer employee questions directly.

There is a credibility problem between employees and management that appears to be growing and could create more serious problems. If, for example, this merger fails to materialize, the employees may maintain their current feelings of alienation to the detriment of the organization.

I know that there are many inherent problems in hashing this subject out in an open forum. However, I would like to suggest that we schedule three Coffee with the President sessions here in the home office next week to test my theory. If you will give me your decision by tomorrow afternoon, I will make the necessary arrangements.

Figure 3.22 ORGANIZATIONAL CHANGE

April 24, 19xx

TO: All Home Office Employees

FROM: President

SUBJECT: PROPOSED MERGER

It has come to my attention that some of you are concerned about the proposed merger. There is no doubt that if the merger materializes, it will affect all of us personally and professionally. However, it

Figure 3.22 Continued

should be viewed as presenting us with new challenges and opportunities rather than a cause for concern.

To help us keep the proper perspective, I would like to discuss this matter with you in person. Therefore, I have scheduled Coffee Klatch sessions next week to which you are invited. The attached schedule outlines the times and location of each session and indicates which meeting you should attend. If you have a scheduling conflict, please contact Mr. Winter immediately so that he can make appropriate adjustments.

I look forward to seeing all of you next week and will be prepared to answer your questions to the best of my ability.

Figure 3.23 BEHAVIOR PROBLEMS

April 24, 19xx

TO: All Employees

FROM: President

As President of this company, I was disappointed and humiliated by the behavior of some [name of firm] employees who attended the meeting on [day]. The discourtesy shown to [individual] was unforgivable. Some employees not only talked incessantly during our speaker's address but also exhibited the height of rudeness by leaving the auditorium before the completion of his speech. To anyone who is guilty of these actions, I want you to know that such behavior will not be tolerated by this firm.

It distresses me to have to write a message such as this to you, and I certainly hope and trust that it will never again be necessary.

Figure 3.24 BENEFIT CHANGES

April 24, 19xx

TO: All Employees

FROM: Director of Benefits

RE: EMPLOYEE HANDBOOK REPLACEMENT PAGES

As a result of major changes in several of our employee benefit plans, some sections of our Employee Handbook have been revised. Please replace the affected sections of your handbook with the enclosed revised setions.

Also enclosed is a benefit summary which will give you a brief overview of the changes. You may want to keep the summary in the front of your handbook for quick reference.

WHEN SHOULD THE PRESIDENT OR HUMAN RESOURCES DEPARTMENT
SEND MEMOS

In small organizations, where employees are accustomed to hearing directly from the president, the only issue is whether the communication tool should be a letter or a memo. If employees are not accustomed to hearing from the president, the problem becomes more complicated. That is primarily because the culture or conventional wisdom is predisposed to seeing the CEO communicate (usually via a letter) that something dramatic is in the works. If the topic is appropriate for the CEO, fine, but frequently, the top executive is used as a scapegoat, whether intentionally or not. Consider this example about cost containment policies.

EXAMPLE: How Using a Letter from the President Caused One Company Problems

---

A company has made modest changes in the employee health care plan, adding health care, cost containment provisions, mandatory second surgical opinions, utilization review programs, and even increased the plan deductible. For the past 18 months, employees have not heard from the president on these topics. The information has come directly from the human resources staff, but the changes have not had a dramatic impact on the employees' out-of-pocket expenses. Likewise, there has not been much change in health care utilization patterns. Now, the organization decides to put sanctions or, as some organizations like to call them, incentives into the health care benefit plan provisions. With the incentives come major cutbacks in benefit payments if employees do not follow the utilization review procedures.

The organization communicates this to employees by having the president send them a letter. The letter talks about the continuing increase in national health care costs, how those costs relate to the national debt, and other equally innocuous statements. There is very little, if any, reference to the impending changes in the company's employee medical plan. The problem is that it is difficult for employees making twenty-five thousand dollars a year to relate to billions of dollars of national debt and health care costs and understand how these billions impact their personal lives and relate them to the company's employee medical plan.

The reason the president writes the letter is not because he is the appropriate person to write the letter, but because he is being used as a scapegoat, intentionally or unintentionally. Why, all of a sudden, is the president sending letters to employees to talk about how the national debt relates to the organization's health care incentives. A better idea is to tell employees how the incentives relate to their pocketbooks. A more appropriate person to write the letter or memo would be the benefit manager, the personnel director, or the human resources vice president.

This scenario is a foolish use of the president's image, and it demonstrates that the prior communication efforts were less than effective.

At the other end of the spectrum, the chairman of a medium-sized communication arts firm has such high visibility with the employees that they would expect him to be the author, no matter what the issue or topic. He, in fact, sends letters and memos to employees almost daily. Others in the organization do too, however, employees tend to look for something from the chairman to reinforce information they receive from any other source.

Most organizations fall between these two extremes. In the earlier sample memo regarding a proposed merger it was not customary for the president to send memos to employees. However, the issue at hand made it appropriate for the memo to come directly from him.

We've already established that your culture will frequently dictate who should send what memos or letters to whom. However, it makes sense to look at this issue a little more closely. Perhaps the easiest way to decide who should send the memos or letters is to identify who has the most hands-on knowledge of the issue or task. Many service organizations have found that a letter or memo from a secretary or administrative staff person can be just as effective as a communication from senior management. If the author is recognized as the person responsible for doing the work, he or she will have the most credibility and will communicate clearly.

Sometimes in an effort to be cooperative and helpful, you may volunteer to be the author of a memo or letter when it is not appropriate. This happens most frequently when the memo should come from an operations manager. By evaluating the topic and thinking about who the appropriate author should be, you can help influence the decision of the author. You will probably be able to notice an increase in memo/letter effectiveness and how they are received if you help identify the appropriate person(s) to write them. Egos must be put to rest in the process.

Figures 3.25 through 3.30 are examples of memos and/or letters written for the specific purpose of communicating to employees. Following each example is a rewritten version of the memo. You decide which is better.

Figure 3.25 EXAMPLE 1—HIRING OUTSIDE SUPPLIER: POORLY WRITTEN

TO: Marketing Coordinating Committee

FROM: John Jones

RE: Retention of a Public Relations Organization

At our meeting on May 28, there appeared to be general agreement that we need professional outside assistance to create a positive image of our consulting practice capabilities among potential clients. Larry's 5/28/87 memo on our Consulting Practice Focus pointed out the need for our organization being recognized as the Best Consulting firm in the area. Larry, Dan, Marty, Jim, and I, in somewhat different ways, expressed the need to achieve greater visibility by use of speeches, seminars, and published articles. I think we all agreed that we need outside professional help, help from a source with media connections, experience in achieving an organization's visibility by getting articles published in important newspapers, magazines, etc.

As I mentioned during the meeting, I had assistance in numerous ways during a long period of years from an individual (name) who is quite knowledgeable of how to get media attention (he worked several years for the Wall Street Journal). He worked for my organization until our merger in March. Dick was able to get me and other staff members quoted in numerous magazines (Forbes, Fortune, Penions and Investment Age, etc.), in newspapers (the L.A. Times and New York Times, among many others) and assisted me and our professional staff continually in writing newsletters, developing and publishing surveys, etc.

Early last month, I contacted Dick and asked him to submit a brief proposal to assist us. Attached for your review is Dick's proposal which is self-explanatory. Having had a very favorable long-term experience with Dick and his organization, I propose that we retain him. Retention of his firm on a monthly basis will give you an opportunity to evaluate his effectiveness without making a long-term commitment.

Figure 3.26 EXAMPLE 1—HIRING OUTSIDE SUPPLIER: IMPROVED VERSION

TO: Marketing Coordinating Committee

FROM: John Jones

RE: Hiring Outside Public Relations Help

As agreed at our May 28 meeting, we need professional public relations assistance to strengthen our visibility and image in the business community.

(Name), with whom I had exceptional success for several years before the merger, has submitted the attached proposal for our consideration.

Having had a very favorable long-term experience with Dick and his organization, I propose that we retain him. As you will see from his proposal, he will provide services on a month-to-month basis which will give us an opportunity to evaluate his effectiveness without making a long-term commitment.

Please let me know by Friday whether or not you concur with my recommendation.

Figure 3.27 EXAMPLE 2—SECURITY PROCEDURES: POORLY WRITTEN

TO: All Employees

FROM: Home Office Security

RE: Indentification Badge Procedure

All persons (employees and visitors) entering the home office complex are required to wear identification badges at all times while on company property. These are to be worn at or above the waist on the front of the body and on an outer garment for clear visibility at all times while on the company premises.

New employees will be issued a permanent home office badge (with their photo) on their first day of work, by the Facilities Operations Department in central plaza.

All visitors and vendors must check in with the Security Office at the reception desk for an appropriate badge. All visitors and vendors must be escorted at all times. All visitor and vendor badges are to be returned to the reception desk prior to leaving the home office premises.

When the badge is forgotten, the employees will need to obtain a temporary employee badge at any reception desk. When the badge is lost, a temporary employee badge will be issued for one week, then a replacement should be obtained from Facilities Operations. Changes in name, building location, appearance (i.e. hair color, glasses/contacts), etc. will require a replacement badge from Facilities Operation.

Terminating employees will receive their paychecks only after returning their badges and credit cards, (if any), to the Security Officer at the reception desk in the foyer of central plaza. Transferring employees are to return their badges to the same location.

Any badges that are found should be given to a Security Officer at one of the reception desks.

The improper use of an identification badge (i.e. loaning it to a friend) is prohibited. Badges may not be altered or changed in any way and may not be used for any purpose other than official company business. For additional information, contact the home office security supervisor, Ext. 0000.

Figure 3.28 EXAMPLE 2—SECURITY PROCEDURES: IMPROVED VERSION

TO: All Employees

FROM: Home Office Security Supervisor - Ext. 0000

RE: Identification Badge Policy

Policy: All persons entering the home office complex are required to wear identification badges at all times while on company property. Badges must be clearly visible and worn as follows:
- at or above the waist
- on the front of the body
- on an outer garment

Only the Facilities Operations Department in central plaza is authorized to issue or replace permanent badges. The Security Office at the reception desk is authorized to issue temporary badges. The following procedures must be followed at all times:

New Employees. If you are a new employee, you will receive a permanent badge on your first day of work.

Forgotten Badges. If you forgot to wear your badge to work, request a temporary employee badge at any reception desk.

Lost/Found Badges. If you lose your badge, you may obtain a temporary employee badge for one week. A permanent replacement badge must be obtained from Facilities Operations. If you find someone else's badge, return it to a Security Officer at one of the reception desks.

Changes. If there is a change in your name, building location, appearance (e.g. hair color, glasses/contacts), you are required to request a replacement badge.

Transfers/Termination. If you transfer to another location or terminate employment for any reason, you must return your badge and credit cards (if any) to the foyer reception desk Security Officer in order to receive your final paycheck.

Misuse/Alterations. Improper use of your badge (e.g. loaning it to a friend) is prohibited. Badges may not be altered or changed in any way and may not be used for any purpose other than official company business.

Figure 3.29 is an excerpt from a letter written by a CEO to retirees. The purpose of his letter was to encourage retirees to write letters to Congress supporting the organization's proposed acquisition. This paragraph was intended to give the retirees enough information to write effective letters to their Congressmen.

Figure 3.29 EXAMPLE 3—RETIREE COMMUNICATION: POORLY WRITTEN

In order to address concerns about the potential adverse impacts of the proposed merger on certain shippers, we made an agreement with XYZ Company that would have provided for the continuation of competition for affected shippers. Considering the substantial, unprecedented level of public benefits that the merger would generate, does it make any sense to deny the benefits that would have been available to the great majority of shippers, employees, and stockholders?

This is a classic example of how eliminating unnecessary words and superfluous prepositional phrases can clarify a message.

Figure 3.30 EXAMPLE 3—RETIREE COMMUNICATION: IMPROVED VERSION

We made an agreement with XYZ Company that would have provided for the continuation of competition for affected shippers. Considering the level of public benefits the merger would generate, does it make sense to deny [these] benefits to the majority of shippers, employees, and stockholders?

SAMPLE LETTERS AND MEMOS COVERING HUMAN RESOURCES COMMUNICATIONS

Like most other human resource functions, communication has very few right or wrong answers, but there are guidelines that relate to fundamental good writing skills. Figures 3.31 through 3.47 are model letters and memos covering a variety of situations.

Figure 3.31 DENY REQUEST FOR RAISE—OPTION 1

April 24, 19xx

Dear

This is to acknowledge your letter of [date]. You are to be commended for your progress during the past two months.

I do believe, however, that your recent request for a raise is premature. It would be more appropriate to discuss a salary increase after you have worked here for six months. If you continue on the same path, I am certain that your timely request will be given careful consideration.

You are doing a fine job, keep up the good work!

Sincerely,

John Doe, Vice President, Manufacturing

Figure 3.32 DENY REQUEST FOR RAISE—OPTION 2

April 24, 19xx

Dear

Although the company appreciates all that you have pointed out in your letter, I do not believe a raise is in order at this time. It is the custom of Wilson & Associates to review all employee benefits and compensation in July, the end of our fiscal year.

Certainly, at that time you will be considered for a salary increase, providing the production figures for your division are significantly increased.

Sincerely,

John Doe, President

Figure 3.33 SERVICE AWARD

April 24, 19xx

Dear

Although all of us at Ashton-Tate are busy, we're never too busy to stop for a moment to recognize a special occasion, your two-year anniversary with Ashton-Tate.

In the two years since you joined the company, a number of significant events have happened, including our move to Torrance; the introduction of new products; the acquisition of MultiMate and Decision Resources, Inc., and surpassing the 200 million dollar mark as a corporation.

I want to take this opportunity to thank you for your personal efforts and contributions during these two years and to recognize your service to Ashton-Tate with this Two-Year Service Award.

Congratulations to you on this milestone and I look forward to working with you over the coming years.

Sincerely,

Edward M. Esber, Chairman/CEO

Figure 3.34 CONDOLENCES

April 24, 19xx

Dear

The loss of a close family member is a very personal experience. We understand these next few weeks will be challenging and want you to know that your friends and colleagues are here to provide whatever support we can.

I have arranged to have your paycheck delivered to your home next Monday and [supervisor name] tells me that [employee name(s)] will handle your most pressing duties until you return. In the meantime, if there is anything else I can do, please call.

On behalf of [name of firm], I would like to express our sincere condolences.

Sincerely,

Vice President, Human Resources

Figure 3.35 CONFIRMATION LETTERS

April 24, 19xx

Dear

This is to confirm that [employee name] is enrolled in our company executive health care program. He is eligible for [% of benefit coverage] of all reasonable and customary charges connected with your professional services.

Figure 3.35 Continued

Enclosed is a copy of our schedule of reasonable and customary charges, our benefit booklet and the necessary claim forms which you must complete and return to the health care administrator.

If you have any other questions, you may contact [name/phone], our benefit claims analyst.

Sincerely,

John Jones, Benefit Manager

Figure 3.36 EMPLOYMENT VERIFICATION

April 24, 19xx

Dear

This letter will confirm that [employee name] is employed as a senior systems analyst with [firm name]. She has been with the company for seven years and in this position for two years.

Her salary is consistent with the data included on your request form. She will be eligible to participate in the new employee incentive plan effective July 1.

Sincerely,

Employment Officer

Figure 3.37 POLICY CHANGE

April 24, 19xx

TO: All Exempt Employees

FROM: Management

SUBJECT: Change in Vacation Policy

This is to provide notice to all [name of firm] employees of our new vacation request policy.

Vacation requests must be given to your supervisor no less than [   ] days prior to your vacation.

This request process will enable us to employ temporary help, if necessary, and to schedule vacations in a manner that will not be disruptive to the company. All other procedures will remain the same. If you need a copy of the entire vacation procedures guide, call [name/phone].

Thank you for your cooperation.

Figure 3.38 MANAGEMENT MEMO

April 24, 19xx

TO: Department Managers

FROM: Vice President, Marketing

SUBJECT: Seminar

A seminar is being held at the Bolten Hotel on June 15 at 1:00 P.M. on selling computerized high technology. It is being conducted by ABC Corporation and should be extremely informative.

We are strongly recommending that every member of the sales force attend this seminar and we will, of course, pay the entrance fees for all those attending.

I would appreciate it if you would encourage everyone to go, and provide me with the names of those who will be attending, no later than June 1st.

Figure 3.39 PROCEDURE STATEMENT

April 24, 19xx

TO: All Employees

FROM: Manager, Office Services

SUBJECT: Ordering Supplies

Recently some of you have not received supplies you requested in a timely manner. I have located the source of the problem and would like to request your cooperation to arrive at a satisfactory solution.

The Problem

Supply requisition forms have not been carefully completed and submitted to Laurie, our order processing clerk.

The Solution

If you will follow these steps, I believe we can solve your problems quickly.

1. Complete the supply requisition form including
   - your name and work location
   - description of supply item
   - cost from supply catalogue
   - supplier from supply catalogue
   - supervisor's signature if request exceeds $25.

2. Hand deliver or send the requisition through inter-office mail directly to Laurie's attention so she receives it before noon on Friday.

3. Laurie will send you a confirmation, advising you when you can expect the supplies.

Except for unusual circumstances, you should expect your supplies to be delivered by noon on the Wednesday after you place your order.

If this new procedure does not solve your specific problem, please call me immediately. If we work together, I'm sure we can meet this challenge.

Figure 3.40 RUMORS

April 24, 19xx

TO: All Employees

FROM: President

SUBJECT: Rumors

Unfortunate rumors have been circulating about John Jones, former manager of our customer service unit.

The Rumor The rumor has several versions, however, the substance of it is that John was fired for political reasons.

The Facts Those of you who know John realize that he is respected by the management of this company. John was not fired. The reason for his departure was personal and as I respect his privacy, I will make no further explanation.

The Results If these rumors persist, John's future, that of our employees, and the organization will suffer needlessly.

I therefore am asking each of you to help by putting these rumors to rest.

Figure 3.41 TRAINING

April 24, 19xx

TO: All Employees

FROM: Vice President, Marketing

SUBJECT: New Service Introduction and Training

On July 1, we will be introducing a new service to our customers which will give us an important edge over our competition.

The new service will be known as FlextraTM. Training and Information classes are currently being scheduled for all employees so you will be acquainted with the new service before it is introduced to the public.

Within the next week your supervisor will advise you of the specific time and place of your Training and Information class. Please mark your calendars so you do not miss it.

Figure 3.42 ANNOUNCING EMPLOYEE SURVEY

July 24, 19xx

TO: All Employees

FROM: Personnel Director

SUBJECT: Company-Wide Survey

As part of our 5-year business planning program which will begin later this year, we would like to have your opinions and ideas about a number of issues including:

- the future of our business
- your career objectives
- our compensation and benefit package
- our communication and training programs

We have engaged the services of an independent survey firm to conduct the survey and submit a report of the results. After the report is completed, you will receive a summary of the results.

Within the next two weeks you will receive a survey questionnaire to complete and return, in confidence, to the survey firm. More details about the survey process will be included.

Please take the time to complete and return the survey. Your input is important to our future.

Figure 3.43 REQUESTING VOLUNTEERS TO GIVE UP PARKING SPACE

November 3, 19xx

TO: First Level Supervisors, Managers and Executives

FROM: Vice President, Public Affairs

SUBJECT: Volunteers Needed

We have donated meeting space to the Thanksgiving for the Needy community service group for the entire day of November 10. Because of the parking space limitations in the building, we are asking you to volunteer your assigned parking space for the convenience of the committee members on that day.

Arrangements have been made with the public parking garage one block west to provide parking for you. The company will pay your parking expense for the day.

If you are willing to volunteer your assigned space on November 10, please contact Janice Harper and she will give you a paid parking chit for the public garage.

We will need approximately eighteen spaces. Your cooperation will be appreciated.

Figure 3.44 REORGANIZATION

March 1, 19xx

TO: All Employees

FROM: Vice President, Corporate Operations

SUBJECT: Reorganization

Effective April 1, our two new business units, ABC Pharmaceuticals and ABC Opticals will be officially launched. As a result, we will have five distinct operating groups instead of three.

The Executive Committee and task force teams from each functional group in the company have worked long hours for the past eight months to develop this new organizational structure.

For the most part, your job will not change significantly although you may be working for a different operating group than you are today. To help you understand the new organization and where you fit, you will be invited to attend one of a series of awareness meetings which will be held over the next two weeks.

Tomorrow you will receive a special edition of *Focus* that will outline the responsibilities of each operating group and include organization charts. Once you have studied the information, write down any questions that come to mind and bring them to your scheduled meeting.

Figure 3.45 SUMMARY OF BENEFIT ENHANCEMENTS

October 1, 19xx

TO: All Employees

FROM: Benefit Manager

SUBJECT: Benefit Enhancements Effective January 1

Following is a summary of benefit enhancements that will be effective January 1.
 Medical
- HMO alternatives available in Connecticut and Northern California
- Medical claims will be processed in the new [name of claims administrator] San Diego office. New Medical ID cards and claims forms will be available December 15

 Dental
- California employees now have three dental plan options

 Long Term Disability
- Your monthly premium will be reduced 30%.
- The maximum monthly benefit has been increased from $7,500 to $10,000.

 Savings Plus Plan
- Enroll, increase, or decrease your contributions twice a year.
- Change your investment options twice a year.

 Voluntary Life Insurance
- Your premiums will be reduced 25-60%, depending on your age.

Watch for your annual enrollment package and make any changes in your benefit elections before December 10.

Figure 3.46 EMPLOYEE ASSISTANCE PROGRAM

September 1, 19xx

TO: All Employees

FROM: Employee Assistance Plan Coordinator

SUBJECT: New Hours and Phone Number

The Employee Assistance Plan (EAP) weekday hours and phone number have changed.
            Hours 8:00 a.m until 6:00 p.m.
            Phone 1-800-970-3800
Remember, emergency assistance can be arranged 24 hours a day.

Please keep this advisory until you receive your new EAP card.

Figure 3.47 PAID TIME-OFF POLICY

August 24, 19xx

TO: All Employees

FROM: Vice President, Human Resources

SUBJECT: New Paid Time-Off Package

During the past year and a half, we have seen an increasing abuse of our sick leave program by some 22% of our employees. The result is that the other 78% are unfairly penalized for their dedication and hard work.

Therefore, effective October 1, we will introduce a new total paid time-off package. The plan has been designed to specifically address the inequities caused by sick leave abusers.

The new package includes
- vacation
- scheduled holidays
- short term disability (formerly sick leave)
- long term disability
- six new personal days
- bereavement and other authorized leaves

You will find details about how the new plan works in the attached brochure. Most of us will find this new package a significant improvement over our prior plans.

HOW TO MEASURE THE COST EFFECTIVENESS OF LETTERS AND MEMOS

Most organizations believe it is cheaper to use letters and memos as primary communication tools. Memos and letters seem cheaper than more sophisticated tools such as audiovisuals, handbooks, or benefit statements because you do not see hard dollars costs. Virtually all the costs connected to sending letters and memos are soft dollars. Soft dollars are primarily time overhead, dictator or sender time, word processing, secretarial or clerical support, reproduction services, and the internal mail room. There are two issues connected with this perception. Time is money, and, if the communication tool doesn't get into the right hands in a timely manner, or does not do an effective job of delivering the message, all those soft dollar costs become very high expenses. They have a direct impact on productivity.

How do you measure the costs of memos and letters? Many studies have demonstrated that a letter or memo is a very expensive proposition. If you want to get immersed in a lot of detail, you can calculate how much it costs to generate one memo or letter on any given topic. Add the time it takes to generate, produce, and distribute the memo. You can do this by multiplying total hours by an average hourly wage. Remember to include direct and indirect compensation and factor in the cost of facilities, equipment, and supplies. You may be amazed at how quickly the dollars add up. Now think about the labor and productivity costs related to the readers when they receive your correspondence. Hidden costs go up in direct proportion to the clarity and effectiveness of the memo. If the memo has to be read more than once to be understood or if it creates unnecessary anxiety among the recipients, the productivity impact can be astronomical. Another cost that is rarely considered arises from poorly executed letters and memos which result in libel suits and other legal actions. Conversely, if the memo is clear, concise, and specific, the average reader can absorb the message in seconds, act on it and move on to more productive activities. Potential legal liabilities can also be reduced. You will not eliminate much of the production costs until you discover the technique of reducing the number of memos and their length.

Cost Cutting Tips For Using Letters And Memos

Effective communication and cost cutting techniques go hand-in-hand. Keeping a message short and simple is your objective. Remember the three keys: What is it? What will it do for me? What does it cost?

CHECKLIST: Ideas to Keep Your Memos to the Point

- be sure the memo or letter is necessary
- focus on only one topic or issue per memo
- state the facts, no more, no less
- keep thoughts in logical order
- use single syllable words
- be sure facts are facts, not opinions
- keep length to less than one page
- be sure distribution list is appropriate to topic

If a memo or letter is unnecessary, it will cost you money. If it is not clear, it will cost you money. If it does not get the desired result, it will cost you money. If it does not get to the right people, it will cost you money.

How To Measure The Success Of Your Message

When memos and letters are properly structured and distributed, you will be able to measure their success by their results. If you do not see the desired results, you can reasonably assume that you were not successful. This is no different than when you use other media to communicate. However, organizations often assume that the reason results were unsatisfactory is the fault of the reader rather than the fault of the writer. Usually, this is not true. Just distributing a letter or memo does not automatically guarantee success. You can quantify effectiveness in much the same way you measure other communication tools. But if you rely heavily on memos and letters as your primary communication vehicles, you should be prepared to measure their results and strive to improve their effectiveness.

CHAPTER 4

WRITING, EDITING, AND PRODUCING EMPLOYEE PUBLICATIONS

Employee publications range from underground rough copy produced by employees themselves, usually by special user's groups, to sophisticated annual reports for employees that look very much like annual reports to stockholders. These publications are distinguished from other printed employee communication tools by the fact that they look and read like a newspaper or magazine. Other communication tools such as handbooks which technically can be considered employee publications are covered in depth in Chapter 5. Some employee publications are authorized by management, some are not. Authorized or otherwise, all represent a valuable communication tool that exists within the organization.

This chapter examines the different types of employee publications and their purpose. You will find guidelines and tips on writing, editing, and producing them as well as how to

- make publications an integral part of your overall human resources communication program
- use editorial policy to improve your publication
- locate resources
- choose the most cost-effective production techniques including a special section on desktop publishing
- determine budgets
- evaluate their effectiveness

You will also find examples and handy worksheets to simplify your publication management tasks

TYPES OF PUBLICATIONS

Learning the precise name for a type of publication can be confusing, given the many hybrid types and variations. What some people call a bulletin may resemble a newsletter to other people. The difference between the two is nothing more than format, how the publication looks. Names are much less important than how employees perceive the publication's value in meeting their needs. What is important to remember is that you have a lot of latitude to design a publication for your specific objectives. With this in mind, consider these types.

CHECKLIST: Ten Types of Publications

Bulletins. Bulletins are usually short documents designed to convey a sense of urgency. They may be published on company letterhead, memo stationery, or a specially designed letterhead that sets them apart from daily internal correspondence.

Newsletters. Newletters fall into two broad categories; general and topic specific. Their purpose is to communicate information about current and future events. General newsletters cover a variety of topics from company business to employee benefits. They are usually four to eight pages in length and are produced on paper with a specially designed masthead and a publication name. Topic specific newsletters usually have names such as *Benefit Briefs* and are dedicated to a specific topic.

News Tabloids. News tabloids are larger than newsletters and frequently resemble industry newspapers or newsstand tabloids like the *National Enquirer*. They usually communicate a broader spectrum of information than newsletters. It is not unusual for these publications to contain feature articles, photographs, illustrations, cartoons, and a variety of columns covering company business and employee interests and activities.

Magazines. Most often, employee magazines are nothing more than newsletters or news tabloids produced in a magazine format. Additionally, special edition magazines may be produced to celebrate a significant event such as the company's 25th anniversary or the merger of two former competitors. Organizations who choose to publish an employee magazine usually commit sufficient budget to the effort for expert design and four-color printing.

Employee Annual Reports. Employee annual reports typically look like magazines or the company's stockholder annual reports. Their purpose is to relate company business issues to employees much as the company does for its stockholders. The primary distinction is that an employee version tries to be more appealing to its employees than to its stockholder's.

Specialty Publications. Specialty publications are designed to serve a need not adequately served by any other communication tool. The most common is a highlight brochure. These brochures are usually topic specific and give the reader more details than they could find in a news or magazine article, but fall short of supplying comprehensive information about the topic. Specialty publications are produced in every size and shape imaginable from photocopied manuscripts to elaborate four-color packages.

Outside Publications You Can Use Internally. Many non-profit and for-profit organizations publish periodicals and other specialty publications specifically designed for employee communication programs. These organizations usually publish their products in such a way as to allow you to imprint your company's name and logo so that it appears to be a company-sponsored publication. Credit unions and other employee organizations also produce publications that could be useful to you. The pros and cons of using outside publications is discussed later in this chapter.

Underground Publications. Underground publications exist in virtually every organization. They are produced by employees to serve a need that is not being met by company-sponsored publications. They are typically very rough, but readers overlook style for content, usefulness, and credibility.

Bargaining Unit Publications. Like any other organization, bargaining units publish a variety of publications for their members. They look company-sponsored, but their editorial slant is distinctively that of the union. Tips on how to capitalize on these publications will be discussed later.

Electronic Publications. More organizations are using electronic media such as computers, video, and telephones as a publication format. Text is prepared in much the same way it would be for a traditional print-based publication. It is then either recorded on computer disc, video, or audio tape in the form of a text file. Employees are able to access the information, at their convenience, by pressing a few buttons on a computer keyboard, video system, or calling a special phone number. Electronic publications are gaining in popularity because they enable organizations to communicate important information more quickly and less expensively.

Including Employee Publications In Your Total Communication Plan

Before you decide *when* to use employee publications, you should be certain they are even necessary in your organization. If the answer is yes, you need to decide what kind of publication you need, how often they should be published, who will do the work, how much they will cost, and how you will evaluate their effectiveness. Following the steps in Chapters 1 and 2 will help you determine how they should fit into your total communication plan. You will find more specific production tips and cost estimating techniques later in this chapter.

Using Publications To Reinforce Your Corporate And Human Resource Messages

Employee publications offer a wealth of communication opportunity management often overlooks. If employees read and respect a publication, they are likely to put a lot of stock in any information that they find in it. Research indicates that the print medium has a stronger influence than any other medium. Its power lies in its perceived veracity. People tend to believe that whatever they see in print is true. The corresponding danger is that if something is first perceived to be true and later is demonstrated not to be, the publication loses credibility. So what you write must be right! These lines from *The Rubaiyat* of Omar Khayyam underscore this idea.

The moving finger writes
And having writ, moves on
Nor all your piety and wit
Can cancel half a line...

Employee publications should not be used to preach to employees, but to relay pertinent information and reinforce management's overall human resource philosophy. The way you use the publications will influence your credibility with the workforce.

How To Choose The Right Type Of Publication To Meet Your Need

The easiest way to determine which type(s) of publications will work best in your organization, is to ask your audience. Find out whether they are reading the publication(s) you are currently producing. If they are, what motivates them to read it? If they aren't, why? Ask their opinion about content and format. Conducting readership surveys or focus group meetings is a good way to find out what type of publication will meet your readers' needs and therefore meet management's needs

> **EXAMPLE: One Publication that Works; One that Does Not**

There are two primary employee publications produced at a community children's hospital. One is professionally designed, typeset, and printed in two colors in an eight-page tabloid size format. The other publication has a simple one-color masthead at the top of an 8-1/2"x11" paper. The rest of the publication is produced on a word processor and printed in black by the hospital's print shop.

The first publication is well-written as well as more inviting and easier to read. But, employees don't read it because it contains what they view as old news or, worse, information that is not relevant to them or their jobs. Most of the articles are written to communicate with the community rather than employees.

The second publication has a higher readership because it tells employees what they want and need to know. It briefly highlights topics such as career development and training opportunities, benefit information, and news about professional knowledge and skills innovations. The second publication is not as effective as it could be, but it comes much closer to meeting employee needs and therefore had more credibility than the first publication. The most effective publication for this organization would be one that combines the best attributes of both publications.

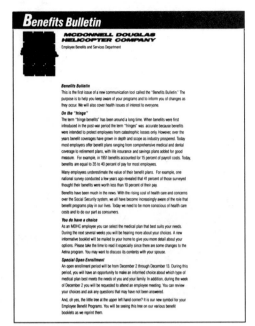

Figure 4.1 Employee Benefits and Services Bulletin Masthead. *Courtesy of McDonnell Douglas.*

BenAlert

A Benefits Publication by Marsh & McLennan Companies, Inc.

July 1988

Retiree Comprehensive Health Plan
New Premiums

Effective July 1, 1988, premium payments will increase for participants in the Retiree Comprehensive Health Plan.

When the Company implemented the current Retiree Comprehensive Health Plan on January 1, 1983, retirees were offered significantly improved benefit coverages – and shared in Plan costs by paying a quarterly premium charge. The Plan is described on page HC-37 of the Health Care Program section of your Benefits Handbook.

Since the current Plan started, the premiums billed to retirees have increased only once: on January 1, 1984. However, the dramatic rise in the cost of medical services and supplies in this country has caused Plan costs (claims) per retiree to triple in the last five years. Therefore, the Company must now raise premium rates again. The increased cost to retirees reflects only part of the higher cost of operating the Plan. The quarterly premium rates for individual and family coverage effective July 1, 1988 are shown below.

Quarterly Costs for Retirees Age 65 or Over:	
For individual coverage	$ 70.00
For family coverage (if all dependents are at least age 65)	$150.00
For family coverage (if any dependent is under age 65)	$195.00
Quarterly Costs for Retirees Under Age 65:	
For individual coverage	$110.00
For family coverage	$235.00

Please note: All of our benefit plans are reviewed from time to time, and the Company has the right to modify or terminate these benefits for current or future retirees. Additionally, the Company has the right to modify the premium rates that are charged to retirees.

Figure 4.2 Employee Benefits Bulletin for Han book Courtesy of Marsh & McLennan.

COMMUNICATOR'S TIP: A Rule of Thumb for Effective Publications

Make sure that what you print in an employee publication contains facts, not opinions. Keep your messages very short and to the point. Make certain the publication's content meets the audience needs. Be sure the format and layout of the publication makes it inviting to read.

BULLETINS: HOW TO CONVEY A SENSE OF URGENCY

To most people, bulletins imply a sense of urgency or something out of the ordinary. To others, bulletins imply periodic and frequent updates on topics of special interest to the audience. Once you have decided what purpose your bulletin should serve, then all that really remains is setting up a formula for producing it. For purposes of this discussion, we are going to assume that the broad definition of bulletins implies briefs that are communicated in a very short time period and are primarily dedicated to announcing or previewing a topic that will be of interest to the audience.

Figures 4.1-4.4 illustrate three approaches to bulletins. While they all deal with benefit topics, they vary in degree of focus.

The McDonnell Douglas Helicopter Company bulletin (Figure 4.1) is an Employee Benefits and Services Department publication. It is used primarily for announcing changes or additions to employee benefits and other employee services such as the employee assistance program. The apple tree logo was designed to be used on every employee benefit communication tool to establish visual continuity. It is used in different sizes and positions, depending on the size and shape of the publication.

The Marsh & McLennan Companies, Inc.'s bulletin (Figure 4.2) is also a topic specific bulletin focusing on benefits. However, is it designed to fit in the employee benefit handbook which is a three-ring 6"x9"

Figure 4.3 Health Care Bulletin Masthead
Courtesy of Morrison Knudson Companies

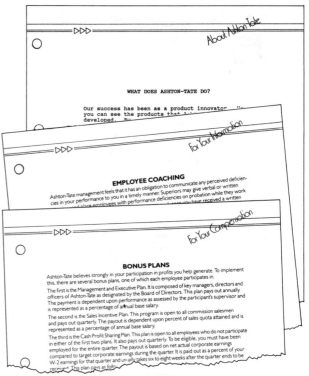

Figure 4.4 Bulletin Mastheads specially designed to be page replacements for the employee handbook. *Courtesy of Ashton Tate.*

binder. This organization has titled their bulletin BenAlert. The illustration of people at the bottom of the page is a visual logo that appears on all Marsh Companies benefit communications.

The Targeted Health Care bulletin masthead (Figure 4.3) was developed by Morrison Knudsen Companies. It is often used like letterhead in that, sometimes, they simply word process a message and print it onto this paper rather than typeset it and give it to the printshop. Notice that it is extremely narrow in scope, dealing only with health care issues.

Ashton-Tate uses an especially effective technique that saves time and money and still allows the firm to communicate quickly and effectively on every human resource issue imaginable. While the illustrations in Figure 4.4 can serve as a bulletin masthead, they have been cleverly designed to be page replacements for the employee handbook. Notice that all three pages have the same graphic treatment, but are distinguished by different headings (e.g. About Ashton-Tate, For Your Information, For Your Compensation). The company has produced topic mastheads for everything from safety to survivor benefits and personal recordkeeping. Whenever an urgent communication need arises, the message can be word processed, printed on the appropriate topic masthead and distributed within hours if necessary. By punching holes in the bulletins, Ashton-Tate's approach also encourages employees to update their employee handbooks with the bulletin.

When To Use Bulletins

By restricting use of the bulletins to urgent or very timely information, they can become a powerful part of your communication program. However, you allow them to become editorial statements, forums for pontification, or if you pack them with too much information, they will lose their effectiveness.

CHECKLIST: Types of Messages Appropriate for Bulletins

Announcing Change. Use bulletins to announce unanticipated organizational, procedural, or administrative changes.

Announcing New Products and Services. Bulletins are very useful ways to advise employees about new products and services *before* they are introduced to clients or the general public.

Crisis Intervention. Briefly explaining the company's position or action plan when an unexpected crisis erupts can be handled efficiently using bulletins.

Reminders. Employees are usually grateful when an organization uses bulletins to remind them of critical dates and deadlines which can affect them personally or professionally.

Helpful Hints For Producing Bulletins

One of the most efficient ways to use bulletins is to develop a masthead which will be repeated for each new edition of the bulletin. You can print tens of thousands, even millions of bulletin mastheads very inexpensively. The more you print, the less each one costs. They become an inventory item not unlike your regular business letterhead. Any time the bulletin format is appropriate, simply pull your inventory, develop your copy, reproduce it on the masthead, and distribute it. It is a simple, efficient process. See Desktop Publishing: A Production Alternative on page 120.

NEWSLETTERS: ALTERNATIVE TYPES AND HOW THEY SHOULD BE USED

Gutenberg invented moveable type in about 1450 A.D. and the first newletter must have appeared soon thereafter. A mistake most organizations make when they decide to produce a newsletter is to do too many things. In other words, their editorial policy is too broad to be realistic. The opposite extreme is when firms produce so many publications that employees don't have time to read them all. Somewhere between these poles lies a workable medium.

There are probably as many newsletters as there are ideas in the world. Like bulletins, newsletters can be found in a variety of sizes and shapes and are produced with varying levels of sophistication. Unlike bulletins, newsletters tend to cover issues in more depth and are rarely useful for communicating time-sensitive information because more lead-time is required to produce and distribute them.

Within organizations, newsletters can usually be classified into two broad categories, general and topic-specific newsletters.

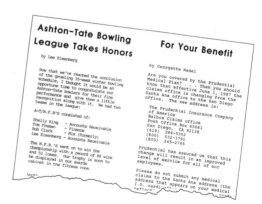

Figure 4.5 ASHTON-TATE'S Newsletter illustrates how to develop a standard masthead that will allow you to have maximum production flexibility. The basic newsletter allows for four pages. If they need more, they simply add one or more sheets in the middle. This is a general newsletter, covering a variety of topics. *Courtesy of Ashton Tate.*

General Newsletters: Communicating A Variety Of Topics

General newsletters are often the only employee publication in an organization and they serve as a mouthpiece for management. Some organizations try to get triple duty from a newsletter by writing it to satisfy the interests of stockholders, employees, and the public media. These are usually ineffective because they aren't targeted to a single well-defined audience. It is quite acceptable to cover a variety of topics in one newsletter, but it is not a good idea to try to serve several audiences who have distinctly different priorities. Everybody ends up dissatisfied.

Most newsletters have banners or mastheads reminiscent of newspapers. Some are very traditional, others take a more lighthearted approach like the *Birds-Eye View* in Figure 4.5. The content of this newsletter is a classic example of a general newsletter targeted to employee interests. It covers

- company business topics
- years of service anniversaries
- employee activities like aerobic classes, bowling leagues, sporting and community service events
- entertainment opportunities such as community theatre tryouts, movie rentals, concert schedules and discount tickets
- human resource issues including compensation and benefits topics and a Questions and Answers column
- miscellaneous topics like photo features, jokes, or cartoons

Since the company relies heavily on employee contributions, the content will usually reflect the current interests of the total audience. As you can see in Figure 4.5, the text is word processed. However, it is reasonably inviting to read because it is set in two columns with sufficient white space and big headlines to attract the reader's attention. Using good design, layout, editorial and writing techniques, you can produce a very effective general newsletter.

Topic Specific Newsletters: Focused Information For Specific Audiences

Topic specific or special interest publications usually are born to serve the perceived needs of a special interest group. Frequently they are produced in a vacuum. Their sponsors believe their topic is so special, it simply cannot be properly communicated by anyone other than themselves. Marketing/sales and benefit newsletters are two such examples. These special topic publications may be necessary because the general employee newsletter does not properly satisfy employee information needs. Over time, though, many organizations find themselves with too many publications which send conflicting messages.

EXAMPLE: The Problem with Too Many Special Interest Publications

For years, a consulting organization produced only two publications, a single topic newsletter and a company news magazine. Each issue of the newsletter was devoted to one professional consulting topic such as health care cost containment. The consultants used the newsletter as a way to keep current with issues surrounding the topic. Because of the newsletter's professional quality, many consultants also used it as a marketing tool for clients and prospective clients. For the most part, this publication was ignored by support and administrative employees. The company news magazine was a general publication which kept employees informed of current and interesting events throughout the organization. This publication was professionally produced, generally well-received, and regularly read by all employees.

As the company grew, pressure to develop new publications addressing special interests of employee groups increased. At first, most of the pressure came from the consulting professionals who felt that their area of expertise was not adequately represented. As the consultants succeeded in instituting new

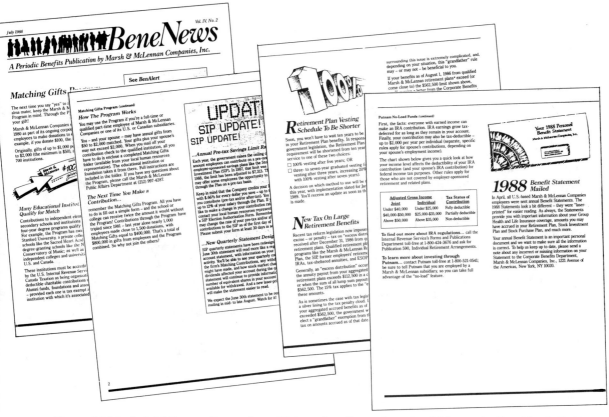

Figure 4.6 Marsh & McLennan Companies publishes a benefit newsletter in addition to the BeneAlert bulletin. Periodic readership surveys help the editors keep the newsletter's focus on target.

publications, technical support and administrative employees perceived an opportunity to initiate publications dedicated to their special needs.

Today, the organization has 15 corporate-authorized publications in circulation, scores of regional and office publications and the number of unauthorized publications, is mind-boggling.

The Problem. There is no way employees can read all the publications and still do any productive work. Even those employees instrumental in getting a new publication into the system have a difficult time of keeping up with what is out there and how it will help them. Most important, the special interest focus detracts from the company focus which could have serious long-term impact on company performance.

The Solution. The organization needs to re-evaluate the audiences and their information needs as they relate to the company's business objectives. This is an example of a good idea taken to the extreme.

Practical Point With the increased use of desktop publishing, there is likely to be an increase in topic specific newsletters because special interest groups will have easy access to this technology. However, desktop publishing can give companies greater production flexibility and potential cost savings. (See *Using Desktop Publishing: A Production Alternative*, pp. 120.)

Compensation and benefit newsletters such as the one shown in Figure 4.6 is the most common type of topic specific publication organizations produce. They usually serve a good purpose because they give you the opportunity to increase the probability that all employees will be aware of pending changes that could affect them personally or financially. As the topic becomes less specific to personal lifestyles and preferences, the readership will decrease. Some organizations have received favorable reviews from employees for newsletters dedicated to topics such as personal health and nutrition or retirement planning. Owens-Corning , for example, created a quarterly health benefit and cost containment newsletter entitled, *For Your Health* which received an impressive 80% positive response to their readership survey. Whether these types of newsletters will work in your organization depends on whether they meet the needs of a majority of your population.

COMMUNICATOR'S TIP: How to Ensure Newsletters
Meet Your Objectives

It is prudent to monitor the value of all your newsletters periodically. The quickest way to test how effective a newsletter is at any given point in time is to publish a readership survey within the publication. If your response is low, the magnitude of your readership, and therefore the publication's value, is suspect. If your response is reasonable or high, study the responses carefully to be certain the newsletter is meeting the needs of your current audience.

Helpful Hints For Producing Newsletters

As with bulletins, one of the most cost-efficient ways to produce newsletters is to develop a masthead which will be repeated for each new edition of the newsletter. The primary difference is that a newsletter is typically more structured. Therefore, while you can print thousands of newsletter mastheads and have them in inventory for the next edition, you need to be more careful about layout and space allocation than for a bulletin. Desktop publishing technology is making this task easier every day.

If you think that the space and layout requirements for topics in your newsletter will vary dramatically from issue to issue, it may be better to obtain professional guidance before you decide to print a million newsletter mastheads. If you envision your newsletter to be similar to the *Birds-Eye View* in Figure 4.5, you can easily produce the mastheads in quantity because you can adjust the length of the text and the number of pages to your specific needs.

NEWS TABLOIDS: FORMAT ALTERNATIVE

The main difference between newsletters and news tabloids varies and has to do with format rather than content. The content is frequently similar to that of general newsletters. Tabloids are larger (e.g. 10" x 13" rather than 8-1/2" x 11), usually have more graphics and photographs, and are almost always professionally typeset. As a result, tabloids will generally take longer to produce and be more costly than newsletters.

Why Organizations Choose News Tabloids Over Traditional Newsletters

The competition for employees' time and attention increases daily. When you are competing with slick consumer magazines, newspapers like *USA Today* and the electronic media, it may seem impossible to attract employees' attention. While tabloids are sometimes developed as a means of attracting more attention and better readership opposite consumer publications, organizations often decide to produce them as a signal for change such as fostering a new identity for the organization or underscoring a strategic change in the way the company looks at its business. Frequently, the reason to use a new format is simply because it is clear that the current format is ignored. Introducing a totally new look to employee publications will encourage employees to take notice quickly.

Helpful Hints For Producing Tabloids

Unlike bulletins and newsletters, it is not practical to create an inventory of tabloid masthead blanks because the size and the use of sophisticated graphics, photographs and 4-color printing, makes the production process much more complex. Therefore, publishing a tabloid requires more planning and resources. Since most organizations do not have all the technical resources necessary to produce a tabloid internally, you will need to find reliable, cost-efficient external resources. Tips on how to find these resources are covered in Chapter 2.

Figure 4.7
NEWS TABLOID

This layout is for the first page of a four-page tabloid. The articles and features are intended to help sall law firms keep up with new ways to build and manage their business. Notice that the headlines, writing style, and layout is much more informal and easy to read than you would expect.

Lawyers' KEYNOTES Casebook

CASE 22 SHOWS HOW $3 MILLION LOSS MIGHT HAVE BEEN AVOIDED

These case studies are one part of our ongoing professional development series.

CASE 22

OBJECTIVE:
Your client is a successful shopping and business center developer who has identified a prime location for a new project in the heart of an established suburb of a dynamic metropolitan area. The objective is to develop a $250 million complex encompassing a four-square block area.

SITUATION:
The city is eager to encourage the development and is therefore amenable to granting necessary variances and offering other support to the developer. The developer begins negotiations to purchase, for a very reasonable market price, the parcels necessary to enable him to proceed with the project. While a substantial number of the parcels in question are controlled by a single owner and already zoned for commercial use, some of the critical parcels are zoned for single family housing and occupied by retired people or long-time residents of the area.

RESULT:
After investing $3 million in conditional escrows, not to speak of the other significant expenses involved in the development process, the developer was forced to abandon the project primarily because he was unable to persuade the homeowners to complete the sale of their critical tracts.

How To Avoid This Kind of Trap

STRATEGY:

Anticipate the needs and fears of your secondary audiences.

PLAN:
The developer failed to recognize the emotional and psychological needs of the homeowners. He could have increased the probability of successfully purchasing the single family parcels by identifitying these unique needs, developing a plan to help meet those needs and properly introducing the plan to this secondary, albeit powerful,

BOOK REVIEW

The Lawyers' Advertising Handbook is a quick, easy guide to help you develop more effective advertising. It includes tips on:
- advertising budgets
- marketing strategies
- effective writing and graphic design
- where to advertise
Check Reader Service Number 43 for more details.

LAWYERS' ADVERTISING HANDBOOK

audience.
Money was not the issue. Their fears and concerns revolved around fear and uncertainty as to how to handle the financial windfall and where they could go if they sold their homes.

IMPLEMENTATION PROCESS:
An effective implementation program might look like this:
- Conduct a sensing survey to identify the perceived and real needs of all property owners.
- Develop an education/information strategic plan targeted to the needs of the audience(s) including:
- an information/planning kit, designed to answer the concerns of the audience with personalized financial models, simple checklists and reputable resources for more help and information
- Identify local real estate and financial planning professionals who could provide personalized counseling.
See Videos, Page 2

Your clients and prospects trust you, but they are most likely intimidated by you as well because they don't understand your highly specialized language or how to access your services. More important, your successful completion of a case may depend heavily on how well the primary and secondary participants understand the issues.
Most clients and other participants are lay people who are inherently suspicisous of things they don't understand. Their insecurity frequently causes them to be antagonistic toward a speedy resolution of a legal issue even though it may be in their best interest.
Unnecessary delays and obstructions cost you money and may unnecessarily compromise your ability to achieve optimum results for your client and yourself.
One way to help improve your chances for handling your cases successfully is to educate your clients. There are various ways to go about it. But the simplest and most cost-effective way may be to use videotapes that are designed to explain the technical subtlies of legal issues in a way that lay people can understand.
Three new education videos designed especially for lawyers' clients have received rave reviews from the firms who have tried them.
See Case 22, Page 3

Table of Contents

Copyright The Creative Guild, April, 1989

April 12, 1989   *1*

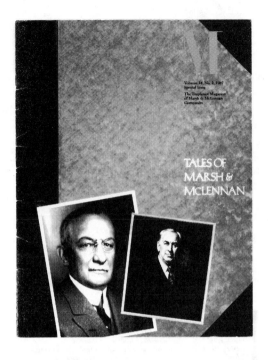

Figure 4.8 EMPLOYEE MAGAZINE This is a special historical perspective edition of the employee magazine *M. Courtesy of Marsh & McLennan.*

EMPLOYEE MAGAZINES: WHAT THEY INCLUDE

When an organization chooses a magazine format for an employee publication, they often decide to add a blaze of color and an enhanced image to their printed communication tools. That is not to say that color is not used in other types of employee publications. However, most employee magazines are designed to send a message of high quality, substance, and permanence to readers.

The graphic and editorial approach used in employee magazines tends to emphasize the company's image of itself and reinforce its business philosophy. Magazines will usually cover a broad range of topics not unlike newsletters and tabloids. However, the way the topics are treated is much like the approach consumer magazines use. For example, a typical employee magazine might include

- *issue-oriented articles* on subjects like AIDS, smoking in the workplace or how the middle-management crunch affects employees' career opportunities
- *how-to articles* on handling problem employees, balancing work and family needs, risk taking and personal financial planning
- *information articles* on company programs such as employee assistance, management training courses, and compensation and benefit issues
- *recognition articles, photo features or columns* about employees on and off the job, departments, plants and divisions, birthdays, service anniversaries, sporting events, and other employee activities

Organizations also use magazines to do in-depth series on significant events such as a milestone in the company's history or to introduce a new organization resulting from an acquisition or merger. On occasion, they may choose to publish a *special edition* such as *The Tales of Marsh & McLennan* in Figure 4.8.

EMPLOYEE ANNUAL REPORTS: HELPING EMPLOYEES SEE THE BUSINESS THE WAY MANAGEMENT DOES

Employee annual reports are really just specialized magazines. Their content and editorial approach is more like a stockholders' annual report than a consumer magazine. The emphasis is on business issues such as growth, profitability, productivity, innovation, the company's future and it's employees. Organizations tend to turn to employee annual reports when they sense that employees need to understand the business and its objectives better or they want employees to see the organization more like management sees it.

Figure 4.9
EMPLOYEE ANNUAL REPORT
The conservative type and graphics used for the cover of this employee annual report are reminiscent of what you would expect the company's stockholder annual report to look like. *Courtesy of Steps, Inc.*

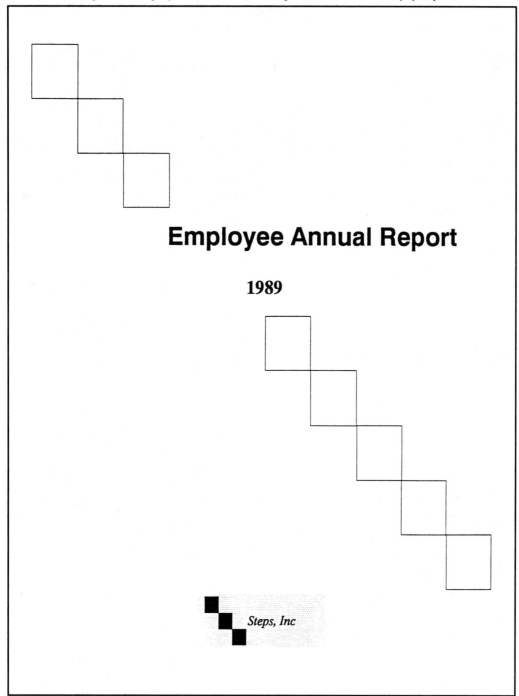

Whether or not employee annual reports are the best way to change employees' perception of the organization is controversial. Some professionals contend that employee annual reports are redundant if the company has benefit plans that include company stock because the employees already receive the stockholders' annual report. The common retort is that not all employees participate in company stock benefit plans and therefore wouldn't receive the stockholders' report. Furthermore, most stockholder reports are difficult to read and less understand.

Practical Point   Before you decide to publish an employee annual report, you should be sure that you have exhausted all other ways to focus employees' attention on the business objectives.

SPECIALTY PUBLICATIONS: FILLING A SPECIFIC NEED

Specialty publications such as highlight brochures comprise another type of employee publication that is almost always topic specific. They usually summarize such topics as a compensation or benefit plan, training or career development programs, an employee assistance program, or the credit union. Highlight brochures are also used in situations where more than one topic is covered, but the information is targeted to a very specific audience. Examples include recruiting brochures and supervisor guides explaining a new policy or procedure.

These tools tend to have a promotional flavor and are often used as interim communication devices, especially when employee decisions are required. This is the most appropriate use for them. In effect, they are an organization's internal marketing tools. Most are designed very much like direct mail sales and advertising brochures. Used as such, they can fill a specific communication need but should not be expected to replace other print-based communication tools. (Figures 4.10 through 4.12.)

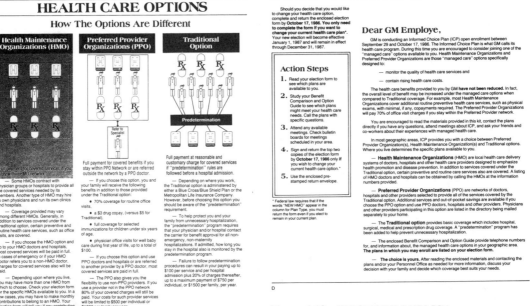

Figure 4.10 SPECIALTY PUBLICA-TIONS One of many tools designed to introduce a new approach to health care benefits, this General Motors brochure graphically illustrates the differences among three types of health care delivery systems. *Courtesy of General Motors.*

Figure 4.11 EMPLOYEE RECRUITING
AWARD BROCHURE   A similar theme with a
different purpose. This brochure promotes an
employee recruiting award program. Employees
earn cash and other prizes for helping successfully recruit new employees. Ashton-Tate chose to
use four colors, elaborate graphics and a handy
small size to increase interest. *Courtesy of
Ashon Tate.*

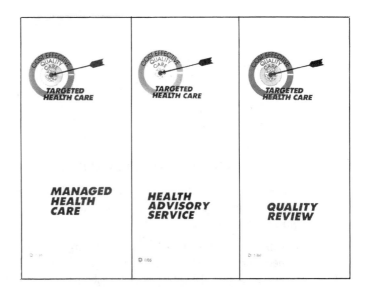

Figure 4.12   COMPANION BROCHURES These
are companion brochures, all relating to different
components of health care. The graphics are
identical, but the topics are different. Morrison
Knudsen distributed them to employees in a
package designed to make it easier to get
acquainted with each issue separately.
Courtesy of Morrison Knudsen.

OUTSIDE PUBLICATIONS: TIMESAVING PUBLICATION SHORT CUTS

To reduce communication planning time and effort, many organizations have discovered the many outside
publications that are marketed for companies to use as employee publications. A publisher does all the
work and the organization buying the publication pays to print their logo on it and then distributes it to
employees. It appears to be a company-sponsored publication. Some, in fact, provide a few pages for
custom articles. Most of these publications are topic specific, focusing on health care, retirement planning,
financial planning and other similar issues.

Where To Find External Publications For Internal Use

Finding ready-made publications is easier than you may think. Business, consumer and trade associations
usually produce generic publications intended to promote their profession. Since these publications are
designed to educate lay audiences, they are usually written in easy-to-understand terms. Similarly,
government agencies and public service or non-profit organizations publish tools designed to help educate
the readers about important issues such as AIDS, tax tips, and free self-help services. There are also many
for-profit companies that specialize in producing educational and information tools on specific topics.
These companies frequently identify themselves as specialists in education and training. Often, you can
find local resources in your yellow pages. In addition, there are publishers who produce directories listing
names and addresses of thousands of such resources. Two prominent newsletter directory publishers are

THE NEWSLETTER CLEARINGHOUSE
       Hudson's Directory
       44 W. Market Street (POB 311)
       Rhinebick, NY 12572
       (914) 876-2081

NEWSLETTERS DIRECTORY
>   Gale Research Company
>   Book Tower
>   Detroit, MI 48226
>   (313) 961-2242

UNDERGROUND PUBLICATIONS: WHAT THEY MEAN TO MANAGEMENT

Underground or unauthorized newsletters are frustrations to any organization. There is risk that they are disseminating inaccurate information or promoting attitudes that are counter to the organization's objectives.

Usually these publications are started to satisfy a specific networking need. The creators see themselves as being misunderstood by management and the rest of the organization. Their perception is that their needs are unique. The problem is that the publications are typically distributed only among the unique user group which does nothing to help the rest of the organization increase its understanding. Underground publications are most frequently found within an organizations's professional ranks such as data processing, engineering, or research and development.

An unusual number of underground publications can be a warning sign for an organization. That is, the formal employee publications are probably not being well-received, and probably don't reflect the needs of employees.

COMMUNICATOR'S TIP: How to Reduce or Eliminate Underground Publications

The easiest way to discourage underground publications is to give the underground publishers a company-sponsored forum such as a column in the employee newsletter.

ELECTRONIC PUBLICATIONS: TAKING ADVANTAGE OF TECHNOLOGY

The technological advances in computers, phone systems and audio and video media during the past few years have made it practical for individuals as well as companies to own sophisticated communication hardware. While it is unlikely that the electronic media will make the printed media obsolete, you can use the technology to your advantage.

The most common use of this technology today is electronic newsletters. They are developed in a variety of formats.

CHECKLIST: Types of Electronic Newsletters

- *Computer-Based.* The simplest form of computer-based newsletters are word processed text files that reside on a computer and are accessed from a PC or computer terminal. It is possible to include graphics and pictures, although more sophisticated hardware is required. Distributing information on PC computer discs is another approach, however the lack of operating system standardization makes this option more problematic.
- *Audio Tapes.* Some organizations have found that audio cassette tapes are an effective way to distribute news to employees. Employees can play them at their leisure at work, at home, or in their car.
- *Phones.* A variety of approaches are available using phone systems. Most rely on some type of dedicated phone numbers which, when accessed, will automatically

play pre-recorded tapes. The phone numbers could be an 800 number that employees call toll-free from anywhere, or they could be part of a voice messaging and mail system where each employee can receive messages in their personal phone mail box.

- *Video.* Video taped news programs can be distributed several ways. Some organizations have broadcasting capabilities similar to a television station with receiving monitors placed in strategic locations throughout the company. Others simply have videotape players and monitors in cafeterias, libraries, or training rooms. Tapes can be produced in a continuous loop so that they play over and over throughout the day. Some organizations have sent video tapes to employees' homes, encouraging them to share the information with their families.

The variety of electronic communication applications is limited only by your imagination. How to produce electronic-based communication tools is discussed in later chapters.

BARGAINING UNIT PUBLICATIONS: WORKING WITH UNIONS TO IMPROVE COMMUNICATION

Like all organizations, unions must have a way to communicate with their membership. Traditionally, they use the same media companies use to communicate with non-union employees.

Bargaining unit publications have been considered off limits by both management and unions. That is because of the adversarial relationship perpetrated by both groups. In the past, neither has considered the potential mutual benefits of cooperative communication activities. This issue could consume a book by itself because the publications are symbolic of much more complicated historical labor relations policies. However, there are opportunities for management and union leadership to capitalize on bargaining unit publications that will meet mutual objectives.

EXAMPLE: Union and Management Share Communication Funds

During negotiations management and union leaders agreed to encourage employee participation in managed health care plans, (HMOs and PPOs). Normally, management would have communicated to its salaried workforce and the union would have announced all these benefits to its members. In this case, both groups agreed to contribute to a fund for cooperative communication and related training activities. A comprehensive plan was developed. The plan determined that all employees, both bargaining and non-bargaining, would receive the same communication tools, and that the union publications would be used to help reinforce the campaign's messages. A union/management task force met regularly, reviewed all communication materials and helped ensure that the messages from all sources were consistent. The result was that all employees perceived a unified commitment to managed care and came to view the change as positive.

This example illustrates how unions and management are beginning to see the mutual benefit of cooperative communication efforts. There are more opportunities to capitalize on union/management cooperation, but you may have to take the first step.

CHECKLIST: Ideas for Initiating Cooperative Communication Activities

---

- Offer unions the opportunity to give input on communication tools that are non-controversial and intended for *all* employees.
- Offer to give unions communication tools to distribute to their membership.

- Ask unions to participate in communication planning sessions.
- Ask unions for their ideas on the best way to communicate a particular issue to their membership as well as non-members.
- Volunteer to give unions articles you have produced for the company newsletter so they can use part or all of them in their own publications.
- Volunteer to produce union versions of material you plan to produce for non-union employees.

These tips are not costly, but, they may buy you a significant amount of goodwill and cooperation. If you initiate an ongoing dialogue with unions about employee communication issues, you have the opportunity to improve union/management relations as well as employee communications.

Practical Point   Begin union/management communication discussions well in advance of negotiations or after you have settled to avoid other emotional and political elements undermining your communication objectives.

FIVE STEPS FOR PLANNING AND PRODUCING PUBLICATIONS

There are five basic steps that will make planning and producing publications easier.

- Matching the type of publication to the appropriate audience
- Establishing an editorial policy for each publication
- Identifying who will do the work
- Determining how much they will cost
- Evaluating their effectiveness periodically

Step 1: How To Get To The Right Audience

Using the guidelines in Chapters 1 and 2, you have probably matched publication needs with the different audiences within your organization. Some, but not all publications should be distributed to all employees. Remember, you have different audiences who have different needs for different types of information.

While most organizations try to evaluate their information and publication needs from the top down, I find it much easier to start from the broadest base your total employee population and work back up through the organization when doing a needs assessment. This approach helps ensure that all employees (don't forget that supervisors, managers, and executives are employees first) get the information they need. Each unique audience then will require only a small amount of additional information to meet their special needs. I can't tell you how often supervisors or field managers say, Let us see, in advance, what you are going to give employees. And, tell us what else we need to know or do to implement and make sure the message is clear. Seems like a very simple, logical request. It is. But most organizations don't remember to do it.

Many organizations get publication happy because they think they have more unique audiences than they really do. This is similar to what happens to a salary administration system over time. An organization may start out with 70 job classifications for 700 employees. But they get caught in the uniqueness trap and soon have 600 job classifications for 800 employees which is wasteful and administratively inefficient. The publication planning worksheet in Figure 4-13 illustrates how you can match your various audiences to the appropriate publications.

Step 2: How To Use Editorial Policies To Give Your Publication A Personality

The purpose of editorial policy or guidelines is to help ensure that confusing messages are not delivered to your audience. Editorial policy also sets standards to help writers understand how the publisher perceives things and to give the publication a consistent *personality* readers can rely upon.

Figure 4.13
PUBLICATION PLANNING WORKSHEET

Use this worksheet to quickly prioritize your publication requirements, itdentify the appropriate audiences and the topics you would cover in each publication.

AUDIENCES
All Employees * Bargaining * Non-Bargaining * Supervisors * Managers * Executives
Other (Research & Development * Sales * Service * Manufacturing * Data Processing)

PUBLICATION NAME	TYPE General or Specific	AUDIENCES	TOPICS
BULLETINS	////////////////////////	////////////////////////	////////////////////////
Ben Alert	Ben Alert	All	Benefits
Targeted Health	Specific	all	Health Care
Management	General	Managers Only	Operations
NEWSLETTERS	////////////////////////	////////////////////////	////////////////////////
Bird's Eye View	General	all	Business & H.R. News
MAGAZINES	////////////////////////	////////////////////////	////////////////////////
SPECIAL	////////////////////////	////////////////////////	////////////////////////
Informed Choice	Specific	All Employees	Health Care
"	"	" Retirees	"
BARGAINING	////////////////////////	////////////////////////	////////////////////////
ELECTRONIC	////////////////////////	////////////////////////	////////////////////////
EXTERNAL	////////////////////////	////////////////////////	////////////////////////
Retirement Planner	Specific	Age 55 and over	Retirement

For example, if the objective of the employee publication is to promote creativity, company activities, and professional development, the editorial policy of the employee publication must have a different style and tone than a publication which is geared to news about people and social events. Tone and writing style must be consistent with the publication's purpose. It is desirable to have an editorial policy for each publication you produce.

You should evaluate each publication to see whether or not it is clear that there is an editorial position for the publication. It is not necessarily wrong to have a combination of business and lifestyle information in a single publication. But if that is the objective, the editorial policy should help dictate how the topics are treated. *Forbes* magazine is a superb example. It is targeted to a relatively sophisticated business audience. Its focus is business. Therefore, its editorial policy dictates the style and approach all business-related topics will follow. But *Forbes* also recognizes more than just the business component of peoples lives. A few years ago, it added a section dedicated to *personal affairs*. In addition to very well researched business analyses, business-trend opinions, and exposé articles which is the main purpose of the publication, the *Personal Affairs* section features short book, movie, and restaurant reviews, vacation tips, and other issues directly related to social and lifestyle topics.

Editorial policy may also influence what the publication looks like. For example, the *Forbes Personal Affairs* section is set apart from the rest of the publication. The writing style and tone, however, is consistent with the rest of the publication. In addition to an appealing, easy-to-follow layout, the popular *Bottom Line Personal* newsletter keeps the publication on track with the following editorial policy which is published in the front of every issue.

PURPOSE

*To help those who are so busy with their careers and businesses
that they don't have time to handle their personal lives effectively.
To bring to them the best information from the most knowledgeable
sources. To select and generate that information free from the influence of advertising. And to give them access to the information
they need quickly, accurately, and efficiently.*

EXAMPLES: How Editorial Policy Influences Employee Publications

---

Writing your editorial policy to be consistent with the readers' needs is the key. IABC Gold Quill Winners (courtesy of *Communication World*) explain how editorial policy influences their employee publications.

Allstate's Quarterly Magazine. *states ...[we] planned editorial content to create strong management-employee realations, to give outstanding managers recognition, and to help managers better understand their work and the industry. ... The success of editorial content was gauged through reader comments and the annual communication survey...*

St. Luke's Texas Heart Institute Monthly Tabloid Newsletter *states Our focus is on good news--employee programs, United Way results, employee and department profiles, patient success stories and health tips. For people on shifts, part-timers and volunteers,* **Currents** *may be their only source of information.*

Bank of America Relocation Brochure *states . . . produce a brochure that would accomplish two purposes: mitigate internal opposition to the [corporate relocation] move, and aid recruitment efforts to offset any attrition.*

```
┌─────────────────────────────────────────────────────────────────────┐
│            CHECKLIST: Publication Managers' Most Common Mistakes       │
└─────────────────────────────────────────────────────────────────────┘
```

The basic goal of any publication is to enhance employees' trust in the organization. By knowing common pitfalls, you can build trust rather than undermining it.

Saying one thing in print, doing something else in practice. Trying to inspire employee's sense of responsibility for improving the company's performance, one firm published a mission statement and clearly invited all employees to offer suggestions on how the company could do a better job. The employees' initial reaction was enthusiastic and management received a lot of practical suggestions. However, they made two serious mistakes. They did not act on any of the suggestions and they did not explain why they did not act on them. In a very short period of time, employee morale worsened dramatically and the company's performance continued to decline.

Failing to have a written editorial policy that is endorsed by management. After considerable research, the human resources department of a medium-sized engineering firm prepared to introduce a newsletter featuring employees at home and at work. The editorial objective was to publicly recognize individuals for unusual contributions to the company and the community. The first issue was well received by everyone except the president who disagreed with the objective and refused to permit further issues.

Failing to relate information in the publication to the organization's business concerns and practices. An extreme example is the case of a company that decided to include short stories written by employees in the company magazine. Unfortunately, the stories were not well-written and employees could not understand why they were published. Employee reaction was hostile, charging the company with wasteful practices and lack of professional business leadership.

Permitting the publication to show bias for a particular individual or group within the organization. Firms whose primary business depends heavily on professionals such as engineers, scientists, accountants, or doctors frequently make the mistake of ignoring the important contributions of technical support and administrative employees. When publications meant for the entire employee population put too much emphasis on the professionals' contributions, the rest of the employee population tends to ignore the publication because it simply doesn't meet their needs.

Using the publication for information that is best suited for another medium. A community hospital decided to terminate a defined benefit retirement plan and replace it with a defined contribution plan. The benefit manager wanted to simply announce the change in the hospital's newsletter. However, the new plan would require employees to make decisions they never had to make before. Helping employees understand how the new plan would work and how to make the decisions required of them requires more thorough explanation than is appropriate for a newsletter article. A highlight brochure with examples and employee meetings are better media for this communication challenge.

Expecting the publication to make magic or be a hit overnight. After working very hard to develop a new publication or revitalize an existing one, it is normal to look for immediate, positive feedback. Occasionally, you will get it. Ordinarily, your audience will reserve judgement to see whether the new approach is a one-time anomaly or represents a consistent standard they can rely upon.

Being penny-wise and pound-foolish with respect to production costs. In order to keep printing costs for a health care enrollment brochure as low as possible, one company printed only 2,000 brochures for distribution to 1,900 employees. What they failed to consider was that they expected to hire 300 new employees in the next 12 months, their recruiters used about 500 brochures a year, and employees do lose copies and need replacements. Inevitably, they ran out of brochures and had to reprint them within 1 month of the first printing. If they had printed 3,000 or 3,500 brochures in the first printing, it would have cost about $800 more than printing 2,000. The reprint cost them only slightly less than the original print run so they paid almost twice as much, trying to save $800.

Trying to make the publication all things to all audiences. The children's hospital example on page 130 illustrates what happens when you try to make one publication satisfy too many audiences.

Permitting the design, layout, writing style, and tone to reflect management preference rather than the intended audience. The president of a well-respected service organization has very specific ideas about how any company-sponsored publication should look. He imposes his authority relentlessly. As a result, no one bothers to argue with him. Nor do they bother with the company publication. They simply created a superb underground network that satisfies their communication needs. In this case, they don't use underground publications. They use the phone, computers, and afterwork get-togethers. Unfortunately, the president doesn't know he is being ignored.

Forgetting to check the effectiveness of the publication periodically. Times change, business conditions change, employees' priorities, perceptions, and needs change. If your publication does not reflect these evolutionary trends, it will lose its effectiveness.

Step 3: How To Identify Who Will Do The Work

Producing an effective employee publication is a time consuming task. It almost always takes more time than most organizations anticipate. It should not be undertaken as a spare time activity. This is not an undertaking to attempt in your spare time! A publication does not have to be someone's only job, but don't underestimate the time it will take from that person's other duties. If you do, both the publication and the other duties will suffer immensely.

Traditional Jobs Required For A Publication   If the scope of your employee publications is big enough, you should consider hiring a full-time editor to manage all publication requirements. This list shows the traditional types of talent required, and the jobs performed to publish an effective employee publication.

Publisher. Overall responsibility for managing the publication process with respect to budgets and editorial policy. Is not usually a specific job in an organization. Could be Human Resource Director, Corporate Communications Director, or the President.

Editor. Ensures continuity with the editorial policy. Gives writers, artists, photographers assignments. Reviews each stage of production process. Edits all copy submitted by writers.

Writers. Selected to write specific articles or columns. May require more than one writer to meet objectives.

Artists. Prepare format layouts, special illustations, prepare type, pictures, artwork, and graphics for reproduction (printing). May require several different artists with specialized skills.

Photographers. Takes photos as specified by editor, artist, or art director.

Production Manager. Coordinates technical and budget process to ensure acceptable final product. This job may be handled by an editor, depending on the complexity of the publication.

Non-Traditional Staffing Resources   Using professional editors, writers, photographers, and artists is usually the way to get the best return for your investment. That does not mean you have to have all these people on staff. Frequently you can use freelancers on a project basis or contract their services for a specific time period. There are probably some resources within your own organization that are at least semi- professional and who would love to contribute to your employee publication. All it takes is a little effort to find them.

Following is a list of potential freelance non-traditional resources for you to consider.

- Employees
- Retirees
- Spouses of Employees or Retirees
- Professional Associations
- Community Service Groups

These people can be considered freelancers in the sense that you use them in the same way you would professional freelancers: have them work on the publication outside of their regular job. You may or may not have to pay for their services.

An easy way to find talent among your employees is to place a help wanted article in your newsletter inviting employees to submit articles, ideas, photos, illustrations, or cartoons for publication. Since people like to see their name in print, you will likely find a few who are also willing to put forth an extra effort to help you publish the newsletter.

Step 4: How To Develop Budgets

Like any other communication tool, employee publication budgets can get away from you if you do not plan and manage them carefully. For some reason, most organizations expect cost overruns. Yet, they are not inevitabilities. Overruns are almost always a direct result of poor planning or poor project management. The first step in determining a sound budget is to write detailed specifications.

Writing Your Specifications Writing good specifications is just another way of writing a plan. You will document technical parameters and identify publication procedures. If you do this carefully, you should only have to do it once and it will be fairly easy to revise and update, if necessary. Figures 4.14 through 4.16 are sample worksheets illustrating how to develop production specifications for different types of publications using a standard print specification worksheet. These worksheets will help you provide the information your production resources need.

- What is the frequency of the publication?
- What size will it be and how many pages will it have?
- Will you use, art, photography, or color?
- Are there special printing requirements such as die-cutting a window in the cover?

COMMUNICATOR'S TIP: Getting Help to Develop Specifications

Artists and printers are best equipped to help you develop specifications. Many printers produce how-to brochures and conduct plant tours and seminars to help their customers understand the technical challenges connected with print production.

Even if you do not complete the worksheets, it is to your advantage to insist that specifications like these are written for every publication. They will help you and all your production resources visualize the finished product and enable you to accurately predict and manage your costs.

CHECKLIST: How to Use a Print Specification Worksheet

Writing specifications is not as difficult as it may first appear. This checklist explains the purpose of each worksheet item.

Description. Writing a brief description of your publication will help you and your resources visualize what the publication should generally look like.

Number of Pages. If you are producing a bulletin, you will have a maximum of two pages (front and back of one sheet). If you are producing a newsletter or magazine, you may have four pages or more. The most efficient number of pages for publications with more than four pages is an even multiple of eight

Figure 4.14
PRINT MEDIA SPECIFICATION WORKSHEET

PROJECT DESCRIPTION
Masthead with Benefit Logo
2-Column Format

No. of Pages	Finished Size	Quantity
2 (front + back)	8 1/2" x 11"	5,000 (1,000 w/text ; 4,000 blank)

PAPER
Cover *N/A*
Text *70# Cameo Dull*
Other *N/A*

NUMBER OF COLORS
Cover *N/A*
Text *2 colors/2 sides*
Other *N/A*

PHOTOGRAPHY/ART/ILLUSTRATIONS/CHARTS
Cover *N/A*	B&W	COLOR
Text *1 Illustration*	B&W	(COLOR)
Other	B&W	COLOR

MECHANICALS (CAMERA-READY ART)
Bleeds *No*
Half-Tones *No*
Screens (Tints) *3 bopes with 10% screens (2 front / 1 back.)*
Other

PRINTING
Color Separations *No*   Bluelines (Proofs) *2 (mark color breaks)*
Color Keys *No*   Varnish *No*   Lamination *No*
Binding *Trim + fold to 8 1/2" x 3 5/8"*
Other   Delivery Date *Aug. 1*
Printer to hold inventory of blanks for future issues.

PRINTER'S ESTIMATES

Printer No. 1 *Gutenberg Press*   Estimate
Printer No. 2 *Jones and Jones*   Estimate
Printer No. 3 *Chasick & Co.*   Estimate

Figure 4.15
PRINT MEDIA SPECIFICATION WORKSHEET

PROJECT NAME	*Focus Newsletter*	DATE

PROJECT DESCRIPTION *Monthly employee newsletter*
A = 8 Pages for Standard Columns and news
B = 8 Pages for Feature Articles

No. of Pages *16* *(8 standard/8 variable)*	Finished Size *8 ½" × 11"*	Quantity *10,000/month*

PAPER
Cover *Self Cover*
Text *70# Vellum*
Other

NUMBER OF COLORS
Cover (*Outside Signature*) *4 Matched PMS over 2 PMS*
Text (*Inside Signature*) *2 Colors / 2 sides*
Other

PHOTOGRAPHY/ART/ILLUSTRATIONS/CHARTS

		B&W	COLOR
Cover (*Outside Signature*)	*4 photos per issue*	(B&W)	COLOR
Text (*Inside Signature*)	*None*	B&W	COLOR
Other (*Inside Signature*)	*2 Charts / Issue*	(B&W)	COLOR
	3 Illustrations / Issue		

MECHANICALS (CAMERA-READY ART)
Bleeds *No*
Half-Tones *4 per issue*
Screens (Tints) *30% of 16 pages have screens of 10%*
Other

PRINTING

Color Separations *No*	Bluelines (Proofs) *2 (mark color breaks)*
Color Keys *1*	Varnish *No* Lamination *No*
Binding *Trim, fold, saddle stitch (staple)*	
Other	Delivery Date *1st Day each Month*

Quote to be based on annual contract; subject
to annual rebid

PRINTER'S ESTIMATES

Printer No. 1 *The Creative Guild*	Estimate
Printer No. 2 *Hot Stuff Printing*	Estimate
Printer No. 3 *ABC Litho*	Estimate

Figure 4.16
PRINT MEDIA SPECIFICATION WORKSHEET

PROJECT NAME *Good Times Annual Report*   DATE

PROJECT DESCRIPTION

Annual Report Magazine for Employees

No. of Pages	Finished Size	Quantity
32 + cover	*8 ½" x 11 "*	*7,500*

PAPER
Cover *Vintage Gloss Cover, 100 basis*
Text *Mountie Opaque Text, 80 #*
Other

NUMBER OF COLORS
Cover *4 colors over 2 colors (process over match)*
Text *3 Colors (black text plus 2 match)*
Other

PHOTOGRAPHY/ART/ILLUSTRATIONS/CHARTS
Cover *1 Full Bleed 4 Color Process (35 mm)* B&W (COLOR)
Text *3 Quarter page; 6 small photos* (B&W) COLOR
Other *3 charts, 1 map, 2 illustrations* (B&W) COLOR

MECHANICALS (CAMERA-READY ART)
Bleeds *Cover - full bleed photo / text - 3 pages full bleed*
Half-Tones *9 - Text*
Screens (Tints) *70 % screen on full bleed pages; misc.*
Other *10 % screens throughout*

PRINTING
Color Separations *1 - Cover*   Bluelines (Proofs) *2*
Color Keys *1*   Varnish *Spot on Cover* Lamination *No*
Binding *Fold, Trim, Saddle Stitch, Pack 200/box*
Other   Delivery Date *March 1*
Drop Ship to 4 locations - N.Y. - 1; Arizona - 1; California - 2

PRINTER'S ESTIMATES

Printer No. 1 *Big Time Colors*   Estimate
Printer No. 2 *Orange Coast Lithography*   Estimate
Printer No. 3 *More for Less Printers*   Estimate

(e.g. 8, 16, 24, 32) because most printing presses are designed to print, fold, and trim all eight pages (or even multiples) in one step. If your publication is twelve pages, the printer has to print eight pages and four pages then collate them.

Finished Size. Finished size refers to the measurements of the final publication. Historical convention says that most publications measure 8-1/2" x 11". The more your publication varies from this standard the more paper waste and printing costs you will have.

Quantity. The printer will use the quantity, number of pages, and finished size to determine how much paper will be required to print your publication. If you plan to print blank bulletin or newsletter mastheads, then imprint them periodically, you need to have two quantities: the total number of blanks you expect to use over a six- or twelve-month period and the quantity you will imprint for each issue.

Paper. There are many different types, weights, and grades of paper. Some kinds of paper are better suited to a particular printing job than others. For example, the paper used in this book would not be a good choice for a slick 4-color magazine. If your publication is to have a cover, it is likely you will need to use a different type of paper stock for the cover than you choose for the text. Your artist and printer can show you paper samples and recommend the best type for your publication.

Number Of Ink Colors. The amount of color you plan to use in your publication will influence the type of paper best suited to the task. Most printers will assume that you will use black ink for text. That counts as one color. If you want two or more colors, you need to decide that in advance. For example, if your publication has a cover, you may decide to use four colors on the outside of the cover, none on the inside of the cover and two colors on all text pages.

Photography. If you plan to use photography in your publication, you need to decide whether it will be black-and-white or color. You also need to have a good idea of how many photographs you will use because they require special handling by your artist and printer, which will impact costs. You will also have to arrange to have the photographs taken, if they do not already exist, which will add to your budget considerations.

Art/Graphics. There are several types of art options you might want to use in a publication, such as charts, graphs, maps, or illustrations. Like photographs, these require special handling and, therefore you should have a good idea of what type and how many you plan to use. For budgeting purposes, you are better advised to overestimate than underestimate your requirements.

Mechanicals. Mechanicals (also known as camera-ready art) are the finished materials the printer needs to prepare your publication for printing. Ideally, the type for each page of your publication is carefully mounted on stiff art boards and marked to indicate where the printer is to put photos or other graphics, where to put different ink colors, and where to fold and trim the publication. In preparing your specifications, you should consider whether you expect to have tinted areas, colors going off the edges of the paper, and pictures as these things will affect how the mechanicals should be prepared.

Printing. In addition to all the above information, your printer will need to know some other details in order to properly estimate how much it will cost to print your publication. If you are using color photographs you will need to have color separations. Your printer will need to know whether you expect him to make the separations or if you will provide them. He will also need to know how many printer's proofs (bluelines or color keys) you expect. Most printers automatically include one proof in their costs. He will also need to know if you want special techniques such as varnish or lamination. Your artist will usually tell you if you need to consider these techniques. You should also be very clear about how and when you want the publication, finished and delivered.

Soft Dollar Costs That Can Hurt Your Budget

In addition to documenting your publications' mechanical specifications, there are two other issues that can impact costs.

Will you use in-house staff? If so, will all or part of their compensation, benefits, and overhead costs be allocated to this publication? Remember, even though in-house staff is often considered soft dollars, there is a cost that should be considered in your budget. If you use outside suppliers (including writers and editors), you can get specific costs from them by showing them your specifications.

How many approvals at how many levels will be required before a publication can be released?   Approvals and revisions can cost time and money. This is probably one of the biggest reasons for cost overruns and should be anticipated in your budget.

Step 5: How To Measure Effectiveness Periodically

Making sure your publications continue to meet your objectives requires periodic monitoring and re-evaluation. There are many ways to test effectiveness. Following are just a few.

Interactive Columns in the Publication
- Question & Answers
- Letters to the Editor
- Contests
- Opinion Polls on a variety of company issues.

Distribution Measurements
- How many copies are produced
- How many are not used
- How many are littering building and grounds
- How many complaints that the publication was not received

Surveys
- Special independent surveys
- Sections of employee attitude and climate surveys

Using the publication itself (presuming it is a periodical such as a magazine or newsletter) is one of the easiest ways to keep on top of how your readers perceive the publication, but there are times when a special survey may be necessary to validate whether you are really meeting your publication objectives.

GUIDELINES FOR ESTIMATING THE COST OF ALL YOUR PUBLICATIONS

As you can see from the budget worksheet shown on the next page, even if you have decided you need more than one employee publication, once specifications have been developed for each, it is not difficult to estimate the total cost of all employee publications and have a solid budget for the year.

You will notice that both the specific and aggregate budgets include contingency expenses. Including these will help you handle unforeseen expenses without destroying your budget or experiencing gross cost overruns.

ANNUAL PUBLICATION BUDGET WORKSHEET				
PUBLICATION	Cost Per Issue	Number of Issues	Sub-Total	TOTAL
Bulletin				
Contingency				
Newsletter				
Contingency				
Magazine				
Contingency				
Special Publications				
Contingency				

COST CUTTING TIPS

Once you have a realistic projection of what your employee publication will cost, there are ways to cut some of those costs. The key to these tips is to start with a carefully developed, realistic budget.

- Produce bulletin mastheads in quantities for the entire year plus 30%.
- Imprint text for each bulletin on the preprinted masthead only as needed and in the quantity needed for that issue.
- Insist on a detailed production schedule for each publication and allow sufficient lead time for each step. Make sure deadlines aren't missed. You and management will be the biggest offenders of missed deadlines and that will inevitably cost you money.
- Avoid making changes after type has been set. Make sure you have all necessary approvals *before* you send a manuscript to typesetting.
- Avoid changes at the printer's proof stage (blueline, brownline, etc.) at all costs. Changes at this point are very, very expensive.
- Insist on written quotes from all suppliers and make certain their specifications match what you gave them.
- Consider giving suppliers contracts to do all publications. This could include single resources, writer's, artists, photographers, typesetters, and printers. Get bids from several people, but tell all suppliers that the successful bidder will get the annual contract.
- Rebid everything periodically to be sure your suppliers are competitive.
- Develop a standard format for each publication so that you can control the number of words, pictures and pages that will be in each issue.

· Avoid odd sizes and shapes. They are more costly and potentially more likely to create production problems. Generally, it is safe to start with 8-1/2" x 11" and specify a size that divides or multiplies evenly. For example: a 5-1/2" x 8-1/2" size is one-half the size of 8-1/2" x 11"; 11" x 17" is twice the size of 8-1/2" x 11".

DESKTOP PUBLISHING: A PRODUCTION ALTERNATIVE

Desktop publishing technology is a combination of computer hardware and software tools. The hardware (e.g. computers and printers) are less important than the software. There are already thousands of computer software application programs that claim to give you desktop publishing capabilities. For the most part, the claims are not false but could be misleading if you are not conversant with computers and software applications.

The most rudimentary type of desktop publishing is word processing. However, when people talk about desktop publishing (commonly referred to as DTP), they are usually referring to the more sophisticated computer-based publication techniques which generate documents that begin to rival professionally typeset and printed publications. The most sophisticated level of desktop publishing combines the best desktop and traditional production technologies. For example, a document will be created on a desktop system, then output through high quality type and graphics processors and printed by a conventional printer.

The more sophisticated the approach, the more you will have to rely on special resources to help you take advantage of the technology. However, if you have access to a computer, a printer, and word-processing software, you already have desktop publishing capability. Figure 4.17 and 4.18 are examples of how you can use desktop publishing to dress up your publications without investing in new hardware or software.

Using DTP To Solve Production Resource Problems

Each day more companies are finding that desktop publishing can be a cost-effective and timesaving way to produce certain employee publications. It can be especially effective for bulletins and newsletters. Alan Frayer, Editor of *WINNING TODAY!*, turned to desktop publishing because the internal production staff was too busy responding to the company's business needs.

> *At one time, our publication was typeset, but increases in [company sales] volume prevented our typesetting department from preparing the newsletter on a timely basis...Desktop publishing, even in the small scale used by our office, allows us to devote our production staff to their normal work. One person can now produce a good quality piece inexpensively...*

Using DTP To Make Your Publications More Inviting To Read

One of the most useful advantages of desktop publishing is that you can make your publications more inviting to read. The training course outline illustrated in Figures 4.19 and 4.20 shows the difference between a traditional word processed page and the same page dressed up with the help of desktop publishing software. Once you have a complete word processed document, it takes only a few minutes to enhance it with desktop publishing techniques.

WINNING TODAY!

The Newsletter for SAVINGS TODAY! People	Vol. III, No. 4

A publication of Savings Today,
Inc. for its employees,
franchises, and licenses.

Alan Frayer
Editor

Mark Dean
Associate Editor

WINNING TODAY! is published monthly
by Savings Today, Inc., 1230 44th
Avenue East, Bradenton, Florida
34203. Reproduction in whole or part
without the written permission of the
publisher is prohibited.

Savings Today, Inc. Management:

Clarence Frayer
Donald Frayer
Arnold McDonald
Jay Clark IV
      Executive Board of Directors
Alan Frayer
      Director of Operations
Cindy Frayer
      Traffic Manager
Mark Dean
      Marketing & Research
Donna Payne
      Production Manager
Milt Frayer
      Supplies & Shipping
Milt Russell
      Regional Supervisor
      Great Lakes Region

SAVINGS TODAY! is a registered trade-
mark of Savings Today, Inc. and is
used with their permission.

SEPTEMBER 1988

In This Issue...

161 franchise areas; 17 states!

Copyright (c) 1988 Savings Today, Inc.

Figure 4.17 COVER OF PUBLICATION PRODUCED BY DESKTOP PUBLISHING. *WINNING TODAY* is produced with an XT-compatible computer, and an Epson LX-800, nine-pin dot matrix printer. They use word processing software (WordPerfect 5.0) which allows them to incorporate graphics from popular graphic programs, like Microsoft's Window Paint. The only things not done in this newsletter with Word-Perfect 5.0 is the newsletter's name and the photographs. The typesetting department screened the photos and provided the masthead type. *Figures 4.17 and 4.18 from WINNING TODAY!, are courtesy of Savings Today, Inc., Bradenton, FL. Alan Frayer, editor.*

Recently, Waran found himself in a position of being compared to other direct mailers. Remembering a lesson on the videotape, Waran "put the shoe on the other foot." Seen in a new light, the customer agreed with Waran's comparison, and purchased the ad.

Waran considers learning an important aspect of the sales business. He's always picking up new ideas, always learning, always ready to improve. This willingness to learn is the reason Waran Jepson will be able to readily adapt to changes in his product and presentation. he knows it pays, and pays well, to be ready to learn.

Copy Writer's Corner

Direct mail is slowly encroaching on classified ads, evident in the appearance of the latest "fad" in fast food advertising: help wanted ads.

DM News reported in their May 1st issue that a McDonald's franchise had "hired Trimark Publishers of Michigan, Inc. to target a 20,000 piece mailing to student neighborhoods" in Ann Arbor, Michigan. The McDonald's/Trimark ad "alerted students to the fact that McDonald's has jobs available." This was followed in August by a full page ad for Burger King, mailed by SAVINGS TODAY! to 15,000 homes in Livonia, Michigan, which combined a brief employment application with six food coupons.

According to *DM News*, F.H. Duern, president of Trimark, quoted the price of a 10,000 piece mailing as "usually just under $400." McDonald's 20,000 piece mailing would then cost almost $800. The article did not mention the size of the ad, but the price familiar with loose coupon mailings to believe the ad was a "long coupon" equivalent to SAVINGS TODAY!'s 1/3 page ad. The price also identifies the ad as a shared mailing, which is Trimark's normal delivery method, something also not mentioned in the article.

Burger King's SAVINGS TODAY! ad, by being a full page ad, offered enough room to provide the incentives that could lead to better response than McDonald's Trimark ad.

Burger King's SAVINGS TODAY! ad, by being a full page ad, offered enough room to provide the incentives that could lead to better response than McDonald's Trimark ad. The six food coupons, along with the many other valuable coupons in the SAVINGS TODAY! book, insures that the book, and the Burger King ad, will be in the public's hands up to three months after mailing. Long after the McDonald's ad has been discarded, the Burger King ad will still be bringing in applicants.

Will direct mail couponing replace classified advertising? If so, it won't be SAVINGS TODAY!, since the majority of classified ads are meant to be short duration ads. They are not the kind of ads that belong in a magazine of such lasting power as SAVINGS TODAY!. In fact, SAVINGS TODAY!'s advertising guidelines do require that ads which contain employment or career opportunities must be predominantly offer oriented. Still, keep in mind that the only thing that prevent similar ideas from becoming popular is choosing not to try. Innovation comes from people who are bold enough to try things that others shrug away. Only trial and time will tell if these innovations will become generally accepted practice.

Winning Bits and Pieces

On occasion, newspapers will print articles regarding the direct mail industry. We smile when we read these, understanding that editorial departments rarely speak with advertising departments in newspapers.

On August 9th, *The Bradenton Herald* reported that, in a survey conducted by the U.S. Postal Service, more than 1 in 4 Americans would like to receive *more* advertising mail. They also reported that the U.S. Postal Service had recently become the nation's third largest advertising medium, trailing only newspapers and television.

The *Sarasota Herald-Tribune* reported recently that shoppers traded in $2.84 billion worth of coupons last year, an 8% increase over 1986 (source: Manufacturers Coupon Control Center).

Our 1987 Franchise of the Year, SAVINGS TODAY! of Sarasota, called Central Clearing a month ago, looking to arrange an ad in St. Petersburg and Ft. Myers, Florida. Unfortunately, at the time both cities were unavailable, but as they become available, Linda Brown has a customer for them.

(left to right) Henry Zielke, Harry Zielke, and Donald Frayer at a picnic, celebrating Harry's purchase of 25 franchises.

Twistee Treat, a franchised ice cream business similar to Dairy Queen, was so impressed with their trial in Sarasota that they want to expand their advertising into other markets. Linda, who would rather forward a lead than hide it, will provide the information when the two areas reopen later this year.

Figure 4-18 INSIDE PAGES Photograph and special use of lines add visual interest to the newsletter.

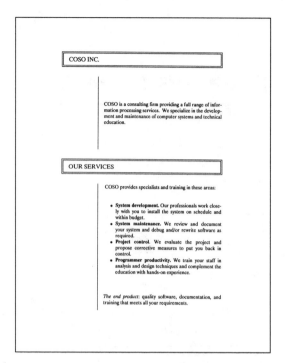

Figure 4.19. WORD PROCESSED COURSE OUTLINE

Figure 4.20 DTP PROCESSED COURSE OUTLINE

The course outline in Figure 4.19 was produced on a word processor and printed on a laser printer. While it is neat and reasonably easy to read, it is less appealing than the same document enhanced with Ventura Publisher Software (Figure 4.20).

Ventura Publisher and Pagemaker are the two most sophisticated IBM-based desktop publishing software programs currently on the market. Both can use text files created by a variety of word processing programs. In addition, you can now get impressive results from popular wordprocessing programs such as Word-Perfect and Microsoft Word.

Three Easy Steps To Enhance Your Word-Processed Documents
STEP 1: Create and edit your text using your word processing software. Do not bother to use your word processor's formatting capabilities (e.g., **boldface,** underlines, *italics*) because you can do that with the desktop publishing software.

STEP 2: When you are satisfied the text is complete and final, use desktop publishing software to enhance the type and layout of your document.

STEP 3: Print your final document. If you need only a small quantity, you can print each copy as an original. If you need large quantities, you can use your copier or printer to mass produce the final document.

The Dangers Of Desktop Publishing
Many of the things that make desktop publishing attractive also make it dangerous.

Unauthorized Publications. Desktop publishing technology will enable anyone with access to the tools to produce a publication that looks good. The better a publication looks, the more likely the readers will assume it is an authorized or company-sponsored publication. If the content conflicts with company policies and goals, readers will be confused and the company may begin to experience unprecedented behavior and employee relations problems. Inviting underground publishers to participate in company-sponsored publications is the best way to reduce the probability of this happening to you.

Gaudy Publications. Because desktop publishing software is so versatile and relatively easy to use, almost anyone who uses a computer can decide to become a desktop publisher. Unfortunately, being able to use a computer does not qualify someone to be a publisher. Most computer-literate people do not have publication design, typesetting, or graphics backgrounds or training. Even skilled writers and other communication professionals often have no sense of design or layout. As a result, many desktop publications miss their mark. They are gaudy, if not ugly, and therefore not inviting to read. Seeking professional guidance to set desktop publication standards and develop standardized templates can help solve this problem.

Increased Cost, Decreased Productivity. Most average computer users will never be able to take full advantage of the power of the desktop publishing software application programs. However, as soon as someone comes out with a new and improved version, everyone will want to upgrade. Usually, the users have not mastered the current version. That costs money. Each time you introduce a new or an improved application program, productivity declines while the user re-learns the program. Careful evaluation of the user's skills and your real needs will help you determine whether or not you need more software or better training or both. It is also advisable to locate outside freelance DTP resources to help handle emergencies or overload. Small DTP publishing companies are springing up daily. Temporary agencies specializing in PC computer operators and your computer hardware and software vendors are also good resources.

No Backup. If you are relying on desktop publishing for one or more of your publications and have only one person who can produce it, you are in trouble. If that person quits or gets sick, you will miss your publication date or have to resort to more expensive alternatives. Try to be sure that you have two or more resources that are skilled with your DTP system and can help out in an unexpected emergency.

No Quality Control. Because desktop-published documents look so good compared to word processed documents, people often forget to review them carefully before they are released. If all else goes well, but you forget to have someone responsible for proofreading, editorial content, and overall quality review, you could be embarrassed when your publication is distributed. Be sure you or a designated person carefully reviews the final document before it is published.

What You Need To Get Started

Hardware and Software. The hardware and software tools available to make desktop publishing a reality in your organization are too varied to itemize. It is likely that you already have some or all of the tools you will need. The best way to evaluate your current and future needs is to make a list of the hardware and software you have and list any hardware or software purchases you expect to make in the next six to twelve months. This will give you a sense of what you will have to work with.

Although you can technically consider yourself ready for desktop publishing if you have a typewriter or word processing system, a personal computer system will give you more options and flexibility. The desktop publishing software application programs you will need depend on the type of hardware you have.

People. Determine whether you currently have someone who knows or can learn how to use the hardware and software to help you meet your desktop publishing objectives. Hiring or training people with computer skills and an aptitude for learning various computer software applications will be a wise investment for the future.

Reading and Resources. To help you keep abreast of the changing technology, you should look for internal and external resources and read as much as you can. Reading books and magazines dedicated to DTP will help you find new resources and give you a sense of the current trends.

Resources To Help You Make The Most Of Desktop Publishing

As each day passes, more resources are made available to help you make the most of desktop publishing. Your most immediate resources are your internal and external communication professionals. In addition, user groups and associations can provide you with a wealth of information and advice. A good place to start is

> *Desktop Publishing Applications Association*
> Courtyard
> Fort Washington Center
> 10737 Indian Head Highway
> Fort Washington, MD 20744
> (301) 292-0060

> *VUNA*
> Ventura Users of North America
> 1 Heath St. West, Ste. 3, 2nd Floor
> Toronto, Ontario
> M4V1T2 Canada

> *The Newsletter Association*
> 1401 Wilson Boulevard
> Arlington, VA 22209

Other useful resources that will help you keep up with hardware and software technology as well as where to find people and services include

> *Publish! The How-to Magazine of Desktop Publishing*
> PCW Communications Inc.
> 501 Second Street
> San Francisco, CA 94107

> *Desktop Publishing*™
> Bove and Rhodes' Inside Report
> P.O. Box 10956
> Palo Alto, CA 94303-0901

CHAPTER 5

STEP-BY-STEP GUIDELINES FOR PREPARING EMPLOYEE HANDBOOKS

Companies provide handbooks for employees in a variety of shapes and sizes and, more importantly, for a variety of reasons. Some organizations develop comprehensive handbooks to give employees information and references on human resource related topics they would like to pursue. Other firms cover only employee benefit programs. This is especially true among companies that are required to have summary plan descriptions. Some organizations opt for two handbooks, one that deals with issues such as company history, work rules, and equal opportunity issues and a separate handbook to describe benefits. A less common format is to produce specialized publications for specific groups such as safety for engineers or hiring policies for managers. What companies must keep in focus when producing handbooks is the purpose they are supposed to achieve. When the need arises, a well-written handbook will serve as a resource for the employee who needs it.

In this chapter, we will focus on three categories of handbooks: comprehensive employee handbooks, topic specific handbooks, and handbooks for special classes of employees.

THREE KEYS TO PLANNING AND PRODUCING A SUCCESSFUL HANDBOOK

Producing any handbook is a major undertaking. The magnitude of the information you include is substantial compared to other communication tools. Three key elements; content, organization (including writing and layout), and format, will influence how easy your handbook is to produce and how successful it will be when it is completed.

EXAMPLE: Why One Company's Handbook Is Still in Draft Form After Three Years

---

An entertainment company decided to develop an employee handbook and assigned a variety of internal staff specialists to write chapters on different topics. Their reasoning was that this would speed up production. When they put all the chapters together, they discovered that many topics were missing because each writer thought that issues should have been covered by someone else. It also became apparent that each writer had a different perception of how the topics should be organized. For example, one chapter had an extensive list of definitions in the beginning and very few helpful subheadings while another had no definitions at all, but many boxed examples and charts.

Since each writer now had ownership in the project, the next few months were spent quarreling over whose approach was best. Three years later, the handbook is still not complete. However, the company has now hired an outside consultant to help them start anew. They are now compiling a comprehensive list of topics to review with the consultant.

Content: What Your Handbook Should Contain

Since handbooks are essentially reference tools, employees expect to use them as such. That means that they will expect a handbook to contain comprehensive coverage of many topics. If you are producing a comprehensive employee handbook, you may have upward of fifty topics whereas in a benefit handbook you may have only ten or twelve topics. The first step in developing your handbook is to decide what information it will cover. The quickest way to do this is to make a comprehensive checklist listing each topic separately. The checklist will help ensure you don't overlook a critical issue and it will simplify your organization and production challenges. You will find topic checklists in this chapter for each type of handbook. Use the worksheet in Figure 5.1 to compile the topics you want to cover.

DESIGNING THE HANDBOOK

How To Produce An Appealing Cover Without Spending A Fortune

You can't tell a book by its cover, but a handbook without an attractive, appealing appearance may never be read. Such is the psychology behind cover design. A cover should suggest that the contents might be worth reading; it should reflect the organization's culture but not be restricted by it. The cover represents what you provide for employees; it should attract them to *their* book and not lull them into thinking this is yet another P.R. tool.

It is worthwhile to make an investment in professional help when you design a cover unless you happen to be a design artist yourself. However, it's equally important not to be awed by what a consultant or artist might tell you is necessary to design a cover. I know of organizations that have needlessly spent tens of thousands of dollars to get a human resource communication logo or handbook cover design. It is not necessary to spend that much money. But it might be necessary to spend $1,500 or $2,000 or even $5,000 to get professional help.

The key to controlling the cost is to be willing to spend enough time with the professionals to help them understand the culture of the organization, and what would and would not be acceptable in design, color, use of your logo, etc. Then you must encourage them to ask questions before they begin creating designs for your approval. Another important issue is quantity. More is not better. Professionals will frequently tell you they will give you a variety of ideas from which you can choose. What usually happens is that you don't really like any of them so you ask the artist to go back and take a piece from this design and a piece from that one and do some new ones. This process can go on indefinitely and as it does your costs and frustration level go up. In some instances you will find a professional who is unwilling to listen carefully to what you wanted and comes back with something that represents specifically what you did not want. Don't pay for it, if you gave clear instructions in the beginning.

If the professional has a thorough understanding of the organization and objectives, he or she should be able to come back with one design that more than satisfies your expectations. Typically that design would be rendered in what is called a comprehensive mock-up (comp) which means it is a detailed prototype of what the finished product will look like.

To help you and the professional ensure you are both on the same wavelength, ask them to sketch what they are talking about right on the spot. You will usually be able to sense that you are both on the right track. Another technique is for you to sketch your idea. Don't worry about whether or not you can draw. The idea is to help them understand you. They will usually be able to pick up the idea and enhance it for you. Using this approach in a first interview can save you a tremendous amount of time and disappointment because as you interact, fuzzy ideas will begin to clarify right before your eyes. If you rely only on words, there is a high probability that how the artist visualizes a concept and how you visualize it are entirely different. By using the sketching technique, you will be able to react to what you see rather than what your imagination sees.

Figure 5.1
EMPLOYEE HANDBOOK TOPIC WORKSHEET

HANDBOOK DESCRIPTION

TOPICS	Check	TOPICS	Check

While it is desirable to have a distinctive cover, it still should be reasonably simple. Remember, you will have to live with it for some time. If it is too busy or too complex, you and your audience will tire of it very quickly. Finally, you need to be sure that your design is something that can be produced at reasonable cost.

CHECKLIST: Budget Tips

Following are things to keep in mind with respect to production costs for designs.

- four-color photographs are inordinately expensive unless you are producing thousands
- intricate designs that have different colors butting up against one another can be a production headache and very difficult to execute perfectly
- metallic inks cost more than conventional ink colors and create other production problems
- blind embossing requires making special dyes and using special materials to get the best effect and therefore can be unnecessarily costly
- insisting on a very detailed comprehensive mock-up will enable you to get an accurate printing estimate so you will not have any surprises when it is time to print your cover

Before you finally accept a cover design, you should be certain that you have complete, detailed specifications and production costs to make certain that it can be produced within your budget limitations. This means having printers and/or binder manufacturers actually look at the comprehensive mock-up and give you very specific quotes.

Organization: How To Make Your Handbook User Friendly

To be effective for employees trying to locate needed information, careful organization and design is critical. Producing a useful handbook requires devoting a great deal of thought to such things as the table of contents, the index, topic headings, and subject divisions. Carefully written text and easy-to-read layouts are also important. Organizing your handbook is relatively simple if you remember that your reader wants to find information fast and wants the information to be complete yet concise. Tables of contents and indices are the most common ways to help readers find the information they are seeking.

Tables of Contents are fairly easy to develop once you know the topics you will cover. You must first decide how detailed to make them. Figures 5.2-5.4 illustrate three levels of detail. The more detailed the Table of Contents, the easier it will be for your reader to locate the information you are trying to communicate.

Indices are more difficult to develop than tables of contents. A retired engineer once told me that he always judged the value of any book by whether or not it had a proper index. However, including an index in your handbook may or may not be worth the time it takes to create, because it is a tedious, time-consuming process. Indices are based on the premise that key words and topics are identified, listed alphabetically, and referenced to every page where they appear. The advantage of an index is that if your reader doesn't see a table of contents listing that clearly highlights the information he or she is seeking, a clue could be found in the index.

CHECKLIST: Quick Tips on How to Create an Index

- *List All Important Topics and Concepts.* Start with the headings and subheadings listed in your table of contents. Then add every main idea that a reader might want

Figure 5.2
SAMPLE TABLE OF CONTENTS No.1—
MINIMUM DETAIL

	PAGES
ABOUT OUR COMPANY	1-13
ABOUT YOU AND YOUR JOB	14-22
ABOUT YOUR PAY AND BENEFITS	23-60
ABOUT YOUR PERSONAL BENEFITS	61-65
MISCELLANEOUS	66-72

Figure 5.3
SAMPLE TABLE OF CONTENTS No. 1—
AVERAGE DETAIL

Figure 5.4
SAMPLE TABLE OF CONTENTS No.1—
BETTER DETAIL

Figure 5.4 (Continued)

to know about. For example, the reader may be looking for the definition of a term such as *vesting* which is used frequently in discussions of retirement and profit sharing summary plans. It is unlikely you would include the exact location of such a definition in the table of contents.

- *Determine How Many Key Topic or Key Word Variations You Need.* Your readers are likely to use more than one approach to look for the information they are seeking. Your challenge is to consider what deductive process might lead the reader to the topic. For example, one reader might look for *vesting, definition of* while another reader might look for *retirement, vesting.* A thorough index could help each reader find the same reference.
- *Prepare Key Topic/Word Cards with Single Subtopic Descriptors.* Use a separate card for each entry that will relate to your key topic or word. For example, you might have several cards for the key topic *Vesting* such as: *Vesting, retirement definition; Vesting, profit sharing definition; Vesting; definition of; Vesting, rules; Vesting, requirements; Vesting, active employees; Vesting, new employees.* In this example, you would have seven references to vesting in your index.
- *Organize Your Index Cards.* After you have created the keyword/subtopic cards, put them in alphabetical order by key topic or word and number them. This will help you determine whether you have too many or too few subtopics and whether you have created unnecessary redundancies for each key topic or word.
- *Edit Your Index Cards.* Eliminate redundancies, add missing subtopics and delete obscure references that may not be clear to your readers. Capitalize all key topics and words. Decide whether the subtopics should be primary or secondary subtopics. Eliminate unncecessary words such as prepositions that do not add to the information value. Add the appropriate page numbers. (*Note:* You will not be able to add page numbers until you have a final page-by-page camera-ready proof of your handbook.)
- *Reorganize, Renumber and Finalize Your Index.* After editing your index cards, realphabetize and number them. Prepare a final index listing from the cards.
- *Typeset and Proof.* When you get the typeset version of your index back from the typesetter or artist, carefully proof the index against the final typeset pages of your handbook.

If the organization of your handbook is comprehensive, logical, and easy to follow, employees are likely to refer to it when they want detailed information about a specific topic. Other organizing tips are covered later under each handbook category.

Page Layouts that Are Inviting to Read. In addition to how the handbook is organized, how the pages look will affect readership. If the pages are crammed with type and look like they will require a major time commitment, employees are likely to close the book, pick up the phone, and ask you to give them the answer to their question.

Since most of the topics you will cover in a handbook are essentially dull and boring, you need to take special care to present them in a manner that is appealing to the eye.

CHECKLIST: Five Keys to Layouts that Invite Readership

- *Use White Space Generously.* Relative to all other costs connected with producing a handbook, paper is cheap. Using wide margins and a little extra space between paragraphs always make the page more inviting to read and will add very few pages to the length of the handbook.

- *Choose Typefaces Carefully.* Fancy typefaces are difficult to read, especially when used for page after page of body copy. Times Roman and Helvetica are two of the most common typefaces recommended for optimum readability. Avoid the temptation to use several different typefaces. Rather than enhance the page, multiple typefaces tend to distract the reader, especially if they are not compatible.
- *Avoid Long Line Measures.* Shorter lines are easier to read than long lines. The reason newspapers and magazines typically lay out pages with multiple columns is to shorten the length of each line. Imagine trying to read your morning newspaper if it was set in a single column.
- *Use Major Headings and Subheadings Frequently.* Headings not only help break up the text visually, they help the reader find the information they want more quickly. This is an especially important consideration with handbooks because it is unlikely your audience will read it from cover to cover.
- *Use Color, Examples and Charts Whenever Possible.* Using a contrasting color for headings, adding clearly marked examples, charts and occasionally illustrations, to your text will enhance the visual interest of your handbook.

Figures 5.5-5.7 illustrate how different layouts affect the readership barometer.

How to Make Boring Topics Come Alive. Most of the topics you would include in an employee handbook are fundamentally lackluster. They will never compete with headline articles from best-selling magazines and newspapers. Even so, you may increase readership with well-chosen words. The key is to select words that have meaning to your readers. This is especially true for heading and subheadings. To illustrate the power of words, read the following examples. These phrases might be headings in an employee handbook. On the left are words which probably mean little to readers. On the right are headings worded to have meaning to employees.

- Severance Pay   Pay Guidelines When You Leave The Company
- Grievances   If You have a Complaint
- Expatriot Policy   If You Work Outside the Country
- Work Rules   You and Your Job
- Eligibility Effective Date   When Benefits Begin
- Accrued Vested Benefit   Your Earned Benefit

The words on the left, for the most part, are technical, human resource-related terms. The words on the right focus on the employee and concepts that will arouse their interest. Choose words with care because they convey many messages. Consider the word grievance. Organizations with a large number of bargaining employees will find that those employees relate to the term grievance very well. The question is, is this wording the most positive way to approach the subject? Complaint is a less negative word than grievance. Saying complaint instead of grievance downplays the negative impact. Think about the meaning that words connote to readers. Your goal is to make topics interesting, compelling, and clear.

Writing for Your Audience and the Law. Writing the text for any human resource communication tool is a challenge because you cannot ignore the legal liabilities inherent in putting words on paper. Yet text written in the convoluted style of attorneys, insurance companies or statutes, will be virtually unintelligible to your audience. Striking the proper balance between readability, liability, and technical accuracy takes skill.

Figure 5.5
HANDBOOK PAGE LAYOUT—EXAMPLE 1
The reader will perceive that this page will be too difficult to read because the line length is too long to make scanning easy.

EVALUATION PERIOD

The first ninety calendar days of your employment or promotion/transfer to a new position are considered your evaluation period. At the end of this period, if your work performance is satisfactory, your status will be changed to that of a regular full-time employee.

PERFORMANCE AND SALARY REVIEWS

At XYZ Company we believe you should get regular feedback on how well you are doing on your job. We have established formal performance review schedules to assure that you and your supervisor discuss how you have done in the past performance period and what you should be doing in the future. You will receive a written evaluation at each of these times.

XYZ Company has positioned itself to be one of the most competitive companies in our industry. Therefore, we are offering a higher rate of pay than our competitors. In return, the company demands a high degree of commitment, dedication and productivity from you. We believe those who perform the best should be rewarded the most. By the same token, we believe if you are not performing up to standard, we should not increase your pay until you are.

We know that starting a new job can be difficult. The first ninety days are a critical period in which you and the company determine whether the match will be mutually satisfactory. To ensure that we both look closely at how the match is working, all employees are to receive written and verbal reviews at the end of their first ninety days of employment, or at the end of their first ninety days in a new position. You are not eligible for a salary increase at the end of this ninety-day evaluation period.

All non-exempt employees receive a written and verbal review in February and August of each year. Non-exempt employees will be rated against specific task standards which will be communicated at hire and semi-annually thereafter. Non-exempt employees are eligible for salary increases at each of these times, but salary increases will be made only when the performance merits an increase.

All exempt employees receive a written and verbal review in February of each year. Exempt employees will be evaluated based upon completion of specific objectives which are negotiated at hire and yearly thereafter. An exempt employee may solicit a renegotiation of these objectives quarterly. Exempt employees are eligible for a salary increase each March, but salary increases will be made only when the performance merits an increase.

Salary increases are determined by your performance, company performance, and economic factors. Each position has a salary range which specifies a minimum and a maximum value for the job, and a midpoint, which represents the salary for a fully experienced person. No person may receive an increase that would result in compensation that is above the maximum rate or below the minimum rate established for the position in which they are employed. These salary ranges are checked on an annual basis to ensure that we are paying salaries that are competitive.

Figure 5.6
HANDBOOK PAGE LAYOUT—EXAMPLE 2

This approach helps employees identify the topics covered in each paragraph. Proper subheadings rather than italicizing the first line of each paragraph would help this layout more.

EVALUATION PERIOD

The first ninety calendar days of your employment or promotion/transfer to a new position are considered your evaluation period. At the end of this period, if your work performance is satisfactory, your status will be changed to that of a regular full-time employee.

PERFORMANCE AND SALARY REVIEWS

At XYZ Company we believe you should get regular feedback on how well you are doing on your job. We have established formal performance review schedules to assure that you and your supervisor discuss how you have done in the past performance period and what you should be doing in the future. You will receive a written evaluation at each of these times.

XYZ Company has positioned itself to be one of the most competitive companies in our industry. Therefore, we are offering a higher rate of pay than our competitors. In return, the company demands a high degree of commitment, dedication and productivity from you. We believe those who perform the best should be rewarded the most. By the same token, we believe if you are not performing up to standard, we should not increase your pay until you are.

We know that starting a new job can be difficult. The first ninety days are a critical period in which you and the company determine whether the match will be mutually satisfactory. To ensure that we both look closely at how the match is working, all employees are to receive written and verbal reviews at the end of their first ninety days of employment, or

at the end of their first ninety days in a new position. You are not eligible for a salary increase at the end of this ninety-day evaluation period.

All non-exempt employees receive a written and verbal review in February and August of each year. Non-exempt employees will be rated against specific task standards which will be communicated at hire and semi-annually thereafter. Non-exempt employees are eligible for salary increases at each of these times, but salary increases will be made only when the performance merits an increase.

All exempt employees receive a written and verbal review in February of each year. Exempt employees will be evaluated based upon completion of specific objectives which are negotiated at hire and yearly thereafter. An exempt employee may solicit a renegotiation of these objectives quarterly. Exempt employees are eligible for a salary increase each March, but salary increases will be made only when the performance merits an increase.

Salary increases are determined by your performance, company performance, and economic factors. Each position has a salary range which specifies a minimum and a maximum value for the job, and a midpoint, which represents the salary for a fully experienced person. No person may receive an increase that would result in compensation that is above the maximum rate or below the minimum rate established for the position in which they are employed. These salary ranges are checked on an annual basis to ensure that we are paying salaries that are competitive.

Figure 5.7
HANDBOOK PAGE LAYOUT—EXAMPLE 3

Splitting the text into three columns and adding vertical column separators makes the page more inviting to read than either Figure 5.5 or Figure 5.6.

EVALUATION PERIOD

The first ninety calendar days of your employment or promotion/transfer to a new position are considered your evaluation period. At the end of this period, if your work performance is satisfactory, your status will be changed to that of a regular full-time employee.

PERFORMANCE AND SALARY REVIEWS

At XYZ Company we believe you should get regular feedback on how well you are doing on your job. We have established formal performance review schedules to assure that you and your supervisor discuss how you have done in the past performance period and what you should be doing in the future. You will receive a written evaluation at each of these times.

XYZ Company has positioned itself to be one of the most competitive companies in our industry. Therefore, we are offering a higher rate of pay than our competitors. In return, the company demands a high degree of commitment, dedication and productivity from you. We believe those who perform the best should be rewarded the most. By the same token, we believe if you are not performing up to standard, we should not increase your pay until you are.

We know that starting a new job can be difficult. The first ninety days are a critical period in which you and the company determine whether the match will be mutually satisfactory. To ensure that we both look closely at how the match is working, all employees are to receive written and verbal reviews at the end of their first ninety days of employment, or at the end of their first ninety days in a new position. You are not eligible for a salary increase at the end of this ninety-day evaluation period.

All non-exempt employees receive a written and verbal review in February and August of each year. Non-exempt employees will be rated against specific task standards which will be communicated at hire and semi-annually thereafter. Non-exempt employees are eligible for salary increases at each of these times, but salary increases will be made only when the performance merits an increase.

All exempt employees receive a written and verbal review in February of each year. Exempt employees will be evaluated based upon completion of specific objectives which are negotiated at hire and yearly thereafter. An exempt employee may solicit a renegotiation of these objectives quarterly. Exempt employees are eligible for a salary increase each March, but salary increases will be made only when the performance merits an increase.

Salary increases are determined by your performance, company performance, and economic factors. Each position has a salary range which specifies a minimum and a maximum value for the job, and a midpoint, which represents the salary for a fully experienced person. No person may receive an increase that would result in compensation that is above the maximum rate or below the minimum rate established for the position in which they are employed. These salary ranges are checked on an annual basis to ensure that we are paying salaries that are competitive.

When planning your handbook, you should give thoughtful attention to your reader's information needs first. While the volume of information contained in a handbook is considerably more than you would include in any other communication tool, the same writing principals apply

- use single syllable words whenever possible
- keep sentences and paragraphs short
- avoid acronyms
- eliminate excessive prepositional phrases
- avoid cross-referencing
- use action verbs liberally
- answer your audience's three basic questions: 1)What is it? 2)What will it do for me? 3)How much does it cost?

Your potential legal liability will depend largely on the specific topic you are addressing (e.g. right to work policies or summary plan descriptions), where you are located, and your company's legal status (e.g. public, private, non-profit). How to reduce your legal liability is covered in more detail later in this chapter.

Where to Look for Good Writers.   Where do you find good writers? You may want to consult a professional writer or use someone in house. If you are fortunate enough to be in a marketplace where freelance writers abound, your task may be simple. Start by asking communication or human resource/benefit consulting firms for referrals. Over the years, such firms have faced needs similar to yours and they may be aware of many good staff or freelance writers. Another approach is to use your internal human resource specialists to produce first drafts of your copy. Once you have a first draft that is technically accurate and complete, you can look for a professional writer or editor to polish the text so that it becomes more readable.

Three types of writers to avoid are

- writers whose primary strength is fiction
- most writers of marketing communication tools
- audio-visual writers

Some retail advertising copywriters might be able to handle the assignment because they are accustomed to dealing with Federal Trade Commission regulations with respect to accurate representation of the products they are selling. This does not mean that all advertising copywriters have the patience to deal with the level of technical detail required for most human resource handbook topics.

Technical writers sometimes can be good, but if they are accustomed to writing in very technical language, they may be able to understand the concepts but not eliminate the complexity. Lawyers, insurance companies, and human resource specialists are usually not good writers for this purpose because they are too knowledgeable about the potential legal liabilities and therefore reticent to simplify the language.

Whether you use internal or external writers, you can increase the probability of getting a good manuscript by developing writer's guidelines. Writer's guidelines will help ensure that whoever is producing the text has some minimum standards against which to measure. Following is a sample.

SAMPLE WRITER'S GUIDELINES

Format
Submit manuscripts in typewritten (double-spaced) format on 8-1/2" x 11" white paper. Sixty-character lines are recommended to allow for reference to source documents in the left margin.

- Identify the document and number each page at the top.
- Use major heads and subheadings liberally.
- Indicate in parenthesis and (CAPITAL LETTERS) where examples, graphics, charts and graphs should appear in the text.

Writing Style and Tone

- The entire manuscript should be written in second person.
- Use as many subheads as necessary to highlight a new subtopic.
- Avoid long sentences and paragraphs.
- Avoid multi-syllable words.
- Do not use technical terms.
- Use bullets to highlight a long list of items.
- Use examples and charts liberally.

Required Technical Information

Depending on the nature of the manuscript (e.g. summary plan descriptions) technical information required by law may be included. In this case, details about the technical information will be provided for inclusion in the manuscript.

Practical Budget And Production Considerations.

The format in which your handbook is finally produced is important to consider early in your planning process because the format will influence cost and how easy the book will be to update. For example: decide whether your handbook will be produced in a three ring binder, spiral bound, stapled or as a series of separate booklets packaged in a folder or box. Also decide what size your handbook will be (e.g. 8-1/2" x 11" or 6" x 9"). These factors, along with your content decisions will help you determine the probable number of pages required, the most effective way to organize the handbook and how much it will cost to produce. Using these three keys, organization, layout, and writing, to plan your handbook will help make the project easier to manage and result in a useful communication tool.

Do You Need More Than One Employee Handbook? If policies and benefits vary for different employee groups, you should consider publishing different versions for each group. However, all versions should look the same and be organized consistently. If your comprehensive handbook becomes an unwieldy tome, you may be better off publishing two or more companion handbooks. They can be designed to look like a set and organized into major topics such as Benefits, Policies, or Company History. Remember, if employees have to struggle to use it, they won't.

HOW TO CREATE COMPREHENSIVE EMPLOYEE HANDBOOKS TO INFORM, NOT OVERWHELM

A comprehensive employee handbook provides employees with details of every aspect of their relationship with the organization. When you reflect on what that means, it is easy to see how a handbook can become an encyclopedia of sorts.

What To Include In A Comprehensive Handbook

If you are developing a comprehensive handbook, you should try to include information that will be useful to employees. An easy way to decide what is appropriate for your handbook is to construct an outline using three or four broad categories. This will help you organize the handbook and logically anticipate the most appropriate size and format. This checklist illustrates one manageable, accessible way to organize a comprehensive handbook. Notice that the topics have been grouped under major headings. Your organization may have other important topics to add to this list, or you may not need everything listed here. Even so, this checklist can get you started on writing a table of contents for your handbook.

ABOUT THE ORGANIZATION
- History
- Description of the Business, its Divisions, and Subsidiaries
- Operating Structure
- Facilities Maps

ABOUT THE EMPLOYEES AND THEIR JOBS
- Statutory Information
- Work Rules
- Grievance Procedures
- Compensation Policies
- Career Development/Training

BENEFITS
- Mandatory Benefits
- Sponsored Benefits
- Personal Benefits

MISCELLANEOUS
- Employee Organizations
- Resources for More Information
- Community Resources

Figure 5.8 illustrates how Ashton-Tate used this approach to develop their comprehensive employee handbook. Note that they have used 13 major categories and 76 sub-categories. The advantage of this approach is that they can add or delete topics quickly and easily without revising the entire handbook.

Keeping Information About The Company Up-To-The-Minute

A comprehensive employee handbook is the most logical place to communicate to employees about the organization. The more employees know and understand about the organization's history, business objectives, and organizational structure, the more they feel part of the organization.

Perhaps the most frustrating thing about producing any document that details the company status is that it is ever changing. People, locations, phone numbers, and organizational structure seem to change daily. The larger and more diverse the organization, the more complicated this problem becomes. That is why many organizations avoid publishing company information in handbooks.

Ashton-Tate, an organization in a constant state of flux due to acquisitions, mergers and aggressive new product development, solved this problem by designing their employee handbook in such a way that company information could be updated quickly and inexpensively.

As you can see from the sample pages shown in Figure 5.9, their solution to communicating fast-paced organizational changes allows them to deal with changes on any topic in the same way.

Communicating Company Policies

Many organizations are reluctant to publish company policies because they are time-consuming to develop, subject to frequent change and they have become the source of increasing legal liability in recent years. Yet, the advantages far outweigh the disadvantages.

TABLE OF CONTENTS

Figure 5.8   COMPREHENSIVE EMPLOYEE HANDBOOK.   Ashton-Tate has chosen a medium level of detail for their employee handbook. *Courtesy of Ashton-Tate.*

Figure 5.9   SAMPLE PAGES FROM THE EMPLOYEE HANDBOOK.

By publishing their handbook in an 8-1/2x11 binder format, Ahston-Tate is able to make updates quickly by simply adding or replacing a page or section that requires change. There is no need to reprint the entire handbook.

Courtesy of Ashton-Tate.

Product Development Centers

East Hartford

        52 Oakland Avenue
    East Hartford, Connecticut 06108
        Phone: (203) 522-2116

Westport

        25 Sylvan Road South
    Westport, Connecticut 06880
        Phone: (203) 222-1974

Glendale

        3800 La Crescenta Avenue
    Glendale, California 91214
        Phone: (818) 957-4411

Sunnyvale

        150 West Iowa
    Sunnyvale, California 94086
        Phone: (408) 735-0742

        471 South Murphy Street
    Sunnyvale, California 94086
        Phone: (408) 773-9591

District Sales Offices:

Canadian District

        #2 Bloor Street W., Suite 700
    Toronto, Ontario Canada M4W 3R1
        Phone: (416) 964-1022

                                    REV 1/87

November, 1985   We outgrow our facilities again and move to new, enlarged corporate headquarters in Torrance, California.

dBASE III PLUS is announced as a successor to dBASE III. dBASE III PLUS is a complete database management system with built in multi-user as well as single-user capabilities.

December, 1985   MultiMate Acquisition Agreement signed and integration of marketing and sales programs begins.

Ashton-Tate employs 856 people!

Announcement of establishment of the new international sales subsidiary in Sydney, Australia.

August, 1986   Ashton-Tate introduces dBASE Mac, an advanced relational database for Apple Computer's MacIntosh.

The first phase of Ashton-Tate's comprehensive service and support program is introduced, including pay-for-support and the removal of copy protection.

September, 1986   The acquisition of Decision Resources, Inc. is completed and Ashton-Tate enters the micro-computer graphics market with established, industry-leading software products.

October, 1986   Ashton-Tate officially announces shipment of its millionth copy of dBASE software, a milestone that ranks dBASE as one of the top two best-selling micro-computer business applications software products of all time.

                                    REV 1/87

October, 1986 (Cont'd)

New president and chief operating officer, Luther Nussbaum, joins Ashton-Tate after successfully guiding Businessland to the top of the computer retail market.

Ashton-Tate introduces RapidFile, its first product targeted at the low-end filer market and final link in the company's direct growth path for users' data management needs.

December, 1986   Ashton-Tate employs 1081 people!

                                    REV 1/87

CHECKLIST: Advantages of Communicating Your Company Policies

- *Provide Consistent Guidelines for Managers and Supervisors.* Managers and supervisors are better able to execute their human resource management responsibilities fairly and consistently and more quickly.
- *Promote Company Philosophy.* Since policy guidelines are the fabric of the organization's culture, reflecting its business and employee relations philosophy, in published policies can help promote the philosophy in a positive way.
- *Clarify Employee Behavior and Performance Expectations.* Employees are able to better understand how and why they are expected to behave in a certain way, reducing potential conflict between supervisors and employees.
- *Decentralize the Decision-Making Process.* You are able to vest decision-making authority to the lowest possible level in the organization and thereby increase efficiency and productivity.
- *Support the Organization's Legal Interests.* Since legislation increasingly dictates employer and employee rights and obligations, it is prudent to be certain employees have the same understanding you do about policies.

The number of policies your organization deems necessary will depend heavily on the nature of your business, the size and mix of your employee population, and your organizational structure. For example, an equipment repair business, operating from one location with 35 employees will require fewer policies than a clothing manufacturer operating with 8,000 employees scattered over 50 states and a few foreign countries.

COMMUNICATOR'S TIP: Rewriting Your Policies for an Employee Handbook

Most company polices are written in third person. Before you publish them in an employee handbook, rewrite them so that the style and tone is more personal and consistent with the other sections of the handbook. The easiest way to personalize the tone of any employee communication tool is to write everything in second person.

CHECKLIST: Over Seventy Policies and Topics You May Want to Include in a Comprehensive Handbook

---

EMPLOYMENT

- Human Resource Management
- Communication
- Business Mission Statement and Objectives
- Equal Opportunity
- Recruitment
- Employee Interview/Selection Process
- Job Posting
- Sexual Harassment
- Physical Exam Requirements
- Substance Abuse
- Smoking
- Rehire
- Layoff
- Leaves of Absence (Authorized, Unauthorized, and Civic Duty)
- Performance Measurement

- Corrective Counseling
- Employee Classifications
- Orientation
- Employment Fees
- Relocation
- Relatives
- Employee Referral
- Termination
- Probation
- Discipline
- Complaint Procedures
- Bargaining Agreements

DIRECT COMPENSATION

- Position Descriptions
- Work Hours, Days, and Weeks
- Payday
- Advances
- Expense Reimbursement
- Overtime
- Shift Differentials
- Bonuses
- Merit Pay
- Salary and Performance Review
- Flex Time
- Salary Administration
- Payroll Deductions
- Meal Period and Rest Period
- Severance Pay
- Garnishment
- Time Records
- Short- and Long-Term Incentives

BENEFITS

- Vacation
- Holidays
- Sick Leave
- Health Care (Medical, Dental, and Vision)
- Short-Term Disability
- Long-Term Disability
- Life Insurance (For Employees and Dependents)
- Accident Insurance (For Employees and Dependents)
- Retirement
- Cash Accumulation and Savings
- Deferred Compensation
- Profit Sharing
- Legal and Financial Counseling

MISCELLANEOUS

- Confidentiality
- Inventions and Patents

- Conflict of Interest
- Gratuities
- Political Activities
- Privacy
- Telephone and Equipment Use
- Professional Memberships
- Educational Assistance
- Conferences and Meetings
- Promotions and Transfers
- Temporary and Part Time Employment
- Safety and Health
- Government Mandated Policies and Procedures
- Expatriate Policies
- Use of Company Facilities
- Business Plan and Objectives
- Right to Change or Discontinue Policies

Figures 5.10-5.13 are sample policy, compensation, benefit, and miscellaneous topic pages from a comprehensive employee handbook. These figures are shown on pages 146 through 149.

TOPIC SPECIFIC HANDBOOKS

Topic specific handbooks are less inclusive versions of their comprehensive counterparts but the fundamentals are the same. Both should be inviting to read, logically organized, and complete enough to serve as reference tools. Topic-specific handbooks are produced more often than comprehensive handbooks, so guidelines to make them more useful follow. A topic-specific handbook is illustrated in Figure 5.14 (p. 150-52).

Benefit Summary Plan Descriptions

Benefit handbooks are the most common of the topic specific handbooks because, thanks to ERISA (the Employee Retirement Income Security Act of 1974), summary plan descriptions are mandatory communication tools. After all these years, you will find no consensus as to what constitutes a qualified summary plan description. Instead, you will encounter so many approaches to summary plan descriptions, that deciding which approach is best for your organization will be tough. The key is to aim for producing a useful, comprehensive communication tool. You will be 99% of the way toward satisfying ERISA regulations and have a better communication document as a result.

CHECKLIST: Five Steps for Preparing Summary Plan Descriptions

- *Locate Your Source Documents.* Collect the benefit plan legal documents (contracts or plan documents) as well as any letters of understanding or administrative procedures which are typically not included specifically in the plan documents.
- *Develop a Comprehensive Outline.* Include every major plan provision (e.g. eligibility, benefit schedule, limitations) you can think of. The more detailed the outline, the easier it will be to write and the more useful it will be to your readers in the form of a Table of Contents. Figure 5.14 is a sample outline for a medical summary plan description.
- *Reorganize the Outline Until the Continuity Is Logical.* It makes more sense for everything pertaining to participant eligibility to be first and plan termination to be last than vice versa, for example.

It's also possible to request an interview with Human Resources to discuss your desired career growth pattern. In the event a suitable opening occurs and the hiring supervisor feels that you are a suitable candidate for the position, you will be referred for an interview.

If you lack the necessary skills for a particular position, you may be referred to Human Resources for career counseling to pursue education or training to develop such skills.

Nine months of service in your current position is required before consideration can be given for a promotion or transfer. Generally, an employee who has received written notice of deficient performance from his/her immediate supervisor is not eligible for transfer or promotion until such time as the immediate supervisor notes that performance has achieved standard and remained there for at least three months.

EMPLOYMENT OF ALIENS

In compliance with the laws covering employment of aliens, you must possess American citizenship or be able to present documentation of your right to work in the United States.

EMPLOYMENT OF MINORS

In compliance with the laws covering employment of minors, you must be legally old enough to work and possess an appropriate state authorization.

EMPLOYMENT OF RELATIVES

While relatives of employees may be considered on the same basis as other applicants for a given job, Ashton-Tate does not encourage the employment of family members. Family members will never be placed under the direct or indirect supervision of each other or under the same supervisor. Family members are spouses, children, parents, sisters, brothers, grandparents, in-laws and step-relations. Present employees who marry will be permitted to continue their employment only if they do not work in a direct supervisory relationship with one another or in the same department.

EMPLOYEE REFERRAL PROGRAM

Ashton-Tate believes that you, as a successful employee, are an excellent source of individuals who can make a significant contribution to our organization. We encourage your referral of associates for employment with Ashton-Tate.

You will be rewarded with $250.00 for each non-exempt referral hired who successfully completes his/her evaluation period and $500.00 for each exempt referral so hired and retained. At the discretion of Human Resources, certain exempt positions will entitle employees to an additional referral bonus.

B-3　　　　　　　　　　　　　　Rev 1/87

Figure 5.10 SAMPLE POLICIES PAGE The policies section is entitled *For Your Information.* That is because the organization wants employees to perceive the policy statements as helpful information rather than rules. Notice that each topic has a clear heading to help the reader identify policy issues quickly.

Like the rest of the handbook, this section is written in second person. Yet, the company's position is direct and leaves little room for subjective interpretation. This approach helps ensure that company policies will be understood and administered consistently at all levels in the organization. *Courtesy of Ashton-Tate.*

EMPLOYMENT CLASSIFICATION:
FULL-TIME, PART-TIME, AND TEMPORARY

FULL-TIME EMPLOYEES are defined as those employees who are hired to work on a regular basis for 30 or more hours a week, and are eligible for all benefits.

PART-TIME EMPLOYEES are defined as those employees who are hired to work on a regular basis for less than 30 hours a week, and are not eligible for benefits.

TEMPORARY EMPLOYEES are defined as those employees holding jobs of limited duration arising out of special projects, abnormal work loads or emergencies. Temporary employees are ineligible for benefits.

IMPORTANT REGULATIONS
CONCERNING PAY AND HOURS WORKED

The Federal Fair Labor Standards Act establishes specific guidelines for determining whether a particular job is or is not subject to Federal Wage and Hour Laws. Positions that must comply with these laws are known as "non-exempt." At Ashton-Tate, all positions are classified as either non-exempt (salaried or hourly) or exempt by an evaluation of the specific job content of each position against government standards.

If your job is non-exempt, Ashton-Tate will pay you overtime at the rate of 1½ times your regular pay for time worked beyond 8 hours in one day, or 40 hours in one week, or up to 8 hours on the 7th day. You will be paid twice your regular rate of pay for hours worked in excess of 12 hours in one day or for hours worked in excess of 8 on the 7th day.

GETTING PAID

Pay periods at Ashton-Tate are dictated by your job classification (exempt or non-exempt).

Non-exempt employees are paid bi-weekly on Fridays for the previous 2-week pay period. Once into the payroll system you may expect a paycheck every other Friday.

Time records must be kept for all non-exempt employees, and it is your responsibility to insure that your hours worked are accurately recorded. All non-exempt employees are required to submit a time card to their supervisor on a bi-weekly basis. Falsification of a time card may be grounds for immediate dismissal.

Exempt employees are paid on the 15th and the last day of each month. If the pay date falls on a weekend, checks are distributed on the preceding Friday.

C-1   Rev 1/87

Figure 5.11 SAMPLE COMPENSATION PAGE   This is one of several pages that explain the company's compensation philosophy. This section not only includes policy statement, but describes specific compensation plan design such as bonuses and deferred compensation plans. Each topic in this section defines employee responsibilities as well as company commitments. *Courtesy of Ashton-Tate.*

For Times When You Are Unable To Work

LONG-TERM DISABILITY

Your long-term disability (LTD) plan guarantees you an income if you are ever disabled and unable to work for an extended period of time.

Most people can appreciate the need for life insurance to protect their family financially when they are gone. However, few people realize the need for disability insurance in case they are ever disabled and unable to work. It's a very real possibility – being alive but unable to bring home a paycheck because of a long-term illness or injury which prevents you from working. Should this happen, your income would be missed.

ELIGIBILITY
As a regular full-time employee, you may enroll for LTD coverage on your first workday.

If you enroll in our LTD plan as soon as you start working for Ashton-Tate, or within 31 days after your first workday, your coverage will be effective from your date of hire.

If you enroll more than 31 days after you become eligible, you will be required to provide evidence of good health. Contact Human Resources for more information.

HOW THE PLAN WORKS
If you become disabled, you receive your remaining salary continuance and then LTD pay begins with the 181st consecutive day of disability. Under LTD you will receive:

- A monthly check equal to 60% of your monthly income. (The maximum monthly benefit is $7,500 or $90,000 annually.)

LTD payments will be made at the end of each calendar month of disability. The first payment will be forwarded through Human Resources; subsequent checks will be sent directly to your home.

COORDINATION WITH SOCIAL SECURITY AND OTHER COVERAGE
LTD benefits will be offset by any benefits you receive from primary Social Security, occupational disease law, Workers' Compensation, "no-fault" legislation or other state-mandated programs providing disability payments. In other words, any payments you receive from those programs will be subtracted from your LTD benefit and you would receive the difference.

G-2   Rev 1/87

For Your Benefit

COMMUNICATIONS AT ASHTON-TATE

In an organization as dynamic as Ashton-Tate, communication is essential. It is the responsibility of each employee to keep informed about what is happening with the Company and the people we serve. Ashton-Tate encourages candid and continuing communication among all employees and is committed to providing information that is timely and accurate.

Your supervisor is the nearest source of information and has the primary responsibility for effective communication between your department and senior management. Your supervisor is responsible for keeping you accurately informed about matters affecting you and your job.

Staff meetings in your department are a good source for accurate, up-to-date information.

Bird's Eye View is Ashton-Tate's employee publication distributed at work to each employee. It covers news of Ashton-Tate people, benefits information, upcoming company sponsored activities, newly hired employees and features on departments and products. *Bird's Eye View* welcomes news items from you.

BULLETIN BOARDS

Information of special interest to all employees is posted regularly on bulletin boards. Employees may not post any information on these bulletin boards without the authorization of Human Resources. All requests to place information on these boards should be made directly to Human Resources.

Human Resources maintains bulletin boards strategically located throughout our facilities. There you will find notices of State and Federal laws, as well as other information and memos regarding changes in policies.

CREDIT UNION

Ashton-Tate is a member of the American Electronics Association Credit Union. This is a full-service credit union that provides savings and checking accounts, automatic teller cards, IRA's, VISA accounts and full-service loans. Applications to join our credit union can be obtained from Human Resources. Membership is available to you immediately upon hire and once a member you retain membership for life as long as a minimum $25.00 is maintained in your account. You will find more detailed information on the credit union and application forms in the Human Resources reception area. The credit union office is open from 9:00 a.m. to 4:00 p.m. and their service staff are always willing to answer your questions and provide additional explanations. A branch office of the AEA Credit Union is located at 6133 Bristol Parkway, Suite 275, Culver City, CA 90230, phone number (213) 641-8913.

COMPUTER PURCHASE

After six months of employment, you will become eligible to participate in Ashton-Tate's employee computer purchase program. At your direction, Ashton-Tate will purchase a computer of your choice for you at its reduced corporate purchasing rate. You must provide 100% of the purchase price at the time of purchase.

Upon completion of one (1) year of service, you are eligible to apply for a bonus in conjunction with the purchase of a microcomputer or peripheral equipment. The hardware bonus is a maximum dollar amount of $1000 and it accrues at a rate of 25% per year according to the

E-1   Rev 1/87

Figure 5.12 SAMPLE BENEFIT PAGES. Ashton-Tate has a non-traditional view of what constitutes benefits. The objective is to help encourage employees to see benefits as a cultural value that goes beyond group insurance and retirement plans.

Since employees frequently do not need or want to know every detail about their traditional benefit plans, this handbook includes benefit overviews like the Long-Term Disability Example, as well as comprehensive summary plan descriptions.
Courtesy of Aston-Tate.

YOUR FAMILY HEALTH RECORD

Use this handy section to keep track of your family's health expenses. A pocket is provided at the end of the section to hold copies of your claims and bills.

The following pages will help you to keep an accurate record of your health expenses. A separate page should be used for each member of your family. Each time you or a dependent goes to a doctor or a hospital, buys prescription drugs or has other health expenses, record the date, the reason for the expense, the amount and to whom it was paid. Then, as you receive your Explanation of Benefits (EOB) statement and benefit check, jot down the amount paid by the company (or companies in the case of more than one insurer) and the amount paid by you. This way you can tell when you have satisfied any deductibles required for the year.

A transparent, plastic pocket is provided at the end of this section to hold copies of claim forms, as well as the Explanation of Benefits statements you receive.

Not only will this record help you in following a course of treatment and in determining your company benefits, it may also come in handy at income tax time for possible deductions of your out-of-pocket expenses.

YOUR PERSONAL PROPERTY RECORD

Use the following pages to record vital information about your important papers and other personal property.

If anything should happen to you, your family would need to know the whereabouts of your important papers and the extent of your personal property. If you don't have a family who could take over your affairs, you should designate someone to be responsible.

When properly filled out, your personal property record will save time, trouble and loss of valuable property if you should become seriously sick, disabled or die. Access to certain information required here could affect the division of your estate or the care and custody of your children in certain situations.

It will only be valid, however, if you keep it up to date. Take time to review it each year.

L-2

Figure 5.13 SAMPLE MISCELLANEOUS PAGES. Providing employees with tools to make their lives less burdened with administrative details is the purpose behind the *For Your Personal Record* section of this handbook. In addition to the medical expense record above, this section includes recordkeeping forms for personal information such as dependent information and work history, survivor protection plans, and company-sponsored plans, credit card records, information about wills, financial statements, real estate, safe deposit boxes, and trust funds. *Courtesy of Aston-Tate.*

PATIENT'S NAME

Date Of Expenses	Paid To	Amount	Reason	A-T Benefit Paid	Amount You Paid	Deductible Remaining

Figure 5.14
SAMPLE CONTENT OUTLINE
MEDICAL SUMMARY PLAN DESCRIPTION

PAGES

BENEFIT HIGHLIGHTS

ELIGIBILITY
Employees
Dependents

WHEN COVERAGE BEGINS
Employees
Dependents
Newborn Children

ENROLLMENT
Employees
Dependents

COST
Company Contributions
Employee Contributions

COST SAVING FEATURES PROGRAM
Preferred Providers
Pre-Hospitalization Review
Special Situations
Out-patient Surgery
Mandatory Procedures
Pre-Admission Testing
Home Health Care
Hospice Care
Weekend Hospital Admissions Exclusion
Patient Management Program
Cost Savings Tips
Alcohol and Drug Abuse

Using a format like this will not only help you organize your summary plan description before you begin writing, it will serve as the framework for your final Table of Contents. You will have to add or delete topics, depending on how your plan is designed. However, this approach will work for every summary plan description you have to write.

Figure 5.14 *(continued)*

PAGES

HOW THE PLAN WORKS

Deductibles

Individual

Family

Hospital

Covered Expenses

Out-of-Pocket Expense Maximums

Expenses Not Covered

Benefit Limitations - Alcohol/Drug

Reinstatement Of Maximum Benefit

Limitations for Pre-existing Conditions

CLAIMS INFORMATION

Claims Policy

How To File A Claim

Release Of Information

Claim Settlement

Proof Of Loss

Decision On Claim

Notice Of Denial

Request For Review

Decision On Review

Denial Of Benefits

Legal Action

The more detail you can give about how the plan works and how to file claims, the more useful your handbook will be to employees.

Figure 5-14 *(continued)*

PAGES

GENERAL INFORMATION
Coordination of Benefits
Medicare Coordination
Subrogation
Extension Of Benefits
Changes In Coverage
Termination Of Coverage
Technical Data
Plan Administrator
Plan Number
Agent For Legal Process
Funding Policy
Type Of Administration
Plan Year
Your Rights Under ERISA

DEFINITIONS

Most of the information listed on this page is required by ERISA either specifically or by inference. If you treat it in the same syle and tone as you do everything else, employees tend to view it as information which they willl probably never need. but is there in case they do.

- *Write Your First Draft.* Start with a blank piece of paper. Translate every provision of the legal document into plain language, following your outline. This step is critical because there may be three or more provisions scattered throughout the legal document referring to participant eligibility. Your objective is to get them all in one place.
- *Annotate Your Draft as You Write.* As you translate and reorganize the legal provisions, make marginal notes on your draft referencing the source document provisions and page numbers (See Figure 5.15). This step is important because as you proceed, you will find that your source documents have conflicting or inaccurate provisions which must be revised. It will also help you quickly locate the source document provision when someone challenges the accuracy of your description.

These guidelines will help you produce a better organized, simpler version of your legal document. It is not yet a good communication tool. The next three steps will help complete the transition from legal document to employee communique.

- *Have Your Drafts Reviewed.* Send copies of your draft to your legal counsel, benefit consultants, insurance carriers, and administrators for peer review. Be sure to tell them you want a response with respect to technical accuracy, not editorial style.
- *Begin Polishing the Text.* This is perhaps the most difficult step because there is a tendency to keep the language very similar to that in the source documents. As you begin to polish the text, focus on *simplifying* the language and developing the style and tone that reflects how your organization wants to communicate. The example in Figure 5.16 illustrates how to transform the technical style of a first draft to a more acceptable human resource style.
- *Test the Final Draft.* Representatives of your intended audience are your most valuable assets to help ensure that your text is easy to understand and complete. Use task forces or ask employees from outside of your department to read your text and provide feedback.

Writing Summary Plan Description Text

Federal regulations govern much of the content and style of summary plan descriptions to help ensure that they are written to be understood by the average plan participant. In that respect, there is no conflict between the government's regulations and your desire to communicate effectively. From the government's point of view, summary plan descriptions must

- be written in a manner calculated to be understood by the average plan participant and beneficiaries
- not mislead, misinform or fail to inform the participant or beneficiary of his/her rights and obligations under the plan provisions
- disclose requirements for plan participation and benefit eligibility including how services are measured, vesting and benefit accrual and any proration rules
- describe the benefits provided
- describe the limitations and exclusions of the plan in the same way benefits are described (e.g. same size type, same completeness of disclosure)
- explain the source of contributions (e.g., employer, employees, employee organizations) and how they are calculated
- disclose any circumstances that could result in denial, forfeiture, or suspension of benefits including a break in service

SOURCE DOCUMENTS	MEDICAL SUMMARY PLAN DESCRIPTION - FIRST DRAFT
HEALTH CARE POLICY Page 123 Policies and Procedures Manual FAMILY HEALTH CARE PLAN DOCUMENT - Sec. II.3a, page 12	**WHAT THIS BENEFIT MEANS TO YOU** The Family Health Care Plan is designed to provide medically necessary, quality health care at a reasonable cost. This plan is a major part of your health care benefits with The Company, which also include dental and vision care (see separate booklets). The Family Health Plan is a comprehensive medical plan with Network Providers which includes designated hospitals, physicians, and other health care providers. Physicians and other providers outside the network are called Non-Network Providers. In most cases, you may choose between enrolling in this plan or in a Health Maintenance Organization (HMO). For more information on HMO enrollment, see page 00.
FAMILY HEALTH CARE PLAN DOCUMENT Sec. II.1,a-e, pages 7-10 CURRENT SPD - Pages 1-3 INSURANCE CONTRACT - Coverage Endorsement Page	**ELIGIBILITY** **Active Full Time Employees** You are eligible to enroll in this plan if you are a Company new normal or regular employee and • have made written application to participate in the plan, • have submitted evidence of good health satisfactory to the Health Care Benefit Department within ninety days prior to your application date, and

Figure 5.15 ANNOTATE ALL SOURCE DOCUMENTS—A SAMPLE. You are likely to have several source documents that you must refer to in order to be certain you have covered all plan design and administrative provisions. This organization has an extensive policies and procedures manual that must be frequently checked to ensure all other source documents are consistent with company policy. Using this source document annotation approach for your first draft will help you when you are ready to have the draft reviewed by legal and other technical resources.

Figure 5.16 MEDICAL SUMMARY PLAN DESCRIPTION

ELIGIBILITY - Section 2H1

Employees as defined in Corporate Policy Statement 19.5.1, General Employment, are eligible for coverage under this plan provided they

    a) have made written application to participate
    b) have submitted evidence of good health satisfactory to the Health Benefit Department within ninety days prior to the date of their enrollment application, and
    c) have not elected to enroll in another company-sponsored health plan
    d) are receiving a regular paycheck from The Company consistent with payroll requirements

The employee may change his/her coverage to another company-sponsored health plan or elect to have no Company-sponsored health care coverage, providing a change of coverage form (Form xxxx) is completed and submitted to Health

The Plan Document does not give employees enough information about eligibility requirements because it refers to other documents.

The summary plan description helps the reader by identifying all the employee classifications and defining the eligibility requirements for each group.

The Plan Document is not logical to an employee because it begins discussing how one may change coverage BEFORE it covers all the employee classifications for eligibility.

A good summary plan description will cover all the eligibility requirements in one section and cover the change options for each group in a separate section.

MEDICAL SUMMARY PLAN DESCRIPTION - FIRST DRAFT

ELIGIBILITY

Active Full Time Employees

You are eligible to enroll in this plan if you are a Company new normal or regular employee,

- have made written application to participate in the plan,
- have submitted evidence of good health satisfactory to the Health Care Benefit Department within ninety days prior to your application date,
- have not enrolled in another company-sponsored plan, and are receiving a regular bi-weekly paycheck from the company.

Part Time Employees

- identify which employee groups are covered or not covered by the plan (e.g. bargaining units, executives, hourly salaried)
- provide a notice of assistance to non-English-speaking participants in their native language
- include provisions of prior plans to the extent they affect the benefits of present participants

In addition, a number of technical information items are required. Because these regulations are so comprehensive, it will be helpful if you expand your writer's guidelines specifically for summary plan descriptions to include the information illustrated in Figures 5.17 and 5.18.

Figure 5.17
WRITER'S GUIDELINES FOR SUMMARY PLAN DESCRIPTIONS

Format

- Submit manuscripts in typewritten (double-spaced) format on 8-1/2" x 11" white paper. Sixty-character lines are recommended to allow for reference to source documents in the left margin.
- The top of each page should include a header which identifies the manuscript name, draft number, page number, and date as illustrated below:

MEDICAL SPD	Page 1
DRAFT 1	October 20, 19xx

- Annotate each paragraph in the left margin with the name, page and section of each source document used.
- Include a detailed table of contents, listing each major heading and subheading in the manuscript.

Writing Style And Tone

Summary plan descriptions must be written in a manner calculated to be understood by the average plan participant or beneficiary. The easiest way to meet this objective is to write to a sixth grade reading level. While most readers will have a higher comprehension level, this approach will help you translate the complex language found in the source documents to a more readable style.

- The entire manuscript should be written in second person.
- Cover all information about a single topic (e.g. eligibility) in one place. Use as many subheads as necessary to highlight a new subtopic.
- Avoid long sentences and paragraphs.
- Avoid multi-syllable words.
- Do not use technical terms.
- Do not reference source documents to give the reader more detail.
- References within the manuscript should be kept to a minimum (e.g. referring to a definition or glossary section is acceptable; referring to another place for more information about eligibility is not acceptable).
- Use bullets to highlight a long list of items such as limitations on benefits.
- Use examples and charts liberally.

If you find discrepancies in the source documents or incomplete information, use CAPITALS TO HIGHLIGHT YOUR QUESTIONS in the manuscript.

Required Technical Information
All summary plan descriptions must include the technical requirements illustrated in Figure 5.18.

EXAMPLE: How a Utility Company Used Focus Groups to Produce a Better Benefit Handbook

---

A public utility sent summary plan descriptions in manuscript form to employees at all levels throughout the organization. The summary plan descriptions were not given to the employees until they had been written, rewritten, technically reviewed, and polished. The first manuscript given to a focus group was a summary plan description for the medical plan. It was double spaced and over 80 pages long. Typeset, it would be 36 pages long in a 5-1/2" x 8-1/2" format.

Employees were asked to read the manuscript, then come to a focus group meeting and offer their opinion of it. A representative from the company's corporate communication staff joined the firm's consultant in conducting the focus group meetings. No other company management representative was present. Employees were told that the purpose of the meetings was not to address issues relating to how policies or benefit plans were constructed, but rather to talk about whether the plan provisions were described clearly and completely.

Employees were asked:

      1) Is there too much information?
      2) Can you understand how the plan works?
      3) Is there missing information?

To which they answered:

      1) No, this is not too long.
      2) Yes, it's easy to understand and why don't you write all of them like this?
      3) There should be more detail about how to follow the right administrative
          procedures.

The results of the focus meetings included some very constructive suggestions on how to make the manuscript better. Using this process will result in a good communication tool that is accurate and complies with ERISA. In the future, it can be updated regularly with minimum effort and expense.

Other Types Of Topic Specific Handbooks
If you do not have a comprehensive handbook, you may find a need for other types of topic specific handbooks. Some of them may be more technical in nature, such as compensation, safety, and policy handbooks. Others may be as simple as an internal phone book or a company resource directory. Regardless of the topic, following the summary plan description steps will enable you to produce a handbook on any topic. Figure 5.19 is a Health Care Services Directory handbook that was developed using this technique.

Figure 5.18

SUMMARY PLAN DESCRIPTION COMPLIANCE CHECKLIST

Plan Name	The name commonly used for the plan. (e.g. retirement plan, Informed Choice Plan).
Plan Sponsor Name and Address	The name and address of the employer, labor organization or other entity sponsoring the plan. If there is more than one sponsor, the name and address of the primary sponsor plus one of the following • list of all other plan sponsors, including addresses and IRS employer identification numbers • statement that complete list of sponsors is available on written request to the plan administrator and may be examined at specified locations during normal business hours • statement that the plan administrator will disclose, upon request, whether a particular employer or organization is a plan sponsor and, if so, disclose address.
IRS Employer I.D. Number and Plan Number	Sponsoring employer's I.D number and number assigned to plan by employer.
Type of Plan	Defined benefit, money purchase, health care, etc.
Type of Plan Administration	Contract administration, joint board of trustees, insurer administration, etc.
Plan Administrator	Name, business address, and business telephone number.
Agent for Legal Process	Name and business address and a statement that service of legal process may be made upon a plan trustee or the plan administrator
Trustees	Name, business address and title of each trustee (both administrative and financial trustees if functions are separate).
Funding Policy	Identify the funding medium through which benefits are provided (e.g. insurance company, trust fund).
Plan Year	Fiscal plan year for recordkeeping purposes.
Claim Procedures	How to file claims for benefits and recourse procedures if claims are denied.
Statement of ERISA Rights	Sample ERISA rights language has been drafted by the Department of Labor.

Figure 5.19

SAMPLE PAGES FROM MEDICAL SUMMARY PLAN DESCRIPTION

MEDICAL SUMMARY PLAN DESCRIPTION - FIRST DRAFT

ELIGIBILITY

Active Full-Time Employees

You are eligible to enroll in this plan if you are a Company new normal or regular employee,

- have made written application to participate in the plan,
- have submitted evidence of good health satisfactory to the Health Care Benefit Department within ninety days prior to your application date,
- have not enrolled in another company-sponsored plan, and
- are receiving a regular bi-weekly paycheck from the company.

Part-Time Employees

If you are a part-time The Company employee working a regularly scheduled minimum of 20 hours a week, you are eligible to enroll in this plan if you pay the required contribution and meet the above eligibility requirements.

Inactive Employees

If you are on an approved inactive status, you may not enroll in the plan until you are actively at work. However, if you are already enrolled in the plan, benefits may be continued during vacation, absences covered by the LTD plan (except as indicated by the "Discharge for Cause" provision), and during approved leaves of absence.

Temporary, Contract and Intermittent Employees

Temporary, contract, and intermittent are not eligible for this coverage.

Retirees and Eligible Dependents or Surviving Spouses

If you retire from The Company before January 1, 1989, see the 1988 Retiree Health Plan Booklet for information on enrollment and special coverage provisions which differ from those for active employees. If you retire on or after January 1, 1989, you will be eligible to enroll in the 1989 The Company Retiree Health Care Plan (see separate booklet).

Dependents

You may enroll eligible dependents in this plan if you are an active new normal, regular or part-time [name of company] employee.

Part-Time Employees and Dependents

If you are a part-time [name of company] employee working a regularly scheduled minimum of 20 hours a week, you can enroll your eligible dependents in this plan.

You must pay the required contribution for coverage (see page 00).

Eligible Dependents (Definition)

Your eligible dependents include:

- Your legal spouse
- Your unmarried children under age 19
- Your unmarried children to age 23 if they are full-time students and are dependent on you for support (proof of full-time student status is required)

(cont.)

Figure 5.19 continued

- Mentally or physically incapacitated children of any age, provided their handicap begins before age 19 and they are dependent on you for support. You must provide proof of the handicap within six months of the child's 19th birthday.

Children who are eligible for coverage include your own or lawfully adopted children and any other children over whom you have legal guardianship, and who depend on you for support and live with you in a parent-child relationship. To be covered, the child must qualify as your dependent for income tax purposes under rules established by the Internal Revenue Service (IRS). Proof of IRS qualification is required.

Who Is Not Eligible

Your dependents are not eligible for coverage under this plan if:

- You are a temporary, intermittent or contract employee
- They are eligible to join [name of company] Employee Health Care Plan
- They are already covered as a dependent under another The Company-sponsored health plan, such as an HMO

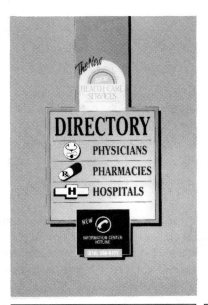

Figure 5.20 SAMPLE TOPIC SPECIFIC HANDBOOK. This topic specific handbook was designed to help employees, retirees, elibigle dependents, and surviving spouses use the southern California Edison Health Care system more effectively.

In addition to maps, addresses, and phone numbers of health care providers, health care consumer tips are found throughout the user-friendly handbook. *Courtesy of Southern California Edison.*

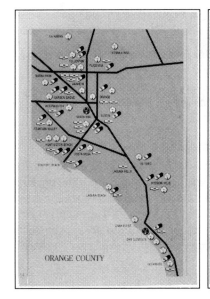

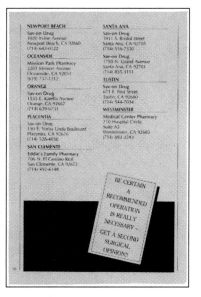

HOW-TO HANDBOOKS FOR MANAGERS AND OTHER SPECIAL GROUPS

Handbooks for managers and other special employee groups are becoming more prevalent. Until recently, dusty, rarely used policies and procedures manuals were the most common reference tools available to managers. Increasing complexities of human resource management underscore the need for better tools that not only serve as reference guides but explain how to use the information.

The primary purpose of specialized handbooks is to provide the users with easy-to-follow steps to accomplish a specific objective and provide helpful tools such as sample letters, memos, handy forms, and checklists.

Typically, they focus on *how to* comply with legislative regulations and *how to* administer various human resource programs. Legislative compliance topics range from discrimination testing for benefit plans to safety and health policies and procedures in the workplace. Human resource management handbooks cover such topics as employee assistance and performance management program administration, benefit enrollment procedures, employee orientation and training and development programs.

CHECKLIST: Reasons to Develop How-To Handbooks

Consider developing how-to handbooks if:

- *Turnover is high or you have a lot of contract or temporary employees.* You can avoid considerable downtime and speed up the learning curve of new hires and temporary employees.
- *You have more than one location.* You can increase the probability that there is a consistent understanding of company objectives and procedures.
- *You have changed old policies and procedures or are implementing new ones.* You can reduce the time necessary to retrain and reorient people to new ways of doing things.
- *You must rely on more than one or two people to help meet compliance or administrative standards.* You can ensure consistency and increase processing efficiency.
- *The topic is so complex that most people in the organization could not be expected to understand it thoroughly.* You can reduce inaccuracies that normally result from incomplete knowledge of the subject.

Eloise McGaw, Co-Director, Performance Management System explains why the Commonwealth of Massachusetts developed a performance management how-to handbook specifically for state managers.

> *...PMS [Performance Management System] is becoming a key
> human resource management activity on which promotions, pay,
> training needs assessment, and a host of other key decisions are
> based. ...without the handbook, it would be impossible to ad-
> minister the program.*

Making How-To Handbooks Into Self-Help Training Guides

Most of the tips described earlier in this chapter are useful for how-to handbooks. The primary difference is that how-to handbooks should take on the appearance of a self-help training guide. The organization and layout should be geared to helping the user locate the issue quickly, provide a concise overview of the objective, and illustrate clearly and specifically what to do and how to do it. The more samples you can provide, the better. The following pages (see Figures 5.21 through 5.26) illustrate how the Common-wealth of Massachusetts successfully communicated a very complex subject through a how-to handbook.

Figures 5.21-5.26 SAMPLE GUIDELINES FOR DEVELOPING HOW-TO HANDBOOKS   The text pages in this handbook have been carefully layed out and written so it is easy for the reader to quickly comprehend the issue. This page effectively summarized the scope of the Performance Management System in an unintimidating way. *Figures 5.21 through 5.26 are courtesy of the Commonwealth of Massachusetts.*

The Performance Management Cycle

There are four major phases that comprise the Performance Management Cycle:
1. Agency Mission, Goal and Objective Setting
2. Performance Planning
3. Monitor and Review Progress
4. Annual Review and Professional Development Plan

Agency Mission, Goal and Objective Setting

"Exactly what are my agency's mission and goals, and what are its priorities this fiscal year?"

Performance Planning

"What results are expected of me in helping my agency achieve its mission, goals and priority objectives. How will my effectiveness be measured?"

"How can I best go about achieving these results?"

Monitor and Review Progress

"How am I doing against my performance objectives?"

"Am I encountering any unforeseen problems? Can my supervisor help me solve these problems?"

Annual Review and Professional Development Plan

"How did I do? Did I meet my performance objectives?"

"What did I do well?"

"Where can I improve my performance?"

"How can I develop and improve as a manager?"

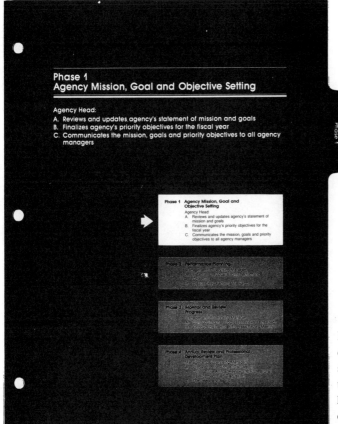

Figure 5.22   Each phase of the program has divider tabs with boxes summarizing major steps in each phase. The phase that the index tab precedes is highlighted. This technique keeps a picture of the entire program in front of the reader.

Guidelines for Writing Sound Performance Objective Statements

"To reduce claim processing errors" is not a well-written objective statement because it is too general. A better statement might be:

"To reduce the total annual error rate for claims processed by the Claims Section from its present 8% to 4% in FY '86."

The second statement represents an improvement. It is more tangible, leaving little or no room for uncertainty. Here are some guidelines for writing and evaluating your objectives:

1. Begin with an Action Verb

These words provide direction to the statement by signifying action or accomplishment of some sort. Examples:
— To increase
— To reduce
— To maintain
— To implement
— To install
— To develop and submit*

2. Relate to a Single Key Result

The action should relate to a single key result so there is a clear picture of when the objective is met. The one key thing that indicates achievement must be clear. For example, "To issue new guidelines for ABC compliance by July 1, 1986" may require several developmental steps, but the *key result* will be the "issuance" of the new guidelines. If *more than one* result is included, the objective is weakened since it may be difficult to verify accomplishment.

* Two or more verbs may be used as long as achievement will be determined on the last used.

2-7

Specify Results Achieved and Reasons for Results

In the *Comments* space next to each priority objective number, the supervising manager specifies the actual results achieved and any factors that affected achievement. This space should be used to explain any *extenuating circumstances* which prevented accomplishment, as well as any other comments on performance against the objective.

Extenuating circumstances should be noted wherever the supervising manager determines that a condition beyond the manager's control led to non-accomplishment. (See the example below.)

Annual Review

B-5

The Example of Deputy Commissioner John Stone

The description below gives an overview of the job duties of a hypothetical Deputy Commissioner.

Example:

John Stone is one of four Deputy Commissioners of the Department of Employment Development. He heads a division, composed of two bureaus, with a combined staff of 20 professional/administrative level and 15 clerical level employees. His primary responsibility is overseeing the administration of the Job Training Program. This program is designed to provide unemployed clients meeting special eligibility criteria, with subsidized on-the-job training opportunities with participating employers. The program is presently budgeted at $5.2 million, 40% of which is from federal grants.

The statements from the "principal accountabilities" section of this Deputy Commissioner's *Management Position Questionnaire* (MPQ) are shown below. Note that these are related to the Commissioner's assignments, but are worded to reflect the ongoing accountabilities of the position.

Accountability Statements on John Stone's MPQ

1. Timely and effective placement of eligible clients within subsidized on-the-job training positions, offered by employers in growth industries.
2. Cost efficiency in the delivery of the Job Training Program services.
3. Client and employer satisfaction with Job Training Program services.
4. Increased public awareness of the Job Training Program, especially in high unemployment areas and in minority communities.
5. Well planned program operations, including substantiated budget and federal grant proposals and subsequent spending plans.
6. Compliance by Division personnel with their administrative functions as part of the agency (e.g., compliance with EEO/AA guidelines).
7. Timely response to special requests for assistance from the Commissioner.

B-2

Action Plan Example 1.

Performance Objective: To develop and implement a plan for receiving employer feedback on the progress of specific clients by 1/15/86

Action Steps	Person Responsible	Planned Completion Date	Actual Completion Date
1. Appoint appropriate Bureau Coordinator and staff to carry out project	J.S.	8/15	
2. Draft plan completed	Coordinator	9/15	
3. Plan approved with necessary changes	J.S.	9/30	
4. Pilot test and evaluation of two employers completed	Coordinator	11/15	
5. Staff briefed on final plan and internal procedures	Bureau Chief	12/15	
6. Full implementation begins	Bureau Chief	1/15	

B-5

Figures 5.23-5.26 illustrate how to include tips, examples and illustrations to help users understand what to do and how to do it.

Get-Acquainted Handbooks To Help New And Temporary Employees

No matter how small the organization, one type of how to handbook that can be very useful is a get-acquainted handbook. A get-acquainted handbook will typically tell new employees and managers how to find and access internal resources such as office services, payroll, benefits, lunch, and rest facilities, as well as basics like how to use the phone system and other office equipment. Since updates are frequently necessary in this type of handbook, it is usually most expedient to produce them in a word processed or desktop publishing format.

WHAT THE LAW HAS TO DO WITH YOUR EMPLOYEE COMMUNICATION PLAN

Thanks to local, state, regional, and federal legislation, being an employer gets more complex with more legal liability each year. Naturally, we've become more careful and concerned about how the words you put down on paper could be construed if you ever ended up in court. Don't dwell on the subject, because the same legislators pass laws requiring employers to communicate to employees in specified ways. In other words, not only do you have to comply with the specific law, in many instances regulations prescribe how you must explain the law to your employees.

Following are just a few examples of how the courts have reacted to some organization's communication efforts.

Sample Court Reactions to Employer Communications

- *Share profits from a profit sharing plan were misrepresented in the employee communication materials.*
- *Life insurance contributions were not paid by the employer as stated in the communications.*
- *Secret severance pay plan must be communicated.*
- *Retiree benefits cannot be reduced without warning.*
- *Notification of conversion privilege in summary plan description is sufficient.*
- *Artificial salaries cannot be used for salesmen's long-term disability benefits.*
- *Plan change must be communicated in advance to adversely affected participants.*
- *Plan participant was not fully informed that he would forfeit survivor benefits by electing disability retirement.*
- *Employer may not discriminate against person with tuberculosis as it is considered a handicap within the meaning and intent of the law.*
- *Employer is guilty of intentionally inflicting emotional distress.*
- *Employer cannot discharge an employee for exercising a statutory right.*
- *Employer did not follow its written grievance procedure.*
- *Employee policies and handbook are part of the employment contract.*

Laws That May Have Specific Disclosure Requirements

There is no way to adequately cover every law on the books in this country. However, following are some of the most common topics that are likely to have specific disclosure rules you must follow.

Recruiting, Employment, Working Conditions, and Terminations. Federal laws such as The Civil Rights Act, The Equal Pay Act, The Employment Act, and The Rehabilitation Act, as well as many state laws affect how you manage and communicate recruiting, employment, working conditions, and termination issues. Specific issues that you should be careful to include are

- Equal Opportunity
- Affirmative Action

- Employee Selection Process
- Sexual Harassment
- Pre-employment Physicals
- Substance Abuse
- Smoking
- Employment Classifications
- Re-employment
- Corrective Counseling
- Performance Management
- Dismissal
- Layoff
- Wrongful Discharge
- Voluntary Resignation
- Grievance Procedures

Compensation and Benefits.   Compensation and benefit plans are also subject to Federal legislation such as the Fair Labor Standards Act, the Equal Pay Act, the Employee Retirement and Income Security Act (ERISA), and many others including the several tax acts that have been passed in recent years. While ERISA, which governs how you must communicate benefit plans, is the most frequently referenced, other federal, state, and local laws such as state disability and worker's compensation cannot be ignored. Other specific issues include

- Workday
- Payday
- Pay Advances
- Paid Time-off
- Overtime
- Performance Reviews
- Salary/Merit Increases
- Payroll Deductions
- Shift Premiums
- Authorized Leaves of Absence
- Expense Reimbursement
- Relocation
- Educational Assistance and Training
- Job Postings
- Inventions and Patents
- Gratuities
- All Qualified and Non-Qualified Employee Benefit Plans

Reducing Your Legal Liability

Do two things to greatly diminish your potential liability

- be honest
- get good technical review

If you tell employees exactly how a situation is, you stand to have fewer problems with them taking you to court. Honesty is therapeutic. People may not like what you tell them, but if they understand it, they will not typically be motivated to do much more than grumble.

How To Satisfy Legal Requirements And Still Meet Your Communication Objectives

Before going to press with any human resource handbook, ask your legal counsel, consultants, and internal specialists to review the text carefully for technical accuracy. Sometimes this means you will have to refine the language more than once to get a satisfactory sign-off from your advisors but it is well worth the effort. A word of caution: Don't let anyone force you into complicating the language you spent so much time trying to simplify.

CHECKLIST: Who Should Review the Text and Why

Following is a checklist of specific reviewers and reasons you should have them read your text carefully before your produce it.

- **Legal Counsel.** If you have to go to court because of something that was included or excluded from an employee communication tool, your legal counsel will have to defend you. Having them review and approve your text before it is published gives both them and you a better opportunity of having a defensible position if you have to go to court.
- **Consultants.** Consultants are not the same as lawyers. They will not have to defend you in court. However, they fulfill a similar function for you. Typically, they have helped you design your human resource policies, compensation and benefit plans. Therefore, they have intimate knowledge of how your plans were intended to work. They also have the benefit of having worked with many organizations and have insight into potential hazards that may have eluded you and your legal counsel.
- **Insurance Companies.** Whether insurance companies are underwriters for a particular kind of risk or benefit plan or only act as third party administrators (TPAs), you will benefit by making sure that their interpretation and your interpretation of their role are described correctly. If they administer a benefit differently than you say they are going to, you may encounter significant employee relations problems. If the communication material you give to employees is in direct conflict with the terms of the insurance contracts, you will end up paying more than you should because you may have no legal recourse to the insurance company.
- **Internal Administrators.** The people responsible for administering your policies and benefit plans internally should be consulted to be sure that what you publish is consistent with internal operations. If there is conflict, you will suffer potential employee relations problems and extra legal liability.
- **Communication Specialists.** No matter who prepares your text, having a fresh pair of eyes look at it is always advisable. Internal or external communication specialists frequently will find inconsistencies or clumsy wording that can be improved.
- **Employees.** Once you are sure you have technically accurate text, your audience is your best source of input with respect to meeting your communication objectives.

How To Reduce Unnecessary Changes In Your Manuscript

Using a large group of reviewers for your text automatically increases the likelihood that numerous changes will be suggested. Someone has to be responsible for deciding whether these changes will be made.

Lawyers, insurance companies, consultants, and other reviewers may ask for changes for the sake of change. Often this is a function of them looking at the text in a technical context. The easiest way to avoid unnecessary changes is to tell them you are not interested in editorial comment, only accuracy. It is usually a good idea to ask specialists to review your first draft and later, your typeset proof, just before it is printed.

Ask for very thorough first draft review because they won't see it again until it is ready for the printer. You will be unwilling to make unnecessary changes at that point. This approach usually helps, but inevitably you will get a lot of changes on the typeset version unless you hold a hard line. The key to keeping changes to a minimum is to clearly communicate to your reviewers what your needs and expectations are with respect to their input.

HOW TO MEASURE THE SUCCESS OF AN EMPLOYEE HANDBOOK

Once you have distributed the handbook, you may experience a major disappointment: silence. After all your hard work, you would like to hear someone say thank you and praise the effort. This doesn't happen very often. So how do you measure the effectiveness of your handbook? One way is through an opinion survey. Other options are less overt. Watch for these signals.

- Are you asked more questions on some subjects and fewer questions on others?
- Are employees asking more informed questions that indicate they know the handbook's content?
- Do you notice a change in behavior or benefit utilization patterns?
- Are supervisors changing the way they ask questions?
- Are supervisors handling more routine questions from employees?

If you can answer yes to these questions, your handbook is probably working as you intended. Remember, a handbook is a reference tool. It may take a while to get employees to use it. But if it is serving the needs of your audience, you will see positive effects over time.

CHAPTER 6

HOW TO MASTER PERSONALIZED COMMUNICATION TECHNIQUES

Personalized communication is a technique that allows you to use information unique to an individual, department, location, or other predefined operating unit. It usually requires computer support, unless the number of versions required is so small that manual personalization is practical.

In the broadest sense, paychecks and W-2 forms are personalized communication tools. In a narrower context, one of the most common personalized tools, and one of the first developed specifically as a employee communication medium, is the benefit statement. As computer technology races forward, and becomes cheaper and more practical for lay people to use and manage, the personalized communication opportunities expand geometrically. For example, today it is possible for a human resource department to produce a newsletter, personalized to every employee in the company. While that is not perhaps the best use of your time, it gives you an idea of the state of the art.

This chapter will give you examples, tips, and ideas about how to exploit the power of computers to produce personalized communication tools. The focus will be on *printed* or hard-copy tools, as distinguished from more sophisticated electronic tools which are covered in chapter 8.

USING COMPUTERS TO DEVELOP MORE EFFECTIVE COMMUNICATION TOOLS

Most organizations have turned to computers to help collect, organize, and maintain information about their employees. The most common data relates to necessary payroll information. Many organizations also maintain data on benefits and other human resource issues that are not directly required to issue a paycheck. This information may be on an internal mainframe, a mini- or micro-computer, or it may be stored on computers managed by outside resources such as banks, payroll services, and specialized consultants. Often firms use some combination of internally and externally managed computer systems.

Taking advantage of employee-specific data allows you to develop very powerful communication tools. Anything that speaks to the intended reader specifically, will get more attention. Reader-specific communication tools also enable you to reduce administrative burdens and control data errors when the reader needs to make changes in organizational or personal data. The challenge is to understand the benefits and limitations connected with these tools.

CHECKLIST: Personalized Communication Ideas You Can Use Today

---

- **Employment Offer Letters**. You can create an offer letter template on your wordprocessor that will permit you to quickly personalize the name and specific compensation and benefit package you are offering the prospective employee.
- **Service, Bonus, Merit, or Special Recognition Awards**. Using only a wordprocessor, you can produce customized letters and recognition documents

quickly and efficiently. These documents can be enhanced if you have desktop publishing capability.

- **Scheduling**. Work, sick leave, and vacation schedules can be published regularly and personalized for departments or operating units whose performance may depend heavily on manpower availability. Spreadsheet and project management application software can make this task a breeze.
- **Earned Vacation, Holiday, and Sick Leave Balances**. Periodic, personalized notes to individuals, reminding them of balances, is a subtle way to communicate with abusers and an nice way to remind hard workers to take some time off.

Personalized communication tools such as these are simple yet very powerful because they focus on the individual and his or her personal needs. These are only a few ideas you can implement almost immediately. Other opportunities are limited only by your imagination.

COMMUNICATOR'S TIP: Using Ready-Made Software to Create Personalized Communication Tools Quickly and Inexpensively

There are many personal computer software products such as project management, forms design, and spreadsheet and data base application programs which include templates you can use for simple, personalized communication tools. Some programs even include complete text files you can use as is or edit with your own application programs. Many of these have been developed by users just like yourself. Since the number of these tools grows almost daily, it will pay to browse through computer magazines, read the direct mail marketing material, and visit your local software store periodically.

The following checklist includes traditional, personalized, communication tools that require more than wordprocessing or spreadsheet capability. Most require larger computer capabilities and more sophisticated expertise than is normally available in most organizations.

CHECKLIST: Personalized Communication Ideas that Take More Time

---

- **Employee Benefit Statements**. Annual personalized summaries of employee benefits have been used by organizations for decades. These tools typically itemize the optimum benefits available to each individual and frequently include employer and employee contributions for each plan.
- **Retirement Plan Statements**. Retirement plan statements vary considerably, depending on the type of plan, how benefits are calculated and the intended audience.
- **Thrift, Profit Sharing, and Stock Plan Statements**. Like retirement plan statements, these personalized tools are unique to the type of plan being communicated. However, since most of these plans permit employee contributions, the amount of detail and the frequency of distribution is usually more than that found in retirement plan statements.
- **Personalized Enrollment Forms**. As organizations have expanded the number of benefit plan options available to employees, they have found that producing personalized enrollment forms simplifies communication to employees and reduces administrative headaches for the employer.

The following pages illustrate different types of personalized communication tools and formats.

Figure 6.1

The Creative Guild

16900 Pineridge Drive
Granada Hills, California 91344

<Date>

<First Name> <Last Name>
<Address>
<City> <State> <Zip>

Dear <Name>:

I am pleased to offer you the position of <position> with The Creative Guild.

The specific components of this offer are as follows:

- You will report directly to <Name>, <Title> and your responsibilities will be those discussed during your interview.
- Your official hire date will be <date> and your base salary for the position will be <monthly base salary amount> monthly. Paychecks are distributed on the second and fourth Fridays of each month.
- You will be eligible to participate in our performance incentive plan which will enable you to earn up to 20% of your base salary. Incentive awards are paid on or about March 1 of the year following the period in which they are earned.
- You are also eligible for the company-paid <list benefits>.
- You may enroll your eligible dependents in the <list voluntary benefit plans> plans. An enrollment form and highlight brochure is included for your convenience.

<Name>, I believe these terms are the ones discussed and agreed upon by <Name of supervisor> and you. If you agree, please indicate your acceptance by signing below and regturning a copy to me.

We are enthusiastic about you joining The Creative Guild and look forward to a mutually rewarding future.

Sincerely,

<Name>
<Title>

Accepted and Agreed:

By:____________________ Date:__________

Figure 6.2

YOUR PERSONAL
VACATION AND HOLIDAY
BALANCE SHEET

TO:

As of <date> our records indicate you have the following vacation and floating holiday balances remaining in your account.

	EARNED	TAKEN	REMAINING
VACATION DAYS			
FLOATING HOLIDAYS			

If you plan to use any vacation days or floating holidays during the next quarter, be sure to complete a time-off schedule, have it approved by your supervisor and return it to Personnel by March 31. If you have any questions, call <name> <phone number>.

Figure 6.3

STAFF PLANNING SCHEDULER

TO: DEPARTMENT:

As of <date> the following employees in your department have scheduled time off, authorized by you, for next month. If you expect the workload in your department will require temporary staffing, please notify <name> <phone> by <date> <Name> will arrange to help you solve your staffing problems.

FROM PERSONNEL RECORDS TIME OFF AUTHORIZED PRIOR TO <DATE>		FOR YOUR USE TIME OFF AUTHORIZED AFTER <DATE>
ADAMS	March 1	
CARTER	March 1, 2, 3, 4, 5	
TAYLOR	March 14, 15	
ZIMMERMAN	March 13, 14, 15, 16	

Figure 6.4

ASHTON·TATE

March 3, 19xx

<name1> <name2>
<street>
<city>, <state> <zip>

Dear <name1>:

On behalf of Ashton-Tate, I'd like to express my appreciation to you for a job well done. Your hard work and dedication to the Company has been brought to my attention by your recent nomination for an Ashton Award. You were among 24 people nominated by their fellow employees for outstanding service to Ashton-Tate.

Because the caliber of nominees was so high, the Ashton Award Committee had a difficult time choosing from among the many qualified nominees. Unfortunately, you were not selected to win the Award this last quarter, however, since the Award is offered every quarter to all employees, you may be nominated again for your oustanding job performance.

For your information, a copy of this letter will be included in your permanent employee record. Additional copies will be forwarded to your immediate Supervisor and your area Vice President. Congratulations on your nomination and keep up the good work!

Sincerely,

Director of Human Resources

JD/bl

cc: <vp>
<supvr>
employee file

20101 Hamilton Avenue
Torrance, California 90502-1319
(213) 329-8000
Telex 664228 ASHTATE TOR

Figures 6.1-6.4 These kinds of templates can be kept on your wordprocessor, ready to be personalized at a moment's notice. *Figure 6.4 is courtesy of Ashton-Tate Company.*

COMPREHENSIVE BENEFIT STATEMENTS

Benefit statements are typically single sheets of paper, dressed up in a variety of shapes, sizes and colors. Their purpose is to summarize an organization's employee benefit package, personalizing benefit levels for each employee. They frequently include salary data as well as company and employee costs for the benefits.

CHECKLIST: Information Typically Included in a Comprehensive Benefit Statement

- medical
- dental
- vision
- life insurance
- personal accident insurance
- disability (short- and long-term)
- savings plan
- retirement plan
- profit sharing plan
- dependent benefits including health care, life insurance and personal accident
- vacations, holidays, and sick leave
- other perks
- salaries and bonuses
- benefit cost estimates

Retirement Plan Statements

Many comprehensive benefit statements include significant retirement plan information. Specialized retirement plan statements are becoming more popular because only a specific portion of employees are interested. Organizations have found these tools particularly useful when used with pre-retirement planning programs. (See Figure 6.8.)

Capital Accumulation Plan Statements

Defined contribution and capital accumulation (e.g. 401(k), profit sharing, stock ownership, thrift, and savings) plans require current and accurate recordkeeping. Since there are legal disclosure requirements and many of these plans allow employees to make investment decisions, the recordkeeper will send periodic statements to active participants. The design and frequency of the statements is usually determined by the employer in cooperation with the recordkeeper.

In addition to the communication value connected with specialized retirement and capital accumulation statements, less information is required about these plans on a comprehensive benefit statement. (See Figure 6.9.)

Compensation/Benefit Enrollment Forms

When organizations began aggressively offering a variety of medical plans to employees, a new administration problem was born: re-enrollments. While organizations have dealt with annual re-enrollments for life insurance, accident, and disability plans for years, there was never enough incentive to develop a specific personalized tool to handle it.

With the variety of health care options available and more flexible compensation plans being implemented every day, personalized enrollment forms are almost a necessity. They are an exceptionally good communication tool in their own right. Not only do they simplify the administrative burdens for organizations, they simplify the decision-making process for employees.

20101 Hamilton Avenue
Torrance, California 90502-1319

◢◣◥ ASHTON·TATE®

Your 1986 Annual Benefit Statement

Figure 6.5 BENEFIT STATEMENT This statement has an overcover with a die-cut window which permits the employee name and address to show, but protects the rest of the personal data. The statement form was designed to be compatible with all other communication tools. It was pre-printed using two colors for the generic information common to all employees. An impact computer printer was used to personalize the information unique to each employee.

Because employees can choose among several medical and dental plans, the health care information was computer printed, depending on which plan the employee enrolled in. *Courtesy of Ashton-Tate.*

HIGHLIGHTS OF YOUR ASHTON-TATE BENEFITS

Your Total Compensation

Your total compensation at Ashton-Tate includes more than your salary. It also includes valuable benefits paid for by the company. Following is a summary of your estimated total compensation as of 12/31/1986.

Benefit	You Contribute	Ashton-Tate Contributes
Medical/Dental/Vision	0	$ 1,269
Basic Life–AD&D Coverage	0	12
Dependent Life Coverage	0	0
Supplemental Life Coverage	0	0
Travel Accident Coverage	0	2
Short Term Disability	197	0
Long Term Disability	117	0
Savings + Plan	0	0
Tuition Reimbursement	0	0
Auto Expense Reimbursement	0	0
Social Security	2,404	2,908

Benefit	You Contribute	Ashton-Tate Contributes
Unemployment Insurance	0	329
Workers Compensation	0	176
Stock Plan 1	0	0
Stock Plan 2	0	0

Total Cost of Benefits	$ 3,122	$ 4,666

Annual Salary ....$ 37,208
Bonus/Commission/
Cash Profit Sharing* .....$ 2,076
Total Cash Compensation ....$ 39,284
Your Total Compensation in 1986 is worth ...$ 43,950
Additional benefits that are part of Your Total Compensation at Ashton-Tate include: Product Purchase Plan, Discount Tickets, Computer Purchase, and the Employee Assistance Program.
*Can include Hardware Bonus and/or Ashton Award.

For Your Health Care

Ashton-Tate's Health Care Program includes Medical, Dental, and Vision Care.

Medical Plan
The Prudential Medical Plan pays 80% of most of your covered medical expenses. Most expenses are subject to a $100 annual deductible. If your covered expenses reach $2,500 in any year, most additional covered expenses will be 100% paid for the remainder of the same year.

deductible to meet, but you must pay a fixed fee for many dental services. Most preventive care is paid in full under the plan.

Dental Plan
You have chosen to enroll in Dental Net, a prepaid dental dental plan. You have no

Vision Care Plan

The Vision Care Plan has a $20 deductible per person with a maximum annual benefit of $150 per person. It covers examinations, all types of corrective lenses, frames and contact lenses. You are covered by this plan after three months of employment.

For Times When You Are Unable To Work

Sick Pay/Short Term Disability
Ashton-Tate pays up to 100% of your basic salary per month for three months and up to 80% for three more months offset by any statutory benefits you may receive.

Long Term Disability (LTD)

Long-Term Disability (LTD) begins on the 181st day you are disabled and pays 60% of your basic monthly earnings up to a maximum of $7,500. Your maximum benefit is ...$ 1,900 Payments continue until you are no longer disabled or reach age 65. LTD payments are reduced by any other disability benefits you receive such as Social Security, other government disability payments, or group plans.

For Time Off

Your vacation time accrues at the rate of 10 days per year. During 1986, nine paid holidays and three personal holidays were provided by the company.

For Your Survivors

Employee Coverage If you should die from any cause while an Ashton-Tate employee, your beneficiary will receive a benefit of 1 times your annual salary or $25,000, whichever is greater, in the amount of ....$ 38,000
In addition, if your death should be accidental, your beneficiary would receive 1 times your annual salary or $25,000, whichever is greater, in the amount of ....$ 38,000
If your accidental death occurs while you are traveling on company business, your beneficiary would receive an additional ....$ 150,000

Dependent Coverage The following benefits would be paid to you if any of your dependents die while covered under the dependent life insurance plan:
Your dependents are not enrolled in this plan.

Covered Spouse ....$ 0
Covered Children: 14 days to 6 months .....$ 0
6 months to 19 years
(23 if student) ....$ 0

For Your Future

Savings Plan The Savings + Plan is designed to help you plan and save for your future. As of November 30, 1986.
Your basic contributions 0%
of base salary were ....$ 0
Your supplemental contributions 0%
of base salary were ....$ 0
The company contributed 25 cents to your account for every dollar of your basic contribution.
You are 100% vested in your own contributions and their earnings.
You are 0% vested in company matching contributions and their earnings.
Your 1986 vested total balance is ....$ 0

The two offering periods ending in 1986 were:
Shares purchased during offering period #1
(ending 1/31/86) 000
Purchase price* .... $ 10.73
Market price value .....$ 20.00
Shares purchased during offering period #2
(ending 7/31/86) 000
Purchase price* ....$ 17.32
Market price value ... $ 22.62
Based on the market price of $44.50 as of 12/31/86, total value of stock purchased was ....$ 000
*Note: Your purchase price reflects 85% of fair market value as of the first day of the offering period. No adjustments were included for the stock dividend paid on January 12, 1987.

As of 12/31/86 you have 0 stock options outstanding, of which 1 are fully vested and exercisable.

Stock Purchase Plan You may purchase Ashton-Tate stock at a 15% employee discount through payroll deductions. Stock purchases are made on the last day of the offering period. As of 12/31/86 you are NOT enrolled in the Ashton-Tate Employee Stock Purchase Plan.

All data as of December 31, 1986

This Statement is specially for:

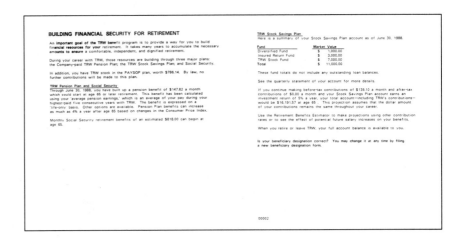

Figure 6.6 BOOKLET STATEMENT. TRW used a booklet format for their statement. The entire text was laser-printed and then assembled into a booklet format for each employee. The company also included an evaluation survey form and an order form which encouraged employees to get a free computer disk that would enable them to do retirement plan projections on a personal computer. *Courtesy of TRW Space & Defense.*

Your PERSONAL Total Compensation Statement

HEALTH CARE

Medical: Our records indicate you are enrolled in: **Equimed Lo 2-Party**	After Deductibles, The Plan Pays:		DEDUCTIBLES	
	Hospital	80%	Per Person	$100
	Outpatient Surgery	100%	Per Family	$200
	Doctor Office Visits	80%	Per Hospital Stay	$100
	Prescription Drugs	80%		

Dental: Our records indicate you are enrolled in: **Equident Lo 2-Party**	After Deductibles, The Plan Pays:		DEDUCTIBLES	
	Basic Services	60%	Preventive	$50/Yr.
	Major services	50%	Major	$50/Yr.
All reimbursements subject to Ususal, Reasonable & Customary (UCR) charges for covered procedures and plan limitations.	Orthodontia	None	Orthodontia	NONE
	Maximum Annual Dental Benefit is $1,000 per person.			

VACATIONS and HOLIDAYS   INCOME SECURITY (All benefits are taxable.)

Vacation Carryover Balance	0 Hours	Current Sick Leave Balance	99 Hours
Current Year Vacation Balance	64 Hours	Short Term Disability	$224/Wk - max. 52 weeks
Current Year Floating Holiday Balance	11 Hours	Long Term Disability	$575 per month
		Benefit ends at retirement and limited to 60% of salary.	

SURVIVOR BENEFITS   LUMP SUM BENEFITS   DEPENDENTS

Basic Life Insurance (1x Salary)		$ 12,000	You have not enrolled
Thrift Plan Balance		2,000	your dependents in the
Retirement Death Benefit		12,000	dependent life or ac-
Social Security Death Benefit		255	cidental death and
Supplemental Life Insurance			dismemberment plans.
SUB-TOTAL to beneficiaries if you die while employed		$ 26,255	
Travel Accident (Under Special Circumstances)		$ 34,000	
TOTAL to beneficiaries if you die while employed		$ 60,255	

FUTURE SECURITY   TOTAL COMPENSATION SUMMARY

Thrift Plan Balance	$2,000 Lump Sum	Your Current Annual Salary	$ 11,494
ESTIMATED Monthly Retirement Plan Benefits		Total Annual Cost of Your Benefits	3,225
$467/MO at 65	**$357/Mo at 62**		
Payable at your normal retirement date, if you continue working for the company. Assumes single life benefit. Benefit would be different if you are married and choose a different payment option when you retire.		TOTAL ANNUAL COMPENSATION	$ 14,719
		Bank's Cost	$13,586
		Your Cost	1,133

IMPORTANT NOTE

This summary is not a guarantee of employment or benefits. Every effort has been made to ensure accuracy based on the company's records. In case of error, this statement does not modify or change the actual benefits to which you may be entitled. If you have questions, please contact the Benefits Department at extension 2233.
INFORMATION CURRENT AS OF 08/01/88

SOCIAL SECURITY NO:	000-00-0010	ESPECIALLY PREPARED FOR:
DATE OF HIRE	04/14/86	
BENEFIT SERVICE DATE:	04/14/86	DEEDEE E. JONES
DEPENDENT MEDICAL COVERAGE:	Yes	

Figure 6.7. SIMPLIFIED STATEMENT. This statement illustrates how you can produce a very simple comprehensive benefit statement. It contains all the information included in the other comprehensive statements, but has much less generic text

Notice the disclaimer at the bottom of this statement. While disclaimers are no guarantee that you will be protected from gross errors or negligence, they should be included somewhere on any personalized employee communication tool you produce. *Courtesy of TRW Space & Defense.*

Figure 6.8 RETIREMENT PLAN STATEMENT

Your
PERSONAL
Retirement Plan
Statement

PREPARED ESPECIALLY FOR:	
DEEDEE E. JONES	Years of Creditable Service: **0 Years** As Of: **08/01/88** You Will be 100% Vested on: **04/14/96**

RETIREMENT PLANNING ASSUMPTIONS

You requested that this projection be calculated based on the following assumptions:

- You will leave the company at age 65
- Your retirement benefits will begin at age 65
- You expect to receive an annual salary increase of 7%

Based on the above assumptions, your projected estimated monthly pension benefit from the company retirement plan would be as follows:

	Your Benefit	%*		Surviving Spouse
For You Alone	$ 1,747	18	NO Survivor Benefits	NONE
For You and Spouse	$ 1,652	17	50% Joint & Survivor	$ 826
For You and Spouse	$ 1,567	16	75% Joint & Survivor	$ 1,175
For You and Spouse	$ 1,491	15	100% Joint & Survivor	$ 1,491

*Your Monthly Benefit Expressed As A Percentage Of Your Projected Final Average Earnings.

The projections in this statement are based on assumptions provided by you. The company gives no assurances or promises that the benefits projected in this model will equal your actual benefits. For a more accurate retirement benefit calculation, consult your Benefits Counselor.

Steps, Inc. STOCK INVESTMENT PLAN

QUARTERLY STATEMENT

PERIOD ENDING

SOCIAL SECURITY NUMBER

John Atwater
1234 Wishner
Hilltop, Kansas 63111

YOUR CURRENT PARTICIPATION STATUS

Your Monthly Contributions	Company Match Per Month	Total Contributions to Date (You and the Company)
BASIC 6% $215.00 SUPPLEMENTAL 0%	$143.33	$8,451.39

YOUR ACCOUNT VALUE

Funds	Your Contribution	Company Contribution	Total Market Value
Company Stock	3,233.19	3,032.70	$6,265.89
Mutual Fund # 1		566.95	$ 566.95
Mutual Fund # 2		565.52	$ 565.52
Fixed Income Fund	2,558.09		$2,558.09
TOTAL	5,791.28	4,165.17	$9,956.45

YOUR WITHDRAWAL CHOICES

	Amount Available	Suspension	Tax Implication
Your Basic Contributions			
Your Matured Contributions	376.66	None	None
Your Unmatured Contributions	4,694.12	3 Months	None
Earned Interest on Above	720.50	6 Months	Taxable
1st 50% Company Matured Account	192.98	9 Months	Taxable
2nd 50% Company Matured Account	192.99	12 Months	Taxable

Figure 6.9

Personalized Financial Planning Tools: The Wave Of The Future

The need to present such data, in a format that resembles a financial planning tool (similar to those provided by brokerage houses, banks, and savings and loans for cash management accounts) is likely to become more prevalent. As employees become more transient and benefit plans become more portable, personalized financial planning statements will probably overpower the more traditional formats.

COLLECTING THE NECESSARY DATA

The amount and type of data you must have available depends on the nature of the personalized communication tool you plan to produce. For example, the data requirements for a comprehensive benefit statement are much more rigorous than the data required for a personalized health care enrollment form.

It is critical that you are knowledgeable about the data you will need. If it is incomplete, inaccurate, or retrieved from several conflicting sources, you can anticipate headaches before you start. The first step in planning a personalized communication tool is to identify all the data you will need and where it will come from.

Payroll Data

Most of the data you will need can be found on your payroll system or can be calculated from that data. There are some noteable exceptions.

- accrued retirement benefits - calculated by the plan actuaries
- projected retirement benefits - calculated by the plan actuaries
- savings, profit sharing, deferred income account balances, and market values - provided by the plan recordkeeper
- health care claims data - available from health care claims administrators
- executive perks - usually available through one or two top level executives and the human resource manager
- all company paid benefits - usually available from the benefit manager in the form of cost or premium schedules

It doesn't matter whether you have the data on your own computer or use a payroll service bureau. If you are handling payroll manually, the task will be bigger, but you could still produce a personalized statement.

Retirement Plan Data

If you have a defined benefit pension plan, you probably have an actuary, a consulting firm, or an insurance company helping you value the plan assets and calculate current and future liabilities. They may also assess retirement benefit calculations. Therefore, they probably will be the best source of data to report on any personalized statement. The types of information you might want from them includes

- normal retirement date
- early retirement date
- current vesting status
- normal benefit payment form
    — if single
    — if married
- accrued vested benefit
- projected benefits at
    — early retirement
    — normal retirement
- valuation date

You might also want a variety of benefit payment amounts at different ages and under different payment options. While it is possible for your statement producer to calculate all of these benefits by using basic payroll data and your plan's provisions, it is better to provide the information after it has been calculated by the actuary, to reduce the likelihood of conflicting results.

Defined Contribution Plan Data

The type of data you will want from your recordkeepers will depend on the type of plan(s) you have. Following are the most common data elements you will want

- current vesting status
- year-to-date company contributions
- accumulated company contributions
- year-to-date employee contributions
- accumulated employee contributions
- all account balances
- current market value of accounts
- amounts eligible for withdrawal (if any)
- date values determined

Because this data is dynamic, you must rely on your recordkeepers to provide it as of a mutually agreed cut-off date.

Where To Look For Other Data

Depending on your communication objective, there may be other data, such as vacations, holidays, employee purchase programs, or medical claims information you would like to include in your personalized statement. You must identify each piece of data and where it will come from. You will also have to be certain it can be provided in a format that is useable. That may mean you have to create manual lists or tables suitable to the programmers. *A word of caution:* Health care claims data is very unreliable and can cause more confusion and employee relations problems than any other type of information. Avoid using it.

Figure 6.10 illustrates the probable data elements you will have to collect and their sources. You will notice that a unique employee identification number (preferably social security number) and the employee's name will be required from every data source. Without these, you will not be able to combine the data.

COMMUNICATOR'S TIP: Understanding the Importance of Confidentiality

Many organizations are concerned about allowing employee data to get into the hands of unauthorized parties. There is good reason to be cautious but it is clear that the number of need to know persons grows every day. Remember that most of the people who will have access to this data either already use it regularly or see it as a collection of numbers to be manipulated. However, it is always good policy to remind anyone who has access to employee data that it must be handled with the utmost care and confidentiality.

How To Make Sure The Data Is Accurate: Six Critical Checkpoints

Whenever you undertake a personalized communication project, the biggest challenge is ensuring data integrity. If an inaccurate statement gets into the hands of an employee you have the potential for a serious employee relations problem, even if the inaccuracies are the employee's fault. The easiest way to ensure good data is to insist on thorough error-checking procedures at every stage of the project. Unfortunately,

Figure 6.10
SAMPLE DATA COLLECTION FORM

DATA DESCRIPTION	LENGTH	DATA FORMAT
Employee Social Security Number (SSN) Employee Last Name Employee First Name Employee Middle Initial Employee Address Employee City Employee State Employee Zip Employee Basic Compensation Employee Supplemental Compensation Bonus Shift Differential Employee Birthdate Employee Hire Date Employee Marriage Date Employee Job Grade Employee Home Phone Employee Pay Status Full/Part-Time Indicator Employee AD&D Code Employee Service Compensation Date Spouse Birthdate Dependent 1 Birthdate Dependent 2 Birthdate Dependent 3 Birthdate Dependent 4 Birthdate Dependent 5 Birthdate Dependent 6 Birthdate Company Division Code Plant Location Code Savings Plan Contribution Rate Deferred Plan Contribution Rate Savings Fixed Income Rate Savings Equity Income Rate Deferred Equity Income Rate Company Dental Contribution Company Medical Contribution Dental Coverage Code Medical Coverage Code Supplemental Life Insurance Code Spouse Life Insurance Code Child Life Insurance Code AD&D Coverage Code FICA Payroll Deduction Amount Supplemental Life Insurance Deduction Amount Thrift Plan Deduction Amount AD&D Deduction Amount Highest Year Salary 1 Highest Year Salary 2 Highest Year Salary 3 Highest Year Salary 4	This column will indicate how many digits will be allowed for each data element. For example: You could need 15 or more digits for the employee's last name but you will only need one digit for the middle initial. This information helps your data processing people determine how to put your data together in a way that it can be used and understood by other programmers and systems analysts.	This column will define what the computer expects to see when it is trying to read the information in one of the data fields. For example, if a data format field like the employee name is expected to be in alpha format, the computer will ignore it if it has numeric values in the field. Similarly, if the computer is looking for a percentage format and encounters something that looks like a date (e.g. yymmdd) field, it thinks there is an error or the field should be ignored. SAMPLE FORMATS INCLUDE: Numeric Alpha Numeric yymmdd (date) Percentage Calculated Value Numeric in Hours Number of Months Constant Value = 12 REMINDER While this may seem like a tedious task, your data processing professionals want and need structured detail to help you achieve your objectives.

this means that you or your staff should carefully review each step. There are six major opportunities to review your data and assumptions before you print.

Dealing with More than One Data Source.   As mentioned earlier, a practical problem connected to using more than one data source is the need to be able to merge the data into one file. The easiest way to get your project off to a good start is to conduct a planning meeting. Be sure that anyone who will have anything to do with the project is represented. This will give you the opportunity to clearly identify responsibilities, clarify outstanding questions or confusion, and establish a good communication base among all the participants. Attendance at such a meeting should be mandatory.

Defining Error Parameters.   The programmers responsible for developing your data and printing programs will need help define acceptable parameters for error checking. Some of the parameters will be obvious.

> - if date of birth is current year...*error*
> - if normal retirement date does not equal date of birth plus sixty-five years...*error*
> - if payroll is deducting for 401(k) but not yet eligible...*error*

More insidious errors can occur because of special exceptions to general rules. This can happen when grandfather clauses, for example, give special status to a certain group of employees. You should document any exceptions.

Identifying a Control Group for Variables.   One way to make your job easier is to define a control group of employees that will represent every possible variable condition you can anticipate. At each step in the production process, you should check the results against the control group to make certain the program can handle the data for each control group employee correctly. For example, short-term disability benefits and costs must be treated differently for an employee residing in California than for one living in New Jersey or Kansas. You should have at least one employee in the control group for each location.

Checking the Calculation Program.   The calculation program or logic is written documentation that tells you what assumptions, formulas, variables, and calculations will be used to manipulate the raw employee data and produce the answers that will ultimately be printed on the personalized form. Some programmers can write this documentation more clearly than others. It is imperative that you carefully review every assumption to be sure the programmer has accurately described the method in which the answers are determined. This document will be used to create the actual program. If there are errors in the logic, there will be errors on the statements. Do not procede until you are satisfied the assumptions are correct and have approved the documentation. Figure 6.11 is a sample of the logic from a benefit statement calculation.

Checking Input Data against Output Data.   Even if you take all the precautions outlined here, it is possible that there will be errors in the output data of one or more employee's. The errors can be a result of inaccurate raw data or a mistake in the programming. This is the point where your control group will be very useful. The best way to use your control group information is to manually calculate every output data item for each control group employee. While this may seem tedious and redundant, it can increase the probability that you have eliminated most errors before the forms are printed. Figure 6.12 is an example of input and output data items for the retirement benefit calculations illustrated in the calculation logic example.

Checking the Print Program.   One final critical checkpoint to insist upon before you print all your statements is the computer print program. Even though you may have validated the output data, the computer print program that tells the computer how to print could have an error. Again, your control group will be very useful. The fastest way to verify the program is to have actual statements produced for the

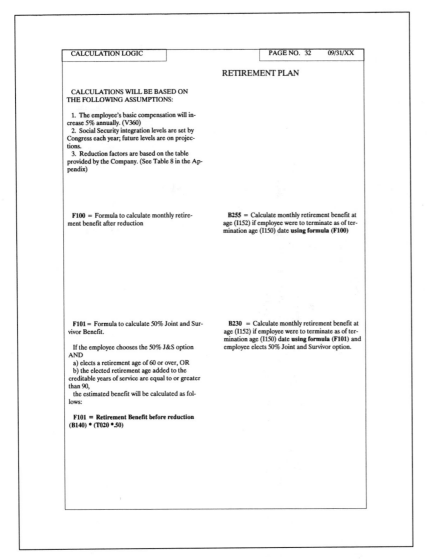

CALCULATION LOGIC | PAGE NO. 32 | 09/31/XX

RETIREMENT PLAN

CALCULATIONS WILL BE BASED ON
THE FOLLOWING ASSUMPTIONS:

1. The employee's basic compensation will increase 5% annually. (V360)
2. Social Security integration levels are set by
Congress each year; future levels are on projections.
3. Reduction factors are based on the table
provided by the Company. (See Table 8 in the Appendix)

F100 = Formula to calculate monthly retirement benefit after reduction

B255 = Calculate monthly retirement benefit at
age (I152) if employee were to terminate as of termination age (I150) date **using formula (F100)**

F101 = Formula to calculate 50% Joint and Survivor Benefit.

If the employee chooses the 50% J&S option
AND
a) elects a retirement age of 60 or over, OR
b) the elected retirement age added to the
creditable years of service are equal to or greater
than 90,
the estimated benefit will be calculated as follows:

**F101 = Retirement Benefit before reduction
(B140) * (T020 *.50)**

B230 = Calculate monthly retirement benefit at
age (I152) if employee were to terminate as of termination age (I150) date **using formula (F101)** and
employee elects 50% Joint and Survivor option.

Figure 6.11 SAMPLE LOGIC CALCULATION. This sample page shows why
you must pay careful attention to detail when developing personalized
communication tools. The left column describes the assumptions and formulas
to be used to calculate benefit values described in the right column. The key
numbers were developed by the programmer to help him keep track of the
types of data elements he would use in each step of the logic and program
development. Key numbers beginning with the letter **F** (e.g. F100 and F101)
tell the programmer to use a specific formula in his calculations. Key numbers
beginning with the letter **T** refer to specific tables which are often necessary to
benefit formulas such as the reduction factor table referred to in this example.
Key numbers beginning with the letter **I** are input values such as retirement
age. Key numbers beginning with the letter **B** refer to calculated benefit values.
In some cases, a formula may use a previously calculated benefit value (e.g.
F101) as well as other factors. If your logic is not carefully constructed, the
results could be grossly inaccurate.

INPUT DATA	DEEDEE E. JONES
DATE OF BIRTH	03/29/60
DATE OF HIRE	04/14/86
BASE SALARY	11,494

OUTPUT DATA	DEEDEE E. JONES
MONTHLY RETIREMENT BENEFIT AGE 65	**1,747**
MONTHLY 50% J&S BENEFIT AGE 65	**1,652**

Figure 6.12 SAMPLE INPUT/OUTPUT DATA SHEET The input data is information provided from your records. The output data the answers that will ultimately appear on your personalized communication tool.

These excerpts from input and output data sheets illustrate how you can easily verify the accuracy of your program. If DeeDee's birthdate, date of hire or salary are incorrect, her projected benefits will be wrong because the calculation logic says you are using those data elements, and others, to calculate her benefit at age sixty-five.

control group. The data on the statement should be checked against the output data elements to be sure they are printed in the right place on the form.

Personalized communication tools can be hazardous both legally and from an employee relations perspective. If you are unwilling or unable to dedicate the time to carefully examine each of the steps described above, you should probably not try to produce personalized communication tools.

FINDING THE RIGHT RESOURCES

It should be clear by now that you will need a variety of specialized resources to help you produce a personalized communication tool. You will need writers, artists, programmers, typesetters, printers, and finishers. Most organizations use outside vendors who have entire staffs dedicated to producing these kinds of tools. The reason is simple. The outside vendors typically can be more efficient because that is their primary job.

The most common outside resources are employee benefit consulting firms. Insurance companies, banks, and payroll or recordkeeping organizations also provide some personalized communication services. As technology races ahead, it will become more practical for organizations to develop these tools internally. However, it is important to objectively evaluate the knowledge base and availability and be wary of any resource that tells you they can produce a complex personalized communication tool in less than six to eight weeks for a cost less than about two dollars per employee. The exception to this guideline is defined contribution recordkeeping statements. These are usually included as part of the administrative service.

QUESTIONS TO ASK OUTSIDE VENDORS

Can you show me samples of tools you have produced for other organizations?

Can you give me references?

Who will be working on the project and what are their credentials?

Can you give me a step-by-step project timeline?

What is expected of me and my organization?

How will you ensure that the information on the finished tool is accurate?

In addition to production resources, you will also have to work closely with the payroll and data processing specialists who manage your data. This may be the toughest part of the project because there is a significant knowledge and communication gap to be bridged between human resources and data processing.

How To Talk With Your Data Processing Department
The most common complaints from the human resource department are that data processing

1) Never has time to help get proper systems set up for us and cannot or will not dedicate the resources to our projects.
2) Takes too long to do anything.
3) Doesn't understand our needs.
4) Is not cooperative; is always saying why something can't be done rather than solving the problem.

Most of the complaints are valid, but can be overcome. Before you can overcome the perceived problems, you must understand the underlying reasons for the behavior. The reasons are

1) Data processing priorities and resources are always dedicated to assignments that directly affect an organization's business such as inventory control, marketing, and management operation reports. Special request from the CEO and CFO will take priority. These priorities are practical.

2) The time it takes to complete a project is always a sensitive issue. Data processing wants protection from criticism against the quality of their work. Human resources frequently cannot define their needs, and writing good programs does take time.

3) Data processing does not understand human resource needs for two reasons
   · human resources doesn't understand data processing needs, and
   · human resources usually can't explain what they want to accomplish.
This is a classic communication problem.

4) Data processing will often say something can't be done because they don't understand the assignment.

The biggest reason for communication problems between data processing and human resources stems from the fact that data processing wants everything precisely defined and unchangeable while human resources wants maximum latitude and the ability to change instantly. These biases are consistent with each professional's requirements.

EXAMPLE

Following is a typical conversation between data processing and human resource professionals.

D.P. What field length (i.e. how many spaces) do you want for the last name?
H.R. 15 or 20.
D.P. Which, 15 or 20?
H.R. How do I know—I only need 15, but I might want 20.
D.P. When you know, get back to me.
H.R. Ok, ok—then make it 20.
D.P. That wastes a lot of space. Why do you want 20 if you only need 15?

Explaining Your Needs In Terms DP Can Understand

Telling a data processing specialist that you want a program that will produce an employee benefit statement is not enough explanation. DP personnel must understand exactly what a program is supposed to do and why.

A SAMPLE ENCOUNTER BETWEEN DP AND HR SPECIALISTS

The human resource director of an international engineering firm wanted data processing to produce an employee benefit statement. He thought he was flattering them by asking them rather than looking for an outside vendor. Data processing would be able to handle the assignment with no problem. But the problems started at the first meeting between the two departments. Human resources showed samples of what they wanted the statment to look like. Data processing couldn't produce a statement like the one proposed because they didn't have all the necessary data on the system.

> **H.R.** What data are you missing?
> **D.P.** The levels of benefits for the medical plans.
> **H.R.** No problem, we can give that to you.
> **D.P.** Sorry, no room on the system to add it.

The Problem	The real problem was that human resources didn't understand enough about computers and programming to suggest how data processing could use the data without putting it into the employee database. Data processing didn't understand the benefit plan enough to recognize that the data under discussion was generic and didn't have to be added to each employee record.
The Solution	Data processing only needed a small file that had the medical information listed for each computer-printed space. The data was the same for all employees so this information was only needed when the statements were being printed. Once this was explained, data processing was content and planning continued. This is a simplified example, but illustrates the importance of understanding between human resources and data processing personnel.

HOW TO DEVELOP BUDGETS

Developing budgets for personalized communication tools is very similar to the process used for other printed materials. You can use the specification and budgeting worksheets included in Chapter 2 to develop your cost estimates. However, there are two factors unique to personalized communication tools you need to consider before you begin your budgeting process: developing specialized computer forms and defining computer and data requirements.

Developing Specialized Computer Forms

Preparing forms on which computer-printed data will finally appear requires much more precision than preparing handbooks or highlight brochures. While computer technology continues to increase the computer's ability to be flexible, computers and data processing professionals demand precision.

Three critical factors to consider when producing tools that are to be personalized by computer are, what the finished form will look like, the printing technique to be used, and camera-ready art preparation.

Finished Form.   Your finished personalized communication tool can be a flat 8-1/2" x 11" sheet of paper, a long form that is folded in an accordian style and stapled inside a special cover, or even a booklet. The complexity of your finished form will impact the flat form size, the type of computer printing process you select (e.g. pin-feed or laser), and how the art will have to be prepared.

Printing Technique.   Personalized communication tools can be produced using a computer printer alone, or by combining traditional and computer printing techniques. In either case, you should be aware of computer printer restrictions with respect to form size.

Form sizes are measured by width and length of their flat, unfinished size. Pin-feed form measurements do not include the pin-hole guides on either side of the paper. The maximum form width is 15 inches. This does not mean that the computer can print across the full 15 inches. It depends on the computer printer. The maximum computer-printed live area is 13 inches.

The length of a pin-feed form usually becomes impractical if it exceeds 28 inches. As the length of a form increases, the risk of damage and waste increases. Twenty-two inches or shorter is better. Printers and finishers may add other limitations because of their finishing equipment.

The most common laser printer form sizes are 8-1/2" x 11" or 8-1/2" x 14" although laser printer techology is fast overcoming these limitations.

Camera-Ready Art. If your form combines traditional and computer printing techniques, you will have to prepare camera-ready art for the traditional printing process. This is a critical process. If it is not prepared correctly, the computer printing will not align properly. To ensure that the art is correct, be sure the artist uses a computer spacing grid to position all typeset copy from top to bottom and left to right. For traditional impact printers, the top to bottom spacing is 1/6". The left to right spacing is 1/10".

If you are producing your statement on a laser printer, both the standardized text and the personalized information can be printed on the page in a one-step process that eliminates the need for traditional camera-ready art. However, the precision factors are still critical.

Defining Computer And Data Requirements

The most significant difference between traditional printed communication tools and personalized tools is the computer and data specifications you must include.

You must be sure all your computer resources understand what you want and that you understand what they need. This is critical whether you are using internal or external computer resources. The following list, although incomplete, shows the type of information that data processing needs to know.

- what you want
- why you want it
- what data is to be reported
- what data is used to get the reported data
- how many possible variables there are for each data element
- what special formulas, tables, and assumptions are used to calculate specific results
- how many sources of data must be used
- what kind of data sources must be used, (e.g. hard copy, PC files, and mainframe files)
- if data is provided on computer tapes or disks, what are the technical specifications of the medium
- how can they locate and identify the right data elements for each task
- if multiple data sources are used, do they all have a common identification code, such as social security number

Preparing to give this type of information to data processing before they ask for it will help you build credibility with them and establish a good communication base. Remember, the less detailed your specifications, the less accurate your cost estimates will be.

Cost Cutting Tips

As with other printed communication tools, what will impact your costs most will be quantities. The higher the quantity, the lower the unit cost.

Complex personalized tools such as benefit statements can be very expensive for small quantities. For example, the total cost to produce a benefit statement for fifteen hundred employees could be twenty thousand dollars or more, which means the cost per employee would be a little over thirteen dollars. If you wanted to produce the same statement for only seven hundred and fifty employees, the per employee cost would be close to twenty-seven dollars. The total cost will not be significantly less for fewer employees because most of the cost is in the preparation, not in the paper and ink used to print the statement.

Another important factor is that the number of data sources has a direct bearing on the cost. The more data sources you must use, the higher the cost. Avoid including unnecessary or superfluous information such as projected retirement benefit calculations covering the five years prior to normal retirement. Most employees are not very interested in that data and it just adds to your programming costs.

The most important cost cutting tip is to remember not to change the rules. Once you have decided on your specifications, stay with them. Every time you change something, your cost basis will increase dramatically.

HOW TO MEASURE THE SUCCESS OF YOUR PERSONALIZED COMMUNICATION PROGRAM

The most common success measurement for personalized communication tools is whether or not employees are eager to receive the most current version of the report. Many organizations find employees consistently asking when the next report will be distributed. If your employees are not asking about it, the reason may be a lack of interest in the information you are providing. This indicates that the tool is probably not as effective as it should be. Conducting a periodic survey is another useful measurement technique. Some organizations include a small survey with the personalized communication tool similar to the one in Figure 6.13.

Other ways to measure success are to watch for signs:

- Are employees challenging the accuracy of the data?
- Are employees more attentive to updating their personal data such as address changes, and dependent status?
- Do you notice any change in voluntary participation patterns?

Personalized communication tools can be powerful motivators if they are designed to meet the needs of your audience. They can increase awareness of the organization's investment in an employee as an individual and influence their sense of ownership and responsibility for managing their total compensation.

We would like your opinion of this year's benefit statement and of the new TRW Retirement Benefits Estimator. Fill out and return this card through intercompany mail.

1. What was the most useful information to you on the Statement? _____

2. How could the Statement be improved next time? _____

3. Did you use the Retirement Benefits Estimator? Yes ☐ No ☐
   If yes, what comments do you have about it? _____

4. What other comments do you have about the Statement? _____

PLEASE TAKE A MINUTE TO ANSWER THESE QUESTIONS

Figure 6.13 SURVEY   This is a classic example of the type of survey measurement tool many organizations include with personalized communications. *Courtesy of TRW Space & Defense*

CHAPTER 7

HOW TO PREPARE AND USE AUDIOVISUAL COMMUNICATION TOOLS

Audiovisual communication is very powerful. Video, film, and slide presentations appeal to more of our senses than does print media. Print compels us to use our imaginations. Understanding the traits of this communication form helps us identify the best times to use it and the best times to use print media.

THE PSYCHOLOGY OF AUDIOVISUAL MEDIA

Because audiovisual media draw on the emotions, they can stimulate and, in fact, manipulate more human senses than can print media. That is not to say that well-written print messages cannot illicit emotion. Clearly, they can. However, an audience has more control over the effect of the printed word than over the immediate impact of an audiovisual experience. When determining the appropriate medium to use in your human resource communication plans, it is important to keep the psychology of this medium in mind. It is a powerful tool that will enable you to establish a consistent, controlled tone to all of your messages and appeal to the emotional needs of your audience. Using the multi-dimensional elements of audiovisual tools enables you to increase the power of any message you wish to send to any specific audience.

CHECKLIST: Ways to Use an Audiovisual to Implement Human Resource Plans

---

There are many situations where using an audiovisual to reinforce other communication tools will help you do a more effective job of implementing human resource plans. Here are just a few.

- *explaining* an important corporate strategy such as a new quality control program or a new organizational structure
- *showing* the company profile to recruits, investors, clients, and community organizations
- *announcing* additions or revisions to company benefit plans
- *educating* employees about policies, procedures, compensation and benefit plans
- *training* supervisors and managers about legal and administrative issues relating to their human resource management responsibilities
- *presenting* your human resource strategies to top management

COMMUNICATOR'S TIP: How to Recognize an Often Overlooked Audiovisual Form

Traditionally, audiovisuals are thought of as movies, slide shows, or videotapes. These tools can be considered controlled mass communication formats. Another more common technique is so prevalent to our social structure that we tend not to think of it as audiovisuals. That is, live person-to-person presentations. If you think about it for a moment, it is easy to see that an individual has all of the components of an audiovisual: sight, sound, motion. The person provides the visual components of the presentation; the body language, appearance, color of clothing, as well as sound. Because the body can move, a speaker can add another dimension, that of motion. Combined, these are the fundamentals of this medium. Speakers can heighten the visual component of person-to-person by adding flip charts, slides, or other props.

TYPES OF AUDIOVISUAL TOOLS AND HOW TO USE THEM

Person-To-Person Techniques

If you can accept the premise that you are an audiovisual tool, you can take advantage of traditional techniques to make your messages more powerful. Imagine yourself as a slide show or videotape. When you are first introduced to the audience, your appearance, demeanor, and clothing establish the tone of the message you are about to impart. Your personality, the tone of your voice and the movement of your body can reinforce your words. Try looking at yourself in the mirror and pretend you are facing an audience to whom you need to communicate a very important message.

Try different techniques. Stand very still, moving your arms, raising and lowering your voice, smiling, or frowning. Similarly, talk into a tape recorder using different tones and approaches to getting your message across. Listen to the tape. Most people are startled by a recording of their own voice and react negatively to it. By recording yourself and playing it back, you will get accustomed to how you sound and learn to modify what you don't like about how you make presentations and express yourself.

When talking to people, become more attentive to how they react to your demeanor and your words. Watch your audience. Listen to their reactions and try different techniques. You will notice that if one approach does not seem to work, you can change your approach until the audience reacts the way you want. This will give you much more power in presentations whether it is one-on-one or in front of thousands.

How Visual Aids Help Improve Person-To-Person Presentation

Once you have practiced and are satisfied with how you present yourself to an audience, look for props to expand your presentation. Flip charts, overheads, and slides are the most obvious tools, but sometimes, using an unusual prop is the best way to drive home a message.

Using an Unconventional Technique to Illustrate Your Point. A benefit manager was trying to illustrate the impact that rising health care services cost had on the organization's purchasing power and its employees. Holding an adult-sized crutch, the manager said, Five years ago, you would have had this if you suffered a broken leg. Then, taking a small child's crutch in hand, he said, Today, the same money will only get you this. The prop was a dramatic visual illustration of declining purchasing power. It also increased the audience's interest and, most likely, retention of the subject.

Using Slides or Overheads Rather than Paper Reports. Studies have repeatedly demonstrated that an audience has a high retention level when some type of audiovisual tool is used to reinforce a message. Pictures, charts, graphs, and illustrations can more effectively and efficiently communicate what would otherwise take masses of words or pages of statistical data.

The benefit and labor relations managers of a community health services organization were challenged with the task of explaining a new paid time off program to several audiences: senior management, operating managers, labor leaders, and selected employee groups.

In the past, they had prepared extensive reports with exhibits for management and labor presentations but realized the reports would not lend themselves to effective communication with operating managers and employees. The time frame in which they had to conduct the various presentations was so compressed they only had time to prepare one set of audiovisual aids. They chose overheads because they knew overhead projectors were easily accessible.

Their solution was to reduce a 25-page report to 7 graphic overheads. The results were gratifying because senior management and the labor leaders endorsed the plan with little discussion and the operating managers and employees were able to understand it well enough to accept it as a positive change.

How To Choose The Best Visual Aid For The Size Of Your Audience

The choice of flip chart, overhead, slides, film, or videotape is primarily determined by the size of your audience. There are many other factors to be considered. (Figure 7.1) is a checklist to help you decide which tool will be more effective.

In general, flip charts are satisfactory and sometimes preferable for small informal groups. For medium or large audiences, overheads or slides will be more appropriate.

COMMUNICATOR'S TIP: Creating Effective Visuals

When deciding what the individual visuals should be, remember that good illustrations are clear, simple, and legible. Meeting these criteria may require such techniques as line drawings, photographs, bar charts, or tables. As an example, a simple line sketch may be better than a detailed shop drawing; a graph may be better than a table. In developing the picture story, keep the following points in mind.

- Limit each visual to one main idea.
- Use progressive disclosure for presenting a list of items.
- Limit text to fifteen or twenty words.
- Leave space between lines.
- Use several simple visuals instead of a single complicated one.
- Maintain a good visual pace.
- If subject is repeated later, provide duplicate visual.
- Display each visual only while pertinent to discussion.
- Visual text should not be identical with oral presentation.

Flip Charts. Lecturer's paper, commercially available in various sizes, is the most common material used in producing flip charts. The largest size pad compatible with available chart easels is recommended. Although good flip charts can be produced using a straight-edge and a large felt pen, more attractive charts can be produced using colored adhesive tapes, clear or colored acetate sheets for overlays, felt pens of various colors, and sheets of transfer letters. To be effective, each flip chart should tell its story clearly, quickly and forcefully. Accordingly, limit each chart to a single idea or concept.

Lettering should be big and bold with no characters less than 7/8 inches. Avoid overcrowding with words and figures. It is a good practice to keep a blank sheet between each flip chart. This way, charts can be removed from view without disclosing a new one until needed.

Overheads (Transparencies or VU-Graphs). Today, transparencies can be produced on many paper copiers and computer-driven plotters. This gives you flexibilty in time and money to prepare effective visuals for small or medium sized audiences. Full color overheads can be made, but you will probably have to go to an outside supplier and they will be more expensive. Production time and expense will be similar to slides.

The same guidelines for preparing flip charts should be used for overheads. They should be clear, concise, bold, and uncrowded. Many people make the mistake of reproducing a transparency from a typed page intended for a printed format. Doing this not only defeats the power of the visual medium, it usually irritates the audience because people can not see it very well. Using oversize typewriter fonts may be acceptable for a small audience. However, even this method tends not to be legible.

Keeping words to a minimum and using graphics wherever possible is the correct way to take advantage of these tools. To avoid the problem of handling the slippery acetate material used for overheads, mount

Figure 7.1
AUDIOVISUAL SELECTION GUIDE

FORMAT TYPE	ADVANTAGES	DISADVANTAGES
FLIP CHARTS	Easy and inexpensive to prepare Easy to change design or numerical order Usable with normal room lighting Cutouts, build-ups and overlays readily created Projection equipment not required	Limited legibility Storage and handling bulk Requires speaker support Not suitable for large audiences
LARGE OVERHEADS	Immediate production and projection No photography required Masters can be used for overheads, paper prints and signs Notes can be added to frames Possible to write on visuals during presentation Bright images can be seen in fully-lighted rooms Special projectionist not required Production equipment is simple and inexpensive Easy to change sequence	Clumsy to handle and transport Good overhead projectors are bulky Too many colors or overlays reduce projection light Bright, blank screen while changing overhead Requires good coordination to talk and show Recorded voice cannot be synchronized Requires speaker support Not suitable for large audiences
35MM SLIDES	Compact handling and transportation Adaptable to prearrangement of sequence Remote control to advance slides Projectors compact and generally available Slides and sound tapes can be fully automated Possible to use two or more projectors Color can be used effectively and economically Suitable for small or large audiences	Information must be converted to 35mm film Any change or error requires a new photograph Room has to be darkened for optimum visibility Cost factor is higher than flip charts or simple overheads
FILM OR VIDEOTAPE	Combines power of color, sound, and motion Ensures accurate, consistent, energetic delivery of message Suitable for any size audience Quality control maximized in unsupervised viewing Portable Speaker support not required	Equipment not standardized, may not be readily available Professional technical expertise required to produce Relatively expensive to change Cannot be produced in a few hours

each one in cardboard frames made for this purpose. Key words and notes may be written on the frame for guidance during the presentation.

35mm Slides. Slides are almost mandatory for presentations to large audiences because they enable communicators to project an image large enough to be easily viewed by the person sitting farthest away from the screen.

Slides are made photographically from either existing materials, or from artwork masters specifically created for slide production. Existing illustrations of almost any size; such as maps, charts, and blueprints can be reproduced for slide production. Even so, it is a fallacy to assume that the larger the original, the better the slide. The detail or text of existing materials is generally too small to provide legible slides. Better quality slides are produced from artwork masters created for this purpose. Like any other visual aid, good slides are designed for viewing, they should not be transparent copies or facsimiles of written pages.

People frequently underestimate the number of overheads or slides they will need in order to make an effective presentation. To ensure that your overheads or slides are most effective, do rough paper layouts for each one. (Figure 7.2) gives you an idea of how to gage the amount of information best suited for each slide and therefore, how many you will really need.

COMMUNICATOR'S TIP: Using Handouts in Your Presentation
Frequently, hard copy handouts are used in presentations. The handouts may be copies of the visual aids or more sophisticated printed support materials. While it is appropriate to give the audience some type of printed material to take with them, many presenters make the mistake of distributing this material prior to the presentation. This is a tactical error because the audience will inevitably flip through the material and you will lose their attention.

CHECKLIST: Power Presentation Tips

- use an outline well marked for slide changes
- use graphics and pictures rather than words whenever possible
- use short words
- try not to ramble
- listen to yourself
- watch your audience for signs of boredom or comprehension problems
- respond to the audience reaction, change pace or style immediately
- encourage audience participation
- relate physically to your visual aids, they should appear to be an integral part of you, not a separate intrusion
- use blanks if you do not have a visual aid to support a point you are discussing

Why Many Visual Aids Don't Get The Job Done
As emphasized earlier, the effectiveness of visual aids is directly related to your ability to use the tool to reinforce your words visually. If the viewer has to read or study the tool to understand it rather than intuitively absorbing the information, you are creating conflict among the senses. It is virtually impossible to concentrate on reading or studying while devoting complete attention to the speaker's words. Unless carefully coordinated, one or the other will get second or third level attention and may even be lost totally.

Figures 7.3 and 7.4 are examples of effective and ineffective visual presentation of the same information.

Figure 7.2 TEMPLATE If you make rough drafts of your slides and keep the information inside a space approximately 5″ x 8″, you will be able to get a good idea of how much information is suitable for each slide and therefore how many slides you will need to deliver you message.

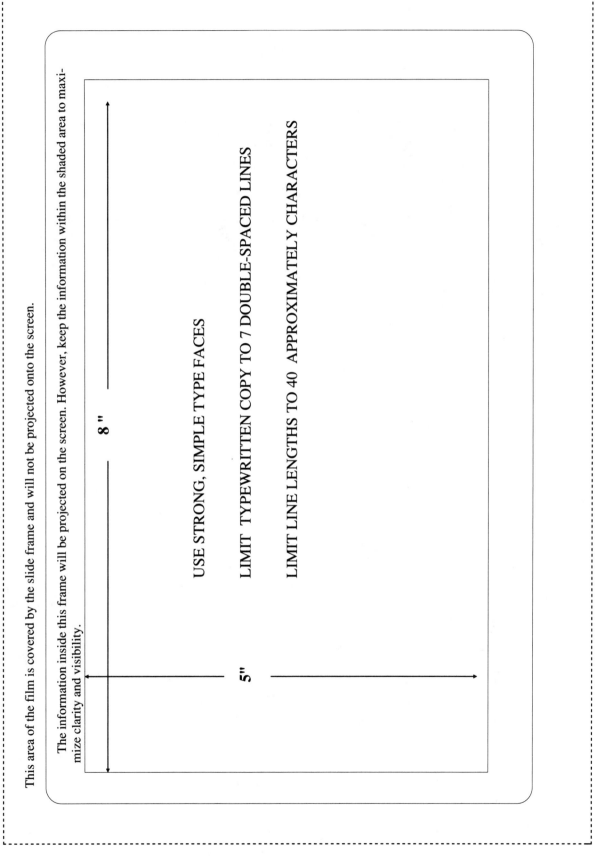

This area of the film is covered by the slide frame and will not be projected onto the screen.

The information inside this frame will be projected on the screen. However, keep the information within the shaded area to maximize clarity and visibility.

8″

5″

USE STRONG, SIMPLE TYPE FACES

LIMIT TYPEWRITTEN COPY TO 7 DOUBLE-SPACED LINES

LIMIT LINE LENGTHS TO 40 APPROXIMATELY CHARACTERS

Figure 7.3 VISUAL PRESENTATION—EXAMPLE. This type of information is more appropriate for the printed medium and is not as effective as the example in Figure 7.4.

PLANT SALES PROJECTIONS

MONTH	PLANT A	PLANT B	PLANT C	PLANT D	PLANT E	PLANT F
January	15,650	2,560	N/A	18,650	46,900	48,210
February	15,790	3,575	N/A	19,500	72,560	50,340
March	16,560	4,550	N/A	20,750	75,660	51,350
April	17,320	5,700	N/A	25,300	80,000	56,130

Figure 7.4 VISUAL PRESENTATION—EXAMPLE This visual illustrates how you can prepare
information so that viewers can grasp the message immediately.

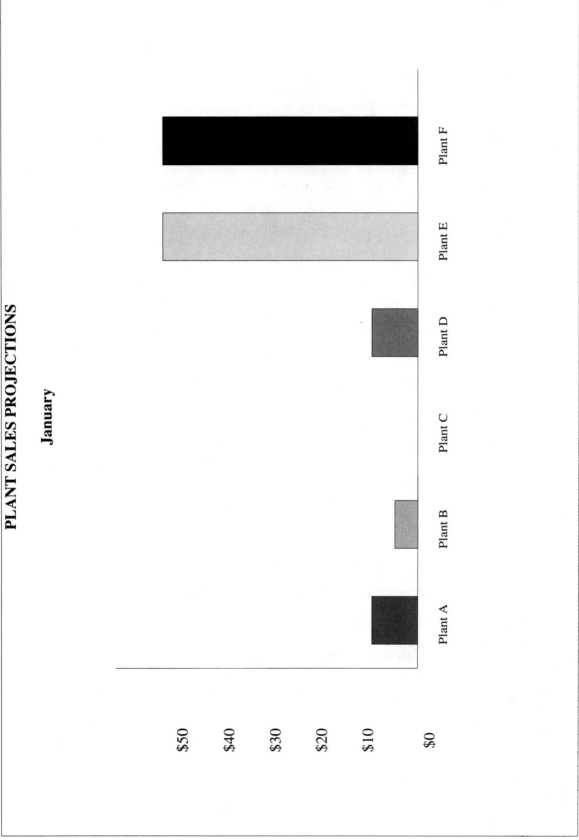

PLANT SALES PROJECTIONS

January

CONTROLLED MASS COMMUNICATION AUDIOVISUAL FORMATS

Controlled audiovisual formats are those types of presentations which are self-contained and do not require a live speaker. They include slides with synchronized audio tapes, filmstrips, film, videotape, videodiscs, computers, or a combination of these options, which is called a multi-media format.

Determining The Best Format For Your Purpose

It is important that you do some research before you decide which format is best for your purpose. While you may be biased in favor of one particular format, this could be the worst choice you could make for a lot of practical reasons. The four most important things to evaluate are

- your current equipment inventory
- your most probable screening facilities
- availability of technical equipment and software support
- the most probable audience size

The more locations or operating units you have to deal with, the more critical these issues become.

Assessing Your AV Equipment Inventory

Even if your organization has a policy regarding the purchase of AV equipment, one or more people have probably overlooked it. Unless you investigate the AV equipment used throughout the organization, you could find yourself with a wonderful audiovisual, and no way to show it. Except for slides and possibly, filmstrips, AV equipment for various media formats may not be standard within your organization. For example, There are three common types of videotape equipment: VHS, Beta, and U-matic. The first two use 1/2" tape, the third uses 3/4" tape. None are directly interchangeable. Finally, the people or departments responsible for showing your audiovisual may borrow equipment from another unit or operating entity and may have very little specific knowledge about the equipment specifications.

The easiest way to inventory the AV equipment is to do a written survey. Figure 7.5 gives you a specification checklist for the most common AV equipment. Beyond the human resource organization, places to expect to find AV equipment include advertising and marketing, training, corporate communication departments and plant or operating unit managers. When completing the inventory, make sure that survey participants are knowledgeable about the equipment.

Assessing Physical Screening Facilities

The audiovisual format you select should accommodate the screening conditions you will encounter most often. A videotape shown on a 25" monitor would not be the appropriate format for an auditorium seating several hundred people. Conversely, a slide or film format would not be the best format for a small 150 to 300 square foot office or meeting room.

Assessing Availability Of Technical Support

The electronic age has forced AV technical expertise upon the layperson. People tend to become accustomed to a specific piece of AV equipment and learn how to operate it well enough to satisfy their personal needs. However, their skill at operating a 1/2" VHS home videocassette player does not necessarily qualify them to operate a multi-media configuration that includes three slide projectors and a videotape player linked together by a computer.

You may find specialized technical support within your organization. Frequently, advertising or training departments have specialists who know how to manage a lot of different types of hardware, and these people are usually available to solve problems. Even so, you need to know how competent other equipment users are. Training classes may be necessary to ensure that people are comfortable enough with the equipment to make use of it.

Figure 7.5 AUDIOVISUAL EQUIPMENT GUIDE

FORMAT TYPE	EQUIPMENT
FLIP CHARTS	Easel Paper Pad or Art Board Colored, Wide, Felt-tip Markers
OVERHEADS	Desktop or Portable Overhead Projector Projection Screen
35MM SLIDES	35mm Slide Projector (with audio jack and synchronized audio-cassette player if slide/tape audio-visual format) Projection Screen Kodak Carousel slide projectors are the most common.
FILM OR VIDEOTAPE	FILM 16mm Manual or Autoload Film Projector (any brand) Projection Screen VIDEOTAPE 1/2" VHS Videotape Player/Recorder and Color Monitor 1/2" Beta Videotape Player/Recorder and Color Monitor 3/4" U-Matic Videotape Player/Recorder and Color Monitor Large Screen Projection Units for Large Audiences Projection Screen for Large Screen Projection

Evaluating The Size Of Your Audience

The topics of your audiovisuals may determine the size of the audience that may be viewing it at any given time. For example, an employee orientation audiovisual for new hires may be shown to only three or four people at a time at the department level. If it is used in a more centralized orientation process, the audience may number over 50. Conversely, if the audiovisual is used for small training sessions, the group's size may average 10 or 12. Your objective is to identify what the most common audience size will be for a specific topic.

HOW TO PRODUCE AUDIOVISUAL TOOLS

As illustrated in the section on person-to-person audiovisual communication, there are many ways to produce low-cost audiovisual aids. Most organizations have production tools such as markers, computer graphics software, acetates and copying machines.

However, these tools will normally not be very useful to you when you are doing complete canned audiovisuals, because your audience has become very quality-conscious about these types of audiovisual productions. Their expectation for the quality of any audiovisual is much higher than it was even a few years ago.

This means that human resource communicators must rely on professional audiovisual experts. You may have internal resources who have this expertise. If you don't, you will be better served to seek outside resources to help you develop and produce an effective audiovisual. The most likely places to find internal audiovisual production expertise is in your advertising, marketing, and training departments. However, just as in print production, the people in these departments have other jobs to do. They may be able to help you achieve your objectives, or only refer you to outside producers.

Guidelines For Developing Professionally Produced Audiovisual Programs

Producing an effective audiovisual program requires two skills: technical expertise and content expertise. It is very difficult to find people who have the combination of both skills. Chances are you have content specialists in house. Finding production specialists requires that you understand the production skills that you will require to do the job. The following list is not comprehensive but illustrates the type of technical expertise necessary to produce an audiovisual. In some cases, one individual may have the expertise to fill two roles. Even more specialized skills may be required for some projects, such as

- Art Director
- Artist
- Writer
- Director
- Photographer
- Assistant Photographer
- Set Designer
- Talent Coordinator
- Recording Engineer
- Editor
- Recording/Editing Technician
- Composer/Musicians
- Sound Technician
- Lighting Technician
- Special Effects Specialist

- Various Production Assistants including Set Decorators, Make-up Artists, Go-fers, Sound and Lighting Assistants
- Producer

COMMUNICATOR'S TIP: One-Stop Shopping Can Save You Time and Money

The easiest way to deal with the technical expertise issue is to hire a producer whose job it will be to assemble the appropriate team of technical experts to get the job done. There are many freelance producers who are eager to help produce your audiovisual and know how to do it for a reasonable cost.

Two handy resource directories that can help you locate producers and other audiovisual specialists in your area are

The Association of Visual Communicators' Membership Directory

>   Association of Visual Communicators
>   900 Palm Avenue, Suite B
>   South Pasadena, CA 91030
>   (818) 441-2274

MPE AudioVisual Source Directory

>   Motion Picture Enterprises Publications, Inc.
>   Tarrytown, N.Y. 10591
>   (212) 245-0969

Determining Program Specifications

Once you have identified your technical and content specialists you must go back to the issue of which media format you are going to use. That will help you determine your program specifications. Your program specifications must be clearly laid out if you are going to be able to manage the production efficiently and control costs. There are two types of program specifications, generic and specific. The generic specifications would be common to any audiovisual format. The specifics would depend on the format selected.

CHECKLIST: Generic Audiovisual Specifications

Length of Completed Show	Ideal maximum is 10-12 minutes
Talent	2 On-camera Actors, 1 Voice-Only Actor
Number of Locations	Plant #1
	Plant #2
	Headquarters
Number of Sites at Each Location	Plant #1- 4
	Plant #2-7
	Headquarters - 1
Music	Use Generic Library Music
Sound Effects	Yes, as needed
Artwork	8 Charts
	2 Maps
Type	Names of Locations and People
Studio	One Day in Studio
Number of Duplicates	7

Ten Basic Production Steps For Audiovisuals

Now that you have defined your program specifications, you are ready to develop a production timetable. While many of the tasks connected with producing the audiovisual will be happening simultaneously, there are ten basic steps in the audiovisual production process.

1. Script
2. Storyboard
3. Casting
4. Technical Crews
5. Shooting
6. Editing
7. Recording, Mixing, and Dubbing
8. First Trial
9. Final Program Master
10. Duplicates

These ten steps can be grouped into four production phases: Creative Concept, Pre-Production, Production and Post-Production.

Creative Concept: How To Tell What The Finished Program Will Look Like

One of the most disconcerting aspects of producing audiovisuals is that you really don't know what the final product will look like until it is finished. By then, it is usually too late to make major changes. There are, however, ways to reduce the risk factor. There are three components that will help you begin to visualize how your finished audiovisual will look.

· a treatment outline
· a shooting script
· a storyboard

Treatment Outline. A treatment outline is simply a narrative describing the creative concept behind the audiovisual. Frequently it will read much like a short story. By insisting on having a treatment outline before the acutal shooting script is developed, you have an opportunity to give the scriptwriter valuable input with respect to style, tone, and acceptable criteria within your organization. (see Figure 7.6.)

Shooting Script. Once you feel comfortable with the treatment outline, an audiovisual writer will need to develop a comprehensive, detailed, shooting script. Without this tool, your audiovisual is in grave danger. The photographers need explicit instructions so they can shoot all the footage necessary. The editors use the same script to figure out how to organize and cut and paste the various scenes together to give you the end product. (see Figure 7.7.)

Storyboard. The storyboard will give you a sense of how words and pictures will be combined. It will not be able to show you all of the nuances that will make your audiovisual great. However, it will give you an impression of the look and flow. Following are excerpts from a treatment outline, a shooting script, and a storyboard for an audiovisual produced for a health care awareness campaign. (Figure 7.8.)

COMMUNICATOR'S TIP: Get Management Approval
Before You Begin

Getting management approval for an audiovisual script is more difficult than getting approval for the printed media, because they cannot see what they are going to get. The key to getting management approval is to be able to provide them with a well-written treatment outline so they have an understanding of the concept. You must also have credibility with them so they are confident that you are going to accurately reflect the organization's policies and image. You will usually be better off if you spend your energy getting approval at the outline stage and do not go back to management until you are ready to show them the

Figure 7.6 TREATMENT OUTLINE

Treatment Outline
for
Continuous Loop Health Care Audiovisual

This audiovisual will be created using selected scenes from the active and retiree audiovisual. It will be produced in a continuous loop format that will enable it to be played in the cafeteria and other selected locations where employees may gather for breaks or after-work meetings.

The show will be similar to the CNN News Channel format with a host who introduces different feature stories. Four major topic categories will feature 1- to 3-minute vignettes related to the Informed Choice Plan and managed health care issues of interest to employees. The categories are:

> ABC Employees Speak Out
>
> Answers to Your Questions
>
> It's Your Choice
>
> Dare to Compare

ABC EMPLOYEES SPEAK OUT

Lifts of employee testimonials will be extracted from the active and retiree versions of the ICP health care audiovisuals.

ANSWERS TO YOUR QUESTIONS

The host will introduce questions submitted by employees through the ICP hotline and answer the questions, supported by animated graphics.

IT'S YOUR CHOICE

Graphic build-ups will illustrate the difference between each type of health care option. Voice-over will encourage employees to decide which is best for them and their families.

Figure 7.7 SHOOTING SCRIPT

ICP CONTINUOUS LOOP AV

ICP LOGO ZOOMS IN FROM IN-
FINITY SETTLES IN UPPER HALF OF
SCREEN. *HEALTH CARE NEWS NET-
WORK* POPS ON UNDER LOGO

WIPE LIKE BOOK PAGE TURNING
TO REVEAL TOPIC HEADING:
**ABC COMPANY PEOPLE SPEAK
OUT**

FREEZE LAST FRAME OF VIGNETTE

WIPE PAGE TURNING TO REVEAL
TOPIC HEADING:
DARE TO COMPARE

WIPE TO NEW PAGE WITH PIX OF
JOHN IN UPPER LEFT QUADRANT.
OTHER PIX OF JOHN POP ON THE
SCREEN . WORDS WIPE ON:
**HIGHEST QUALITY CARE
LOWEST POSSIBLE COST**

ZOOM INTO ONE PIX OF JOHN AND
CROSS FADE TO ECU OF COM-
PARISON CHECK LIST. HAND
HOLDING PENCIL POINTS TO EACH
ISSUE AND CHECKS OFF THE ITEM
AS VOICE OVER EXPLAINS THE DIF-
FERENCES AMONG THE PLANS.

PAGE 4
MUSIC UP AND UNDER

V.O. There is a growing interest in health care management. People like you are making important decisions about what they expect from health care providers and their health benefit plans. ABC people across the country are joining the movement and speaking out.

(INSERT ONE VIGNETTE FROM ACTIVE VERSION OF EMPLOYEE MEETING AV)

INSERT ONE VIGNETTE FROM RETIREE VERSION OF MEETING AV)

V.O. Watch for more ideas from other ABC people about what they are doing to begin managing their own health care needs.

V.O. You can manage your health care needs better if you dare to compare.

V.O. John, a (insert job title), at (insert division or plant name), in (insert city name), will probably need major surgery next year. He wants to be sure he has the highest quality care at the lowest possible cost.

Since this is his opportunity to choose the health care plan that will best suit his needs, he is evaluating each option very careful- ly. Here's how he did it.

First, he compared how each plan would evaluate his need for surgery.

If he is enrolled in the Traditional plan, he must be sure that his doctor gets authorization for the surgery or his coverage may be reduced.

If he is enrolled in the PPO plan and his doctors are preferred providers, they will be sure there is no better alternative to surgery before they recommend it. John can use a non-preferred provider and have the surgery if he thinks it is necessary, but his coverage may be reduced.

Figure 7.8 STORYBOARD A storyboard will not show you every detail and nuance that will make your audiovisual come to life. It is intended only as a rough sketch to help you visualize selected concepts and transitions.

ICP CONTINUOUS LOOP AV

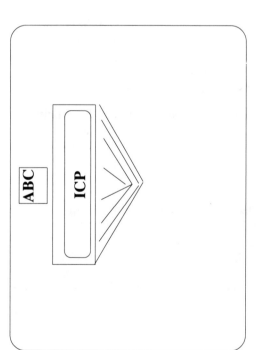

(MUSIC UP AND UNDER)

STORYBOARD

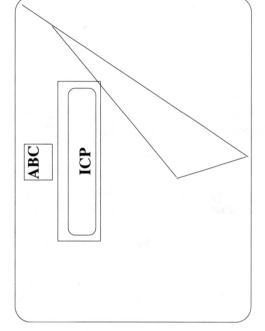

V.O. There is a growing interest in health care management. People like you are making.....

finished product. More audiovisuals have ended in the middle of the project because management was unable to deal with the vagaries of the audiovisual production process.

Pre-Production: Getting Ready To Shoot

Before you can begin production, you must select the talent (e.g. actors and actresses) who will make your audiovisual come alive and assemble the technical crews.

Casting.   Once your script is final, you must choose your actors and actresses. This is commonly referred to as casting.

If your audiovisual is a slide/tape show, it may not be necessary to engage professional talent for the slides, but you will have to choose off-camera talent to record the narration. Normally, a producer will provide you with selection of audio cassette tapes with various voices from which to choose. On occasion, you might want to listen to a variety of narrators read part of your script although you can get a better idea of how they will sound by listening to the tapes.

If your audiovisual is to be produced on film or videotape, you will have to choose on-camera talent and perhaps voice-over talent as well. You can look at portfolios of pictures to do the initial selection of on-camera talent and then either look at videotapes or conduct live tryouts to make final decisions about which talent will be most appropriate for your audiovisual. If you also need voice-over talent, you may use your on-camera spokespersons or select a different individual for the voice-over narration.

COMMUNICATOR'S TIP: Using Professional Actors Will Save Time and Money

Always use professional actors and actresses. It is penny-wise and pound-foolish to try to save money using non-professional talent for your audiovisual. No matter how clever the producer, director, and editors are, the results will be amateurish at best. If you *absolutely* must use a company spokesperson, ask the writer or producer to help you develop the script in such a way that the company spokesperson's remarks are voice-over rather than on-camera. If the spokesperson *absolutely* must be on camera, allow plenty of time for rehearsal and expect your costs to increase dramatically.

Assembling Technical Crews.   Your producer will determine what kind of technical expertise (e.g. cinematographers, lighting and sound technicians, and post-production engineers) will be required to produce your audiovisual. Normally, you will not have to know much about who is selected or what their specific jobs will be.

Production

Once the talent and technical crews have been identified, the process of shooting and recording your audiovisual can begin. The producer will manage all the scheduling details and will normally invite you to be present when the actual work begins. While the production process can be interesting, it is also tedious because preparing to shoot one scene can consume hours. It can also be confusing if you are not familiar with production techniques because, frequently, scenes are not shot in sequence because the producer and director are trying to manage the production process in the most efficient, cost-effective way.

Post-Production

After shooting, voice-over recording, music selection, and art and graphics have been completed, the post-production task of putting them all together begins. The simplest way to understand the post-production process is to think of it as a very sophisticated cut and paste exercise. The shooting and recording sessions will have generated hundreds of feet of film or tape which must be edited, organized, and merged with the other elements, such as music, sound effects, and graphics. The result will be what is called a first trial or final program master. This will be the first time you will be able to see what your audiovisual actually looks like. If you are not satisfied with the results, additional time and expense will be necessary to make changes. If you are satisfied, you will be ready to order duplicates.

Figure 7.9 GLOSSARY OF AV TERMS

Like any other profession, AV has its own vocabulary of terms that may be unfamiliar to you. Following is a list of the common ones.

Artwork—any visual element that is not a photograph

A Burn—photographic process of combining one image over a base image or background

Composite—an image that is created from two or more separate sources which are intended to be viewed simultaneously

Field (Live Area)—the area to be photographed and projected in the final format

Frame—the actual picture area of a slide or one picture segment of a film or videotape

MOS Motion Over Sound—where the soundtrack and pictures are not necessarily from the same source

SOF Sound On Film—where the sound is a live, synchronized part of the picture, such as when you see an actor speaking

Talent—actor or other person featured in the audiovisual

VO Voice Over—when you hear the actor's voice but do not see him or her

LS Long Shot—where the primary scene is viewed from a distance

MLS Medium Long Shot—closer view of the primary scene

SFX Sound Effects—added to the sound track to enhance the perception of reality

CU Close Up—a close view of the primary scene

MCU Medium Close Up—a wider, but still relatively close view

ECU Extreme Close Up—a very close view, e.g. only eyes instead of entire face

Mixing—the procedure of combining several different soundtrack sources such as voice, music, and sound effects

Dubbing—the process of making videotape (or audio tape) copies of the finished audiovisual

Dupes—duplicate copies of finished audiovisual

Sync—the process of synchronizing the soundtrack with the picture

First Trial—The proof of the finished show which must be approved before copies are made

TV Cut-Off—the percentage of the total picture area that is lost when the image is viewed on a television screen

HOW TO DEVELOP BUDGETS

If you do not insist on a thorough, detailed budget for your audiovisual, you can count on the cost being three times what you expected. The easiest way to establish and control an audiovisual budget is to use both the detailed specifications you developed early on and a production budget form. Audiovisual professionals are very creative and more interested in the end product than the cost. This is not an indictment, just the truth. Working with the professionals on budget issues before you begin will help ensure that you and they have considered all the possiblities that can impact your costs. The form in Figure 7.10 can be used in conjunction with your specifications to work with your producers in developing a budget.

Why Videotape Is Not Necessarily More Expensive Than A Slide/Tape Show

Audiovisual producers have a tendency to tell you that film or videotape will be considerably more expensive than a slide show with a synchronized audio tape. This is simply not true. The major difference between the formats is the raw materials used. The real cost in developing an effective audiovisual in any format is all the up-front creative and planning costs. Furthermore, there are trade-offs among the different formats. For example, the raw cost of buying videotape may appear to be more than the cost of thirty rolls of slide film. However, there is no need to develop a videotape. Slides must be processed or developed which is in addition to the cost of the unexposed rolls of film. If you aren't satisfied with the results, you must incur additional expense to redo them.

Cost Cutting Tips

- Use professional actors; they save time and money.
- Use voice-over actors rather than on-camera actors.
- Use stock footage available from other departments in your organization or libraries rather than reshoot something that already exists.
- Minimize shooting on multiple locations.
- Minimize using splashy special effects.
- Make sure that you shoot more film or videotape than you think you will ever need.
- Find ways to amortize your costs.

How To Amortize Costs

There are two ways to effectively amortize costs. The first way is to think beyond your immediate need and consider other situations where the audiovisual might be useful. For example, If you want to produce an orientation audiovisual that summarizes the organization's history, the way it is organized, the business it is in, and highlight the compensation and benefit policies, you can use it for more than just employee orientation. It can be used for recruiting and training. If done properly, it can even be used for community awareness and public relations.

Another way to amortize the cost is to produce the audiovisual in modular form. By structuring it in modules, you have the flexibility of using one or more components to produce additional shows. For example: One organization wanted to develop an audiovisual to help employees, retirees, future new hires, and plant supervisors understand the company's health care program and the various benefit plan options available. Initially, the organization considered producing one audiovisual to meet all these needs. The treatment outline was developed and a cost of seventy thousand dollars was estimated. While the budgeted cost was not inordinate for the proposed show, the resulting product had some problems. It would not be as effective if it had to be generic rather than address the perceptions and needs of each of the three primary audiences separately. Furthermore, because the audiovisual would be distributed to many locations, it was probable that not all employees or retirees would have an opportunity to view the show in scheduled

FOCUS III
PRODUCTIONS

7500 Topanga Canyon Boulevard, Canoga Park, California 91303 (818) 704-6676
P.O. Box 2870, Canoga Park, California 91306 FAX: (818) 594-5041

```
VIDEO PRODUCTION BUDGET

CLIENT:  ABC Company, Inc.

PROJECT: Employee Benefits Presentation

Produce 16-minute video presentation describing new
employee benefits program for professionals.  Includes
script, production design, 3 days original photography (1
day location, 2 days on stage), casting, 3 principal
performers, set design & construction, props, costumes,
original music, editing, through completion of 1" video
master and protection master.

100 VHS release copies, labeled, in albums.


==============================================================
BUDGET SUMMARY                                           PRICE
==============================================================
Creative Development   .....................     7,085.00
Crew   .....................................     9,068.00
Equipment & Supplies   .....................     4,062.00
Talent   ...................................     1,912.00
Soundstage   ...............................     4,771.00
Location Expenses   ........................       313.00
Props & Wardrobe   .........................     1,102.00
Pre-Production & Wrap   ....................     1,805.00
Post Production   ..........................     5,258.00
--------------------------------------------------------------
TOTAL PRODUCTION                               $35,376.00
--------------------------------------------------------------
Release Copies   ..........................       573.00




PAYMENT SCHEDULE
--------------------------------------------------------------
Before Work Begins                              17,688.00
Upon Completion of Principal Photography         8,844.00
Upon Completion of Editing                       8,844.00
Upon Delivery of Release Copies                    573.00
```

Figure 7.10 LOW BUDGET AV This budget format is a handy tool to help
you work with your audiovisual producer in developing a budget. In addition to
providing a description of the services to be provided, the major production
steps are costed separately. If you want more detail, you simply have to ask.
However, most people find this type of budget summary adequate. *Figures
7.10-7.12 are courtesy of Focus III Productions.*

```
VIDEO PRODUCTION BUDGET

CLIENT:  ABC Company, Inc.

PROJECT: Employee Benefits Presentation

Produce 16-minute video presentation describing new
employee benefits program for professionals.  Includes
script, production design, 3 days original photography (1
day location, 2 days on stage), casting, 3 principal
performers, set design & construction, props, costumes,
original music, editing, through completion of 1" video
master and protection master.

100 VHS release copies, labeled, in albums.

======================================================
BUDGET SUMMARY                                    PRICE
======================================================
Creative Development   .....................    7,625.00
Crew  ......................................    17,735.00
Equipment & Supplies   .....................     7,799.00
Talent  ....................................     3,915.00
Soundstage   ...............................     8,822.00
Location Expenses   ........................     2,722.00
Props & Wardrobe   .........................     3,951.00
Pre-Production & Wrap   ....................      4,113.00
Post Production   ..........................     15,758.00
------------------------------------------------------
TOTAL PRODUCTION                            $72,440.00
------------------------------------------------------
Release Copies    ..........................      573.00


PAYMENT SCHEDULE
------------------------------------------------------
Before Work Begins                             36,220.00
Upon Completion of Principal Photography       18,110.00
Upon Completion of Editing                     18,110.00
Upon Delivery of Release Copies                   573.00
```

Figure 7.11 MEDIUM BUDGET AV At first glance, this appears to be the same show as budgeted in Figure 7.10. The difference between the two is that this show will use more exotic and sophisticated production techniques. This requires more sophisticated and talented expertise in every phase of the production process. The actors are also more well-known and therefore able to command above-scale wages.

Comparing the two budgets underscores the importance of working closely with your producer to be certain you both understand the cost implications of each phase of the production process.

```
VIDEO PRODUCTION BUDGET

CLIENT:  ABC Company, Inc.

PROJECT: Employee Benefits Presentation

Produce 14-minute video presentation describing new
employee benefits program for professionals.  Includes
script, production design, 8 days original photography (3
day location, 5 days on stage), casting, 12 principal
performers, 25 extras, set design & construction, props,
costumes, original music, editing, through completion of 1"
video master and protection master.

100 VHS release copies, labeled, in albums.

========================================================
BUDGET SUMMARY                                      PRICE
========================================================
Creative Development   .....................     11,650.00
Crew  ......................................     38,590.00
Equipment & Supplies   .....................     15,407.00
Talent  ....................................     10,581.00
Soundstage   ...............................      9,984.00
Location Expenses   ........................      9,601.00
Props & Wardrobe   .........................     11,383.00
Pre-Production & Wrap   ....................       7,736.00
Post Production   ..........................     21,682.00
--------------------------------------------------------
TOTAL PRODUCTION                            $136,614.00
--------------------------------------------------------
Release Copies    ..........................       573.00


PAYMENT SCHEDULE
--------------------------------------------------------
Before Work Begins                             68,307.00
Upon Completion of Principal Photography       34,154.00
Upon Completion of Editing                     34,153.00
Upon Delivery of Release Copies                   573.00
```

Figure 7.12 HIGHER BUDGET AV This show is planned to be shorter than the first two, but cost nearly four times what the first show cost. Again the level of sophisticated production techniques will be higher. In addition the number of production days and the number of principal performers and extras are much higher. The company is paying for things they feel are worth the additional expense.

IMPORTANT NOTE All three of these audiovisuals will be good values. They are included to help illustrate that you can't produce *Gone With The Wind* on your local car dealer's TV commercial production budget.

meetings. While the basic concept of the show was good for all three audiences, these issues would have made the show less effective and therefore the return on investment was questionable. By rethinking the production process and considering how to produce the show in modules, three shows were ultimately produced for only slightly more than the original budget for one show. The three shows were

- a specific show directed to active employees and probable new hires
- a show directed at the retirees
- a show developed to be shown in lunch rooms and other gathering places such as employment offices and retiree centers.

The methodology was very simple. They developed an opening and closing module that talked about concepts and issues that were common to all audiences. The active show had a module in the center that had issues specific to the active and new hire audience. The retiree show had a module in the center that focused on retiree needs and perceptions. The third show was structured in the format of a news/information program such as *60 Minutes*. It was edited so that it could be running in a continuous loop and people would not have to stay and watch the entire show to get the most substantive parts of the information. Since the production was planned to have three modular versions, there was no need to duplicate much of the scripting and no need to have three different shooting schedules. Everything was done at one time. When all of the footage was shot, it was then only a matter of selecting the right footage and putting it together in different formats in the editing room.

How To Measure Audiovisual Success

Like measuring the success of any communication tool, the ultimate test is whether or not it achieved your objectives. Because audiovisuals are an emotional media, you can almost always tell how it was received by observing the audience reaction during and after the show. If there is a general positive feeling, you will know that you have hit the right combination of emotional responses within your audience. After its initial introduction, if you see that it is used on an ongoing basis, you can be satisfied it has perceived value by the audience and the primary users.

CHAPTER 8

IDEAS FOR DEVELOPING INTERACTIVE COMPUTER-BASED COMMUNICATIONS

Personal computers, internal, computer-based, communication systems, electronic mail-boxes, comprehensive electronic databases, interactive video, and artificial intelligence systems are proliferating, and these advances can enable you to communicate better and faster than you ever thought possible. Innovations in computer technology and new communication applications for the computer arise so rapidly that much of the information would be obsolete before it could be published. Therefore, the purpose of this chapter is to familiarize you with some general information, provide tips and ideas about how to develop interactive communication tools, and encourage you to take advantage of computer technology in human resouce communication.

USING THE COMPUTER AS AN EMPLOYEE COMMUNICATION MEDIUM

Personal computers have transformed a highly specialized technological data management tool into a viable communication medium. The cost of computers has dropped so dramatically, it is becoming common to find one or more personal computers in the home. Families with school-age children are seeing computers heading birthday and Christmas wish lists instead of dolls and toy trucks. Older employees who have never touched a computer are contemplating PC purchases as a way to pass time and remain productive after retirement. As software applications become more user-friendly, the mystery of computers has been replaced with the discovery that virtually anyone can use a computer to

- communicate across the country or throughout the world,
- learn new skills,
- manage personal and business affairs,
- make complex decisions more easily, and
- entertain themselves and others.

You can capitalize on these trends to add a new dimension to your human resource communication efforts.

Getting Messages Out Faster With Electronic Mail

Electronic mail is a relatively simple computer function whose primary purpose is to enable people to communicate faster. For some time, organizations have used a form of electronic mail to communicate among offices and divisions at the supervisor or management level. The concept is to post work and production schedules, bulletins, news items, and other data, such as sales reports, on a central computer. Authorized users are able to access this information and even make additions or changes from their desks. The advantages are that

- the information is readily available any time of the day or night
- the information can be kept current more easily

- remote users can have the information at the same time that a user in the adjacent office gets it
- several layers of bureaucracy such as typists, reproduction, and internal and external mail services can be eliminated
- the incremental cost for using the computers as a communication tool is negligible because the communication technology is an inherent component of most computer hardware and software applications

For these reasons organizations are expanding the base of users who can access a central computer from terminals or PCs at their desks and use the electronic mail utilities to communicate and share information throughout the organization instantaneously.

Recently human resource professionals have discovered that they can use the same technology to communicate with all employees as an alternative to paper-based newsletters and bulletins. The only difference between electronic mail capabilities as a personal rather than an employee communication medium is that employee communication messages must be prepared with the same care that traditional communication tools require.

How A Community Hospital Uses Electronic Mail Technology To Produce An Employee Newsletter

Hospitals have a difficult time keeping all employees informed about issues relating to their jobs, benefits, and professional topics because they are twenty-four-hour service operations. Memos, bulletins, and newsletters frequently are lost or destroyed after being read by the first employee. Consequently, subsequent employees may never know of their existence.

With the help of their internal data processing staff, a hospital's human resource director developed a simple way to keep all employees informed of new developments. A special place on the computer was designated for an employee *NEWS* file. The human resource department can write employee news items on their wordprocessor and send it to the *NEWS* file. Employees can go to any terminal or PC in the hospital, type the word news at the system prompt, hit the enter (or return), key, and see the most current human resource news items appear on the screen immediately. The employees do not have to know anything about using a computer in order to use the medium.

Virtually any organization with even one PC can use this approach to eliminate paper and make information more accessible to employees.

The diagram in Figure 8.1 illustrates how an electronic mail utility works. Figure 8.2 illustrates how the traditional print-based communication process works. Comparing the two will help you decide whether or not electronic mail is a communication option you should consider.

Increasing Retention With The Learn-At-Your-Own Speed Approach

As personal computers become more prevalent in the working environment, more commercial applications have been developed to enable individuals to learn new skills at their own speed. The most common reason for promoting this approach is that it eliminates or reduces the need for people trainers. Another aspect is that the computer creates an interactive process that increases retention level. The most common example is that most computer-based word processing programs now have learn-as-you-go tutorials included within them. While in certain situations it may be desirable to send an employee to an extensive training course or have an in-house employee devote time teaching another employee, it is no longer mandatory. The on-line training concepts developed by commercial software developers can be invaluable to human resource professionals who want to capitalize on the power of computer technology as a training and education tool.

Figure 8.1 ELECTRONIC MAIL PROCESS

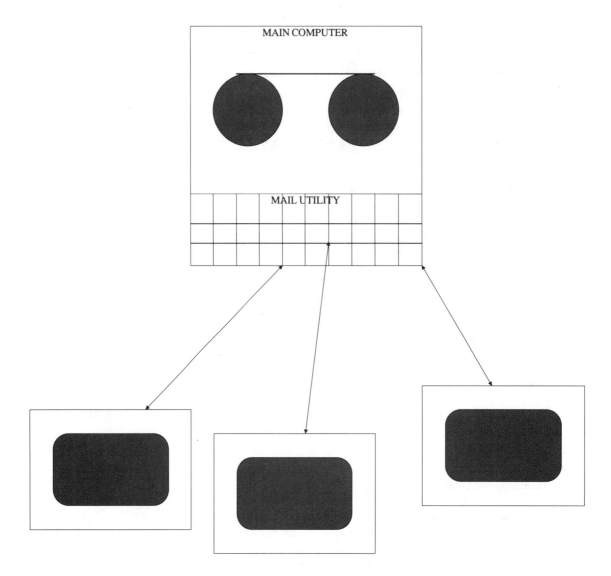

   Space for electronic mailboxes is allocated on the main computer. Remote users can create and send mail to one or more users and pick up messages from their own mailbox any time of the day or night by calling the main computer from their PC or terminal. The same principle will allow you to post information in a single file that all employees can access.

Figure 8.2 PRINT-BASED COMMUNICATION PROCESS

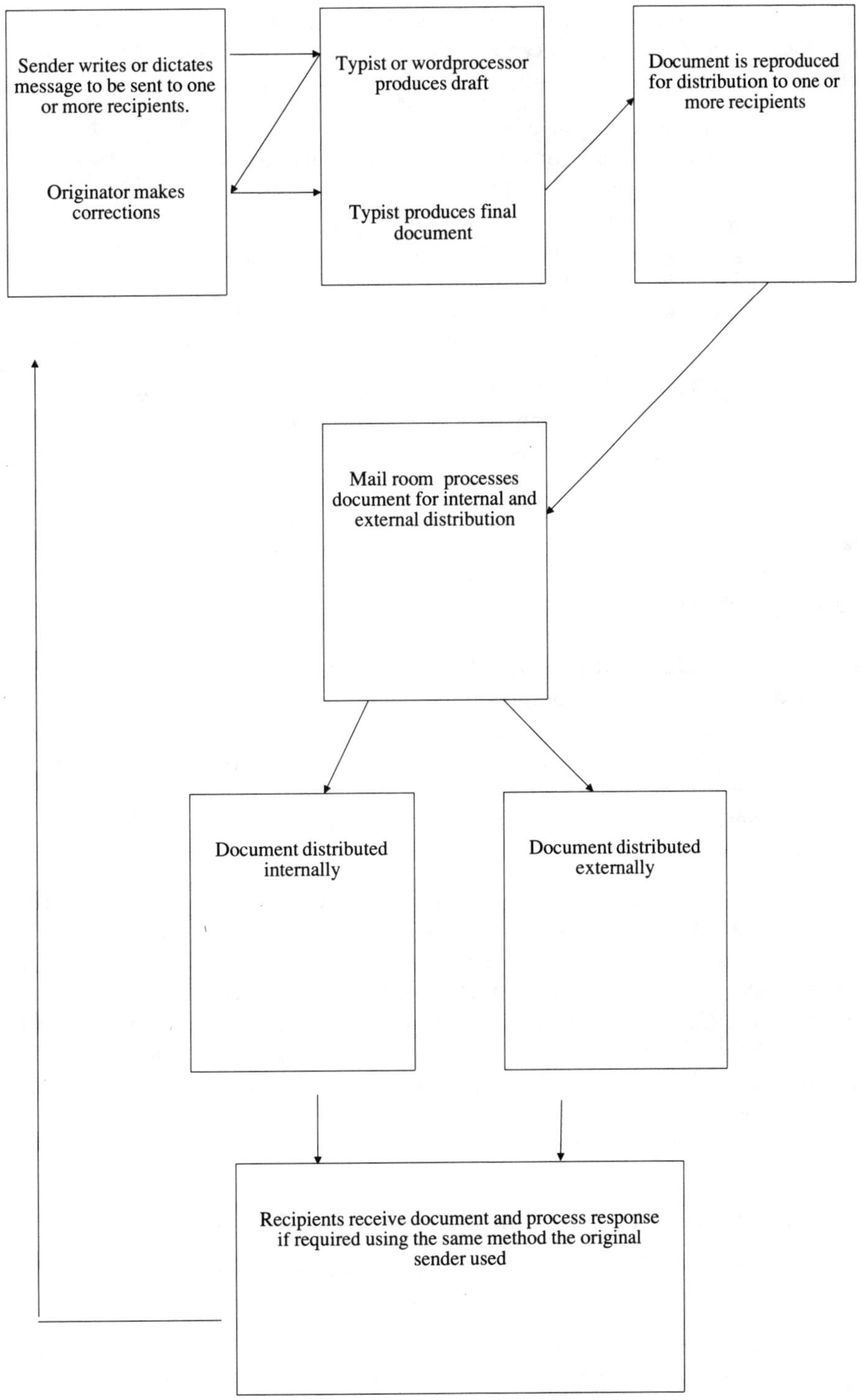

Sender writes or dictates message to be sent to one or more recipients.

Originator makes corrections

Typist or wordprocessor produces draft

Typist produces final document

Document is reproduced for distribution to one or more recipients

Mail room processes document for internal and external distribution

Document distributed internally

Document distributed externally

Recipients receive document and process response if required using the same method the original sender used

---

CHECKLIST: Ideas for Computerized Training

Simple, menu-based, computer programs can give supervisors, managers, human resource administrators, and employees an efficient way to get acquainted with your policies and procedural guidelines, how to administer them, which forms are required, implementation schedules, and scores of other useful tips to make their jobs easier. The programs can include routines that will enable users to print out reports, communication tools, and completed forms. Here are just a few ideas for computer-based training tools.

- Administering policies and procedures
- Administering compensation and performance plans
- Administering benefit plans
- Meeting compliance guidelines
- Calculating retirement benefits
- Conducting benefit enrollment programs
- Form letters and memos that can be personalized
- On-line directory of company resources, phone numbers, and addresses

COMMUNICATOR'S TIP: How Employees Will See Benefit Statements In The Year 2000

The most obvious application of computer software for hands-on employee use is an electronic-based, benefit statement. Without a doubt, PCs and terminals will be able to virtually replace traditional personalized communication tools in the not too distant future. The obvious advantage is that much of the traditional production requirements of printing forms will be eliminated. Other computer-based tools (e.g. what if retirement modeling, benefit comparison evaluations, enrollment processing) are gaining favor and being used within organizations now.

Improving Employee Decision-Making With Computer Programs

Organizations are demonstrating a tendency to transfer decision-making power back into the hands of employees on such issues as total compensation and flexible benefit programs. Computer-based tools can help employees analyze their decisions. For example, some organizations have already developed proprietary software that enables employees to see the effects of participating in a 401(k) program. The programs are designed to let them try what if scenarios until they have a good understanding of what that decision will mean to their current and future financial plans.

Some organizations with manufacturing- or production-oriented employee populations mistakenly view computer-based, interactive communication tools as useless investments. In fact, there is no basis for this assumption. The fundamentals behind a computer-based communication tool are no different than the computer- and video-based games successfully marketed in the consumer marketplace. It is, in fact, highly probable that a blue-collar work force is more adept and comfortable with these games than a white-collar work force, and are more likely to perceive the games as a healthy diversion from their real world trials and tribulations. One of the most valuable psychological advantages of interactive communication tools is the user's perception of control. This perception melds comfortably with organizations' desire to shift personal decision-making back to employees.

TYPES OF INTERACTIVE EMPLOYEE COMMUNICATION PROGRAMS

One of the most promising prospects for interactive computer programs is that they will eliminate or simplify much of the administrative duties currently required of human resource professionals.

Most of the proprietary or specialized, interactive computer programs currently being developed for employees emulate the paper-based, personalized communication tools such as benefit statements, retirement and savings plan statements, and personalized enrollment forms. In addition, financial and retirement planning modeling programs are gaining popularity. Interactive communication programs can be as simple or as complex as you like. The key is deciding what you want the system to do. Figures 8.3 and 8.4 outline the objectives and parameters one organization established for an administrative interactive document system. Figures 8.5 and 8.6 summarize how the Federal Reserve Bank of San Francisco defined a comprehensive, interactive, employee communication system.

Designing Your Program To Be User-Friendly

Since it is almost impossible to predict how any given person will interpret and respond to the prompts on a computer program, developing and testing a computer program requires more time up front than does a written document. Extra time is required to ensure that the results will be accurate and that the computer will be non-threatening. However, paper-based production activities are virtually eliminated as the computer program will be able to generate a paper copy on demand. Some organizations are even developing programs that will generate benefit plan enrollment forms after employees have made their decisions. The primary difference between these computer-based tools and their paper-based counterparts is that the computer program must be designed to interface with lay mentality that may be uncomfortable with computer technology.

Like audiovisuals, it is very difficult to understand exactly what the finished product will look like until it is completed. Furthermore, it is virtually impossible to illustrate the power of this tool using the printed media. However, the following pages (see Figures 8.7 and 8.13) illustrate different types of user-friendly screens extracted from employee-based interactive communication tools.

Which Computer Is Right?

The three most common types of computers are mainframes, mini computers and micro computers (personal computers or PCs). Lay people using a mini or mainframe won't know the difference between the two. In either case, they will have only a computer terminal at their desk, in contrast to PC users who will also have the computer's central processing unit nearby. Currently most interactive employee communication programs are developed for use on personal computers. As technology becomes more sophisticated and as more computers are installed in organizations, we can expect more widespread use of minis and mainframes for human resource communication. The right computer for your organization depends entirely on what your current and planned system needs are. Preparing to develop an employee computer-based communication tool is very similar to developing audiovisual tools. You have to do some research before you start.

A STEP-BY-STEP GUIDE TO STARTING A COMPUTER-BASED COMMUNICATION PROGRAM

There are four steps you must take before you can start developing a computer-based communication program.

Step 1: Hardware Inventory Assessment

Your most important task before embarking on an employee, computer-based, communication program is to understand your hardware inventory. The key questions you will need to answer are:

- What kind of computers do you have?
- Who manages the computer systems now?
- Are the computers accessible by a large number of employees?
- Will you be willing or able to invest in more hardware?

Figure 8.3 INTERACTIVE DOCUMENT SYSTEM OBJECTIVE STATEMENT. This is an objective statement for an interactive document system to enable benefit administrators review, modify, and publish summary plan descriptions and benefit plan documents more quickly.

Objective

Write comprehensive Summary Plan Descriptions for 17 plans.

Develop a computer-based system that will

- reduce administration connected with updating SPDs and plan documents,
- provide an audit trail as administration and provision interpretation changes,
- permit on-line access to each document through a user-friendly menu, and
- provide hardcopy output capability for review and publication purposes, and
- increase the opportunity for timely compliance with IRC Section 89 basic qualification tests.

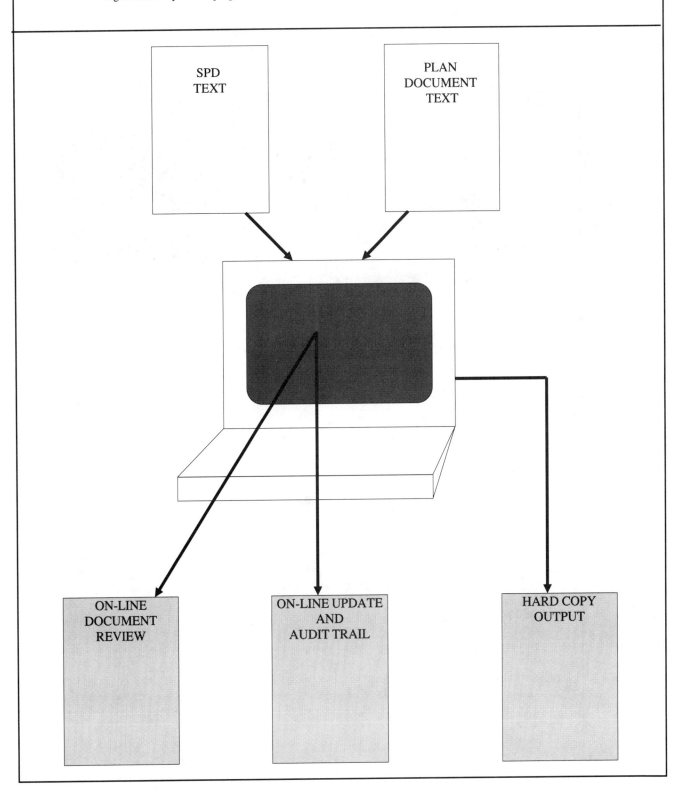

Figure 8.4A INTERACTIVE DOCUMENT SYSTEM MODEL This figure graphically illustrates how the organization expects the program to work.

SPD
TEXT

PLAN
DOCUMENT
TEXT

ON-LINE
DOCUMENT
REVIEW

ON-LINE UPDATE
AND
AUDIT TRAIL

HARD COPY
OUTPUT

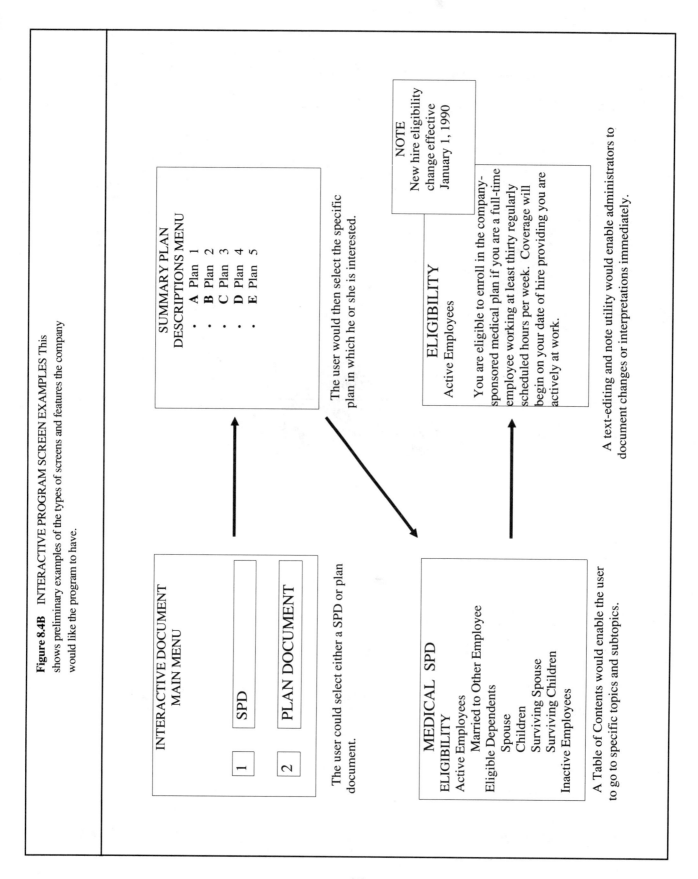

Figure 8.4B INTERACTIVE PROGRAM SCREEN EXAMPLES This shows preliminary examples of the types of screens and features the company would like the program to have.

INTERACTIVE DOCUMENT
MAIN MENU

1   SPD

2   PLAN DOCUMENT

The user could select either a SPD or plan document.

SUMMARY PLAN
DESCRIPTIONS MENU

- **A**   Plan   1
- **B**   Plan   2
- **C**   Plan   3
- **D**   Plan   4
- **E**   Plan   5

The user would then select the specific plan in which he or she is interested.

MEDICAL   SPD

ELIGIBILITY
Active Employees
    Married to Other Employee
Eligible Dependents
    Spouse
    Children
    Surviving Spouse
    Surviving Children
Inactive Employees

A Table of Contents would enable the user to go to specific topics and subtopics.

NOTE
New hire eligibility
change effective
January 1, 1990

ELIGIBILITY
Active Employees

You are eligible to enroll in the company-sponsored medical plan if you are a full-time employee working at least thirty regularly scheduled hours per week. Coverage will begin on your date of hire providing you are actively at work.

A text-editing and note utility would enable administrators to document changes or interpretations immediately.

218

Figure 8.5   INTERACTIVE EMPLOYEE COMMUNICATION SYSTEM Figures 8.5 and 6 explain a comprehensive employee communication system. Both programs were designed to operate on IBM PC compatible computers.

INTERACTIVE EMPLOYEE COMMUNICATION SYSTEM

WHAT IS IT?

For Employees

A computer-based interactive benefit communication system designed to allow employees to access and review personalized compensation and benefit data, compare and model different benefit scenarios, generate customized output, make enrollment decisions and output payroll coded enrollment forms.

For Administration

Reduces redundant paper. The system also allows authorized personnel to access each employee's extract file records, add or change personal and dependent data, modify variable text files such as benefit bulletins, employee contribution rates, and social security integration tables.

Another option which was considered but not implemented was to provide the facility for the program to provide computerized enrollment data to other benefit recordkeeping systems and carriers.

Exhibit I illustrates how the system works.

WHAT WILL IT DO?

Program Parameters

The program includes the necessary assumptions, formulas, tables, eligibility and cost criteria to calculate and/or display employee-specific benefit levels and costs (company and/or employee). Employees can:

- review their current coverage under each plan
- print a personalized total compensation statement, current within 45 days of the access date
- review and compare health care coverages and costs
- print health care benefit comparisons
- review other voluntary benefit options such as personal accident
- perform "what if" modeling for retirement and 401(k) plans
- print modeling results
- change or select new coverage
- print enrollment forms
- review personal and dependent data files
- print personal and dependent data change forms

Figure 8.5 (*continued*)

Data Input

Employee data resides in three separate files - the payroll masterfile, the retirement salary
history file and a special system file that maintains vacation and sick leave balances. The
three data sources are merged into an extract file on the mainframe which is downloaded to
a dedicated PC workstation located in the benefit department.

The only data that is not resident on any internal system file is the 401(k) account balances.
Employees are permitted to input this data item if they wish.

HOW DOES IT WORK?

Interactive Capabilities

After the employee passes the security tests and basic data have been accessed by the system, the program will allow employees to choose from a menu of options...current benefits,
benefit comparisons and modeling, personal data and enrollment options. Since open enrollment periods vary, depending on the plan, the program does not allow access to the
enrollment programs unless it recognizes the current date as falling within the allowed open
enrollment period.

Benefits included are:
- basic life and accidental death and dismemberment insurance
- all health care options
- sick leave
- short term disability
- long-term disability
- personal accident
- employee savings program...401(k)
- retirement plan
- vacation and holidays

Output Data

The program is designed to permit screen and hardcopy output.

Documentation

Documentation includes a detailed calculation logic, which identifies each program assumption, and all formulas, tables and data elements necessary to generate the desired result,
hard copy of all user interface screens, program code and administrative procedures guide.

Figure 8.6 INTERACTIVE EMPLOYEE COMMUNICATION SYSTEM FLOW CHART

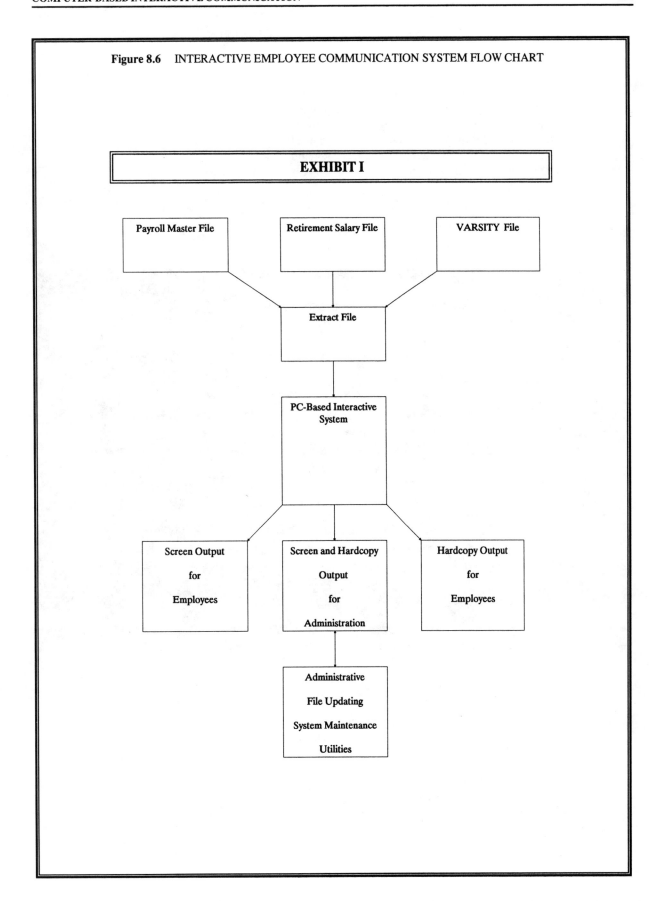

Figure 8.7 USER-FRIENDLY TUTOR SCREEN

It is difficult to get more user-friendly than this program. This single screen tells employees virtually everything they need to know in order to navigate through the program successfully. If the user forgets any of the instructions while using the program, they will get help prompts and reminders at the moment they make a mistake.

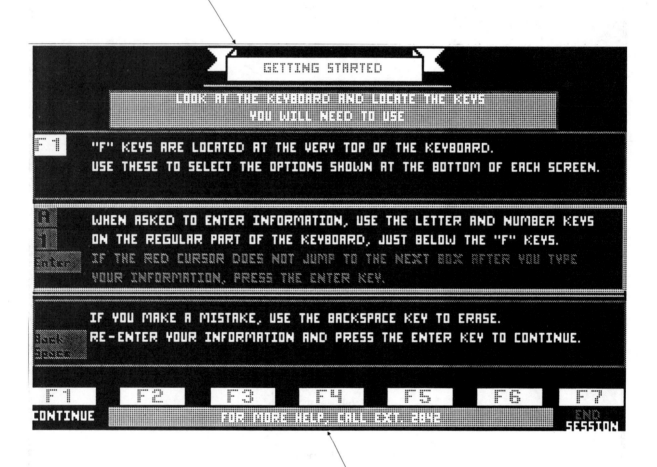

The user's attention is focused on the bottom of the screen. This format continues throughout the program to reduce user confusion.

Figure 8.8 HARD COPY OUTPUT EMPLOYEE BENEFIT STATEMENT

The interactive program reformats the information shown on the screens in Figure 8.8 and sends it to a laser printer so employees may take their personal benefit statement with them.

The interactive program resides on a dedicated PC located in the Benefits Office. The personal data is extracted from the bank's master file which resides on a mainframe and is downloaded to the PC once a month.

Both the screen and hard copy output show the employee the value of their total compensation package.

The hard copy report emphasizes the fact that the statement does *not* guarantee employment or benefits and encourages employees to contact the Benefits Department if they detect an error.

```
                          A B C   C O R P O R A T I O N
              Y O U R   P E R S O N A L   B E N E F I T   S T A T E M E N T

HEALTH CARE COVERAGE          After deductibles, the plan pays           DEDUCTIBLES
Medical: Our records indicate Hospital                  80%      Per person          $100
you are enrolled in :         Outpatient Surgery       100%      Per family          $200
Equimed to Two-Party          Doctor Office Visits      80%      Per hospital stay   $100
                              Prescription Drugs        80%

Dental: Our records indicate  After deductibles, the plan pays   DEDUCTIBLES PER PERSON
you are enrolled in :         Basic Services            60%      Preventive  $50/annual
Equident to Two-Party         Major Services        50%/$ Limited Major      $50/annual
                              Orthodontia              NONE      Orthodontia NONE
           Maximum Annual Dental Benefit $1,000.00 per person
All reimbursement is subject to Usual, Customary, and Reasonable (UCR) Charges
for covered procedures and plan limitations.

VACATION and HOLIDAYS               INCOME SECURITY (All benefits are taxable)
Vacation Carryover Balance  0 hours  Current Sick Leave Balance  99 hours
Current Year Vacation Balance  64 hours  Short Term Disability (UCD)  $ 224/wk - max. 52 weeks
Current Year Floating Holiday  11 hours  Long Term Disability         $ 575 per month
          Balance                        Benefit ends at retirement and is limited to 60% of
                                         salary including Social Security benefit entitlement

LIFE INSURANCE AND SURVIVOR BENEFITS   LUMP SUM BENEFITS      LUMP SUM BENEFITS
                                                              SPOUSE      CHILD
Life and Survivor (1 X Salary)         $  12,000   Eligible survivors MAY receive
Thrift Plan Balance (entered by You)   $  10,000   monthly L&S benefit of 40% of your
Retirement Active Service Benefit (1 X Salary)  $  12,000   salary.  One year of service
Social Security Death Benefit          $     255   necessary for this benefit.
Supplemental Life                      $             $         $
SUBTOTAL TO BENEFICIARIES in event of death  $  34,255
PLUS Accidental Death and Dismemberment (AD&D)
Travel Accident (Under Special Circumstances)   $  34,000
    TOTAL TO BENEFICIARIES in event of death     $  68,255

FUTURE SECURITY        Thrift Plan Balance (entered by You) $  10,000  Lump Sum

Estimated MONTHLY Retirement Plan Benefit $  476/Mo. at 65   357/Mo. at 62   274/Mo. at 60
Payable at your normal retirement date, if you continue working for the Bank.  Assumes single
life benefit with a conservative 3% salary increase.  The benefit would be different if you are
married and elected other than a single life benefit payment option when you retire.

TOTAL COMPENSATION SUMMARY
Your Current Annual Salary         $  11,494
Total Annual Cost of Your ABC Benefits  $   3,225    Bank's Cost   $  13,586
TOTAL ANNUAL COMPENSATION          $  14,719         Your Cost     $   1,133

             IMPORTANT NOTE
This summary is not a guarantee of employment or benefits.  Every effort has been made to
ensure accuracy based on the Bank's records and the data you may have entered when using this
program.  In case of error, this statement does not modify or change the actual benefits to
which you may be entitled.  If you have questions, please contact the Benefits Department at
extension 2842.  (Information current as of 08/02/87 )

ESPECIALLY PREPARED FOR:        SOCIAL SECURITY NO.:        000-00-0010
DEEDEE E. JONES                 DATE OF HIRE:               04/14/86
                                BENEFIT SERVICE DATE:       04/14/86
                                DEPENDENT MEDICAL COVERAGE: Yes
```

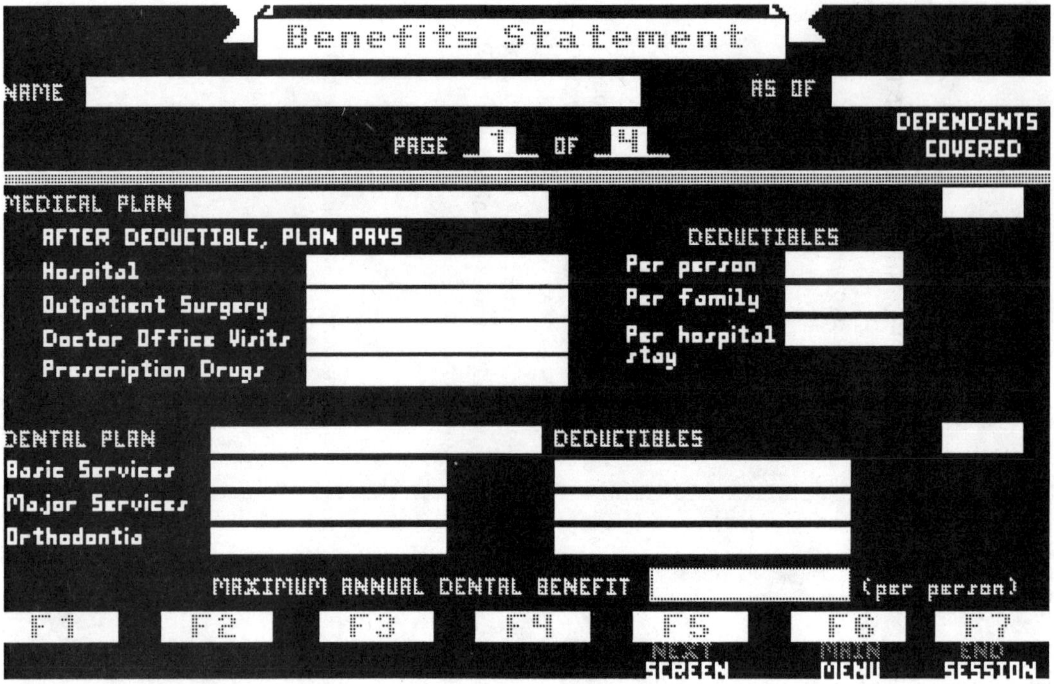

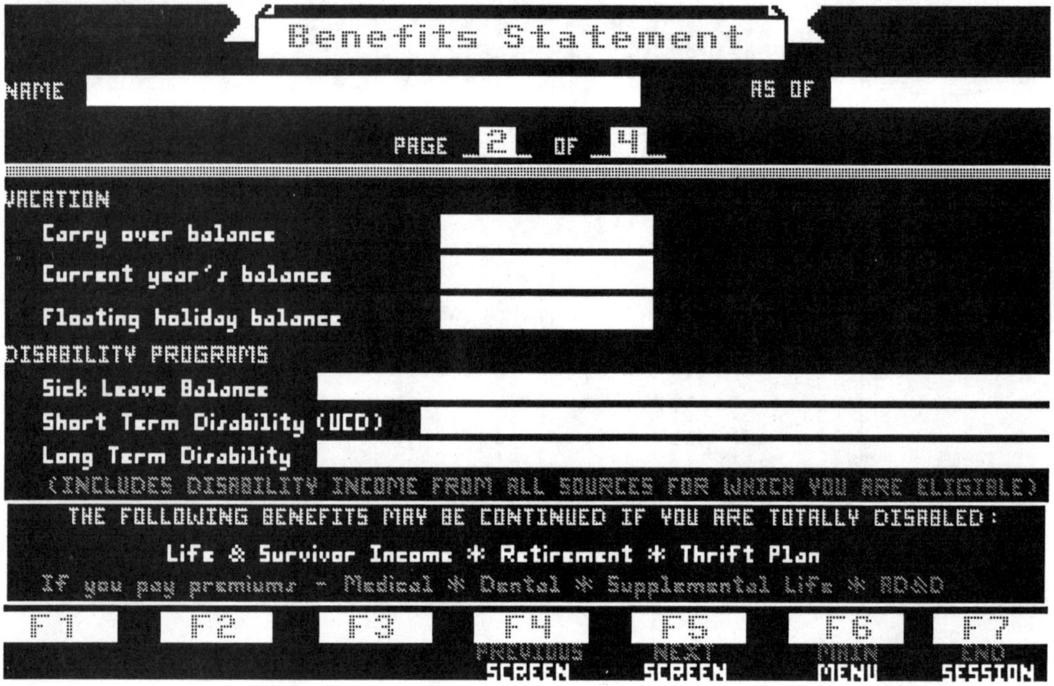

Figure 8-9 BENEFIT STATEMENT COMPUTER SCREENS These four screens comprise the on-line benefit statement employees can view on the interactive employee communication system at the Federal Reserve Bank of San Francisco, District 12. When an employee successfully accesses the system by inputing the appropriate security codes, he or she may choose from several options. If they choose the benefit statement, the system will automatically show these screens, one at a time, with the employee's personal data showing in the white boxes. The words and F-key illustrations at the bottom of the screen help the user move through the program easily. The employee may choose a hard copy printout of his or her benefit statement (see Figure 8.8) by pressing the F5 key on screen number 4. *Courtesy of Federal Reserve Bank of San Francisco, District 12.*

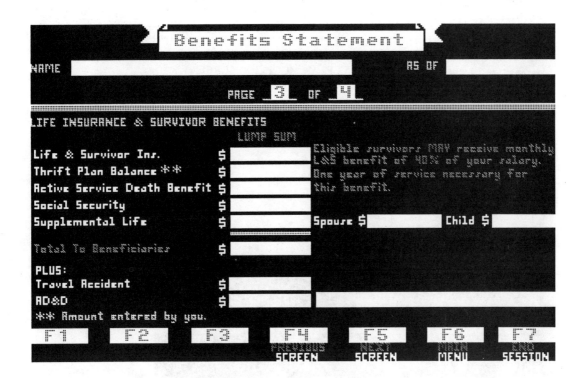

Benefits Statement

NAME [   ]   AS OF [   ]

PAGE [3] OF [4]

LIFE INSURANCE & SURVIVOR BENEFITS

LUMP SUM

Life & Survivor Ins.	$ [ ]	Eligible survivors MAY receive monthly
Thrift Plan Balance **	$ [ ]	L&S benefit of 40% of your salary.
Active Service Death Benefit	$ [ ]	One year of service necessary for
Social Security	$ [ ]	this benefit.
Supplemental Life	$ [ ]	Spouse $ [ ] Child $ [ ]
Total To Beneficiaries	$ [ ]	

PLUS:

Travel Accident	$ [ ]
AD&D	$ [ ]

** Amount entered by you.

F1	F2	F3	F4	F5	F6	F7
			PREVIOUS SCREEN	NEXT SCREEN	MAIN MENU	END SESSION

Benefits Statement

NAME [   ]   AS OF [   ]

PAGE [4] OF [4]

FUTURE SECURITY

		Savings	Def. Comp.
Thrift Plan Balance $ [ ]		Contrib. % [ ]	Contrib. % [ ]

Annual Bank Match (60% match to 6% of salary) $ [   ]

RETIREMENT BENEFIT ESTIMATES IF YOU CONTINUE WORKING FOR THE BANK

At Age 65 - Single Life Max. Benefit $ [   ]
At Age 62 - Single Life Max. Benefit $ [   ]
At Age 60 - Single Life Max. Benefit $ [   ]

TOTAL COMPENSATION SUMMARY

Salary	$ [ ]
Benefits	$ [ ]

YOUR TOTAL COMPENSATION $ [   ]   BANK PAYS $ [   ]

YOU PAY $ [   ]

F1	F2	F3	F4	F5	F6	F7
Thrift Detail	Retirement Detail		PREVIOUS SCREEN	PRINT Statement	MAIN MENU	END SESSION

Figure 8.10   RETIREMENT PLAN MODELING SCREEN

This program tells the user their
creditable service as of the current date
and on what date they will be one hundred
percent vested in the retirement plan. This
helps employees remember their current
status in the plan .

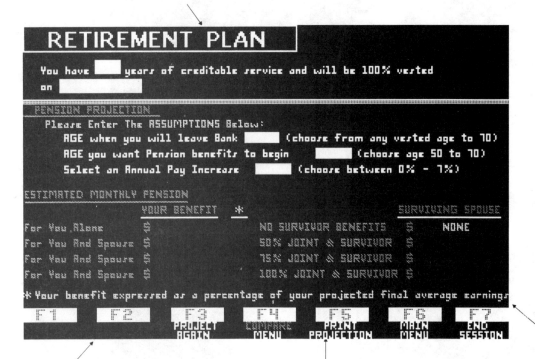

This section lets the user decide what assumptions are to be used to calculate
retirement benefits. The prompts at the
right of the white boxes help employees
remember valid options. If the employees
choose an invalid option, the program
asks him or her to try again.

Using the employee-defined assumptions, the program then calculates
estimated monthly pension benefits based
on the company's retirement plan formula.
If the employee is single, only one number
will be displayed. If the employee is married, all numbers for the different
scenarios will be displayed.

The prompts at the bottom of
the screen give the employee options to print hard copy output,
do another projection, move to
another part of the program, or
quit.

1988 TRW RETIREMENT BENEFIT ESTIMATOR

INPUT SCREEN

INFORMATION FROM YOUR BENEFIT STATEMENT

Birth Date (MO/DAY/YR):   Credited Service:

Annual Salary : $ Average Retirement Benefit: $ /month

Stock Saving Plan Account Balance $

YOUR ASSUMPTIONS ABOUT THE FUTURE

Retirement Date (MO/YR):   Future Annual Salary Growth: %

Stock Savings Plan Contributions: Before Tax: %   After Tax: %

Stock Saving Plan Annual Investment Return: %

Figure 8.11A RETIREMENT BENEFIT ESTIMATOR—INPUT SCREEN

Facsimilie of TRW Interactive Input Screen

This program was designed to be used with TRW's traditional benefit statement. Employees must request a floppy disk for their personal use and are encouraged to input the data shown on their traditional benefit statement, following the screen instructions of the program.

When the data has been input, and they press the enter key, a results screen will appear showing the assumptions they used, the estimated account balance of their stock savings plan at retirement and estimated monthly benefits from the TRW Pension Plan and Social Security. The program will also allow them to print a hard copy of the results. *Courtesy of TRW Space & Defense.*

1988 TRW RETIREMENT BENEFIT ESTIMATOR

RESULTS SCREEN

PERSONAL INFORMATION

Retirement Date: January, 2001

Retirement Age: 58

Salary at Retirement: $ 94,153

Salary Growth: 10%

SSP Contributions: 0.0% Before Tax
0% After Tax

SSP Investment Return: 0.00%

YOUR ESTIMATED RETIREMENT BENEFITS

LUMP-SUM BENEFIT
Stock Savings Plan Account: $ 0

MONTHLY BENEFITS
From TRW Pension Plan: $2,449 (as a life-only benefit)
From Social Security: $1,096 (first available at age 62)
TOTAL: $3,545 (45% of final salary of $7,846 a month)

Figure 8.11B RETIREMENT BENEFIT ESTIMATOR—RESULTS SCREEN

FACSIMILE EXCERPT FROM TRW RETIREMENT ESTIMATOR RESULTS SCREEN

The program calculates the benefits based on the plan provisions and the user's input. It also cautions that the projections are only estimates and that the employee's actual benefits will be calculated at retirement. *Courtesy of TRW Space & Defense.*

Figure 8.12 THRIFT PLAN MODELING SCREEN *Courtesy of Federal Reserve Bank of San Francisco, District 12.*

This program tells the user what account balance he or she entered, what percent of salary is currently contributed to the plan by the employee and whether or not it is taxable, what investment vehicle(s) he or she has chosen and the current rate of return on the fixed income fund.

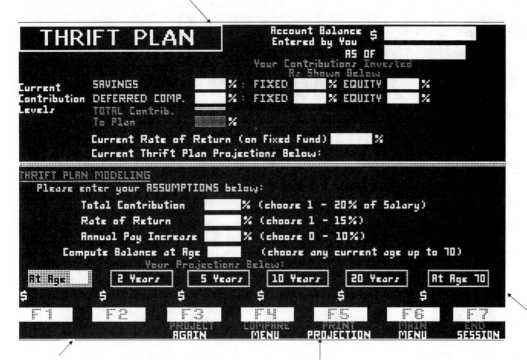

The employee can choose the assumption upon which future account balances will be calculated.

The program uses the plan provisions and legal parameters to calculate the future account balances.

The prompts at the bottom of the screen give the employee options to print hard copy output, do another projection, move to another part of the program, or quit.

Figure 8.13   MEDICAL COMPARISON SCREEN *Courtesy of Federal Reserve Bank of San Francisco, District 12.*

Companies are encouraging employees to consider a number of health care benefit plans and choose one that is best suited to their personal needs. To help employees compare benefits and costs of various plans, this program gives them an interactive matrix. The first column of the matrix is automatically filled in because the program knows which plan the employee is enrolled in and what the benefits and costs are for that plan.

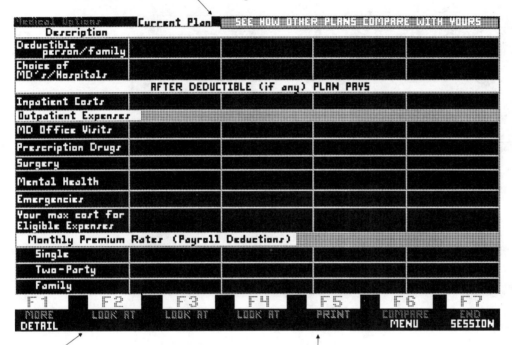

The plans the employee can compare are shown below the F-Key graphics at the bottom of the screen. The employee can compare as few or as many plans as he or she wishes. Each time an F-Key is pressed, another column of data will appear on the screen.

The prompts at the bottom of the screen give the employee options to print hard copy output, do another projection, move to another part of the program, or quit.

Some organizations have already established common area computer systems so that employees can access them easily. Frequently, the investment in additional hardware is minimal and computer hardware gets less expensive every day. The checklist in Figure 8.14 summarizes the kind of hardware inventory information you need

---

CHECKLIST: Computer Hardware Inventory Considerations

- **Types And Numbers Of Computers**. The types of computers in your organization may range from mainframes to PCs and may influence what kind of program you can develop. Different types may not be compatible. For example, you have to purchase additional hardware and software to enable an Apple MacIntosh and IBM PC to use the same program.
- **Kinds Of Monitors.** If you have both monochrome and color monitors, your program may have to be designed to run on both. Since monitors have different levels of resolution, your program must be able to address the lowest common denominator in order to work properly on all of them.
- **Graphics Capabilities**. Computers must have special adaptors in order to run programs that use graphics as well as text. Since graphics give you more ability to make your program interesting and user-friendly, it is desirable to be sure your computers have graphics capabilities.
- **Memory And Disk Drives**. Most interactive programs will require at least two or three megabytes of memory. Memory capacity and disk drives are transparent to people using terminals connected to minis and mainframes. However, they are a visible part of PCs. If your program is complex and is to run on a PC, the computer should have a speedy hard disk. If it is a simpler program that could be distributed to employees on a floppy disk, you will have to be sure that the distribution disks are compatible with the most common type of floppy disk drive on your PCs.
- **Communication Capabilities.** Computers can talk to one another or share information via phone lines, which require the computers to have modems, or by being physically connected with cables. In addition, each computer must have communication software. Unless you plan to install an interactive program on a PC, you should know whether or not your computers can communicate and share information.
- **Printers.** If you want your program to produce hard copy, you will need to have a printer connected to the computer. Different types of printers require different types of instructions from the computer. You must know what kind of printer will be used for output so the program can be written to communicate properly with it. For example, if the program thinks it is sending print instructions to a dot matrix printer, but you installed a laser printer, you will not get satisfactory results.

While this checklist may seem formidable, if you have computers you have people who know how to use them and can help you compile your hardware inventory. Once you have a sense of the practical issue of hardware availability, you need to re-evaluate your communication needs.

Step 2: Communication Needs Assessment

As with any other communication tool, developing a computer-based program because your competitor down the street does it, is not a good reason. You should be able and willing to invest the time to evaluate whether or not the tool will be practical in your current working environment. The easiest way is to write an objective statement.

- A tool to train branch personnel how to process loan applications.
- A tool to facilitate customer education about proper use of a specific piece of equipment.
- An on-line employee benefit statement that can be viewed and printed on demand.
- A communication hotline that enables employees to get immediate answers to their questions.

Expanding the statement and illustrating how it might work (see Figures 8.3 through 8.6) will help you clarify your needs and the practicality of your vision. If you have determined that a computer-based communication tool is good for your organization, it is critical that you spend some time developing an implementation and administration plan to be sure that it will do the job intended. Figure 8.14 summarizes five major steps for developing an interactive computer program.

Programmers call this a flow chart (see Figure 8.15). It is a simple one in that it does not illustrate every conceivable branch that could occur in the program. As you can see, the program is not linear in nature which is why it is important to carefully define your program objectives.

Step 3: Implementation And Administration Of A Computer-Based Communication Program

Like any other communication tool, your computer program will need to be updated periodically. Therefore, it must be developed with that fact in mind. Organizations whose employees already use computers in their day-to-day work may find that the easiest way to implement and update the program is to distribute individual floppy disks to employees and send out periodic revisions. Most organizations, however, prefer to use techniques that are easier to manage such as loaning computers with the program installed to employees to take home or setting up special libraries or computer rooms and encouraging employees to go there to become familiar with the new software. Another popular approach is to set up kiosks or work stations that are tied into mini or mainframe computers and then encourage employees to schedule times to use the work stations.

Because the technology is relatively untested in the employee environment, organizations with multiple locations may want to introduce a pilot program in one location before making it available to all employees. This will give you an opportunity to evaluate the program, how employees use it, and what the appropriate access and/or distribution process should be.

Step 4: Getting Management To Say Yes

In proposing any new program, gaining management approval depends on how well you prepare your presentation. If your superiors are uncomfortable with computers, they will be more difficult to convince. In addition to justifying the program financially, perhaps the easiest way to get management's endorsement is to set them down in front of the computer to use a prototype program themselves. Senior management may be the group most reluctant to try a program, yet once they agree, they tend to see the value of the tool quickly and become personally interested in the program.

Whether or not you can cost-justify the program depends on how you are currently spending time and money for a specific task or communication goal. It is unlikely you can justify computer-based programs for one-time or short-term communication objectives. However, for ongoing and administrative-intensive communication activities, computers offer some very attractive options. For example, if you are currently

Figure 8.14 FIVE STEPS FOR DEVELOPING AN INTERACTIVE COMPUTER PROGRAM

GETTING STARTED

Planning is the most important part of any project. Following is an oversimplified summary of the the major project steps necessary to develop and implement an interactive employee communication system.

STEP I...Planning

- Confirm Program Objectives and Scope of the Project
- Identify Internal Systems and Systems Capabilities
- Confirm Benefit Plans to be Included
- Identify Resources and Primary Responsibilities
- Establish Timetable
- Establish Budget

STEP II...Design Stage

- Develop Creative Concept (Theme/Title/Graphics)
- Develop System Flow Chart
- Develop Preliminary Screens and Text
- Develop Preliminary Calculation Logic
- Develop Administrative Training Program
- Design User and Administrative Brochures/Worksheets
- Develop User Awareness/Information Campaign

STEP III...First Review Stage

- Approve Creative Concept (Theme/Title/Graphics)
- Finalize Screens and Text
- Finalize Calculation Logic
- Approve User Brochure/Worksheets

STEP IV...Programming & Testing

- Develop Program
- Alpha Test
- Revise as Necessary
- Beta Test
- Finalize Documentation

STEP V...Implementation

- Produce User Brochure/Worksheets
- Conduct Administrative Training
- Implement User Awareness/Information Campaign
- Go Online

Figure 8.15   PROGRAM FLOW CHART

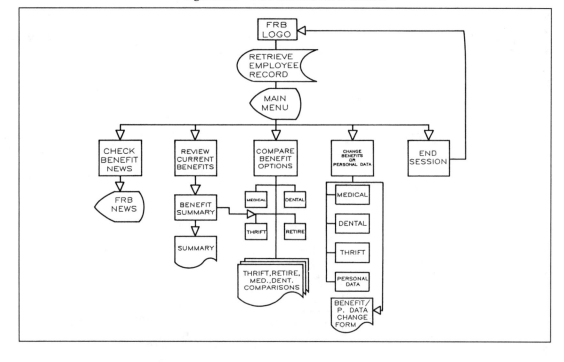

producing a traditional paper-based benefit statement, the external supplier costs and internal staff time required every year to collect data, validate each step of the data manipulation process, and manage production could be virtually eliminated with an interactive system that allows employees to punch a few buttons and get their own statement whenever they want it. The initial setup time and expense could be significant, but the ongoing expenses and administrative time would drop dramatically.

KEEPING PACE WITH THE LEADING EDGE

Interactive Video
Interactive videos combine the power of live action audiovisuals and interactive computer programs. A videotape or videodisk player is connected to a computer system and the computer program operates like any other computer-based communication program but it is enhanced with the ability to show live action audiovisuals on the same screen as the computer program prompts. The technology to produce interactive videos is here today but still relatively expensive for human resource applications. They are most commonly used in the entertainment industry and for very sophisticated training. Some organizations have used this combined technology for employee communication tools. However, these organizations typically have a great deal of experience with both audiovisuals and computers.

Artificial Intelligence
For years, computer professionals have been convinced that there is a way to successfully emulate human intelligence on the computer. Many rudimentary artificial intelligence programs appear in the marketplace today. This area will be a focus for computer professionals and software developers for some time to come. Even now a few organizations' human resource departments are developing programs that use the theory of artificial intelligence to create expert systems and databases which will enable them to reduce the time

INTERACTIVE COMMUNICATION BUDGETING WORKSHEET		
DESCRIPTION	**PROJECT COST**	**TOTAL COST**
DESIGN		
Creative Concept		
Screen Design/Text		
System Flow Chart		
Preliminary Program Logic		
SYSTEM DEVELOPMENT		
Final Program Logic		
Program Coding		
Alpha (1st) Test		
Refine Program		
Beta (2nd) Test		
Final Programming		
Final Documentation		
HARDWARE/SOFTWARE		
Hardware Purchases		
Software Purchases		
TRAINING		
User Guides		
Administrator's Guides		
Training Sessions		
EMPLOYEE INTRODUCTION		
Promotion Materials		
User Guides		
OTHER		

Figure 8.16 INTERACTIVE BUDGETING WORKSHEET. This budget
worksheet is designed to help summarize the various development and production elements you must consider if you are developing an interactive
communication system. The specification and budget examples in Chapter 2
can be useful to itemize the cost elements in more detail. Your biggest costs
will be in system design and development.

and administrative burden connected with producing employee communication tools. The most prominent area affected right now is summary plan descriptions for benefit plans. Keeping pace with the leading edge of this technology is really very simple. As you become more comfortable with the concepts and see more application opportunities, your imagination will take over and you will be one of the creators of the leading edge.

HOW TO DEVELOP BUDGETS

Developing budgets for interactive communication tools is extremely difficult. This is primarily because there is no way to anticipate a particular programming or user problem until it occurs. The easiest way to develop cost estimates is to use personalized communication specifications and estimating techniques and then increase your anticipated time and expense by a complexity factor (e.g. expenses + [time]x 3). The complexity factor is just another way of emphasizing that you will inevitably underestimate the time required to complete the project. The budget worksheet in Figure 8.16 can help you determine what your probable cost would be.

Cost Cutting Tips
Trying to use short cuts in this medium will probably cost you more than you could ever save. The key to controlling costs is to plan very carefully and avoid the tendency to expand the scope of your program's capabilities once you begin production. Every time you change one component of a program, it will likely impact several other components and you may not discover the insidious effect until it is too late.

Evaluating The Success Of An Interactive Communication Program
Like all other communication media, if employees are not satisfied with a computer program, you will hear about it. Unlike all other media, you can easily measure the effectiveness of the program by using the computer itself. For example, your program can have a little routine built into it that counts how often the communication program is accessed and what options are used and when. You can periodically check the counter to see employee-use patterns. Think of it as a mini-audit. The information can appear on the computer screen or you can ask for printed reports. Another way to measure employee opinions is to include an interactive employee survey option on your program menu. The computer can ask employees questions such as how the program works, if it is user-friendly, if they like it, and what could be done to improve it.

CHAPTER 9

INTEGRATING COLLATERAL MATERIALS INTO YOUR COMMUNICATION PROGRAM

Collateral communication tools can be almost anything from napkins to health fairs. The term collateral is used because these tools are used in conjunction with other communication tools rather than standing alone. Collateral material has a place in your communication program because it gives you a relatively inexpensive way to reinforce a campaign or to establish a readily identifiable image. Following are some examples of the more conventional collateral materials which organizations have used to supplement communication messages.

CHECKLIST: Eighteen Examples of Collateral Material

This list is by no means all inclusive; the options are limited only by your imagination

- *Payroll stuffers* are similar to the promotional leaflets you receive with bank and credit card statements. They usually have very little information on them but rather, are intended to attract the reader's attention to a specific issue or event. If you distribute paychecks in envelopes the leaflets can be stuffed into the envelope with the paycheck. If you use presealed paychecks, you can distribute the flyers by hand with the paychecks or create special envelopes with motivational messages on them about the issue you are trying to promote.
- *Posters* can be produced in a variety of sizes. They need not be huge, but they must stand out from other notices you may post on bulletin boards and other appropriate locations. The most effective posters are colorful, graphically interesting and have very few words.
- *Mastheads* or stationery with an identifiable theme are useful for attracting attention to the topic when you need to send periodic updates and answer questions about a particular issue. Company's have found mastheads so useful that they have become almost a standard tool in many communication programs.
- *Buttons* with slogans are popular when organizations are seeking to encourage participation in special events such as stop smoking campaigns, United Way contribution campaigns, or enrollment in managed health care programs. The buttons are usually distributed after an employee has attended a special meeting or signed up to participate in a specific event.
- *Pens* with communication themes or slogans have the benefit of being perceived as useful items and are likely to be kept rather than discarded. The idea is that the

recipients will have a constant, albeit, subliminal reminder of the issue you are communicating.

- *Telephone hot lines* help organizations handle batteries of employee questions more efficiently. Typically a specific phone number is designated and employees are encouraged to call the number if they have questions or need help. The phone number may be answered by an individual whose only job is to respond to the questions and calls for help or employees may encounter a recording that gives them basic information and directs them where to go for additional information. Computer technology has helped increase the interest in telephone hot lines because it is now possible for an employee to dial the number, follow prerecorded instructions, and receive personalized information, such as the balance in their 401(k) plan or how many vacation days they have used.

- *Health fairs* have been useful to organizations trying to improve employee awareness and responsibility for better health care practices. They are organized in the same manner as any other fair, with booths and attractions focusing on health. Often local doctors and other health care providers are invited to participate and to provide free services, such as blood pressure and other testing, that can be done outside the doctor's office or a hospital environment. Health care associations like the American Cancer Society, American Heart Association, and local hospitals participate, providing health care education and consumer awareness service. The fairs are usually held from one to three days to give employees an opportunity to attend and bring their families. Many organizations conduct health fairs in conjunction with annual health care benefit enrollment periods.

- *Note pads*, like pens and other stationery items are inexpensive ways to give employees a useful item that will reinforce a communication theme or message for a prolonged period after the focused communication activity is over.

- *Balloons* and other traditional promotional gimmicks used by consumer advertisers can add interest and variety to a communication campaign.

- *Keychains* can be considered promotional gimmicks, but are useful and have the same subtle impact as pens and stationery items.

- *Cafeteria place mats, table tents, and napkins* can reinforce a communication message and are especially useful as reminders about employee meetings and other deadlines which they must meet.

- *Bumper stickers*, like balloons, are gimmicky but have been used successfully to promote a company-wide campaign focusing on issues like quality and productivity improvement and meeting increased sales targets.

- *Coupons* are accepted as a bartering tool or exchange alternative for money. Companies can use them in the same way to encourage employees to trade in their coupon for something in return, such as a benefit statement, a financial planner workbook, or a free visit to the local health gym.

- *Coffee cups* are another popular way of sending a message that has longevity.

- *Notebooks* and binders, customized with a communication or campaign theme, are particularly useful for preparing inexpensive, but nicely packaged administrative support material for managers and supervisors.

- *Paper weights, letter openers, post-it notes* and myriad other practical items can be used as collateral material to reinforce your communication message.

- *Computer software* is becoming a very effective way to stimulate interest and communicate to employees because the information can be personalized.

Figure 9.1   RECRUITING PIECE

Figure 9.2   EMPLOYMENT THANK YOU CARD

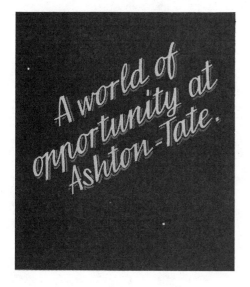

Figure 9.1 is the outside cover of a recruiting piece developed by Ashton Tate. It opens to a 16"x18" poster-like piece that promotes the company, career opportunities and benefits. This is a particularly appealing example of a collateral piece that appeals to the college market.

Figure 9.2 is sent to applicants and is cleverly designed to look like a custom thank you card. *Courtesy of Ashton-Tate.*

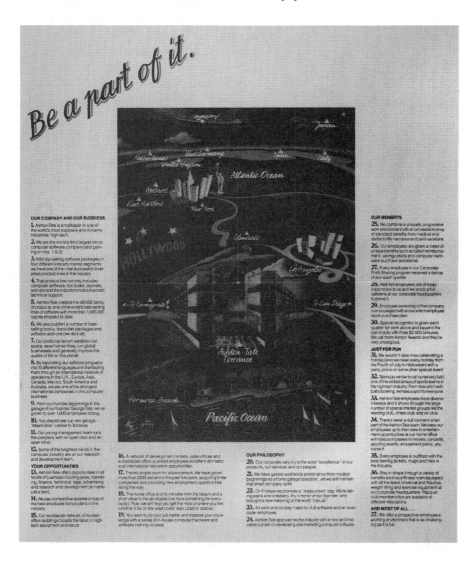

Figure 9.3. INFORMED CHOICE BUTTON is a button distributed to General Motors employees and retirees who attended health care awareness meetings which introduced the new Informed Choice, Health Care Plans. *Courtesy of General Motors*

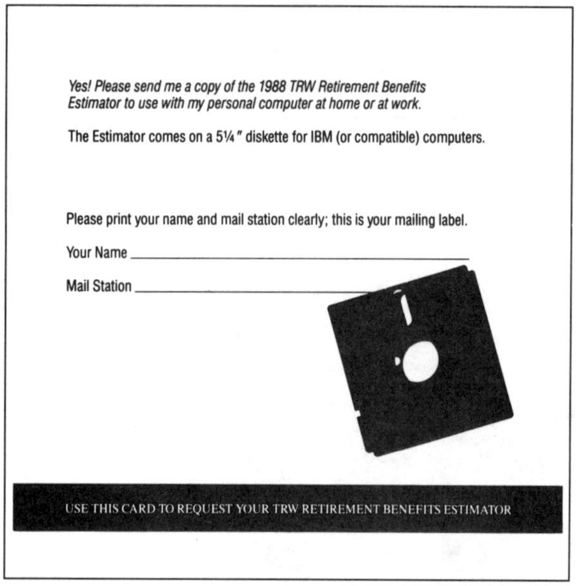

Yes! Please send me a copy of the 1988 TRW Retirement Benefits Estimator to use with my personal computer at home or at work.

The Estimator comes on a 5¼" diskette for IBM (or compatible) computers.

Please print your name and mail station clearly; this is your mailing label.

Your Name _____

Mail Station _____

USE THIS CARD TO REQUEST YOUR TRW RETIREMENT BENEFITS ESTIMATOR

Figure 9.4 ANNUAL BENEFITS STATEMENT COUPON is a coupon employees received with their annual benefit statement promoting a retirement plan benefit estimator software program. It was designed so their name and mail station address would show through the window of the floppy disk envelope.

Figure 9.5 DISK MAILING ENVELOPE used when the disk was sent to the employee. *Courtesy of TRW Space & Defense.*

Benefits

The 1988 TRW Retirement Benefits Estimator

- *Calendars* that highlight important company events, enrollment deadlines, and employee meetings are usually welcome communication tools. Some organizations publish annual calendars but the most common practice is to publish them month by month so unexpected or unplanned events can be highlighted.

WHEN TO USE COLLATERAL MATERIALS

The biggest danger in using collateral materials is overkill; it is possible to get overly enamored with them. Like all other communication program elements, the use of collateral materials should be carefully planned. Otherwise your audience will perceive them as gimmicks. Some of the most common and appropriate times to use collateral materials are

- pre-announcements for special enrollments
- behavior incentives
- reinforcing organizational messages
- teasers to announce coming changes
- safety programs
- performance or productivity programs
- product or service development or improvement programs
- acquisitions, mergers, or divestitures
- health care consumer utilization practices

TIPS FOR PLANNING A PROGRAM WITH COLLATERAL MATERIALS

Collateral materials are only components of your total communication strategy, but they can enhance the effectiveness of a specific communication objective. Conventional collateral materials such as bulletin mastheads can be used as collateral for an ongoing communication effort such as benefit update bulletins. Alternatively, they may be designed for a specific one-time campaign such as keeping employees informed about a pending acquisition. Less conventional tools, like balloons or coffee cups, are usually reserved for one-time campaigns. However, some companies have discovered a way to convert a one-time idea into an ongoing communication strategy.

EXAMPLE: How a Professional Services Firm Used Umbrellas for Several One-Time Campaigns

---

As part of the strategy to communicate its first major merger, a professional services organization decided to give employees umbrellas imprinted with the combined company names on the day the merger was final. A little tag was attached to each umbrella explaining that the umbrellas were symbolic of the broader coverage the new firm could offer its clients and the additional resources the combined companies could offer employees. As a result of the positive response to the first umbrella campaign, the company decided to make it a permanent part of their acquisition and merger communication strategy. Some employees now have four umbrellas, all identical except for the company name which changed for each campaign.

Developing A Collateral Material Strategy For Your Communication Plan

When you are considering collateral materials for a specific communication effort, it is important to be certain they will add value to your overall objectives. If they are used indiscriminately, they can distract from your primary message and could cause embarrassment by becoming the target of employee ridicule.

Figure 9.6
COLLATERAL PLANNING WORKSHEET

PROJECT DESCRIPTION	
COMMUNICATION OBJECTIVES	
STRATEGY	
PROCESS	
COLLATERAL MATERIALS	
HOW MATERIALS ARE TO BE USED	

Figure 9.7
COLLATERAL PLANNING WORKSHEET

PROJECT DESCRIPTION	
Pre-Announcements for Special Enrollment	
COMMUNICATION OBJECTIVES	Encourage enrollment in deferred compensation plan
STRATEGY	Promote special enrollment campaign Build interest in employee meetings
PROCESS	Use series of collateral materials to attract attention and build interest in attending enrollment meetings
COLLATERAL MATERIALS	Posters (series of three) Payroll stuffers (series of two) Meeting schedule reminder for desks Enrollment meeting attendance buttons
HOW MATERIALS ARE TO BE USED	*POSTERS* - A different poster was displayed each week for three weeks prior to scheduled employee meetings. The first poster was simply a colorful campaign theme graphic with the words, Take the Bite Out of Taxes. Each subsequent poster had a little more information, focusing attention on the upcoming enrollment meetings. *PAYROLL STUFFERS* - Simple little flyers, using the campaign graphics and drawing attention to the impact of the new plan on employees' paychecks were distributed with paychecks for the two pay periods immediately preceding the enrollment meetings. *MEETING SCHEDULE REMINDER FOR DESKS* - A campaign theme design cut-out and assemble desktop meeting reminder was published in the employee newsletter. *ENROLLMENT MEETING ATTENDANCE BUTTONS* - A campaign theme I Enrolled...Have *you*? button was distributed to each employee who attended an enrollment meeting.

Figure 9.8
COLLATERAL PLANNING WORKSHEET

PROJECT DESCRIPTION Behavior Incentives	
COMMUNICATION OBJECTIVES	Quality Control Improvement
STRATEGY	Reward employees for improved quality control
PROCESS	Use series of collateral materials to promote individual or group contributions to quality improvement
COLLATERAL MATERIALS	Posters (monthly) Recognition pins Employee publication Cash award
HOW MATERIALS ARE TO BE USED	*POSTERS* - A generic campaign theme poster was designed to publicize the quality control contribution of an individual or group. *RECOGNITION PINS* - Recognition pins, similar to those used for length-of-service achievements, were designed and awarded to individuals who were recognized as monthly quality control contributors. *EMPLOYEE PUBLICATION* - A quality control feature column was established to publicize the individual or group that received recognition for their quality control contributions. *CASH AWARD PROGRAM* - An annual cash award program was developed to recognize the individual or group that made the most significant contribution to the organization's financial results through their quality control efforts.

One way to avoid this trap is to use a worksheet like the one in Figure 9.6. It is designed to help you integrate your collateral material ideas into your communication plan. The process is a mini version of developing a total communication strategy.

TWO PRACTICAL EXAMPLES FOR USING COLLATERAL MATERIAL

Following are two examples of how a variety of collateral materials can be used to reinforce your communication objectives.

HOW TO DEVELOP BUDGETS

For the most part, developing budgets for collateral communication materials is no different than the process you would use for any specific communication tool. The keys to successful budgeting are:

- careful planning
- detailed specifications
- competitive bidding
- ongoing project management

Developing Specifications

Developing specifications for your collateral materials depends on the medium you are using. For conventional printed, audio-visual, or computer-based tools, the process is identical to that described in other chapters. For unconventional tools such as award pins, cash compensation, or balloons, you will have to adjust your budgeting methodology to the specific circumstance. The easiest way to develop budgets for these kinds of materials is to seek advice from suppliers and in-house resources who have the professional expertise to guide you. For example, if you want to use a cash award, internal or external incentive compensation professionals should be consulted. If you would like to use balloons, it will be well worth your time to talk with marketing specialists and suppliers who can explain the balloon production process and tell you what variables will affect pricing decisions. Figure 9.9 is a sample specification and budget planning worksheet for a communication plan to introduce a team compensation incentive plan.

Finding Suppliers

Finding suppliers for non-traditional collateral materials can seem overwhelming at first. However, if you take a moment to reflect, you will probably find resources within your organization who can help you locate the most appropriate suppliers. If you want to use some kind of award pin, for example, the person responsible for service awards might be a good resource to start with. If you are looking for pens that you can have customized for your communication campaign, you might talk to your office supply purchaser. You can also use the Yellow Pages, your advertising and marketing professionals, or your communication consultants for guidance and referrals.

Cost Cutting Tips

The value of seeking internal advice is that your organization may have already established purchasing power that will help you get what you need at a lower cost than if you try to do it yourself.

Figure 9.9
SPECIFICATION AND BUDGET PLANNING WORKSHEET

PROJECT DESCRIPTION

Communication tools to introduce Team Compensation Plan

QUANTITY	DESCRIPTION	COST
50	*POSTERS* Design, writing, typesetting, printing 8-1/2 x 11" , 2 colors/1 side	$ 135.00
1,000	*HIGHLIGHT BROCHURES WITH* *FOLD-OUT SCORECARD* Design, writing, typesetting, printing 8 pages + Cover 5-1/2 x 8-1/2" finished size 2 colors/2 sides throughout	10,000.00
2,500	*CUBES OF NOTEPAPER FOR DESKS* Design, typesetting, printing 3" sheet paper cubes with target chart	3,000.00
50	*MEETING LEADER GUIDES* Design, write, and produce 1" ring binders with slip sheet covers in 2 colors 36 pages, desk top published	500.00

HOW TO MEASURE THE SUCCESS OF COLLATERAL MATERIALS

Measuring the individual success of collateral materials is difficult because they are ancillary tools. It is probable that you cannot define a cost/benefit ratio for specific collateral materials unless you are willing to do a thorough market-test analysis. The hard and soft dollar costs connected with such an analysis probably cannot be justified. Therefore, you will find it easier to include the cost of collateral materials in a total communication budget.

CHAPTER 10

EDUCATION AND TRAINING

Worker education, training, and retraining is a high priority with organizations today. Yet a recent survey indicated that only 48% of the employees surveyed believed that their companies' efforts were sufficient to help them meet the demands of their job, much less the decision-making responsibilities companies are shifting back to employees.

THE DIFFERENCE BETWEEN EDUCATION AND TRAINING

Many organizations have formal or quasi-formal education and training programs designed to focus on issues connected with their primary business. In the context of this discussion, education is defined as communication or awareness-building challenges as opposed to academic educational assistance programs. As organizations decide that they must transfer decision-making responsibilities back to employees in areas such as career development, total compensation, and future financial security, they recognize that their success will depend on how well they educate employees about their options.

Usually, organizations do not consider education and training as an integral or even necessary component of their human resource *communication* tasks. This is unfortunate because most communication activities require human support for maximum effectiveness. The human support responsibilities, formal or informal, usually reside with supervisors, managers, and human resource staffs. Preparing these people to proactively support communication activities accomplishes two tasks: 1) It helps facilitate the education and training task at hand, and 2) it enables you to maximize these tasks and communication opportunities.

KEYS TO MAXIMIZING COMMUNICATION, EDUCATION, AND TRAINING OPPORTUNITIES

To the extent that your human communication support system is not compatible with your education and training objectives, you run the risk of employees receiving mixed messages.

EXAMPLE: How One Company Missed a Training/Education/Communication Opportunity

A small manufacturing organization decided to make dramatic changes in their basic compensation and performance evaluation system. However, because of budget constraints, they decided to simply circulate a policy and administration guide to supervisors rather than conduct formal employee education and supervisor training meetings. The result was disastrous. The employees didn't hear about the new system until supervisors used it as an excuse to justify their performance review. The policy guide did not give supervisors sufficient information to enable them to deal with employee concerns and questions. So the supervisors interpreted the new policies based on their limited knowledge and reinforced employee concerns and negative reactions to the new policies. Supervisors felt inadequately prepared to explain the new policies and exhibited resentment rather than support for enforcing the new guidelines.

The company clearly lost a significant opportunity to effectively use the most powerful communication tools at their disposal, education and training, to implement the new plan successfully.

Communication Vs. Education And Training

Communication, education, and training should not be separated into distinct functions. They are interdependent. Usually, however, training professionals lack certain skills that communication professionals have and vice versa. Training professionals, for example, are usually not as technically skilled at making the most of different communication media and fussing with awareness-building educational issues, while communication professionals are frequently inexperienced in developing and using effective training models and interpersonal techniques. The obvious solution is to integrate them.

Throughout this book, you will find awareness-building educational examples because they are an integral part of human resource communication activities. Therefore, this chapter will focus on training programs, how to structure and develop them, budgeting issues, and how to measure their effectiveness.

Sharing Resources And Budgets

It is common for each human resource function (e.g. compensation, benefits, employment, and recruiting) to have primary responsibility for communicating issues specific to their specialty. This tends to be true because these people are the content specialists and are intimately familiar with potential legal and employee-relations problems that can arise from inaccurate or inappropriate communication. However, as the lines separating these functions get fuzzier, it is more important for the content specialists to draw on the skills and knowledge of their colleagues and other professionals inside and outside the organization. The most obvious practical advantage is that they can share resources and budgets which translate into increased productivity and reduced expenses. This evolutionary process will affect training goals and needs as well.

Why You Can Expect More Requests For Training Support

There are basically three types of training challenges facing organizations today.

- *practical skills training* such as how to perform a specific manufacturing, repair, or sales task or how to use a computer, or improve writing or interpersonal skills
- *administrative procedural training* such as how to document, process, and communicate policies and procedures, and how to comply with government regulations
- *management training* to prepare people for additional supervisory and team building responsibilities

The type and intensity of training required depends on the nature of your current and future business objectives. For example, if you plan to venture into the exploding Pacific Rim business environment, teaching employees the cultural and practical nuances of doing business with Japan is mandatory and not something that can be learned in a one- or two-day training session. Conversely, training people to complete government-required compliance documents often can be done in less than half a day.

Small organizations and large organizations that are downsizing and decentralizing must rely on many people to make operating and resource allocation decisions. More often than not, employees find that they have these expanded responsibilities and no experience or training to help them do the job. If an organization expects its employees to successfully take on additional responsibilities, it must be prepared to provide adequate training.

There is an ever-increasing need for retraining because some skills are becoming less important and others more important in today's world. For example, shorthand is much less important for secretaries and clerical staff than the ability to use wordprocessors and other PC software, and gaining computer literacy is not limited to clerks, typists, secretaries, and programmers. More and more executives are seeing that they need and want to personally access the power of computers to support their information and decision-making needs.

Fifteen Training Program Ideas You May Have to Develop

The above examples emphasize why human resource professionals can expect more and more requests for help in developing and managing their organization's training needs. Following are only a few types of training programs that you may be faced with developing.

- Executive incentive programs
- New location start-ups
- Downsizing
- Benefit plan enrollment and administration
- Salary administration programs
- Performance review systems
- Equal opportunity compliance
- Safety programs design and administration
- Employee communication techniques
- Team building
- Electronic information processing
- Interpersonal skills development
- Compensation and benefit compliance and administration
- Succession development and planning
- Basic, intermediate, and advanced computer application skills

PREPARING TO MEET NEW TRAINING CHALLENGES

Meeting your current and future training challenges requires that you become familiar with internal and external resources, know how to help develop course outlines, curricula, and materials, and can manage all these functions within some budget constraints.

Internal Training Facilities: Using Untapped Skills And Resources

If you have professional training resources within your organization, they can be extremely valuable resources. In some cases, they may be able to assume responsibility for developing training programs for you. However, like other internal resources, they are probably not staffed to provide unlimited support and will usually be required to focus on the organization's business-related training requirements for such functions as sales, manufacturing or maintenance. They are usually eager to offer advice and counsel. Also ask them for any tips and models they may have to help you develop training tools appropriate to your needs. This will save you from having to start from scratch and learn through trial and error.

Often internal training professionals may have developed a training course for another purpose that you can modify for your specific requirements. A supervisor training program might include modules on leadership, time management, financial management, business planning, recruiting, and compensation and benefits policies. If, for example, you needed to communicate a new compensation and performance management program, you might be able to modify the leadership and compensation modules of the supervisor training program to provide specialized training.

External Training Resources: Are Boilerplate Tools Really Less Expensive?

Thousands of prepackaged training tools and programs are available in the marketplace. They cover virtually any subject you can imagine and use every kind of media imaginable, from printed workbooks to audio-visuals to computer software. The appeal of prepackaged training tools is that they are perceived to provide everything you need for a very small price. There are two significant issues, however, that will determine whether a prepackaged or boilerplate training tool is less expensive than custom programs. These are: 1. Quality, and 2. Applicability.

Tips For Judging The Quality Of Prepackaged Training Tools

It is time-consuming and often difficult to evaluate the quality of a prepackaged training tool. Quality is so subjective that about the only way to get a feel for it is to interview previous users to see whether they would use it again and whether it helped them achieve the desired results. Even then, unless you can establish that the needs, audience, and objectives are very close to yours, you will not be certain the tool will be right for you.

Determining The Applicability Of A Boilerplate Package To Your Needs

How you plan to use the training tool can impact its usefulness, even if it has credibility with respect to quality. For example, an organization decided to purchase an audio-visual and companion workbook that was promoted as a wellness educational tool. The quality of the tool was excellent. The question then became how they intended to use it. More importantly, why did they want to promote wellness? The real reason was to control the utilization and cost of their health care benefit program.

Their idea was that showing the audio-visual to employees and giving them each a workbook, constituted a wellness program that would teach employees to take better care of themselves, and would result in lower medical expenses. A missing key was how the organization would be able to measure the results of their investment. The problem was that there was no direct connection between their real objective and the wellness training tool. The audiovisual and workbook alone would not qualify as a training program. They were only generic tools that, at best, could be used within the framework of a health care cost management training program.

A training program is not a training program unless you have some method of measuring results. This means that even if you find a prepackaged program that will meet your needs, you will still have to administer it so that you can track results.

Traditional Resources For Training Materials

If you do not have internal resources to develop or administer training programs, you can find external resources that can do it for you. The two most traditional external resources are training and education producers and training consultants. The distinction between these two resources is that the producers are less likely to provide ongoing support. The main thrust of their business is to develop a turnkey program and leave you to deal with maintenance and administration. Conversely, consultants are less likely to provide high quality support tools such as audiovisuals and printed materials. Their orientation focuses more on problem-solving techniques.

Non-Traditional Resources Of Training Packages

Other external resources have developed the ability to provide specialized training program assistance. Examples include compensation, benefit, communication, human resource consultants, health care providers, insurance companies, financial institutions, third party administrators, trade associations, and employer coalitions. In most cases, the training tools they develop are directly related to their products and services.

Figure 10.1   TRAINING COURSE VENDORS

There are myriad training specialists and suppliers. Finding those who can provide the specific services you need can be a challenging task. A handy guide that can make the job easier is the Marketplace Directory published by TRAINING, The Magazine of Human Resources Development. It is a comprehensive training resource directory which lists nearly 2,000 training program suppliers. It is divided into seven major sections which will help you find a variety of resources for almost any training need you can imagine.

- Training Equipment and Supplies - Identifies suppliers of training hardware, presentation equipment, media packaging and other training-related products.

- Training Programs and Services - Lists training program suppliers by subject matter and identifies whether they provide off-the-shelf or custom- designed programs.

- Supplier Catalog Pages - Features advertising catalog-type pages providing additional details about suppliers' products and services.

- Production Facilities and Services - Provides names and addresses of production support companies. Organized by state.

- Training Sites - Includes state-by-state listings of off-site training facilities with a summary of key amenities such as number of meeting rooms and capacity, number of guest rooms, audiovisual capabilities, and recreation facilities.

- Training and Human Resource Development Associations - Lists national training and human resources development organizations.

In addition, a Company Directory section has an alphabetical listing of the suppliers and training specialists found in the other sections of the directory. This guide is the equivalent of a trainer's yellow pages.

Figure 10.2   TRAINING PROGRAM EVALUATION WORKSHEET

	PROGRAM A	PROGRAM B	PROGRAM C
PRICE			
TYPE OF PROGRAM			
NUMBER OF MODULES			
COURSE LENGTH			

COURSE MATERIALS
    Workbooks
    AVs
    Pre-reading
    Other
    Other
    Other
COURSE LEADERS			

OTHER			

VENDOR
    Name
    Address
    City, State, Zip
    Phone
    Contact			

Pages 252 and 253 list external training program resources (Figure 10.1) and a worksheet (Figure 10.2) that can help you evaluate the types of programs you are considering.

HOW TO DEVELOP BUDGETS

Regardless of how simple or sophisticated your training requirements may be, it is wise to develop budgets. The budgeting process is similar to that of any other communication tool or program. You must start with objectives, specific guidelines, and insist on detailed quotes. If you have a formal, internal, training function, they can help you. By discussing your needs and objectives with them, you may discover that they are working on programs upon which you can piggyback. For example, parts of a financial management training program might be modified for a human resource department budget training program.

Developing Specific Guidelines For A Training Program

The more detailed your training guidelines, the more likely you will be to develop a meaningful budget and control costs. The first place to begin is to develop a course profile. The profile should include:

- *Purpose or objective statement.* The general purpose of any training program is to help the participants improve their knowledge base or skill level with respect to a specific issue or task. In addition, your objective statement should define specific results you expect to achieve such as *Accurately complete benefit forms for the Internal Revenue Service* or *Provide participants with basic tools to implement new team building techniques.*
- *Target audience definition.* Your objective statement will help you define your target audience. In some cases, the audience may be easily identified. If the course objective is to teach participants a specific task, only those who are expected to perform the task (e.g. payroll processing) would need the training. On the other hand, if your objective is to acquaint people with staff resources such as payroll, compensation, benefits, and legal and medical departments, your primary audience might be operations supervisors and managers. Your training program would likely focus on what each department does and how the supervisors and managers should interface with them. You could change the emphasis of the course slightly for all employees and focus on what each department does and how their supervisor uses the resources to give employees proper counsel and guidance. It could also be modified and included as part of a new hire orientation program.
- *Program format.* The success of your training program depends on being able to see positive results from your efforts. There is no one right format for training programs because different topics and expected results require different training techniques. The most common program formats include classroom, individual study, and project or task force assignments. The elapsed time of the program could be two hours or two months. Organizations frequently make the mistake of using a classroom environment and try to do too much in too little time. If the topic is complex, it is best to break it into several segments using different program and instructional formats for each segment.
- *Instructional method.* Regardless of the topic or training objective, successful programs most often use a five-step approach to providing the instruction: explanation, demonstration, practice, critique and feedback, and developing action plans. Lectures without interactive participation are almost guaranteed to fail.

- *Curriculum and course materials*. The curriculum is simply an outline of order and methods to be used to conduct the course. Regardless of the length and complexity of the course, developing a curriculum outline will help keep the delivery organized and easier for the course leader and students to follow. Course materials are limited only by your imagination. Some form of every medium discussed in this book would be considered potential course materials. The most traditional tools are: workbooks, audio-visuals, and reading materials. The more creative you are with respect to providing course materials, the more interesting the course will be.

Figures 10.3 and 10.4 are sample course outlines. Figure 10.5 is a sample case study exercise used for the utilization review training program outlined in Figure 10.4.

EXAMPLE: How One Firm Used Unconventional Course Materials to Drive Home a Message

---

- A benefit consulting firm thought it would be useful for their actuaries and group insurance consultants to understand how slide/tape audiovisuals were produced because they were always complaining that the slide shows their clients needed took too long and cost too much money. The course leaders were communication professionals. They followed the five-step instruction approach and provided a small workbook. However, most of the full day course was devoted to a hands-on exercise. When participants arrived, they found the classroom filled with all kinds of strange equipment: six slide projectors, six tape players, six light boxes, and stacks and stacks of slides.
- After a discussion of audiovisual basics, the participants were divided into teams and told to use the slides and other equipment to produce an audiovisual. In addition to learning that audiovisual production is more difficult than home movies, the participants learned some team building techniques and came away with new approaches to problem-solving and a new sense of their latent creative abilities.
- *Course leaders*. Choosing the right course leader is not always easy. He or she must be knowledgable enough about the topic to be credible. Course leaders must also have strong leadership skills and be able to successfully encourage student participation. In addition, they have to be monitors, timekeepers, housekeepers, supply officers, and problem solvers. If your obvious course leader is strong on content but short on interpersonal or leadership skills, you should send him or her to a leadership training course or consider a different or co-course leader who can bring those critical skills to the program.

Once you have profiled the training program objectives, you can fill in the detail that will help you define the costs. There are 5 primary cost areas to consider when you are creating program guidelines.

- Student costs
- Instructor costs
- Facilities costs
- Administrative costs
- Instructional development costs

The cost estimate worksheet in Figure 10.6 highlights some of the variables that can impact the total cost of your training program.

Figure 10.3   SAMPLE COURSE OUTLINE: DEVELOPING COMMUNICATION SKILLS

PURPOSE

Develop interpersonal communication skills.

- Define communication
- Describe communication process and channels
- Examine barriers to effective communication
- Assess listening skills and habits
- Identify techniques to improve listening skills

TARGET AUDIENCE

First line supervisors who have not attended a basic program in interpersonal communication. Maximum 15 participants per session.

FORMAT

This program requires approximately 12 hours of classroom time. It can be given in two consecutive days or in three 1/2-day sessions.

INSTRUCTIONAL METHODS

Explanation is approximately 40% of the session while application practice is approximately 60%. The instructional format is

- Explanation - Course Leader
- Demonstration - Course Leader and participants
- Practice - participant teams of 3 to 5
- Critique and feedback - teams
- Application (recommendations and action plans) - Course Leader and participants

CURRICULUM

Section 1

- Communication - role and definition
- Assessment (team)
- Communication process, chain, channels, modes
- Application: communication exercises

Section 2

- Barriers
- Interpersonal communication factors
- Listening guidelines
- Application: listening tests

Figure 10.3 (*con't*)   SAMPLE COURSE OUTLINE: DEVELOPING COMMUNICATION SKILLS

Section 3

- Ten keys to effective listening
- Assessment (team)
- Application: recommendations and action plans

COSTS

Use the following guidelines for budgeting.

- Course materials - $100 per participant
- Course leader travel and expenses - Est. $900
- Meeting facilities, food and equipment rental fees

Figure 10.4   SAMPLE COURSE: HEALTH CARE UTILIZATION REVIEW PROGRAM

SAMPLE COURSE OUTLINE: HELPING EMPLOYEES UNDERSTAND UTILIZATION REVIEW

TOPIC

Health Care Utilization Review for Benefit Representatives and First Line Supervisors

INTRODUCTION

Reasons for Utilization Review

- Change in health care delivery system
- Technology
- Rising health care costs
- Need to monitor costs and enforce medical necessity to maintain current benefit levels

Utilization Review Components

- Pre-admission
- Concurrent
- Retrospective

CASE STUDIES

Evaluate Employee Perceptions. Use three UR case studies to show how to cope with problems.

SPEAKER/AUDIO-VISUAL

Utilization Review Organization Representative

- How and Why UR Process Works
- Common Communication Problems
  - UR Organization and Physicians
  - UR Organization and Employee
  - Physician and Employee

BREAK

ROLE PLAYING

Refer to Case Studies. Use each case study to have work groups show how they would deal with the case. Identify a work group leader. Allow twenty minutes to solve the problem.

Feedback and Critique. Each work group will present their approach.

WRAP-UP AND QUESTIONS AND ANSWERS

Figure 10.5 SAMPLE COURSE: CASE STUDY

SAMPLE UTILIZATION REVIEW CASE STUDY

BACKGROUND

A patient is admitted to the hospital for a hysterectomy. The patient's recovery is slower than might have been expected. She had a higher fever, experienced more than normal postoperative nausea and vomiting and required IV antibiotics to treat unexpected infection.

After several days, the patient's temperature returns to normal, the infection is gone and she is able to walk without assistance. She is eating well but still feels very tired and complains of continuing aches and pains.

These aches and pains are, in fact, normal for a postoperative hysterectomy patient. But she believes, as would many patients, that this indicates a need for continued hospitalization. Also, she is fearful about going home and having a relapse after her rocky recovery.

CURRENT SITUATION

The utilization review organization looks at the case for continued stay. The reviewer questions the need for continued stay as the patient is walking without assistance, eating well, her temperature is normal and IV's discontinued. The reviewer asks the physician for additional documentation as to why the patient needs to be in the hospital.

THE PROBLEM

The physician states that the patient could be discharged on the following day but that she does not want to be discharged. The utilization review representative and physician jointly agree that the patient should be given a denial letter.

The patient calls the benefit office and states, I'm being thrown out of the hospital. I've worked at this company for 25 years and can't believe I'm being treated this way. There's no one to take care of me when I get home. What are you going to do about this?

ASSIGNMENT

1. How can you intervene to help dissipate the employees' anger?

2. What information will you need from the employee to verify circumstances with the utilization review organization?

3. What should you explain to the employee about how the utilization review program works?

4. What should you explain to the employee about the company medical plan benefits?

5. What should you explain to the employee about the company philosophy regarding health care expenditures?

6. What will your action plan be to resolve the problem and how will you explain this to the employee?

Figure 10.6   TRAINING BUDGET WORKSHEET

COST AREA	AMOUNT
STUDENTS	
Salary	
Housing/Meals	
Travel	
TOTAL STUDENT COST	$
INSTRUCTORS	
Salary	
Housing/Meals	
Travel	
TOTAL INST. COST	$
FACILITIES	
Rent/Overhead	
Equipment	
Special Services	
Supplies	
TOTAL FACILITY COST	$
ADMINISTRATIVE	
Management Line	
Clerical Line	
Staff Management	
Staff Clerical	
Supplies	
TOTAL ADMIN COST	$
TRAINING COURSE	
Project Leader	
Course Design	
Content Review	
Production Costs	
Materials Costs	
Evaluation Cost	
TOTAL COURSE COST	$
TOTAL TRAINING BUDGET	$

HOW TO MEASURE SUCCESS

The two most effective ways to measure the success of your training programs are to use participant evaluation forms for immediate feedback and to monitor the things you expect to change within your organization as a result of the training program. The evaluation forms will alert you to whether or not you can expect to see productive results. If the participants do not evaluate the course favorably, you will see no change in productivity or behavior patterns and must look for ways to improve the course or replace it with one that is more relevant to the needs of the participants. If the course review is favorable, you can reasonably expect to see positive results. If you do not, you should follow up with participants to locate the source of the problem. Figure 10.7 is a sample evaluation form that you can customize for your purposes.

Figure 10.7
SAMPLE COURSE EVALUATION FORM

Please help us improve this course. Complete this form and leave it with the Course Leader before you leave. You will receive a summary of all evaluations within the next two weeks. Thank you for your participation.

SUBJECT CONTENT

	TOO MUCH	BALANCE	NOT ENOUGH
Theoretical			
Practical			

SUBJECT LEVEL

	TOO EASY	JUST RIGHT	TOO DIFFICULT

PRESENTATION

	VERY EFFECTIVE	SOMEWHAT EFFECTIVE	NOT EFFECTIVE
Organization			
Participation			
Emphasis of Key Points			
Visual Aids (if used)			
Course Material			

List 2 or 3 things you liked *best* about the course.

List 2 or 3 things you liked *least* about the course.

Please indicate your overall reaction to the course by circling the number in the appropriate box on the scale below.

EXCELLENT	GOOD	FAIR	POOR

Your suggestions for improving the course would be appreciated.

CHAPTER 11

HOW TO HANDLE COMMUNICATION AT MULTIPLE LOCATIONS

The moment you find you must develop a communication program for more than one location, you know your communication task has become more complex. Still, you have probably dealt with multi-location challenges in many other day-to-day activities and are up to the task. Frequently, organizations assume that they can disregard any additional challenges brought on by multi-locations as they produce their communication tools. Nothing could be further from the truth. The more locations you are dealing with the more complex your communication challenge becomes. Operating styles, cultural biases and perceptions, employee demographics, and administrative variables will be different in virtually every location. The communication approach that works in one location very likely will not be as successful in another location. Few organizations are equipped to deal effectively with all the challenges connected with communicating in multiple locations. However, stress and risk factors connected with the communication challenges can be kept in check. The first step is to recognize the potential pitfalls and plan ahead.

CHECKLIST: Potential Pitfalls of Multi-Location Communication Plans

- *Demographic Differences.* If your communication approach is designed to the demographic audience of only one location, it probably only will be effective in that location.
- *Cultural Differences.* The cultural mix of your audience will vary significantly by location. Heritage, local customs, and lifestyle patterns in Southern California bear little resemblance to those in Michigan, for example.
- *Management Styles.* Managers significantly influence employee perceptions and the way things happen in their territory. No two managers approach the same problem or challenge in the same way. The way managers communicate and support communication efforts is usually directly related to their personal success relative to the firm's organizational goals and objectives.
- *Different Businesses.* The nature of the primary business influences demographics, cultures, perceptions, management styles, and administrative processes. The more diversified an organization is with respect to its businesses, the more difficult it is to find common denominators upon which to build a communication program. The challenges of a manufacturing operation are not the same as those facing a service organization.
- *Administrative Feasibility.* Each location will typically develop administrative procedures that are unique to their special circumstances. While each location may conform to organizational reporting and administrative requirements, they may do it differently. Typically, this is a function of budgets, staffing, and equipment requirements.

- *Perception Differences.* Employee perceptions are directly influenced by all of the issues as well as individual experience. Perceptions will vary in relation to the frequency and direct impact of each of these variables.

SOLUTIONS FOR OVERCOMING DIFFERENCES AMONG LOCATIONS

When developing a communication plan that must serve several locations, evaluate the problems you may encounter by location before you decide on the communication technique, tone, style, and media you propose to use. You may have to use different approaches for each location. If it is impractical to customize your program for each location, find the most common denominators that are likely to be successful in spite of the variables. The easiest way to accomplish this is to group the potential pitfalls into two convenient categories: people issues (e.g. demographics, cultural and perception differences) and organizational issues (e.g. management styles, different businesses and administrative feasibility). Local laws may also enter into the equation.

Solutions That Will Work With The People Part Of Your Communication Plan

- *Audience Demographics, Cultural and Perception Differences.* Communication techniques that work well with a young, single, primarily male, upwardly mobile audience living in Southern California will not be as effective with a middle-aged, married, primarily female group, born, raised, and working in LaGrange, Georgia.
- *The optimum solution* is to design communication tools and techniques to appeal to each audience specifically. Most organizations do not have the time or money to devote to this approach.
- *A common denominator solution* is to clearly structure your communication tools into sections that address the interests of each audience. For example, you can use practical examples of how the communication topic affects each audience. Practical examples could include testimonials or dummy stories of real or prototype people who fit the profiles of your various audiences.
- *Using a variety of media* is another way to tackle the problem. The audience in LaGrange is more likely to read and study information in printed media such as newsletters and booklets while the Southern California audience in this example is more likely to respond to audio-visuals and interactive or personalized communication tools. By using all these media, you have a better chance of appealing to very diverse audiences.

EXAMPLE: How One Employer Created One Solution for Two Distinct Audiences

---

A small, but diversified manufacturing and distribution company decided to terminate its defined benefit retirement plan and replace it with a defined contribution savings plan. Their employee population was dispersed among four major locations and almost equally divided between two distinct audiences: age fifty and over, long service males who were looking forward to retirement and income security; and eager young men, between the ages of twenty and thirty-five, who were most interested in career growth and cash accumulation. The only obvious common denominator between the two groups was a tendency toward a conservative lifestyle.

Since it was not practical to produce multiple versions of the communication tools, the organization decided to capitalize on the conservative nature of both audiences and develop and use a variety of media to illustrate how the new plan would benefit each of the audiences. The media selected were

- an announcement letter which accompanied mandatory disclosure documents and invited employees to special information meetings
- an enrollment kit which included a highlight brochure, a personalized, future financial security statement, and an enrollment form
- an audio-visual to be used in employee meetings
- employee meetings

The audio-visual and the highlight brochure were designed around a family story theme in which a representative employee nearing retirement and his spouse explained why the new plan was good for them *and* their son who was an up-and-coming young manager in the company. This theme was credible because it was not unusual for two or three generations of a family to have worked for the company.

The older employees were most interested in projected monthly retirement benefits and the younger employees were more interested in the capital accumulation features of the plan. So it was relatively simple to focus the information on the personalized, future financial security to the interests of each employee.

Solutions That Will Work With The Organizational Part Of Your Program

Just as one communication technique will not be effective for all audiences, your implementation plan may not be equally effective from one location to another.

- *Management Styles, Different Businesses, and Administrative Feasibility.* The organizational differences among various locations can hinder your communication objectives unless you gain support from local managers.
- *The optimum solution* is to structure your communication plan to suit the organizational biases of each location. Whether or not this is practical, depends on the nature of your business. If your main location is a manufacturing plant and your remote locations are small sales or services offices, it would be nearly impossible to satisfy the perceived or real needs of every location. On the other hand, if each location has standardized operating procedures (e.g. a restaurant chain, one-hour photoprocessing plant, a tax preparation service), developing standardized communication tools with some implementation flexibility may be possible.
- *The common denominator solution* is to invite your remote location managers to participate in the communication *planning* process. By inviting their participation, you are likely to get them to take ownership in the plan and you will frequently get good ideas for designing effective communication tools that will suit everyone's needs. While you can get input by using written and phone survey techniques, a more effective way is to convene a planning meeting. Getting the managers together in one room will almost always result in each one offering reasonable compromises that will enable you to develop a plan that will suit each location's needs and *your* objectives.

Dealing With The *I Hate Corporate* Syndrome

In most organizations home office management constantly faces credibility issues from the rank and file employees, particularly if the employees are working at a different location. This is because home office management is remote at best and, at worst, unknown by the majority of the individuals who enable the organization to function. Over time, this sense of alienation develops into the *I Hate Corporate* syndrome. Even small companies with only two or three locations must contend with this problem because it is only natural for the more remote entities to feel that the home office doesn't understand their unique problems. By association, human resource professionals are viewed as an extension of home office management.

The more locations there are within an organization, the more severe the credibility issues. However, it is possible to change this perception.

Presumably, you are in your current position because you have demonstrated professional skills and a global understanding of the organization's goals. Yet, if you forsake or ignore the field location's needs in favor of headquarter responsibilities, you will have increasing difficulty in achieving your total communication objectives. Political, ego, and performance issues provide important clues to understanding your audience in the field. Invest the time and energy to get acquainted with the cultures and biases of each location. Remember, most of their actions and reactions are based in their perceptions of how home office decisions support or detract from their ability to succeed.

How To Really Get Support At Various Locations

The quickest and easiest way to get a sense for the local environment is to talk with the managers, supervisors, human resource representatives and employees regularly. Ask specific questions about how things are done, what works best for them and then solicit advice about how you can give them more or better support. It is important to be very candid, that you may not be able to accommodate everyone's wishes, but will do what you can to take specific issues and needs into account.

This approach will at least get you the opportunity to try. At best you will find yourself with more local support and participation than you expected. Frequently, field locations will offer to do more than you really need from them. Never turn them down. Following is a checklist of tips that can help you build a sense of cooperation and local ownership.

CHECKLIST: Building Support in the Field

- Make frequent phone calls to ask how things are going.
- Visit the location as often as practical (no less than once a year).
- Ask for opinions and advice on the best way to achieve objectives at a specific location.
- Position yourself as a network facilitator.
- Share good solutions one location devises with other locations.
- Informally communicate upcoming programs as soon as possible and solicit advice and opinions about the best way to handle them at the location.
- Ask for volunteer help to review plans, creative concepts, and copy before it is final.
- Invite location representatives to serve on project task forces.
- Sponsor headquarter meetings periodically.
- Try to use advice and input so that the locations recognize their contributions in the final product.
- Promote location contributions to senior management.
- Accept any help a location offers.

Negotiating With Locations

You will never be able to conduct a successful system-wide communication program without local support. The only way to get local support is to recognize that you have to communicate with them frequently. So your communication plan will have to include special communication activities from you to one or more field management levels.

> **EXAMPLE: How One Organization Compromised a System-Wide Communication Opportunity**

A company based in the mid-west decided to implement a system-wide flexible benefit program. Two east coast locations and four west coast locations, in addition to the home office location, would be affected. The home office engaged a consulting firm to help them manage this very complex undertaking. Each location embraced the new plan concept but communicated to the home office that they would need additional support to smoothly integrate the new program into their environments. The home office acknowledged their concerns and promised assistance.

As the project progressed, the locations became increasingly nervous because, in spite of their queries, no response or assistance was forthcoming from the home office or its consultants. In desperation, three of the west coast locations combined resources and engaged a local consulting firm to help them solve their immediate local problems without jeopardizing the system-wide program. When the system-wide program was finally introduced, the remote locations suffered more problems than were necessary because they were not adequately prepared. The three locations that hired their own consultant fared somewhat better than the others, but they were unhappy because they were not included in the system-wide planning and implementation process. Worse, they will offer only token support for future home office communication plans. The following flow chart (Figure 11.1) illustrates why you need to develop several communication plans when you have multiple locations, before you can get to the rank and file employee.

How To Maintain Consistency *And* Flexibility In Multi-Location Communication Projects

Perhaps the biggest challenge in developing and implementing a system-wide communication program is solving this dilemma: How do you keep your message consistent and yet allow for local flexibility?

First, you must recognize that you won't be able to do it unless you have cooperation from the field. Second, you must develop a plan that considers as many potential local variables as possible.

Developing One Plan With 2-200 Variables

The major difference between developing a plan for a single location and multiple locations is the number of variables you have to consider. The easiest way to get a global picture is to develop a spreadsheet or matrix that itemizes the critical issues and the probable impact at each location. (See Figures 11.2 and 11.3) The first items in the matrix should be those things which must be consistent throughout the organization, such as

- policy statements
- project objective statements
- organization/program image
- communication message
- administrative forms and procedures

Acceptable variables might include:

- quantities
- demographic profiles
- media selection
- content details
- administrative capabilities
- distribution procedures

Both lists could be much longer, depending on the complexity of your organization, the communication project objectives, and the resources available at headquarters and each location. This type of matrix will give you a broad indication of your probable challenges. Each of these categories will have multiple

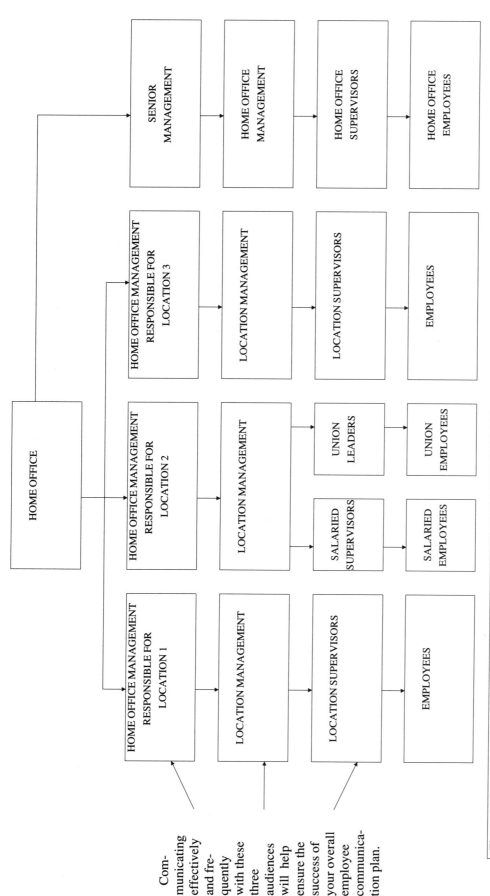

Figure 11.1 FLOW CHART As discussed in Chapters 1 and 2, it is important to recognize that you have several audiences with which to communicate within the general employee population. As this flow chart illustrates, when you are dealing with multiple locations, your audiences multiply rapidly.

COMMUNICATOR'S TIP

It is particularly important to remember that the various audiences at remote locations will have different perceptions and priorities from the audiences in your home office. Avoid developing a communication plan for your home office audiences and trying to export it to the field unless you involve local management in the planning process.

Figure 11.2   MULTIPLE LOCATION ANALYSIS SPREADSHEET

NON-VARIABLE COMMUNICATION ISSUES SYSTEM-WIDE HEALTH CARE	IMPACT ON LOCATIONS		
	LOCATION 1	LOCATION 2	LOCATION 3
COMPANY POLICY OBJECTIVE Contain Health Care Costs	Reduce costs by 1%	Non-lowest cost in market	Reduce costs by 5%
PROJECT OBJECTIVE Encourage participation in managed health care options (HMO/PPO)	Needs local endorsement	No options yet available	Needs local endorsement
ORGANIZATION/PROGRAM IMAGE Provide quality health care at reasonable cost.	Use corporate communication theme	Use corporate communication theme	Use corporate communication theme
COMMUNICATION IMAGE Employees must perceive objectives as reasonable	Reinforce at local level	Reinforce at local level	Reinforce at local level
ADMINISTRATIVE FORMS AND PROCEDURES 1) Implement U.R. program 2) Employees to communicate with doctor about U.R. 3) Local managers to verify enrollment in health care plan	1) Provide contact for local managements 2) Tips for employees 3) Send employees list with enrollments to Corp.	1) Provide contact for local managements 2) Tips for employees 3) N/A – No option, defaults to plan #1	1) Provide contact for local management 2) Tips for employees 3) Send employees list with enrollment to Corp.

Figure 11.2 *(continued)* MULTIPLE LOCATION ANALYSIS SPREADSHEET

VARIABLE COMMUNICATION ISSUES	IMPACT ON LOCATIONS		
System-Wide Health Care	LOCATION 1	LOCATION 2	LOCATION 3
QUANTITIES *Enrollment Kits / AVs / Extra Enrollment Forms*	300 3 100	250 1 100	500 3 100
DEMOGRAPHIC PROFILES			
Age	35	27	40
Sex	F 90%	80% M	50% M / 50% F
Marital Status	Married	50% married ~50% single	50% married
Salary	$18,000	$40,000	$32,000
Length of Service	4 years	2 years	6 years
Education	High School	Professional/Engineer	Some College
MEDIA SELECTION			
Printed Media	Review for 2 options	Generic	Review for 3 options
Audiovisuals	Generic	Generic	Generic
Personalized Tools	Generic		Generic
Interactive Computer Tools	Yes	No	Yes
Meetings	Yes	No	Yes
Other			
CONTENT DETAILS *Training for new H.R. program*	Yes	Yes	Yes
ADMINISTRATIVE CAPABILITIES	Adequate	Adequate	Adequate
DISTRIBUTION PROCEDURES	Mail to Home / Meetings	Distribute Internally	Mail to Home / Meetings

269

Figure 11.3 MULTIPLE LOCATION ANALYSIS SPREADSHEET

NON-VARIABLE COMMUNICATION ISSUES *Pilot Plan*	IMPACT ON LOCATIONS		
	LOCATION 1	LOCATION 2	LOCATION 3
COMPANY POLICY OBJECTIVE *Increase Location Quality, Productivity and Delivery*	Maintain current standard as minimum performance measure	N/A	N/A
PROJECT OBJECTIVE *Introduce Gainsharing Plan*	Set Performance and bonus standards	N/A	N/A
ORGANIZATION/PROGRAM IMAGE *Pilot for Location*	Create Performance Measurement Theme	N/A	N/A
COMMUNICATION IMAGE *Teamwork Pays*	Local plants to determine with Corporate approval	N/A	N/A
ADMINISTRATIVE FORMS AND PROCEDURES *Measurement Formulas / Methods* *Reporting Standards · Employee · Home Office* *Payout Methods*	Plant and Home Office. Home office to provide systems and procedure guides.	N/A	N/A

270

Figure 11.3 (*continued*) MULTIPLE LOCATION ANALYSIS SPREADSHEET

VARIABLE COMMUNICATION ISSUES

	IMPACT ON LOCATIONS		
	LOCATION 1	LOCATION 2	LOCATION 3
QUANTITIES	*Brochures / Note Pads Posters Train Trainers*	N/A	N/A

DEMOGRAPHIC PROFILES
  Age
  Sex
  Marital Status
  Salary
  Length of Service
  Education
	1,000
	25
	50
	
	20 – 40
	60% F / 40% M
	50% Married
	$12 K – $40 K
	2 years
	H.S. – Engineering Degree		

MEDIA SELECTION
  Printed Media
  Audio-visuals
  Personalized Tools
  Interactive Computer Tools
  Meetings
  Other
	Interactive > Dept. Quarter		

CONTENT DETAILS	*Measurement standards & Rewards for team performance*		
ADMINISTRATIVE CAPABILITIES	*Forms for Quarterly Reports to Home Office P.C. Database*		
DISTRIBUTION PROCEDURES	*Internal Mail Monthly Seminars Plant Meetings Quarterly Performance Review*		

subsets. The more you know, the easier it will be to anticipate potential problems and find solutions. Building this overview matrix will be an invaluable communication tool to help you enlist support and ownership from each location.

The easiest way to get local support is to draw employees into the planning process. Show them your communication plan matrix. They will see the need to endorse certain generic or nonvariable issues, even if it makes their jobs a little more difficult. Frequently, they will be willing and able to offer suggestions that will be acceptable compromises to everyone.

On occasion, a certain location may have legitimate special needs that will require extra effort and expense. If they are able to see the overall picture, but still feel a need for additional tools or services, they are often willing to pay for them. A simple example exists where four locations have slide/audio sync equipment for audio-visuals. The fifth location uses videotape. It would not be unreasonable for the fifth location to insist on a videotape format and would probably be willing to pay for the conversion costs if you will agree to do it for them.

HOW TO DEVELOP PILOT PROGRAMS WITH ONE OR TWO LOCATIONS

Pilot programs can be especially valuable in two situations:

- when you want to institute a new communication program but encounter wholesale resistance from the field, and
- when one field location or business wants a special program that you or other locations are resisting.

In the first case, you should not waste your time trying to get consensus for your idea. Find a single location that seems to be responsive to the concept. Focus on the potential benefits to that group alone and try to work out an arrangement that will allow you to try the idea. If the program succeeds, persuading other units or locations to consider using it will be easier. In the second situation, offer your support and resources to help test the program. In most cases, the location will volunteer to do most of the work, but will check with you periodically, share their work and progress with you, and ask your opinion.

If your organization is comprised of different businesses, you are likely to encounter even more call for diverse communication approaches. In most cases, these requests are valid. The communication needs of a manufacturing facility are clearly different than the needs of a computer systems group. Even if you believe the needs in a given situation are similar, you may not be able to overcome cultural egos. The simple solution is to work with one entity to develop a pilot program. Later, it may make sense to tailor the pilot program for another, unrelated business entity.

Figure 11.4 shows how to use your planning matrix to outline a pilot program introducing a productivity and gainsharing plan. If the plan is successful, you can use the spreadsheet to analyze whether or not the same approach will work in location number two or three. Figures 11.5 and 11.6 show how pilot program material can be adapted to more than one location. The Southern California version was developed with the idea that it could be flexible enough to meet the needs of the Arizona location and still maintain the image and message standards the division wanted to project to all employees.

Figure 11.4 MULTIPLE LOCATION ANALYSIS SPREADSHEET

NON-VARIABLE COMMUNICATION ISSUES	IMPACT ON LOCATIONS		
	LOCATION 1	LOCATION 2	LOCATION 3
COMPANY POLICY OBJECTIVE			
PROJECT OBJECTIVE			
ORGANIZATION/PROGRAM IMAGE			
COMMUNICATION IMAGE			
ADMINISTRATIVE FORMS AND PROCEDURES			

Figure 11.4 *(continued)* MULTIPLE LOCATION ANALYSIS SPREADSHEET

VARIABLE COMMUNICATION ISSUES	IMPACT ON LOCATIONS		
	LOCATION 1	LOCATION 2	LOCATION 3
QUANTITIES			
DEMOGRAPHIC PROFILES 　　Age 　　Sex 　　Marital Status 　　Salary 　　Length of Service 　　Education			
MEDIA SELECTION 　　Printed Media 　　Audio-visuals 　　Personalized Tools 　　Interactive Computer Tools 　　Meetings 　　Other			
CONTENT DETAILS			
ADMINISTRATIVE CAPABILITIES			
DISTRIBUTION PROCEDURES			

Figures 11.5 and 11.6 SAMPLE PILOT PROGRAM: ADAPTING PRINTED MATERIALS FOR MORE THAN ONE LOCATION

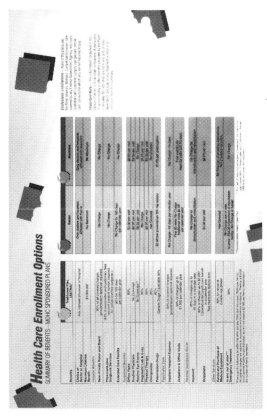

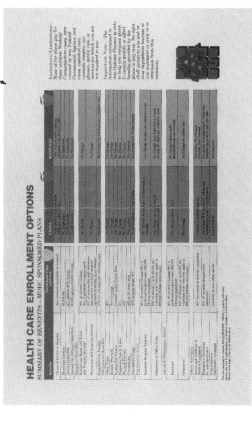

Figure 11.6 The health care options of each location are different. The comparison spreadsheet format, however, easily meets the needs of both locations. The integrity of the communication theme and approach have been maintained while allowing flexibility to meet the specific needs of each location.

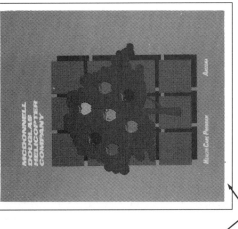

Figure 11.5 This division has two primary locations. The difference between the covers of their health care enrollment kits is the location name. Division theme and image are the same.

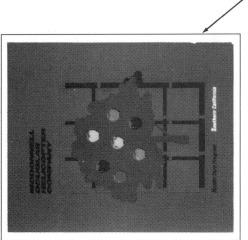

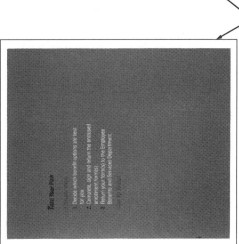

Figure 11.5 (*continued*) Instructions on the inside cover differ because administrative procedures between the two locations are slightly different. *Courtesy of McDonnell Douglas.*

CHAPTER 12

WORKABLE IDEAS FOR HANDLING EXTERNAL COMMUNICATIONS

External communication is generally considered to be any message directed outside the organization. In the broadest sense, this includes mass news media, community relations, trade and professional associations, consumers, and the financial community. Most organizations separate the outside communication function from that of the human resource function. While this may be logical from the organization's perspective, the way information is communicated outside the organization can have dramatic impact on your responsibilities and activities for communicating human resource issues.

```
EXAMPLE: How the Outside World Influences Your Job
```

Employees naturally learn some information about your organization from outside sources. Anytime a news article surfaces outside the organization, you can be sure employees pay attention to it. They also expect the organization to be communicating internally. This example about news of a firm's acquisition illustrates the point.

A consultant visited a client to discuss a communication program to explain the firms's new compensation program. In the lobby, the consultant noticed a great commotion and a large gathering of employees around a bulletin board. An employee had posted a newspaper article explaining the pending sale of the organization to a venture capitalist. This was the first employees heard about the sale and they reacted with great apprehension. In the consultant's meeting, the human resource people were aware of the article but astounded to learn that employees were up in arms about it. Instead of planning the compensation communication program that day, they embroiled the consultant in a discussion about how to deal with the communication crisis at hand. The moral: Even if you are not prepared to respond quickly and candidly to issues surfacing outside the organization, the grapevine begins working immediately. An organization caught unaware can lose credibility, productivity, and valued employees.

In addition to your internal communication responsibilities, you should be prepared to deal with external communication issues. If you are prepared, you can use them to your advantage rather than be placed in a reactionary role like the example just described. In this chapter we will examine the two most common sources of external communication that can affect the human resource function, tips on how to work with them, and external communication ideas that can enhance your internal communication objectives. We will also discuss ideas for planning crisis communication strategies long before you need them.

UNDERSTANDING THE HUMAN RESOURCE ROLE IN EXTERNAL COMMUNICATION

Most employees do not like to see the organization they work for embarrassed in public because the embarrassment extends to them personally. Even good news can cause ill will, as in the example about employees learning of a proposed acquisition from a newspaper. Generally, employees viewed the acquisition as positive, but these people had cause to be angry since they learned the news from an outside source. Imagine their embarrassment if friends or relatives asked about the acquisition before the employee even knew of it.

What does this mean to you as a human resource professional? It means that you must interact with and understand the roles of the specialists in external communication. Usually, they will not focus on coordinating their external roles with internal communication just as you may not think much about external communication unless it adversely affects human resource issues. Most organizations have three types of external communication specialists.

Types Of External Communicators

- **Public Relations.** This function usually deals with the news media and attempts to project a positive image of the organization to the outside world.
- **Advertising.** This function is primarily responsible for promoting a positive image of the organization through paid promotion of its products or services.
- **Marketing.** Marketing often focuses on target sales or expansion objectives and frequently deals with both the news and paid advertising media to promote the company's image.

Of the three, you will interface most often with public relations professionals because their view of the organization is broader than revenue and profits. Their responsibilities are much broader as well and include

- Preparing news releases for the media
- Writing and placing feature articles about all aspects of the company
- Providing the media with background information about the company
- Representing the organization with various publics such as special interest groups, community groups as well as the print and broadcast media
- Training company spokespersons
- Producing promotional material such as brochures
- Staging and conducting press conferences and other public meetings

Two other groups also contribute to the firm's external image.

- **Management.** Managers function as formal ambassadors and sources of information to the outside world.
- **Employees.** The people who work for a company serve as informal ambassadors and sources of information to the outside world.

Establishing better and more frequent communication between yourself and external communication specialists and keeping your ambassadors informed will serve you well when company activities become highly visible externally.

The news media and special interest groups are probably the most formidable external forces that can impact human resource communication. Learning to use them to your advantage can complement your internal communication goals.

WAYS TO USE THE NEWS MEDIA TO YOUR ADVANTAGE

Of all the external communication sources, you will most frequently encounter challenges and opportunities with the news media. Understanding how the media works will enable you to turn challenging situations into opportunities.

What The News Media Wants To Know

The news media is in the business of covering news. News is defined, like any other product or service, as that which generates revenue and profits. The direct consumers dictate what sells and what doesn't sell. Frequently what an organization thinks is news is not considered marketable by the media. From the media's perspective, there are two types of news: hard news and soft news. Hard news usually has some financial, social, moral, or tragedy-related shock value. It also tends to have a sense of immediacy or is presented as a well-researched exposé. Following are sample hard news headlines that directly affect an organization's human resource image. (Figure 12.1)

The media treats hard news and soft news differently. If a firm gets a new business contract, that is soft news (see Figure 12.1) and the media may give it a few lines of exposure for one day. Or, if a soft news story is published, it will most often take the form of a one-time feature article or broadcast. Conversely, hard news like alleged overpricing or an unfriendly takeover bid can get feature exposure, perhaps for days, weeks or months.

This doesn't mean that the media is only interested in bad news. Innovative business, management and human resource programs can warrant feature media exposure as long as they can appeal to the media consumers which means they must have broad readership appeal.

Turning Hard News Angles Into Soft News Opportunities

Different media focus on different consumer markets, such as local, national, trade, professional, or financial and their focus will determine what they cover. For example, what may be feature news material to a local newspaper or business trade publication, may be too narrowly focused to appeal to a national publication. The key to using the media to your advantage is to know what kind of information is considered news, be able to distinguish between hard news and soft news, and identify topics that can be converted into positive publicity for the organization and its human resource function. The following chart summarizes company information that generally interests the media and human resource topic ideas you can use. (Figure 12.2)

Dealing With The Media In Hard News Situations

If you do not have a dedicated PR professional, it will be much more difficult to attract the media's interest because cultivating reporters and editors is time-consuming. One way to keep your company's name in front of them is to distribute news releases with a hard news focus.

Writing Effective News Releases

The media receives thousands of news releases a day, most of which are discarded quickly. The best way to draw attention to your news release is to focus on facts and hard news issues.

Tips for Writing Effective News Releases

- **Tell the Story Completely, Yet Concisely.** Answer seven basic questions: who, when, where, why, what, how, and how much.
- **Identify a Company Contact.** Be sure to include the name, address, and phone number of an authorized person in your organization who can provide more information.

HARD NEWS HEADLINES

Company Official Accused of Fraud

Company Denies Benefits to Employees with AIDS

125 Employees Lose Jobs

Unions Charge Employee Survey Is Biased

Pension Benefit Scandal Jeopardizes Retiree's Livelihood

New Plant Opening Boon For Recession-Plagued Town

Medicare Seeks Big Cuts In Professional Fees

Soft news tends to be more informational in tone and style than hard news. The following headlines are examples of how the media perceives and treats soft news stories.

SOFT NEWS HEADLINES

Pre-Retirement Seminars Gain Popularity With Employers

Day Care Centers At Work

Dealing With The Aging Workforce

Trends in Union/Management Relations

What Employees Want More Than Pay

Computers Change the Way Companies Communicate With Employees

Figure 12.1   SAMPLE HARD AND SOFT NEWS HEADLINES

Figure 12.2 HUMAN RESOURCE TOPIC IDEAS

Type of Information	Factual Angle Hard News	Human Resource Angle Soft News
Financial health of the organization	Sales and profits up 20%	Gainsharing plan increases productivity
Operational problems and opportunities	New product delivery schedule delayed	Employee quality control groups improve product image
Growth strategies	Company plans expansion to Japan	Employees learn how to do business in Japan
Community involvement and contributions	Clean-up day saves community $10,000	ABC company employees lead clean-up day charge
Management strengths and weaknesses	New president expected to solve woes of struggling company	New suggestion program rewards employees and company

- **Keep to the Facts.** Avoid trying to write a story. That is the reporter's job. If your news release is fuzzy rather than factual, it will raise suspicion rather than interest.
- **Be Sure Your News Is Timely.** Old news is no news as far as the media is concerned unless you are dealing with a historical publication.
- **Include Professional Photos.** Good photos get published and can frequently stimulate interest in your story. You must be careful not to include photos if they are not appropriate or if they are not of professional quality because they will detract from your message rather than enhance it.

Figures 12.3 through 12.6 are excerpts from news releases that illustrate how to write news releases with hard news angles and some sample photographs that show how pictures can add interest to your news release.

How To Manage Media Relations Successfully

Whenever possible, you should try to have your public relations specialists field potentially volatile interviews. They are trained to handle the media. But you should be sure they have as much information as possible with respect to any human resource-related facts. If you do not have a full-time specialist, you can still enhance your company's media relations image by knowing what to expect and how to manage media encounters.

COMMUNICATOR'S TIP:
Eight Ideas for a More Effective Encounter with the Media

Members of the media tend to ask hard questions, the kind you would rather not have to answer. Yet, avoiding the hard questions only sets you up for harder ones. Of course, at times you cannot answer a question as completely as your interviewer would like. In these instances, you are better off explaining why. Following are some tips that will make your relationship with the media favorable and help you avoid bad publicity.

1. Ask the interviewer to explain the purpose of the story and focus on answering questions that help meet their goals.
2. Do your homework so you can anticipate questions.
3. Be prepared with answers to probable questions and include as much statistical data as possible.
4. Be candid, never evasive.
5. Help the interviewer understand the broader issues of the topic.
6. Explain why you cannot answer a question at the time (e.g. We haven't made a final decision) and offer to give more specifics as soon as possible.
7. Offer suggestions for research sources and other interviewees, both inside and outside your organization.
8. Encourage the interviewer to call you back to confirm or reconfirm the information you supplied.

The biggest mistake you can make is to be evasive, dishonest, or incomplete when answering questions.

News Release

Contact: Don Gingery
312/948-7400

FOR IMMEDIATE RELEASE
October 5, 1988

or

Sandy Lincoln
312/948-7400

ONE YEAR LATER: ANOTHER STOCK MARKET DEBACLE?

Most Investment Managers Think Chances are Slim;

Most Favor Limiting or Banning Program Trading

New York, New York -- One year after Black Monday, a William M. Mercer
Meidinger Hansen, Incorporated (MMH) survey of the country's leading
investment managers reveals some interesting attitudes on a range of
issues of concerning the U.S. financial system:

- 58 of 101 managers, almost three out of five, thought there was a
  25 percent or less change of another market crash. However, 19
  percent indicated a 75 percent or better probability that the
  October, 1988 crash could be repeated. The other 20 percent saw
  a 50-50 possibility.

- 60 of the managers said they favored restrictions on limiting or
  banning program trading, again three out of five, while 39 said
  they did not.

WILLIAM M.
MERCER MEIDINGER HANSEN
INCORPORATED

1211 Avenue of the Americas • New York, NY 10036-8855 • 212 997-8126

Figure 12.3 NEWS RELEASES:
SURVEY STATISTICS The media loves
statistics and surveys. These two news
releases provide not only survey statistics, but
are structured to give the media some ideas
for articles on human resource trends. While
the news releases were developed by the
consulting firm that conducted the surveys,
the media is often interested in different
points of view and specific examples from
participant companies. If you are a survey
participant or conduct surveys of your own,
don't overlook their internal and external
communication opportunities.

News Release

Contact: Joyce Cain
(312/948-7400)

FOR IMMEDIATE RELEASE
September 23, 1988

LEGAL SALARIES CONTINUE TO SHOW ABOVE-AVERAGE GROWTH

New York, NY -- Salaries for attorneys continue to grow faster than
those for jobs in most other functional areas, according to the 1988
edition of the Finance, Accounting and Legal Compensation Survey. The
average salary for an Attorney within a corporation has risen 8.1% since
1987, from $49,200 to $53,200. Managing attorneys show an even larger
increase of 9.4%, from $80,200 to $87,700 in 1988.

Salaries for finance and accounting positions, while showing
less aggressive growth, are keeping ahead of inflation, with a few jobs
moving well ahead. Corporate Investment Relations Executives show an
average increase from $74,100 in 1987 to $84,500 in 1988. Investment
Specialist salaries show movement of 9.8%, from $39,600 to $43,500.

The Finance, Accounting and Legal Compensation Survey,
published annually since 1980 by William M. Mercer Meidinger Hansen,
Incorporated, this year contains data submitted by 1,040 companies on
48,440 individual salary rates.

WILLIAM M.
MERCER MEIDINGER HANSEN
INCORPORATED

1211 Avenue of the Americas • New York, NY 10036-8855 • 212 997-8126

Figure 12.4B. NEWS RELEASE ANNOUNCING MERGER

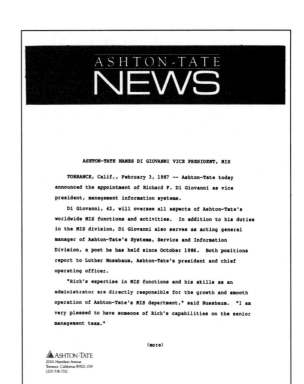

WILLIAM M. MERCER - Meidinger   **News Release**

1211 Avenue of the Americas • New York, NY 10036 • 212 997-7171

Contact:
Virginia F. Decker
William M. Mercer-Meidinger, Incorporated
(212) 997-8076

Bobbie Stirnichuk
A. S. Hansen, Inc.
(312) 948-7400, ext. 2860

FOR RELEASE: December 8, 1986

**WILLIAM M. MERCER-MEIDINGER AND A. S. HANSEN
ANNOUNCE PLANS TO MERGE**

NEW YORK, N.Y. and CHICAGO, IL. -- William M. Mercer-Meidinger, Incorporated, a wholly-owned subsidiary of Marsh & McLennan Companies, Inc., and A. S. Hansen, Inc. have signed a letter of intent to combine their two employee benefit, actuarial and compensation consulting organizations. The combined firm is expected to have revenues in 1987 exceeding $400 million.

   The board of directors of A. S. Hansen has approved the principal terms of the proposed merger which calls for a total price of $45 million consisting of Marsh & McLennan Companies, Inc. stock and a small amount of cash equivalents. The two companies have signed a letter of intent to merge; but the final combination of the firms remains subject to execution and approval by the parties of a definitive merger agreement, approval by the board of Marsh & McLennan Companies, Inc., the approval of Hansen shareholders, and satisfaction of certain regulatory requirements and other conditions.

A Marsh & McLennan Company

Figure 12.4A NEWS RELEASE ANNOUNCING NEW VICE PRESIDENT

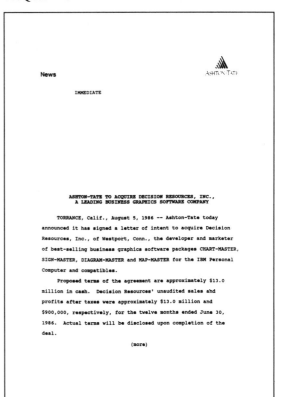

ASHTON-TATE NEWS

ASHTON-TATE NAMES DI GIOVANNI VICE PRESIDENT, MIS

TORRANCE, Calif., February 3, 1987 -- Ashton-Tate today announced the appointment of Richard F. Di Giovanni as vice president, management information systems.

   Di Giovanni, 42, will oversee all aspects of Ashton-Tate's worldwide MIS functions and activities. In addition to his duties in the MIS division, Di Giovanni also serves as acting general manager of Ashton-Tate's Systems, Service and Information Division, a post he has held since October 1986. Both positions report to Luther Nussbaum, Ashton-Tate's president and chief operating officer.

   "Rich's expertise in MIS functions and his skills as an administrator are directly responsible for the growth and smooth operation of Ashton-Tate's MIS department," said Nussbaum. "I am very pleased to have someone of Rich's capabilities on the senior management team."

(more)

ASHTON-TATE
20101 Hamilton Avenue
Torrance, California 90502-1319
(213) 538-7312

Figure 12.4C NEWS RELEASE ANNOUNCING ACQUISITION

News   ASHTON-TATE

IMMEDIATE

**ASHTON-TATE TO ACQUIRE DECISION RESOURCES, INC.,
A LEADING BUSINESS GRAPHICS SOFTWARE COMPANY**

TORRANCE, Calif., August 5, 1986 -- Ashton-Tate today announced it has signed a letter of intent to acquire Decision Resources, Inc., of Westport, Conn., the developer and marketer of best-selling business graphics software packages CHART-MASTER, SIGN-MASTER, DIAGRAM-MASTER and MAP-MASTER for the IBM Personal Computer and compatibles.

   Proposed terms of the agreement are approximately $13.0 million in cash. Decision Resources' unaudited sales and profits after taxes were approximately $13.0 million and $900,000, respectively, for the twelve months ended June 30, 1986. Actual terms will be disclosed upon completion of the deal.

(more)

Figures 12.4 A, B, C

The media is always sensitive to organizational change. While the announcement of a new Vice President will generally get less attention than acquisition or merger releases, the media recognizes that any organizational change can signal interesting news about a company or an industry.

COMMUNICATOR'S TIP

Remember, organizational change is a significant communication issue internally as well as externally.

Photograph showing a hand and numbered thumb wheels used in computer switching devices.

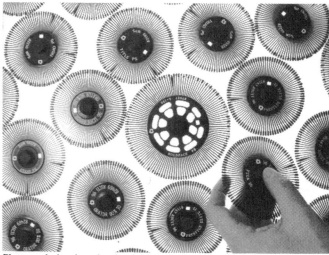

Photograph showing a hand and daisy wheels used on printers

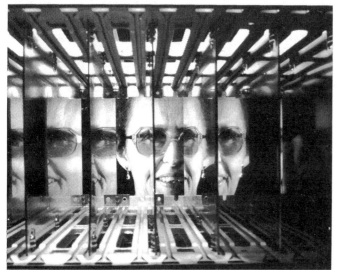

Photograph showing a woman inspecting a component rack for a radio system at Motorola in Schaumburg III.

Photograph showing a man inspecting a circuit design.

Photograph showing a woman inspecting airbags at a TRW facility in Michigan.

Figure 12.5 HOW PHOTOS OF AN ORDINARY SUBJECT CAN CAPTURE ATTENTION. Including photographs with your news releases or sending photos instead of text can get media attention. However, don't expect amateur snapshots to do the trick. Ken Love, a Chicago-based professional photographer and President of Imagery Source, Inc. keeps his clients abreast of the types of photos wire service and newspaper photo editors are seeking. These examples of his work illustrate how a creative photograph of an average or boring subject can capture attention. Ken's philosophy is to show people something from a new perspective. It works. Dick O'Donnell, PR manager for Software Publishing Corp., Mountainview, California reported in *O'Dwyer's PR Services Report*/April 1988 that ''he has used Love about a dozen times, and every time his photographs have produced in excess of fifty clips...'' Photos *Courtesy of Ken Love/Imagery Source Inc.,*

WILLIAM M. MERCER - Meidinger   **News Release**

1211 Avenue of the Americas · New York, NY 10036 · 212 997-7171

Contact: Virginia Decker
212/997-8076

FOR RELEASE: August 26, 1986

MERCER-MEIDINGER CAPTURES TOP AWARDS
IN BENEFITS COMMUNICATION COMPETITION

NEW YORK, NY -- William M. Mercer-Meidinger, Incorporated today announced that it had captured four of the 15 possible awards in the 14th annual Business Insurance competition recognizing "outstanding accomplishments in employee benefits communications." The awards were presented on August 4, 1986 in New York.

Out of a field of 174 entrants in five basic communication areas, the interactive computer software package designed by Mercer-Meidinger for the Hanes Group (Winston-Salem, NC) won first-place in the computer communications category. Third prize in that competition was awarded to Mercer-Meidinger for the interactive retirement planning program the firm developed for Santa Fe Southern Pacific Co. (Chicago, IL).

The interactive program developed for the Hanes Group helped that company's employees make decisions about participation in a new 401(k) retirement savings plan. Speaking about the design philosophy behind the winning program, Mercer-Meidinger communication consultant, Karen Greenbaum said, "Advances in computer technology have proven quite useful in communicating benefit programs in which employees may choose between a number of alternatives."

A Marsh & McLennan Company

News   ASHTON·TATE

For release: IMMEDIATE

Contact: Jeanne Jalan
Ashton-Tate
(213) 538-7783

Velina Houston
Miller Communications
(213) 822-4669

ASHTON-TATE ANNOUNCES NEW, COMPREHENSIVE
CORPORATE & GOVERNMENT SERVICE PROGRAM

TORRANCE, Calif., June 1, 1987 -- Ashton-Tate Corporation today announced a new, comprehensive service program designed to meet the software support and service needs of its corporate and government customers.

The Corporate and Government Service Program, which replaces the company's former Corporate Support Program, allows users to select services from a menu of options. In addition, two cost-saving service packages are available: the Technical Support II Plus Package, which is directed toward in-depth technical support, and the Comprehensive Services Plan, which is a combination of all the services provided.

"Since the launch of our original support and services program last August, we studied the issues surrounding support and service, and carefully researched the strengths and weaknesses of our original program," said Luther J. Nussbaum, Ashton-Tate president and chief operating officer.

"We have taken our customers' feedback, and expanded and enhanced the quality and scope of support and services Ashton-

(more)

Figure 12.6 EXAMPLES OF APPROPRIATE INTERNAL COMMUNICATION OPPORTUNITIES
The media will generally respond to releases that focus on special recognition or programs that signal an innovative approach to a traditional dilemma. While these are examples of very soft news stories, they are designed to keep the companies names in front of the media. Both topics are good examples of appropriate internal communication opportunities. *Figure 12.6B is courtesy of Ashton-Tate.*

WHAT TO DO WHEN THE PRESS CALLS YOU

If a magazine, newspaper, or the broadcast media is developing a general interest article on human resource trends, you may be the most appropriate person to respond because they are usually looking for facts and a recognized level of expertise. And, in spite of the fact that the topic may be considered a soft news story, they will typically ask some very hard questions. You should not be intimidated by the press, but it makes sense to be prepared if you are called upon to represent your organization.

In addition to specialists like yourself, the media is often interested in getting different points of view on an issue and may ask to interview others in your organization. For anyone who does not deal with the press frequently, their first experience can be traumatic. To help company representatives who are authorized to deal with the press feel more comfortable, you may want to consider implementing a press relations policy and publishing a handy set of guidelines. Your policy can establish who is authorized to speak to the press and the guidelines can help interviewees handle press interviews and unexpected encounters more comfortably.

COMMUNICATOR'S TIP:
Good Media Relations Information Is Good for Everyone

Even if your policy limits the people who are authorized to speak to the press about company matters, it is a good idea to expose all employees to the policy and the guidelines. They will feel part of the inner circle and may save you an embarrassing moment or two if they are accidently interviewed as a person on the street.

USING SPECIAL INTEREST GROUPS TO SUPPORT INTERNAL COMMUNICATION OBJECTIVES

Second to the news media, special interest groups can have significant influence over your external image and therefore your internal communication challenges.

Helpful Insights Into The Motives Of Special Interest Groups

Most organizations must contend with both friendly and antagonistic external special interest groups. Each group has a reason to add or withdraw its support of the organization. To the extent any special interest group enlists employee recognition and support, the human resource communication function is affected. Some examples of potentially forceful special interest groups include:

- **Bargaining groups.** Bargaining groups are always looking for opportunities to enhance their image as necessary to the well-being of employees and society. To the extent they can gain favorable publicity by working with management, they will. To the extent they find it more advantageous to their cause to embarrass management, they will.
- **Environmentalists.** While most people today are concerned about protecting our environment, organized environmental groups are proactively looking for organizations that are either model good guys or model bad guys. They are especially relentless if they discover work situations that may be hazardous to people's health which quickly becomes a troublesome human resource issue.
- **Equal opportunity activists.** These groups focus on discrimination issues such as age, sex, race, and disability. You only need look at all the federal legislation regulating human resource management practices to understand their power.
- **Community service organizations.** Because community service groups rely primarily on volunteer service and monetary donations, they often look to local

Figure 12.7   SAMPLE GUIDELINES: WHAT TO DO WHEN THE PRESS CALLS

RESPOND QUICKLY

Reporters are usually on deadline, so a request should be handled immediately. A quick response is appreciated and might result in a quote; a tardy one is often worthless, as the story has been filed without your input.

What If:

You're tied up with assignments or meetings and can't get back to a reporter?

Enlist the help of another qualified person who will return the call and respond with the appropriate information.

RESEARCH RESPONSE

Although reporters are often in a hurry, they understand that you may not have the needed information at your fingertips. Rather than providing a weak answer, or even worse, guess, ask some questions to determine the reporter's specific questions and story angle. Then arrange a mutually convenient time to discuss the issue when you have the needed information at hand.

What If:

You don't know the answer to the question?

Call back, but refer the reporter to another (non- competitive) information source in your business community or to a colleague in another location. Such referrals solidify your cooperative reputation and increase chances that the reporter will try you again on another story.

Figure 12.7 *(con't)*

What If:
You don't know the person who's most likely to have an answer for a reporter's question?

It's important to direct reporters thoughtfully to the right source. Call (NAME AND PHONE NUMBER) for suggestions.

DO YOUR HOMEWORK

Learn everything you can about the subject under discussion so that you can speak authoritatively and avoid factual errors. Prepare an outline of points you want to cover and take pains to provide accurate information. Reporters consider credibility the most important attribute in a good press contact, and not only will misinformation be devastating in print, but credibility with the reporter and readers will be diminished greatly.

SPEAK SLOWLY AND IN PLAIN ENGLISH

Reporters take notes during interviews and will find your remarks more useful if they are ordered, concise, and in language he or she can understand. Try to avoid technical phrases and jargon and use full association names rather than the many acronyms we use. Answer questions directly and try to turn negative responses, if appropriate, into positive statements.

MAXIMIZE CHANCES FOR QUOTES

Pepper your responses with a few remarks you've rehearsed to provide spice or special interest.

Figure 12.7 (*con't*)

Anecdotes will make your remarks more colorful, and color can be as important a consideration to a reporter as the information value of your response to questions.

USE "REAL LIFE" EXAMPLES

When responding to a press inquiry, try to use specific examples. Reporters write better stories, even if they're covering bad news, when actual scenarios are included. If possible, provide examples of developments at companies in your city.

AVOID *NO COMMENT* AND *OFF THE RECORD*

Whatever you say, under any circumstances, it's fair for a reporter to use in a story. But there may be times when you are unable to make certain information public. When this happens, be honest. Say that you're unable to comment on a question and explain why. Remember there really is no such thing as an *off- the-record* comment. If you agree to speak with a reporter, you are tacitly communicating your willingness to be quoted.

BROADEN HORIZONS

In developing a story, reporters are generally seeking new information as well as confirmation of what they have already heard. While you may be asked to confirm a specific fact or respond to a specific question, it is important not only to be responsive but also to use the reporter's line of questioning as a springboard to get into a related but different area which you feel is important. By doing so, you may improve your chances of being quoted.

Figure 12.7 (*con't*)

CLARIFY DIPLOMATICALLY

Don't hesitate to tell a reporter he or she has got a detail wrong or is pursuing a weak story angle, but do so in a way that broadens the writer's knowledge and points out a realistic slant for the story.

PROVIDE BACKGROUND MATERIALS

If you think that additional background information will help a reporter write a better story, quickly forward information on the subject. This is particularly useful when a reporter is covering a technical topic with which he or she has little prior understanding. Whenever possible, to enhance the firm's image, use published company information to provide background.

business for endorsements and support. Since employees are frequently active in one community service activity or another, most organizations recognize that supporting community service activities is an easy way to promote favorable public sentiment and human resource goals.

- **Highly marketable professional groups such as engineers or data processing specialists.** Encouraging participation in professional organizations and acting as sponsors for some of their activities can be an effective way to increase the employees' stature among their peers which translates to a special pride and loyalty that is hard to compete with.
- **Competitors.** The easiest way for competitors to sabotage your human resource goals is to communicate better than you do, internally and externally.

If these groups believe their cause is supported and furthered by an organization, they will proactively publicize that fact. Conversely, if they see an opportunity to get publicity by embarrassing an organization, they are not reluctant to pursue that end vigorously. In either case, the human resource communication challenges can be monumental.

Five Ideas For Gaining Support From Special Interest Groups

- Encourage frequent and open dialogue with special interest groups.
- Offer to co-sponsor activities that will benefit the group as well as your organization.
- Communicate with them when you are planning something that could affect their interests, positively or negatively.
- Ask for their advice.
- Publicly give them credit for their support whenever possible.

BENEFITS OF WELL-COORDINATED INTERNAL AND EXTERNAL COMMUNICATION

Returning to our example about the ill-planned announcement of a firm's acquisition, let's examine the internal and external communication issues the situation raised.

External Issues. This was a hard news story for the local press. Because many questions were left unanswered in the first article, the company could expect the press to follow up with questions like:

- Where will the company headquarters be?
- How will jobs here be affected?
- What will the business focus be?
- Why was the company sold?
- When the new owners take over, who will run the company?
- What will happen to the plans for adding the new research facility?

Internal Issues. Employees were taken by surprise. Their first reaction was shock. The second reaction was anger. They were asking the same questions the press was asking. In a situation like this, employees are less likely to be talking to you and more likely to be talking to one another, speculating wildly, firing up the grapevine, and thinking about looking for other employment.

Obviously, both internal and external audiences expect answers. If the answers are not consistent or if they are slow in coming, the organization can expect a major credibility crisis, internally and externally. Given the situation, how could the press relations and human relations issues have been better managed?

The nature of an acquisition or merger is such that, in the early stages, it is difficult to develop a predictable communication timetable. Legal and financial complexities as well as government and company management approvals almost always take longer than anticipated. However, this organization could have taken two simple steps to minimize the negative impact of the acquisition announcement.

Step 1. Prepare internal and external announcements to be released to the employees and the media simultaneously. The lag time between the media's receipt of the news release and the article appearing in the newspaper would have ensured that employees heard about it from the company first.

Step 2. Provide employees and the media with at least weekly updates. Even if the updates said nothing more than *"...nothing has changed because we are still waiting for the legal documents to be completed...,"* frequent, but honest communication has a calming effect.

TIPS FOR COORDINATING INTERNAL AND EXTERNAL COMMUNICATION ACTIVITIES

There are three keys that can help you coordinate internal and external communication activities.

Get Acquainted And Share Information. Get to know the external communication specialists within your organization, influential media, and special interest group representatives outside the company. Attending seminars and meetings sponsored by these groups is a good way to start getting acquainted. Show an interest in their objectives and share your ideas and objectives with them. The better you know one another, the more likely you can work together for mutually beneficial results.

Consider The Impact An Internal Decision Will Have On The Outside World. Some of your human resource decisions will be of little or no interest to the outside world. Others, like a reduction in force, will. As you are developing your internal communication plan, make a checklist of outside audiences who might have an interest in your action. For example, the media, bargaining groups, and professional groups would likely have some strong opinions about you laying off two hundred and fifty employees. The techniques described earlier and the development of a strategy to deal with outside forces effectively should be an integral part of your total communication plan.

Consider The Impact An External Decision Will Have On Your Employees. The most important tip to remember is that no matter what the issue, you will have substantially less human resource problems if you make sure your employees know as much or more than any external source and they hear about it from you first.

Chapter 13

WRITING EFFECTIVE REPORTS

A report is a type of communication medium. Reports are typically longer than other organizational communication tools, such as memos, and are used because the topic requires more space than is appropriate for a memo.

There are two types of reports.

- Reports which are brief, factual, and require little or no explanation such as daily sales volumes or plant production reports.
- Reports which are based on volumes of research or specialized knowledge, and often require interpretation or recommendations such as how to design and implement a performance incentive plan.

We will focus on the second category. The fundamentals of good writing which have been covered in previous chapters apply to report writing, however, the majority of this book focuses on employee communication techniques and media. The thing that distinguishes reports from employee communication is that reports are most often prepared for top management or other audiences whose perspectives are quite different from employee perspectives.

This chapter will review the expectations and needs of your audience and provide tips for organizing your reports. It will give examples of how to visually enhance your reports with charts and graphs, how to change the appearance of your report by using different formats, and how to turn your reports into effective presentations.

GETTING TO KNOW YOUR AUDIENCE

Knowing your audience is key to preparing effective reports. In most cases, your audience will fall into one of five categories.

- colleagues
- operation managers
- top management
- board of directors
- stockholders

It is likely that a report on a major issue will be submitted to each of these audience categories and will therefore have to be modified for each audience. How well you address the needs and expectations of each audience will determine the success of your reports.

CHECKLIST: Tips for Targeting Reports to Audience Expectations

Like you, your audiences suffer daily from information overload. They are deluged with memos, letters, proposals, and reports, not to speak of newspapers, magazines, solicitations and all manner of junk mail.

While reports are generally perceived to be required reading, it is important to remember that your report will get more attention if it is tailored to the recipient's probable frame of reference.

Colleagues. Those who have staff positions and are more or less at your level in the organization are most likely to have needs and expectations similar to yours. They will be most interested in:

- whether the report has any direct impact on their department,
- whether their workload or responsibilities will be increased or decreased,
- whether their staffing needs will be affected, and
- whether their budget will affected.

They typically will not be interested in:

- historical details,
- details of your knowledge and expertise on the topic (that is assumed), and
- financial details unless they directly affect their budget.

Operation Managers. Operation managers will look for information that directly affects their ability to achieve revenue, expense, and profitability objectives. They are instinctively suspicious of staff or corporate-generated reports and expect to find evidence that their operational freedom or power will be compromised. This is especially true if the operation is logistically separated from the corporate location.

Like your colleagues, operation managers are not likely to be very interested in historical details or the expert issues connected with the topic. However, unlike your colleagues, they will probably want to scrutinize the financial implications more carefully.

Top Management. It is not a shocking revelation to say that top management is most interested in the bottom line. After the bottom line, they look for anything that could be unsettling to the board of directors or stockholders. Finally, top management will want just enough information to be satisfied that the report is based on sound research and is consistent with the company's strategic goals.

Board of Directors. Other than company annual reports, boards of directors generally do not spend much time on reports unless it makes recommendations which require their approval. Their interest is similar to that of top management. In large organizations, boards typically expect the reports submitted to them to be concise but well-researched and documented. In small companies, boards are frequently less formal in their demeanor and rely heavily on the president to deal with reports.

Stockholders. Reports to stockholders are heavily regulated. You must provide information in a prescribed manner. Stockholders are most interested in the effect any company action will have on the price of the stock and dividends. While it is not likely that you will have to prepare stockholder reports, it is prudent to think of their perspective when you are preparing reports for top management or the board of directors.

If you are sensitive to the biases and priorities of the audience to whom you are writing, you can develop effective reports with a minimum of effort.

TECHNIQUES FOR ORGANIZING YOUR REPORTS

None of your audiences will want to wade through a report the size of this book, but it is amazing how often managers produce such a tone. Frequently this is because he or she subconsciously wants the recipient to appreciate the energy, research, and analysis required to prepare the report. Another reason reports tend to have more bulk than substance is that the writer has not taken time to get organized before starting to write. Proper planning and organization before you start writing will help improve the effectiveness of any report.

CHECKLIST: Four Steps to Planning Your Report

Organize Your Thoughts First.   Before you commit anything to paper, think about your report.

Ask yourself these questions:

- What is the purpose of the report; to inform, persuade, or recommend?
- Who is the primary audience; what is their probable position on the topic; what are their expectations and biases?
- What results do you want to achieve; increased visibility, more responsibility, or approval to act on the report's recommendations?
- Is there any reason for you to expect resistance to the report? If so, what form might that resistance take and from what source?

Once you have thought through these issues and answered the questions, you will be better prepared to begin constructing the framework of your report.

Outline.   Prepare an outline of what you think the report should contain. Approaching the outline development in several stages is usually easiest.

- **Select the major issues to be addressed first.** Try to limit the major issues to five or less. The most effective reports have no more than five major sections. In the final analysis, it is possible to write an effective report using only three major sections which will always meet your reader's need by answering the three key questions: 1) What is it? 2) What will it do for me? 3) How much does it cost?

If your first try produces more than five major sections, review each one carefully. Usually you will find that some of the items are more appropriately handled as a subsection. This process will help you begin to fill in your outline.

- **Once you are satisfied with the major topics to be covered in your report, add at least two subtopics under each major head.** If you can't think of two subtopics, that is a signal that what you thought was a major section really is a subset of another section. If you have more than five subtopics, that is a signal that you may be trying to provide your reader with too much information.
- **The third level of your outline (i.e. subtopics of subtopics) should be approached in much the same manner as you approach the second level.** Two or three subsets are most effective. If you have too few third level topics, the second level topic may not be appropriate or necessary. If you have too many, you are probably trying to provide too much information.

At this level of your outline, it is usually easy to identify information that is more appropriately handled as an exhibit in an appendix.

You can create as many levels to your outline as you feel comfortable with. However, three levels is usually sufficient to give you a realistic view of what your finished report will look like. Using the outline as the

Figure 13.1   MAJOR TOPIC OUTLINE—FIRST LEVEL

INTRODUCTION

TECHNIQUES FOR ORGANIZING YOUR
REPORTS

USING GRAPHICS TO ENHANCE THE
QUALITY OF YOUR REPORT

EFFECTIVE FORMATS FOR POWERFUL
REPORTS

TURNING YOUR REPORTS INTO WINNING
PRESENTATIONS

Figure 13.2   EXAMPLE OUTLINE—SECOND LEVEL

INTRODUCTION
Getting To Know Your Audience
Tips For Targeting Reports To Audience Expectations

TECHNIQUES FOR ORGANIZING YOUR REPORTS
Four Steps To Planning Your Report
Writing The Report

USING GRAPHICS TO ENHANCE THE QUALITY
OF YOUR REPORT
How Charts And Graphs Will Improve Your Report
Tips On How To Prepare Charts And Graphs

EFFECTIVE FORMATS FOR POWERFUL REPORTS
Executive Summary
Body Of The Report
Appendices
Packaging

TURNING YOUR REPORTS INTO WINNING
PRESENTATIONS
How To Keep Your Audience's Attention
How To Plan Your Presentation

Figure 13.3   EXAMPLE OUTLINE—THIRD LEVEL

INTRODUCTION
Getting To Know Your Audience
Tips For Targeting Reports To Audience Expectations
- Colleagues
- Operation managers
- Top management
- Board of directors
- Stockholders

TECHNIQUES FOR ORGANIZING YOUR REPORTS
Four Steps To Planning Your Report
- Organize your thought first
- Outline
- Diagrams
- Put last things first
- Writing the report

USING GRAPHICS TO ENHANCE THE QUALITY OF YOUR REPORT
How Charts And Graphs Will Improve Your Report
- Financial tables
- Case study examples

Tips On How To Prepare Charts And Graphs

EFFECTIVE FORMATS FOR POWERFUL REPORTS
Executive summary
Body of the report
Appendices
Packaging
- Reproduction options
- Binding options

TURNING YOUR REPORTS INTO WINNING PRESENTATIONS
How To Keep Your Audience's Attention
How To Plan Your Presentation
- Content preparation
- Meeting preparation
- Making the presentation

Figure 13.4   HOW TO USE DIAGRAMS TO HELP THINK THROUGH REPORTS

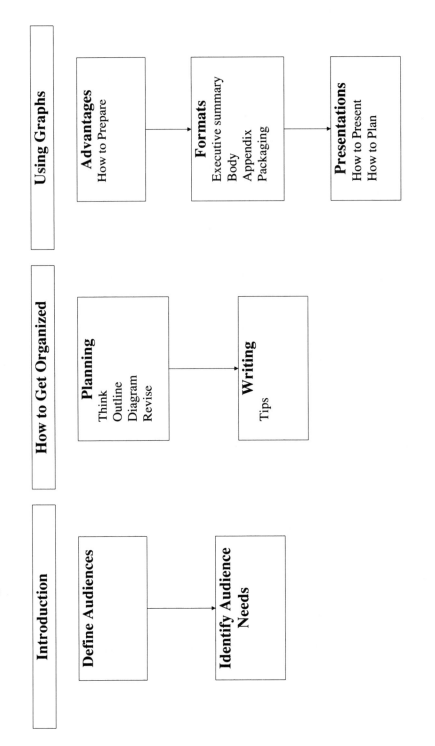

Introduction

Define Audiences

Identify Audience Needs

How to Get Organized

Planning
Think
Outline
Diagram
Revise

Writing
Tips

Using Graphs

Advantages
How to Prepare

Formats
Executive summary
Body
Appendix
Packaging

Presentations
How to Present
How to Plan

This diagram illustrates how you can draw pictures to help outline your report. Notice that this version of the diagram has presentations as a section under the major heading Using Charts and Graphs. Looking at the diagram, it became obvious that it was more sensible to make a separate section entitled Presentations.

framework when you begin writing. It will enable you to complete your report more quickly because it will prevent you from being sidetracked from your objectives.

Figures 13.1, 13.2, and 13.3 illustrate how the three-step outline approach was used to develop this chapter.

Occasionally, the complexity of issues surrounding a report are such that it is almost impossible to develop a useful outline. Or, you may just be having a bad day and find it difficult to focus on the issue well enough to prepare a logical outline. Illustrating the issues in the form of a diagram can often help break writer's block.

Diagrams. Drawing pictures is an effective technique to use when you are not satisfied with the results of your outlining efforts. Unless you are an artist, *pictures* will probably mean lines, boxes, and circles, but artistic skill is not the point. Using graphic techniques to develop an outline can often help you see the challenge more clearly than using word-based outlines. Figure 13.4 illustrates how to use diagrams to help develop the framework for your report.

Put Last Things First. When you think you have a good framework with which to begin writing, revisit your outline. Most likely it will look something like this:

- Background
- Problem or Challenge
- Research and Analysis
- Recommendations
- Financial Implications

Figure 13.5   EXAMPLE: TRADITIONAL APPROACH TO ORGANIZING A REPORT

In brief, a report recommending a new compensation structure based on the above outline would read something like:

Proposed Compensation Plan Restructure

Background	For the past 10 years we have limited our performance incentive plan to employees of salary grade xxx and above. Exhibit A illustrates the 5-year history of incentive payments opposite company growth, profitability targets, and actual performance.
Challenge or Problem	In the past two years we have experienced a flattening of growth and profits. We have also lost key research people, sales employees, and promising recruits to the competition.
Analysis	Our growth and profitability depends on attracting and retaining specialized research and sales staff. The pool of talent for these people is very small. A big reason we are encountering staffing problems is because our performance incentive plan is not available to these key employees who are generally employed at a lower level in the organization. Therefore, it is clear our current compensation package is not competitive.
Recommendations	Based on our analysis, we should restructure our base and incentive compensation plans to include more lower level employees.
Financial Impact	Cost estimates to implement the recommendations in this report are based on recent surveys of our competition as well as a thorough analysis of the probable return on our investment if the recommendations are implemented.

Figure 13.6 EXAMPLE: EXECUTIVE SUMMARY APPROACH TO ORGANIZING A REPORT

A more effective report will present these issues in reverse order in the form of an executive summary. It should not be more than three pages long.

One page is better. Top management wants to read a report that goes something like this:

Proposed Compensation Plan Restructure

Financial Implications and Recommendations   It will cost us $xxxx and require six months to design and implement an improved base salary and incentive plan which will expand the number of employees eligible to participate. The proposed plan would be performance-based and tie compensation to company profitability rather than the current plan which pays employees bonuses based on title and tenure. The total compensation budget would remain the same because the available compensation dollars would be reallocated to reward employees most able to give us a better return on our investment.

Challenge/Problem and Research/Analysis   Improving our growth and profitability performance depends heavily on our ability to attract and retain key research and sales talent. Our competitors have already installed performance incentive plans which are favorably received by the people we are trying to recruit and those we have recently lost to the competition.

Background   The Exhibits A and B in the Appendix of this report provide the details substantiating the recommendations contained in this report.

Writing The Report

Once you have the framework of your report, you are ready to begin writing. The style, tone, and format your report should take depends on your personal style, the audience, and the topic. *Remember, smaller and simpler is better.*

CHECKLIST: Common Writing Mistakes To Avoid

Excess is the biggest sin in reports.   The little word *too* says it all. Avoid:

- *too* many words
- words that are *too* big
- *too* much detail

Use an active rather than passive voice.   The active voice will make your writing more crisp and easier to read.

Use periods generously.   Avoid sentences that are two or three lines long.

Use bullet points whenever possible.   This technique makes the report appear less formidable without sacrificing important information.

Use graphics in place of words.   Look for opportunities to replace words with charts, graphs, simple tables, or an illustration. Your report will be more visually inviting and interesting to read.

USING GRAPHICS TO ENHANCE THE QUALITY OF YOUR REPORT

Most people like charts and graphs but are reluctant to undertake creating them. One reason is that many managers perceive the task of preparing any type of illustration as outside their experience or skill level. Dr. Joel N. Orr, a well-known author, lecturer, and computer graphics consultant, says:

> To put it simply, managers are just not pictorate—they are not
> literate in pictures.*

However, as Figures 13.7 and 13.8 illustrate, it is often easier to explain a complex idea using pictures or examples rather than words. Another important benefit is that a graphically-oriented report is likely to be given priority over one which the recipient must take extra time to read carefully.*

How Charts And Graphs Will Improve Your Report

Charts and graphs are not only effective tools to enhance your reports, they can often replace hundreds of words you would otherwise have to write and rewrite. After you have completed your report outline and before you begin writing, look for opportunities to use pictures rather than words and make notations in your outline. As you begin writing, when you come to a chart notation, you will find that you find it unnecessary to write three pages of text to make your point. In fact, you may need only one or two paragraphs to introduce the graphic.

People who are unaccustomed to using visual presentations think of only three types: pie charts, bar charts, and line graphs. While you can illustrate many ideas using hundreds of variations of these types, don't limit your illustration opportunities to just these three. The templates in Figures 13.9 through 13.16 are just a few ideas you can use to add punch to your reports.

In addition to traditional charts and graphs, two other techniques that make your report more effective are graphically enhanced financial tables and case study examples.

> **Financial Tables.** Contrary to popular belief, massive financial tables do not add credibility to your report if the reader has to study them for more than ten seconds to understand what they are trying to illustrate. However, if you compress the amount of data to be displayed, put a frame around it, and even add shading in appropriate places, it becomes a useful addition to your report. A better solution is to create graphs of the key points you want to make.

> **Case Study Examples.** Case study examples are especially useful when you must explain how a complex formula works (e.g. changing benefit formulas for your retirement plan, showing how various decisions will affect the Profit and Loss statement.)

Tips On How To Prepare Charts And Graphs

While you are drafting your report, you can sketch rough representations of what you would like your chart or graph to illustrate. It doesn't matter whether you think you can draw, try it; it can be fun as well as productive. Like writing, you may redo your charts several times before you are satisfied. As you are beginning to lay out your illustrations, remember the following tips.

- Avoid using more than five segments for pie charts because they begin looking cluttered. If you need more than five segments, try a different illustration format.
- Limit yourself to one typeface for all words on your chart. Using several type styles distracts the reader.

*Presentation Products Magazine, November/December 1988

Figure 13.7   SAMPLE EXECUTIVE COMPENSATION REPORT TEXT

Total Compensation

Historically, long-term compensation at ABC Company has been through stock options which have provided a relatively less significant compensation component to the broad executive group. Currently, salaries are below market while total cash compensation is at or above market average.

It is important for the very senior executive group, who must take a long-term, strategic, business perspective to be rewarded for long-term performance gains.

For the larger executive group who has more of an operational focus, and for whom stock options have been a relatively small component of total compensation, the shift from one hundred percent bonus opportunity to a higher base and lower at-risk compensation has the advantage of increasing their pensionable earnings base, as well as decreasing risk associated with their annual compensation. An increase in potential total cash compensation (the increase in base not being completely offset by a decrease in incentive opportunity) can also be utilized to offset the absence of a long-term incentive opportunity.

Any increases in potential bonuses are for those executives with the greatest likelihood of increasing corporate earnings. The portion of bonuses which switch from corporate to unit or individual performance targets are only paid for measurable performance improvements, and again place the largest opportunities with those most able to contribute to corporate success.

Notice that the text from this report is difficult to comprehend without studying it carefully. The graphic in Figure 13.8 can help the reader visualize the points made in the text. The text could also be edited to make it more readable.

Figure 13.8   GRAPHIC ILLUSTRATION

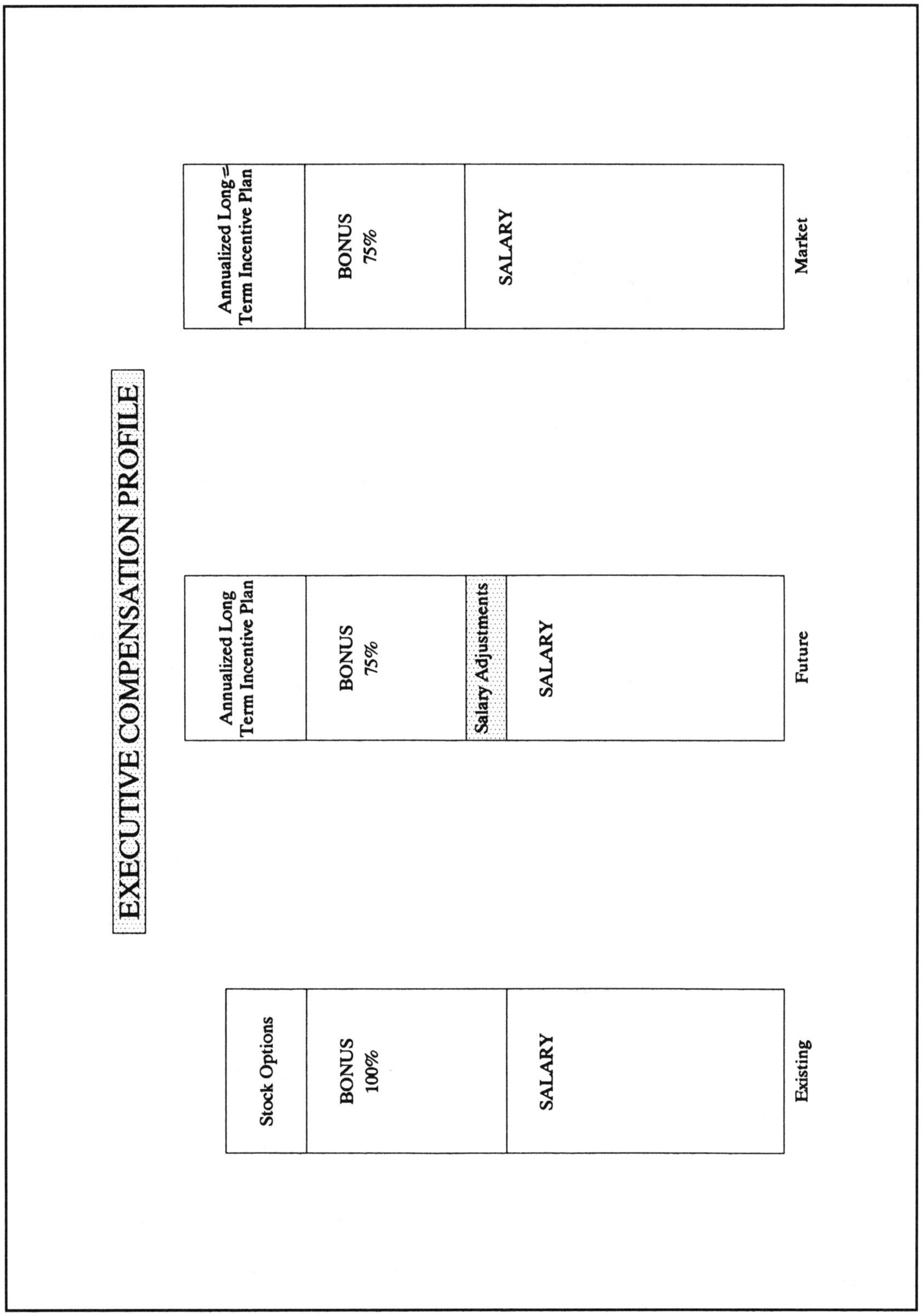

EXECUTIVE COMPENSATION PROFILE

Stock Options	Annualized Long Term Incentive Plan	Annualized Long= Term Incentive Plan
BONUS 100%	BONUS 75%	BONUS 75%
	Salary Adjustments	
SALARY	SALARY	SALARY
Existing	Future	Market

Figure 13.9–13.16   TEMPLATES TO USE TO ADD PUNCH TO REPORTS

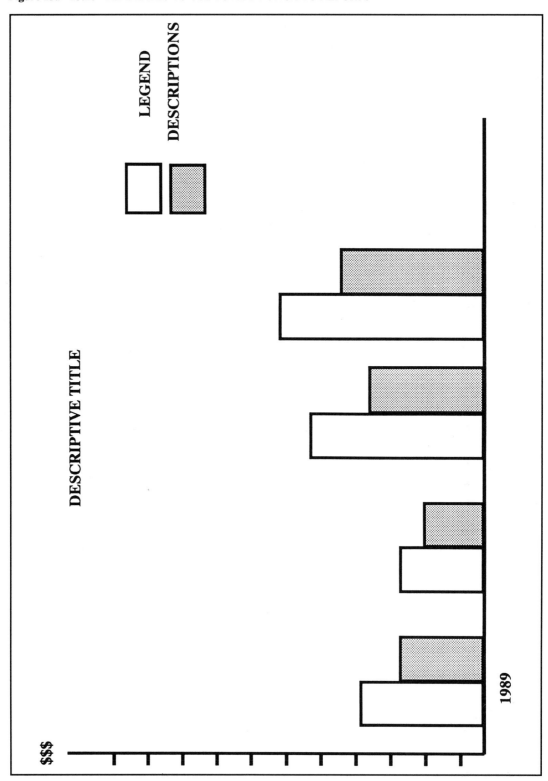

Figure 13.10

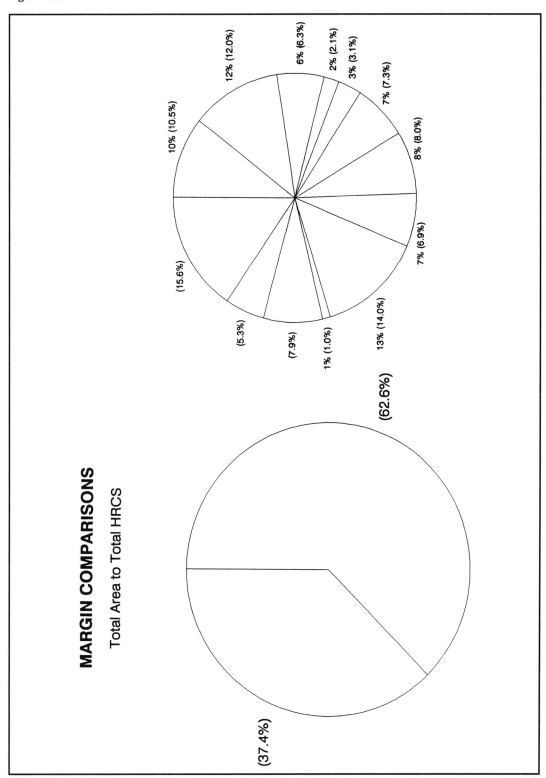

MARGIN COMPARISONS
Total Area to Total HRCS

Figure 13.11

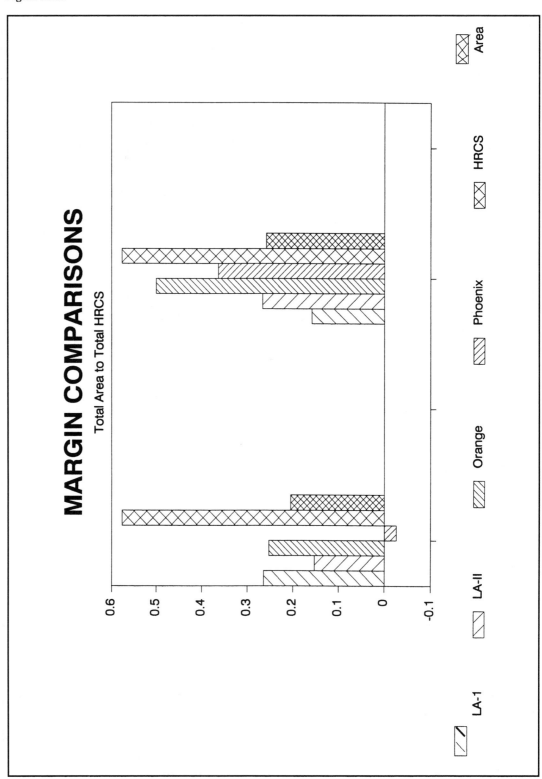

Figure 13.12

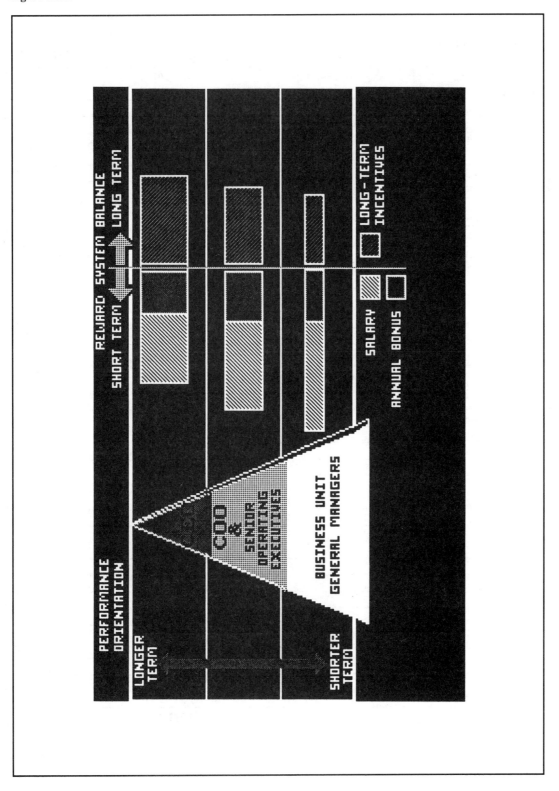

Figure 13.13

12-May-89			
	Unit I	**Unit II**	**Unit III**
Percent to Gross Revenue	3%	91%	7%
REVENUE			
INTRA-UNIT			
Products	4,327.68	132,249.08	10,203.60
Service			
VENDOR ACCT 782	18.00	19,164.19	631.90
VENDOR/CRC		(4,884.10)	
VENDOR AC-CRUAL/CRC			
TOTAL REVENUE	4,309.68	117,968.99	9,571.70
Percent to Total Revenue	3%	92%	7%
EXPENSES			
COMP	398.56	12,179.42	939.70
BENEFITS	116.52	3,560.87	274.74
TR/CLIENT			
TR/NON-CLIENT	29.77	0.00	0.00
SUB/TRAVEL			
ENT/CLIENT			
SUB/ENTERTAIN			
EXEC AUTO	14.89	454.90	35.10
OTHER	0.00	0.00	0.00
FAC/EQUIP	83.36	2,547.45	196.55
COMM	74.43	2,274.51	175.49
TAX/INS	14.89	454.90	35.10
OUT/SERVICES	0.00	0.00	0.00
CRC TIME	2,650.00	3,900.00	
CRC ACCRUAL			4,050.00
EDP TIME			
EDP ACCRUAL			
CII TIME			
CII ACCRUAL			
MISC	4.47	136.47	10.53
SUB-TOTAL	3,394.33	25,735.98	5,734.74
ALLO/SERV	257.95	7,882.54	608.17
119.09	3,639.22	280.78	
TOTAL EXPENSES	3,771.36	37,257.74	6,623.70
NOI	538.32	80,711.25	2,948.00
Margin	0.12	0.68	0.31

Figure 13.14

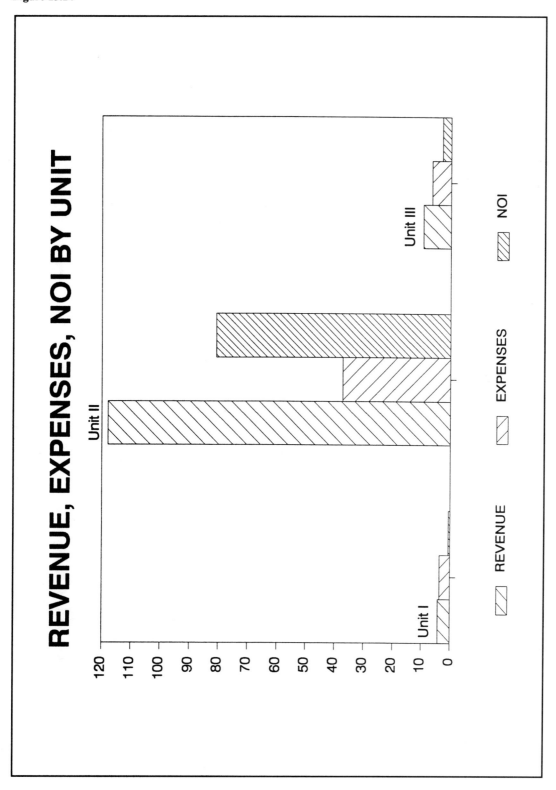

REVENUE, EXPENSES, NOI BY UNIT

Figure 13.15

```
=====================================================================
P&L BY UNIT FOR      01-Jan-89
=====================================================================
                            Unit I        Unit II      Unit III
    Percent to Gross Revenue        3%            91%           7%
=====================================================================
***************
REVENUE
***************

INTRA-UNIT
Products                    4,327.68    132,249.08    10,203.60
Service
  VENDOR ACCT 782              18.00     19,164.19       631.90
  VENDOR/CRC                             (4,884.10)
  VENDOR ACCRUAL/CRC
acctg reconciliation
TOTAL REVENUE               4,309.68    117,968.99     9,571.70
    Percent to Total Revenue       3%           92%           7%
***************
EXPENSES
***************

COMP                          398.56     12,179.42       939.70
BENEFITS                      116.52      3,560.87       274.74
TR/CLIENT
TR/NON-CLIENT                  29.77          0.00         0.00
  SUB/TRAVEL
ENT/CLIENT
ENT/NON-CLIENT                  7.44        227.45        17.55
  SUB/ENTERTAIN
EXEC AUTO                      14.89        454.90        35.10
OTHER                           0.00          0.00         0.00
FAC/EQUIP                      83.36      2,547.45       196.55
COMM                           74.43      2,274.51       175.49
TAX/INS                        14.89        454.90        35.10
OUT/SERVICES                    0.00          0.00         0.00
SERV/PURCH/SOLD
  CRC TIME                  2,650.00      3,900.00
  CRC ACCRUAL                                          4,050.00
  EDP TIME
  EDP ACCRUAL
  CII TIME
  CII ACCRUAL
MISC                            4.47        136.47        10.53
  SUB-TOTAL                 3,394.33     25,735.98     5,734.74
ALLO/SERV                     257.95      7,882.54       608.17
HOME OFFICE OP                119.09      3,639.22       280.78
  TOTAL EXPENSES            3,771.36     37,257.74     6,623.70

NOI                           538.32     80,711.25     2,948.00
                                0.12          0.68         0.31
```

Figure 13.16

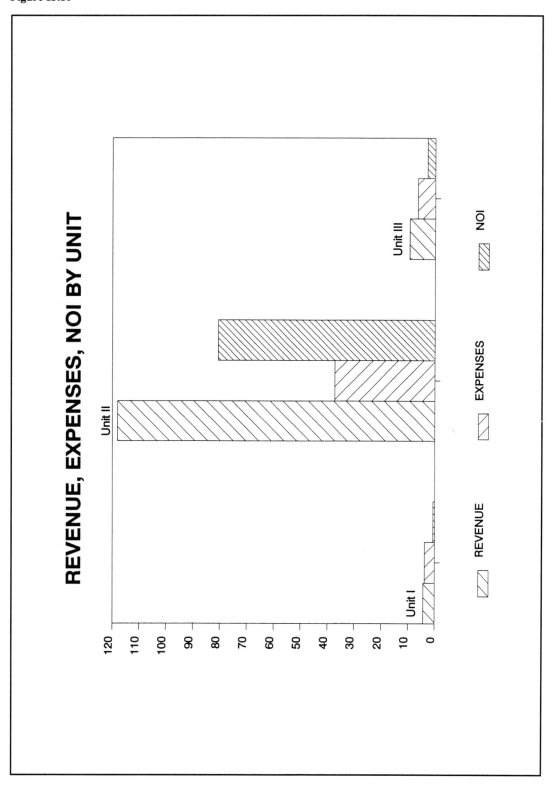

- Try to use only one or two sizes of type in any given graphic.
- When illustrating financial data in bar charts or line graphs, statistical precision is less important that relative relationships. This is especially true if statistical precision makes the chart so small it must be studied to be understood.
- Use boldface, rather than italics, for emphasis whenever possible. Avoid underlining, as it adds clutter to the visual, rather than showing emphasis.
- If you use color, shading, or crosshatching to distinguish different components, include carefully placed and labeled legends to help the reader. Use the color or shading consistently, throughout your report, from one graphic to the next.
- Be careful to keep your graphic simple. Don't use a three-dimensional bar chart if, for example, the second and third dimensions are there for aesthetic rather than practical reasons.

The tips in Chapter 7 for preparing slides also are useful for preparing illustrations for your reports.

EFFECTIVE FORMATS FOR POWERFUL REPORTS

The best format for your report depends on your audience, the purpose, and the topic. However, there are four components that are repeatedly mentioned as most often determining the recipient's perception of an effective report. They are

- an executive summary,
- a logical, tightly written body of the report,
- appropriate detail presented in an appendix, and
- user-friendly packaging.

Executive Summary

Most managers admit that the longer the document, the less likely they are to give it immediate and thorough attention. The rule of thumb is: if it is two paragraphs long, *all* of it is read immediately; if it is two pages long, *some* of it is read immediately to determine whether it is worth spending more time with; if it is three pages or longer, *it goes to the bottom of the stack of things to do*. Given this behavior pattern, it is obvious why a concise, well-written, executive summary can influence the effectiveness of your report.

Body Of The Report

If the executive summary is effective, most readers will bypass the body of the report and go directly to the appendices to *review or double-check* the data used for drawing the conclusions presented in the executive summary. For those who want to read the body of the report, it will be most effective if it merely expands the details required to support the conclusions presented in the executive summary without superfluous text. This is the place to use charts and graphs liberally.

Appendices

Appendices are the place for more comprehensive research and analytical detail. If the executive summary and body of the report are credible, this section provides information for the few readers who enjoy pouring over 132 lines of financial detail or those who want to confirm that your what if scenarios include every possible variable. The information included in the appendix should be just as carefully prepared as every other section of your report because this data is the substance of your report's conclusions. However, the audience you are addressing in this section will be significantly smaller. Those who are truly interested in this section will judge you on how well this section is prepared. Don't succumb to the temptation of making this section any less professional than the executive summary or the body of the report.

Packaging

We all have heard the old saw, You can't tell a book by its cover.

While most of us would agree, the cover (i.e. packaging), nevertheless has a significant influence over whether or not the recipient will open the document. No matter how expertly your report is prepared, if your packaging is substandard or inappropriate, you have compromised its effectiveness before the intended audience turns to page one. Packaging includes how the text of the report is reproduced as well as how it is bound. Most organizations are aware of the myriad packaging techniques available to them, ranging from professionally typeset and printed booklets to stapled photocopying. Neither of these extremes is likely to enhance the effectiveness of your report.

Reproduction Options. Photocopying your report is an acceptable reproduction process, providing your photocopier produces clean copies. Otherwise, you might want to consider a $3.95 investment in having your local quick printer reproduce the text for you. Or, if you have a laser printer or letter-quality printer, you might want to produce original copies for each recipient.

Layout Options More important to the reproduction is how the report looks on the page. With the wordprocessing and computer-graphics tools available today, there is no excuse for any report looking less than 100% professionally produced. Most of the popular wordprocessing programs enable you to output documents that look typeset to the untrained eye. Desktop publishing programs give you even more options to enhance the look of your final report. The computer-based financial analysis and graphics programs give you outstanding charts and graphs. Failing to take advantage of the technology available to you will compromise the effectiveness of your report.

Figures 13.17 through 13.22 are samples that will help you visualize how the layout or format can influence readers' perception of your report no matter how good the content.

Binding Options. While it is not necessary to have specialized equipment on your premises to professionally package your report, you probably have the tools to bind your reports professionally and cost effectively. Binding options include: professionally printed and stapled booklets, hard-bound book binding, multi-ring binders, plastic-sealed products, spiral binding, or stapled photocopies. Deciding which binding approach to use is easier than determining how to reproduce the report because any binding approach that does not enable the user to open the report and have it remain flat, is not acceptable. Consequently, the most favored binding approaches are multi-ring binders or spiral binding.

You can refer to other chapters in this book for more detailed production tips.

TURNING YOUR REPORTS INTO WINNING PRESENTATIONS

You may be called upon to present the findings of your report. Even if you have reduced your report to only a few pages with easy-to-follow graphics, you should be prepared to simplify it even more for presentation purposes. The easiest way to simplify your report for presentation is to think of it as a slide show. It is not important whether you actually use slides or choose another medium such as overheads or flip charts to support your presentation. The important point is that you must reduce all your narrative to a few key points and be certain that each point, as well as your charts and graphs, can be understood at a glance. Your dialogue will fill in all the detail. Referring to the slide preparation tips and guidelines in Chapter 7 will help. Figures 13.23 through 13.29 show how you can add visual interest to your report presentations. Depending on your audience, you may want to have hard copy of your presentation visuals to distribute as well as additional copies of your formal report.

Figure 13.17–13.22   SAMPLE LAYOUTS

Chapter XIII

Writing Effective Reports

A report is a type of communication medium. Reports are typically longer than other organizational communication tools such as memos and are used in lieu of memos because the topic requires more space than is appropriate for a memo.

There are two types of reports.

- Reports which are brief, factual and require little or no explanation such as daily sales volumes or plant production reports.

- Reports which are based on volumes of research, specialized knowledge, and often require interpretation or recommendations such as how to design and implement a performance incentive plan.

This chapter will focus on the second category. The fundamentals of good writing which have been covered in previous chapters apply to report writing as well. However, the majority of this book focuses on employee communication techniques and media. The thing that distinguishes reports from employee communication is that reports are most often prepared for top management or other audiences whose perspectives are quite different than employee perpectives.

This chapter will review the expectations and needs of your audience, provide tips for organizing your reports, give examples of how to visually enhance your reports with charts and graphs or change the appearance of your report by using differnt formats and how to turn your reports into effective presentations.

Getting to Know Your Audience

Knowing your audience is key to preparing effective reports. In most cases, your audience will fall into one of five categories:

- colleagues
- operation managers
- top management
- board of directors
- stockholders

It is likely that a report on a major issue will submitted to each of these audience categories and will have to be modified for each audience. How well you address the needs and expectations of each audience will determine the success of your reports.

Checklist: Tips for Targeting Reports to Audience

Expectations

Like you, your audiences suffer daily from information overload. They are deluged with memos, letters, proposals and reports not to speak of newspapers, magazines, solicitations and all manner of junk mail. While reports are generally perceived to be "required reading", it is important to remember that your report will get

Figure 13.18

Chapter XIII

Writing Effective Reports

A report is a type of communication medium. Reports are typically longer than other organizational communication tools such as memos and are used in lieu of memos because the topic requires more space than is appropriate for a memo.

There are two types of reports.

- Reports which are brief, factual and require little or no explanation such as daily sales volumes or plant production reports.

- Reports which are based on volumes of research, specialized knowledge, and often require interpretation or recommendations such as how to design and implement a performance incentive plan.

This chapter will focus on the second category. The fundamentals of good writing which have been covered in previous chapters apply to report writing as well. However, the majority of this book focuses on employee communication techniques and media. The thing that distinguishes reports from employee communication is that reports are most often prepared for top management or other audiences whose perspectives are quite different than employee perpectives.

This chapter will review the expectations and needs of your audience, provide tips for organizing your reports, give examples of how to visually enhance your reports with charts and graphs or change the appearance of your report by using differnt formats and how to turn your reports into effective presentations.

Figure 13.19

Chapter XIII

Writing Effective Reports

A report is a type of communication medium. Reports are typically longer than other organizational communication tools such as memos and are used in lieu of memos because the topic requires more space than is appropriate for a memo. There are two types of reports.

- Reports which are brief, factual and require little or no explanation such as daily sales volumes or plant production reports.

- Reports which are based on volumes of research, specialized knowledge, and often require interpretation or recommendations such as how to design and implement a performance incentive plan.

This chapter will focus on the second category. The fundamentals of good writing which have been covered in previous chapters apply to report writing as well. However, the majority of this book focuses on employee communication techniques and media. The thing that distinguishes reports from employee communication is that reports are most often prepared for top management or other audiences whose perspectives are quite different than employee perpectives.

This chapter will review the expectations and needs of your audience, provide tips for organizing your reports, give examples of how to visually enhance your reports with charts and graphs or change the appearance of your report by using differnt formats and how to turn your reports into effective presentations.

Getting to Know Your Audience

Knowing your audience is key to preparing effective reports. In most cases, your audience will fall into one of five categories:

- colleagues
- operation managers
- top management
- board of directors
- stockholders

Figure 13.20

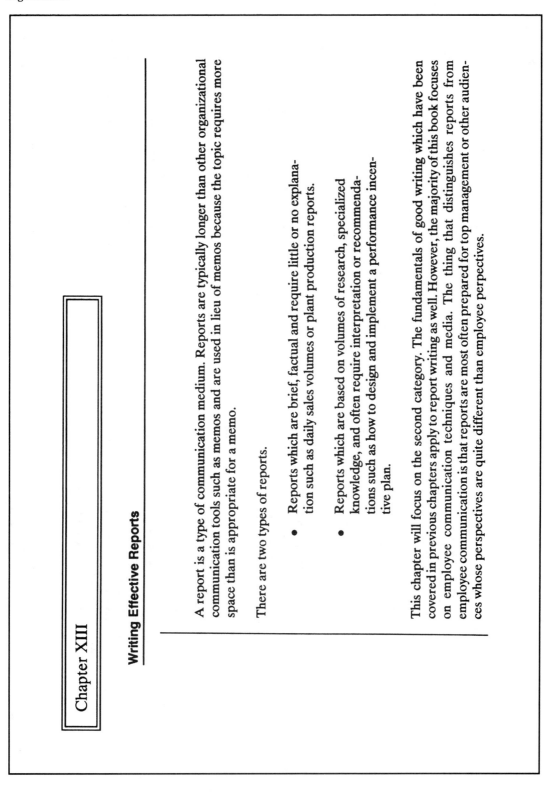

Chapter XIII

Writing Effective Reports

A report is a type of communication medium. Reports are typically longer than other organizational communication tools such as memos and are used in lieu of memos because the topic requires more space than is appropriate for a memo.

There are two types of reports.

- Reports which are brief, factual and require little or no explanation such as daily sales volumes or plant production reports.

- Reports which are based on volumes of research, specialized knowledge, and often require interpretation or recommendations such as how to design and implement a performance incentive plan.

This chapter will focus on the second category. The fundamentals of good writing which have been covered in previous chapters apply to report writing as well. However, the majority of this book focuses on employee communication techniques and media. The thing that distinguishes reports from employee communication is that reports are most often prepared for top management or other audiences whose perspectives are quite different than employee perpectives.

Figure 13.21

Chapter XIII

Writing Effective Reports

A report is a type of communication medium. Reports are typically longer than other organizational communication tools such as memos and are used in lieu of memos because the topic requires more space than is appropriate for a memo.

There are two types of reports.

- Reports which are brief, factual and require little or no explanation such as daily sales volumes or plant production reports.

- Reports which are based on volumes of research, specialized knowledge, and often require interpretation or recommendations such as how to design and implement a performance incentive plan.

This chapter will focus on the second category. The fundamentals of good writing which have been covered in previous chapters apply to report writing as well. However, the majority of this book focuses on employee communication techniques and media. The thing that distinguishes reports from employee communication is that reports are most often prepared for top management or other audiences whose perspectives are quite different than employee perpectives.

This chapter will review the expectations and needs of your audience, provide tips for organizing your reports, give examples of how to visually enhance your reports

with charts and graphs or change the appearance of your report by using differnt formats and how to turn your reports into effective presentations.

Getting to Know Your Audience

Knowing your audience is key to preparing effective reports. In most cases, your audience will fall into one of five categories:

- colleagues
- operation managers
- top management
- board of directors
- stockholders

It is likely that a report on a major issue will submitted to each of these audience categories and will have to be modified for each audience. How well you address the needs and expectations of each audience will determine the success of your reports.

Checklist: Tips for Targeting Reports to Audience

Expectations

Like you, your audiences suffer daily from information overload. They are deluged with memos, letters, proposals and reports not to speak of newspapers, magazines, solicitations and all manner of junk mail. While reports are generally perceived to be "required reading", it is important to remember that your report will get more

Figure 13.22

Chapter XIII

Writing Effective Reports

A report is a type of communication medium. Reports are typically longer than other organizational communication tools such as memos and are used in lieu of memos because the topic requires more space than is appropriate for a memo.

There are two types of reports.

- Reports which are brief, factual and require little or no explanation such as daily sales volumes or plant production reports.

- Reports which are based on volumes of research, specialized knowledge, and often require interpretation or recommendations such as how to design and implement a performance incentive plan.

This chapter will focus on the second category. The fundamentals of good writing which have been covered in previous chapters apply to report writing as well. However, the majority of this book focuses on employee communication techniques and media. The thing that distinguishes reports from employee communication is that reports are most often prepared for top management or other audiences whose perspectives are quite different than employee perpectives.

This chapter will review the expectations and needs of your audience, provide tips for organizing your reports, give examples of how to visually enhance your reports with charts and graphs or change the appearance of your report by using differnt formats and how to turn your reports into effective presentations.

Getting to Know Your Audience

Knowing your audience is key to preparing effective reports. In most cases, your audience will fall into one of five categories:

- colleagues

- operation managers

- top management

- board of directors

- stockholders

It is likely that a report on a major issue will submitted to each of these audience categories and will have to be modified for each audience. How well you address the needs and expectations of each audience will determine the success of your reports.

Checklist: Tips for Targeting Reports to Audience

Expectations

Like you, your audiences suffer daily from information overload. They are deluged with memos, letters, proposals and reports not to speak of newspapers, magazines, solicitations and all manner of junk mail. While

Figure 13.23–13.29   SAMPLES TO ADD VISUAL INTEREST TO REPORTS

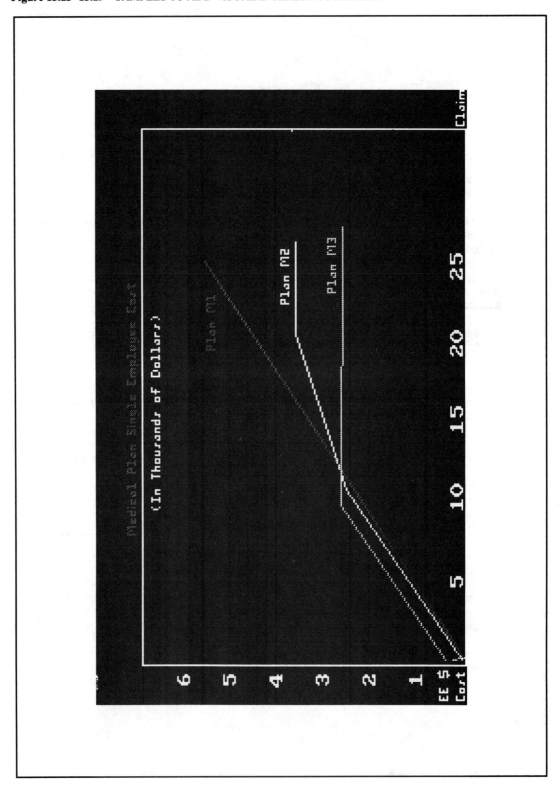

Figure 13.24

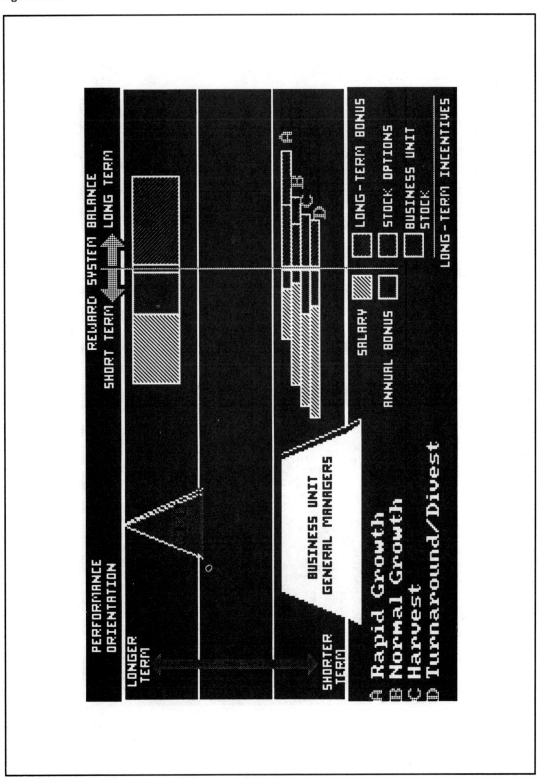

Figure 13.25

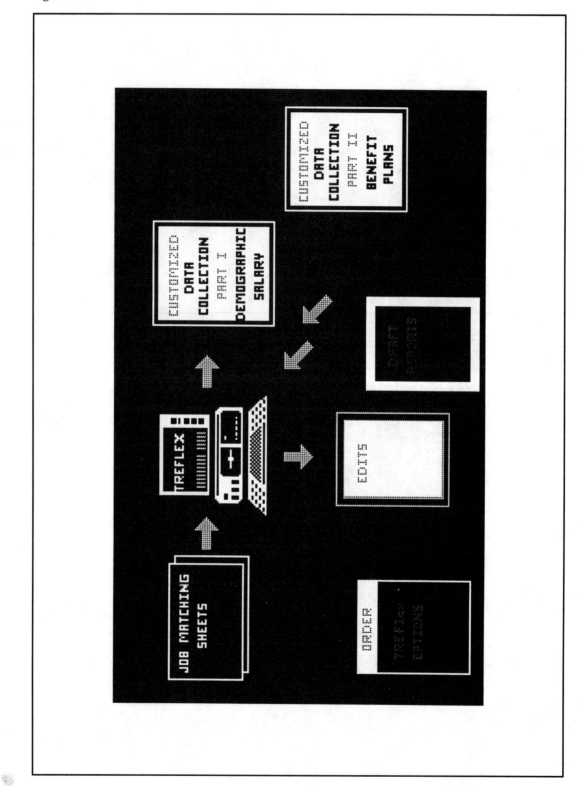

Figure 13.26

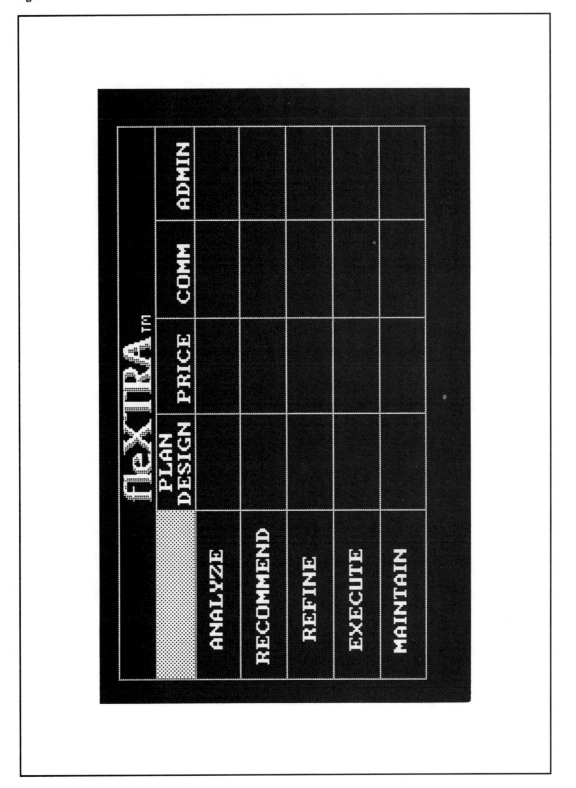

Figure 13.27

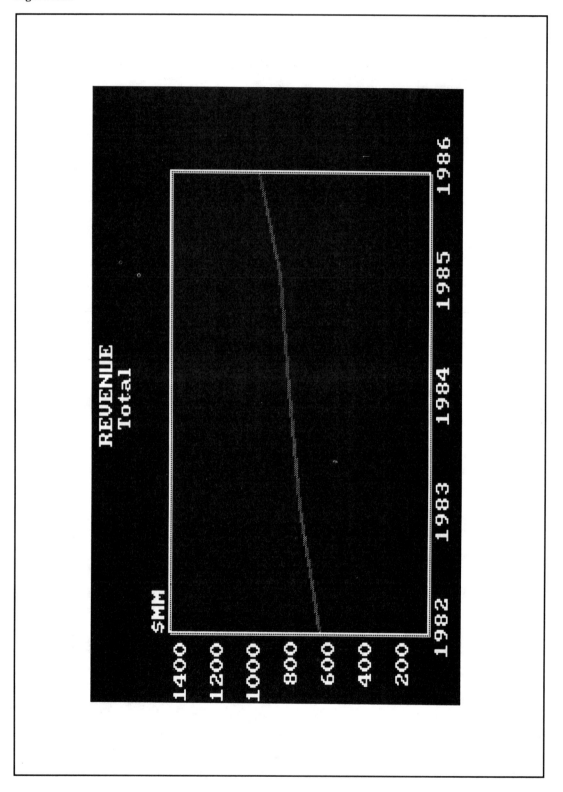

Figure 13.28

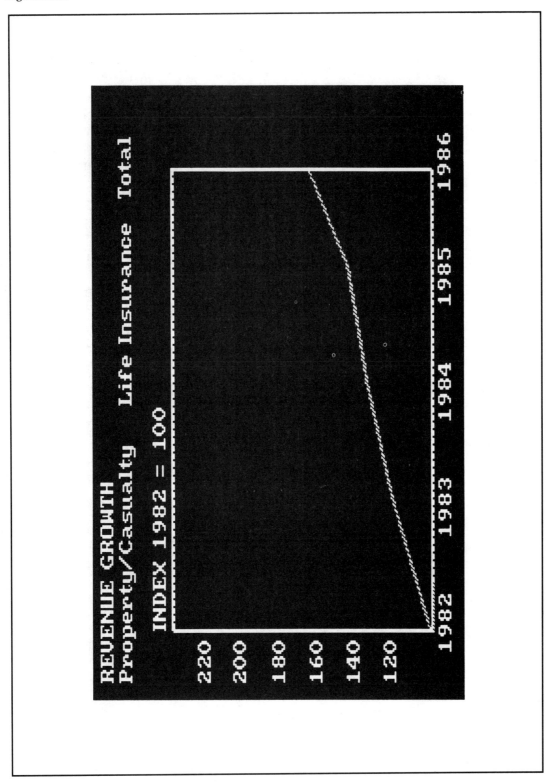

Figure 13.29

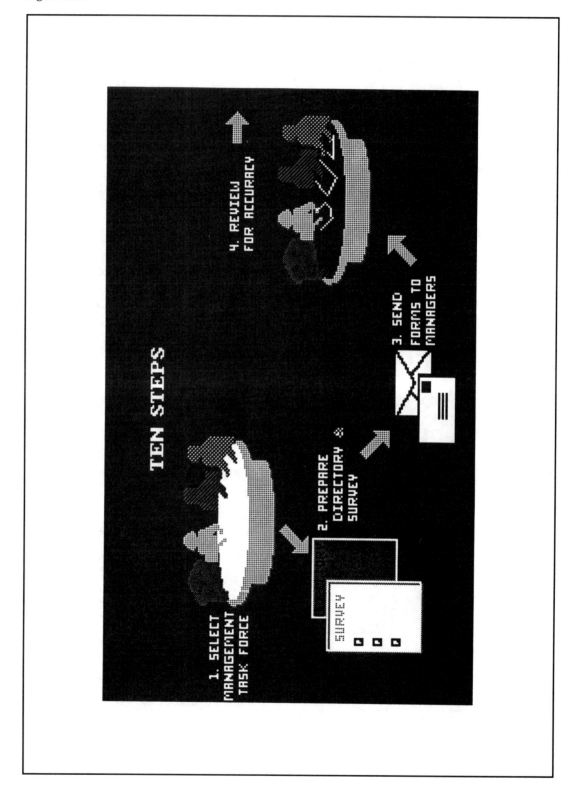

CHECKLIST: How To Plan Your Presentation

Content Preparation

1. Practice your presentation using your visual aids so you will feel comfortable with them.

2. Make a list of questions you might expect from each person in your audience.

3. Study the questions and prepare answers for each.

4. If you encounter questions which you are not confident in answering on the spot, admit that you are not sure. Advise that you will get back with the answer within a short period of time.

5. If you are using an example to illustrate a point, try to anticipate other scenarios a meeting participant might think of and use another example with different assumptions than were included in your presentation. This will make it easier for you to quickly and confidently show how other scenarios can impact the results.

Meeting Preparation

1. Check out the meeting facility *before* the meeting. Things to look for include
   - Space for overhead or slide projector at one of the room and a screen or plain white wall at the other end
   - Proper electrical outlets to plug in the audio-visual equipment and turn off room lights (You may need adapter plugs or extension cords.)
   - Shades or drapes to control outside light if the room has windows
   - Proper seating arrangement so all attendees can see the audio-visual *and* you as you speak
   - An area where you can store extra handouts and your personal belongings

2. Make a list of everything you will need to have at the meeting such as
   - Supply of extra handouts, especially worksheets and examples
   - Audio-visual equipment (overhead and/or slide projector)
   - Your presentation script
   - Extra notepads and pencils or pens
   - Chalk or felt pens for chalkboard/flip chart

3. Put the supplies you are taking in separate folders or envelopes, prominently marked so you can find them easily.

4. Plan to be at your meeting location at least a half-hour early so you will have time to prepare and remedy any last minute oversights.

Agenda For Making The Presentation

1. Opening Remarks
   - Introduce yourself and anyone who may be there to help you. Welcome the attendees and explain what will be happening during the meeting.
   - State or restate the meeting objectives.
   - Give attendees the time schedule for the meeting (e.g. in the next half hour, we will... or by 2:00 p.m. you will know the details of...).

2. Crisp but Personal Presentation

3. Question and Answer Period
  - Open the meeting to questions. Don't ask if there are any questions. Instead ask has this presentation (or discussion) explained the plan to your satisfaction. If there are no questions, share some questions that others have asked along with the answers. Use some of the questions you anticipated *might have been asked.*
  - Offer to respond to anyone who may think of questions later. Encourage them to bring questions to you at any time.

At All Times Be Friendly and Enthusiastic

INDEX